THE WAR
FOR A NATION

Warfare and History

GENERAL EDITOR: JEREMY BLACK
Professor of History, University of Exeter

A Naval History of World War I
Paul G. Halpern

Medieval Naval Warfare,
1000–1500
Susan Rose

Air Power in the Age of Total
War
John Buckley

Modern Chinese Warfare,
1795–1989
Bruce A. Elleman

English Warfare, 1511–1642
Mark Charles Fissell

Modern Insurgencies and
Counter-Insurgencies
Ian F. Beckett

European Warfare, 1494–1660
Jeremy Black

Mughal Warfare
J.J. L. Gommans

European Warfare, 1660–1815
Jeremy Black

Naval Warfare, 1815–1914
Lawrence Sondhaus

European and Native American
Warfare, 1675–1795
Armstrong Starkey

Ottoman Warfare, 1500–1700
Rhoads Murphey

Frontiersmen
Anthony Clayton

Samurai, Warfare and the State
in Early Medieval Japan
Karl F. Friday

German Armies
Peter Wilson

Seapower And Naval Warfare,
1650–1830
Dr. Richard Harding

Israel's Wars
Ahron Bregman

The Armies of the Caliphs
Hugh Kennedy

Medieval Chinese Warfare,
300–900
David Graff

The Balkan Wars, 1912–1913
Richard C. Hall

THE WAR
FOR A NATION

THE AMERICAN CIVIL WAR

SUSAN-MARY GRANT

Routledge
Taylor & Francis Group
New York   London

Routledge is an imprint of the
Taylor & Francis Group, an informa business

Routledge
Taylor & Francis Group
270 Madison Avenue
New York, NY 10016

Routledge
Taylor & Francis Group
2 Park Square
Milton Park, Abingdon
Oxon OX14 4RN

© 2006 by Susan-Mary Grant
Routledge is an imprint of Taylor & Francis Group, an Informa business

Printed in the United States of America on acid-free paper
10 9 8 7 6 5 4 3 2 1

International Standard Book Number-10: 0-415-97990-0 (Softcover) 0-415-97989-7 (Hardcover)
International Standard Book Number-13: 978-0-415-97990-0 (Softcover) 978-0-415-97989-4 (Hardcover)

Library of Congress Cataloging-in-Publication Data

Grant, Susan-Mary.
    The war for a nation : the American Civil War / by Susan-Mary Grant.
        p. cm. -- (Warfare and history)
    Includes bibliographical references and index.
    ISBN 0-415-97989-7 (hb) -- ISBN 0-415-97990-0 (pb)
    1. United States--History--Civil War, 1861-1865.   I. Title. II. Series.

E468.G74 2006
973.7--dc22   2006002089

Visit the Taylor & Francis Web site at
http://www.taylorandfrancis.com

and the Routledge Web site at
http://www.routledge-ny.com

Contents

Acknowledgments   vii

Introduction   ix

Chapter 1   Portents   1

Chapter 2   Divisions   29

Chapter 3   The Road to Perdition   53

Chapter 4   All Quiet Along the Potomac   77

Chapter 5   Battle Cry of Freedom   107

Chapter 6   Into the West   139

Chapter 7   The People Embodied   167

Chapter 8   "Lee's Miserables"   193

Conclusion: Death of a President, Birth of a Nation   223

Endnotes   227

Short Guide to Secondary Reading   245

Index   249

Acknowledgments

This book offers a short introduction to the major war in American history, the war that made the American nation: the Civil War of 1861 to 1865. There are a great many books on this subject, but this one is designed to provide the reader with an overall perspective of Civil War America in all its complexity and crisis, and to this end, it incorporates not just familiar material but original research into unpublished Civil War soldiers' letters and diaries. This aspect of the work would not have been possible without the help and support of the Gilder Lehrman Institute of American History who awarded me a fellowship enabling me to study its holdings of soldiers' letters at the Pierpont Morgan Library in New York from 2000 to 2001. I wish to thank the Institute, in particular James Basker and Lesley Hermann, for its generous support of a foreign scholar with a fascination for the American Civil War. At the Pierpont Morgan Library itself, I would like to thank Leslie Fields, then the assistant curator of the collection, for her help and guidance, and also the library staff, especially Ms. Inge Dupont, who was always more than helpful; it was an absolute pleasure to work there. The library staff at the *Caroliniana* at the University of South Carolina were also unfailingly helpful in helping me identify a great deal of material on my flying visit to them in 2005, a visit I could not have made without the help and extremely generous hospitality of Don H. Doyle and Marjorie Spruill, who not only put up with me but took me to visit Civil War sites in South Carolina and in Nashville, Tennessee. In Tennessee I also greatly benefited from the help of Richard Blackett, who showed me around Stones River and helped me understand the battle that was fought there.

Of course, this book would not have been written had Jeremy Black not accepted it for his series on *Warfare and History*, and I am extremely fortunate that he gave me this opportunity, although I will never work with either his speed or efficiency. Without the intervention of Jeremy Boulton of the University of Newcastle, where I currently teach, the time to complete the book would not have been available, and I am very grateful for his support of my work. Martin Crawford of Keele University bravely read the typescript, and I very much value his comments; any errors, naturally, are entirely my own and have nothing to do with him. I want, too, to thank Andrew Haughton, who will no doubt not be pleased that the Army of Tennessee is not the central subject here, but he is the best person to bounce ideas off generally. I also want to thank Jay Kleinberg of Brunel University, who is an inspiration. Her constant encouragement of, and challenges to, my work has been extremely valuable. The editors at Routledge have been more than patient in the course of this project, and I want to thank Vicky Peters and my new American editor, Kimberly Guinta, for their help on and encouragement of this book.

I am conscious—acutely so—that my doctoral supervisor, the late Peter J. Parish, wrote a far more detailed study of this conflict with which a short treatment such as this cannot hope to compare. Nevertheless, it is because of him that I developed an interest in the Civil War in the first place, and I will always be grateful for the guidance he gave me, a guidance I sorely miss.

Introduction

The American Civil War was the most destructive conflict—to date—endured by the American nation, a self-inflicted wound that took some 620,000 American lives but that held that nation together as a single nation that would, many years after the Civil War ended, become the most powerful nation on earth. This much is well known. What is sometimes overlooked is the fact that the Civil War was not just America's, but the nineteenth century's most devastating war. Positioned between the Napoleonic Wars that were waged between 1798 and 1815, and the killing fields—or trenches—of the First World War, it is the more remarkable that America's internecine struggle often takes second place to military matters in Europe, as if the Civil War had occurred in a vacuum, neither developing from, nor setting precedence for, the conflicts that flanked it. This is not to say that Europeans were not interested in America's Civil War at the time. They certainly were, but sometimes more from the perspective of not entirely benevolent onlookers, waiting to see if the modern world's first great experiment in republican democracy would implode. Modern-day Europeans do not expect America to come apart—the Civil War's outcome ensured that it would not—but they remain fascinated by the war itself. The interest in the conflict from the other side of the Atlantic is testament to its importance, and its continuing centrality, to those who seek to understand America, its development as a nation, and the underlying tensions that run below, or sometimes clearly on, the surface of American life.[1]

Despite the level of interest, and the wealth of publications on the war, confusion remains, outside the academy at least, as to whether the Civil

War was the first "modern war." The many excellent studies available on almost every aspect of the war make it hard—and the sheer volume makes it even harder—for the more casual reader to gain a comprehensive, but brief, overview of how the war began, how it was fought, what issues were at stake, why it ended, and how and when it did. There are a great many in-depth studies of the war, including many studies of individual battles or generals. This book offers a shorter overview of the war, utilizing mainly original historical sources, to provide a brief, but detailed, narrative of the Civil War. It seeks to introduce the military history of the war to readers who might be apprehensive of military history in general and who may never before have thought about how military history is, in fact, social history enacted on battlefields. The American military—indeed any military—is not a machine, but a group of individuals struggling through the circumstances in which they find themselves. This is true of all wars, but of the American Civil War it is truer than many other conflicts. The Civil War was a war fought mainly by volunteer troops, a "people's contest," in Abraham Lincoln's phrase, in which the rights of the people, North and South, black and white, were challenged, defended, and fought over from opposite positions. The American Civil War was not a war of conquest but a conflict of ideals. For the Union, the American republican experiment was at stake; for the Confederacy, it was the right to secede from that experiment and to establish a separate nation. This work attempts to do justice to both sides of that equation.

What this book is not, is a synthesis. It does not attempt to explain or even enter the arena of Civil War historiography. The focus throughout is on the war itself, not on what its participants made of it afterward nor what the several generations of Americans and American historians have made of it since. Unlike many shorter treatments of the Civil War, this book provides notes, wherever possible, directly from the original sources, in order to make it easier for readers to go directly to that source, should they so wish. To this end the notes are, for the most part, restricted to identifying direct quotes: the "The Short Guide to Secondary Reading" at the end of the book contains suggestions for where to go from here in the study of the Civil War. Although unpublished material is used, most of the material quoted is readily available either online, as with the *Official Records of the War of the Rebellion* and the *Official Records of the Union and Confederate Navies*, or in easily accessible printed form, such as Elisha Hunt Rhodes's (Union) diary or Sam Watkins's (Confederate) memoirs. Wherever possible, I have sought to allow the Civil War's participants, both on and off the battlefield, to speak for themselves, to attempt to convey their reactions to, and experiences of, the war as it was being fought, avoiding as much as possible the many post-war debates that sought to apportion blame or praise to individual generals at specific points in their Civil War careers.

Avoiding the pitfalls of hindsight is especially tricky when dealing either with antebellum America or with the war itself, and extracting the individual from the, by now, overwhelming mountain of secondary works surrounding him or her is well-nigh impossible. Nevertheless, that is what I have tried to do, and leave to readers the opportunity to lose themselves—if not their minds—in the voluminous historiography over McClellan's abilities as a general or the reasons behind Lee's decision to assault the center of the Union line on the third day at Gettysburg. In a short treatment such as this, it is also impossible to do full, or even partial, justice to the campaigns themselves, to the issues surrounding them, and to the people involved. Battle descriptions here are, unlike most of the battles themselves, short and to the point, conveying the battles' basic structure, development, outcome, and place within the broader context of the war. Again, there is no shortage of studies of individual campaigns and individual battles that detail these far more extensively than any overarching treatment of the war can ever hope to do. This study does attempt to give equal weight to the Western and Eastern (or Virginian) Theaters, but inevitably not every aspect of the war can be covered: I only dip my toes into the water of the war at sea, and I am fully aware that I am in and out of the Shenandoah faster than even Stonewall Jackson managed.

In seeking to offer the general reader a flavor of as much of the war as possible, I am also aware that I have rushed through, completely flanked, or simply not mentioned events, people, and places that were—that are—important. Throughout, the main intention has been to highlight the origins and general thrust of the war, from its long-term and more immediate origins in the secession winter of 1860–61 to its conclusion by focusing on the way it was fought, the type of people who fought it, and the weaponry they fought it with. These elements are set within the broader context of the motivations, expectations, and experiences of soldiers and civilians as the war grew in scope and in brutality to provide a clear picture of its impact on the political, military, and social arenas of nineteenth-century America at war. I have sought to give clear information to readers on subjects that can often seem confusing, not least the naming of Civil War field armies, and their relative positions at various points in the conflict. If Lincoln gets more coverage than Jefferson Davis, that is because I believe this reflects the reality of a war during which the president of the Union was frequently called upon to define and defend the Union cause whereas the president of the Confederacy, to the detriment of the Confederate cause in the end, never really explained in any satisfactory way—certainly not to the thousands of Southerners called upon to bear its sacrifice—what the South was fighting for. Lincoln came to symbolize the Northern war effort; in Walt Whitman's words, "UNIONISM, in its truest and amplest sense, form'd the hard-pan of his character." Secession, however, did not do the same for Davis. The individual who best exemplified the tortuous struggle between loyalty to state and loyalty to nation was Robert E. Lee. It was Lee, not Jefferson Davis, who came to symbolize the Confederacy. Davis is therefore a shadowy figure in this work, which seeks to keep the focus on those who actually fought for the South in the field.[2]

The structure of the book is broadly chronological, with a few exceptions. The origins of the Civil War can be traced back to America's origins as a nation—with hindsight, obviously—so the opening chapter, "Portents," provides a brief overview of the growth of both a national and a more dangerously sectional ideology in the period from America's founding to John Brown's raid on Harpers Ferry in 1859, but the chapter stresses that from the perspective of the time, war was neither foreseen nor seriously anticipated. Chapter 2, "Divisions," focuses on the election of 1860, the subsequent secession of much of the South from the Union, and the birth of the Confederacy, ending with the fall of Fort Sumter and the arrival of the first escaped slaves at Fort Monroe in 1861. Chapter 3, "The Road to Perdition," describes the raising of the Civil War armies in the war's early stages, the kind of war it was expected to be, and the basic weaponry used by both sides; it ends with the first major engagement of the war, First Bull Run/Manassas. Chapter 4, "All Quiet Along the Potomac," as its title suggests, explores George B. McClellan's ill-fated Peninsula Campaign, but also explains the importance of the blockade and the war at sea in the context of Union diplomatic relations at the start of the war and covers the first major engagement in the Western Theater, Shiloh, and sets out why it was so important for the Union to gain control of the Mississippi and its tributaries. Chapter 5, "Battle Cry of Freedom," looks at the issue of emancipation in the second year of the war: it looks at Antietam, the battle that enabled Lincoln to issue his Preliminary Emancipation Proclamation, and explores the raising of African-American regiments and the general experiences of black troops in the Civil War. Chapter 6, "Into the West," juxtaposes events in the Western and Eastern Theaters, but not chronologically, as that would have involved too much jumping backward and forward over the Appalachians. The three main Civil War battles in the East—Fredericksburg, Chancellorsville, and Gettysburg—are therefore placed, as I believe they should be, in the broader context of the Confederate advance in the West, culminating with Stones River and the fall of Vicksburg.

This work does move beyond battlefields. Chapter 7, "The People Embodied," contrasts the political situation in the Union with that of the Confederacy, the reaction to conscription, and the experiences of women in the war—both on and off the battlefield. Chapter 8, "Lee's Miserables," begins with two of the Western Theater's most significant battles, Chickamauga and Chattanooga, the better to trace the evolution of the war from one of pitched battles to one of, effectively, trench warfare (although not exactly in the modern sense), the emergence of Grant and Sherman out of the West, and the development of a more structured, persistent, and aggressive method of warfare that, in the end, brought down the Confederacy. Throughout, the purpose of this work is to introduce and explain—if only in part, and more briefly than the historian in me would wish—the most significant war in the history of the American nation; I want to show how Americans at the time reacted to the reality of a conflict that challenged all they held most dear, and what that conflict entailed. English journalist Edward Dicey was guilty of some understatement when he remarked that "no nation in the world has gone through such a baptism of war as the people of the United States underwent ... With the men of the Revolution," he observed, "the memories of the revolutionary wars had died out. Two generations had passed away to whom war was little more than a name." The Civil War's more complex legacy, however, ensures that, even today, at the start of the twenty-first century, it remains so much more than the name of a war in America.[3]

Union, Confederacy, and Border States

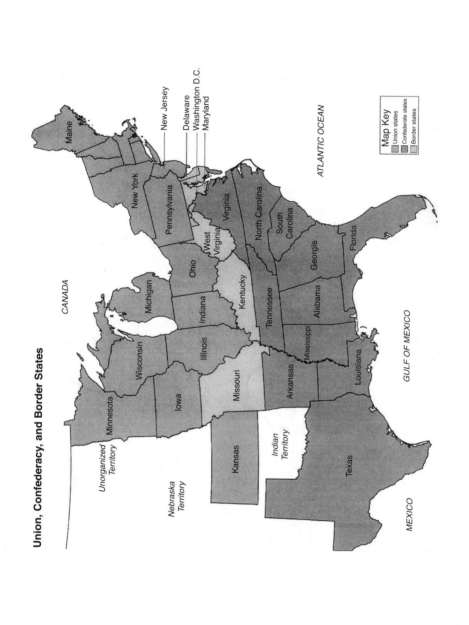

CANADA

Unorganized
Territory

Nebraska
Territory

Minnesota

Wisconsin

Michigan

Iowa

Illinois

Indiana

Ohio

Pennsylvania

New York

Maine

New Jersey

Delaware

Washington D.C.

Maryland

Kansas

Indian
Territory

Missouri

Kentucky

West
Virginia

Virginia

North Carolina

South
Carolina

Tennessee

Arkansas

Mississippi

Alabama

Georgia

Florida

Louisiana

Texas

MEXICO

GULF OF MEXICO

ATLANTIC OCEAN

Map Key
Union states
Confederate states
Border states

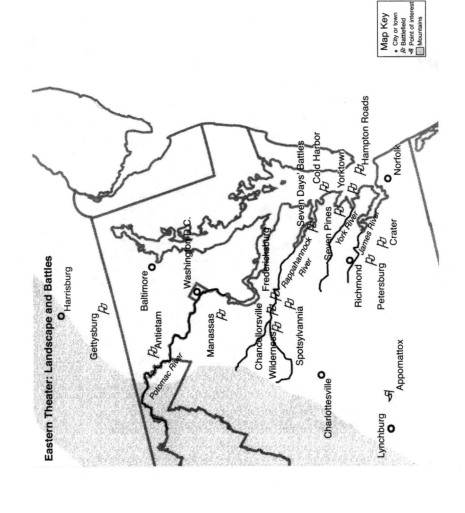

Eastern Theater: Landscape and Battles

Harrisburg

Gettysburg

Baltimore

Antietam

Washington, D.C.

Manassas

Potomac River

Chancellorsville

Fredericksburg

Wilderness

Spotsylvania

Rappahannock River

Charlottesville

Seven Pines

Seven Days' Battles

Cold Harbor

Yorktown

Hampton Roads

York River

James River

Richmond

Petersburg

Crater

Norfolk

Lynchburg

Appomattox

Map Key

• City or town

⚑ Battlefield

⚑ Point of interest

▨ Mountains

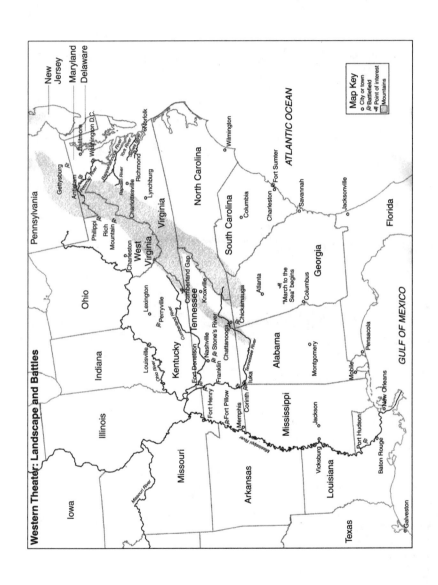

Western Theater: Landscape and Battles

Map Key
○ City or town
⚔ Battlefield
▼ Point of interest
▓ Mountains

CHAPTER 1

Portents

Hanging from the beam,
Slowly swaying (such the law),
Gaunt the shadow on your green,
Shenandoah!
The cut is on the crown,
(Lo, John Brown),
And the scabs shall heal no more.

...

Hidden in the cap
Is the anguish none can draw;
So your future veils its face,
Shenandoah!
But the streaming beard is shown
(Weird John Brown),
The meteor of the war.

—Herman Melville, "The Portent," 1859[1]

Prescience is frequently a gift that only hindsight makes tangible, and so it was with the origins of the American Civil War. Before the colonies had even made the break with Great Britain, before, indeed, they were even full-fledged colonies, the specter of sectional division between North and South had, apparently, been identified. The early colonizer Captain John Smith had, in 1631, already detected "the seed of envy, and the rust of covetousness" in the relationship between the Virginia and New England settlements, recognizing that "some would have all men advance Virginia to the ruine of New-England; and others the losse of Virginia to sustaine New-England." Smith deplored this, noting the original intention that "the two Colonies should be planted, as now they be, for the better strengthening of each other against all occurrences." Once the colonies became more established, and especially following the American Revolution, state loyalties were a source of pride and concern in almost equal measure. During the Federal Convention of 1787, Gouverneur Morris announced, perhaps somewhat prematurely in the circumstances, that, in his opinion, "State attachments and State importance have been the bane of this country." America's first president, George Washington, addressed Morris's concerns in his famous "Farewell Address" of 1796, and reminded his audience that they were citizens "by birth or choice, of a common country, that country has a right to concentrate your affections. The name of 'American,' which belongs to you, in your national capacity, must always exalt the just pride of patriotism, more than any appellation derived from local distinctions." Washington's audience heeded the lesson. "Americans everywhere," Donald Ratcliffe noted, "adapted traditional street celebrations into rituals that legitimized the new order; the toasts—initially always thirteen in number—offered at public festivals expressed national rather than provincial pride." Some thirty years later, however, French visitor and commentator on America, Alexis de Tocqueville concluded that the "Union is a vast body, which presents no definite object to patriotic feeling." The states, by contrast, were "identified with the soil; with the right of property and the domestic affections; with the recollections of the past, the labours of the present, and the hopes of the future." American patriotism, as Tocqueville saw it in the 1830s, was "still directed to the state and has not passed over to the Union."[2]

During the early years of the American republic, predictions of disunion were both common and widespread, so much so, as Linda Kerber has noted, that it "was the persistence of union which excited surprise rather than recurring secessionist sentiment." Street festivals may have represented self-conscious expressions of the desire for a coherent American nationalism, but they took place in a shifting environment in which it was perhaps unreasonable to expect individuals to don new national garments when, until just a few years previously, the old ones had suited just fine. Nevertheless, in seeking to establish a wholly new form of government, eighteenth- and early-nineteenth-century Americans were acutely conscious of the need to pull a disparate group of states into a single functioning Union, to create, in effect, a nation in a very short space of time. Whether they actually achieved this remains a matter of debate. Some argue, as David Waldstreicher has done, that "Americans practiced nationalism before they had a fully developed national state" or, in John Murrin's memorable phrase, that the American nation was initially a "roof without walls." The Articles of Confederation treated each state as a discrete entity, describing the relationship between them as no more than "a firm league of friendship," voluntarily entered into, with the understanding that each state would be respectful of the sovereign rights, freedom, and independence of all other individual states. The desire to improve on the Articles, to create, in the words of the Constitution, "a more perfect Union," shows that Americans were conscious of the need for something more than "friendship" between the Union's constituent parts. The Constitution, in short, provided a framework for balancing not just the three branches of American government but also national and state power; however, in its implementation it never fully eradicated what Daniel Boorstin identified as the "continuing secessionist tradition" that remained a feature of American political and cultural discourse until the Civil War.[3]

State loyalties, despite Morris's and Tocqueville's concerns on the matter, were not the biggest barrier to national unity in late-eighteenth- and early-nineteenth-century America. That individuals expressed stronger attachment to their state than to a vague and inchoate Union was hardly surprising; nor was it especially suspect in terms of the political validity and practical effectiveness of that Union. In any case, the original thirteen states were soon joined by other, newer states, some too new, in fact, for any long-established localism to be an issue. In just under a decade, between 1810 and 1819, no fewer than five new states entered the Union. The American population was both growing fast and surging westward across the Appalachian-Allegheny mountain chain.

Population growth—natural and from immigrant arrivals—and westward expansion would continue to define the period up to the Civil War. By the eve of the war, the original thirteen states had become thirty-three, with three states joining the Union during the Civil War itself: Kansas, West Virginia, and Nevada. By that time, over half the population lived in the trans-Appalachian region. Places that had been no more than frontier towns in 1810 had become booming cities: Cincinnati, for example, the smallest designated "urban place" in the 1810 census, with a population of two and half thousand, had, within a decade, become a city and trebled its population; in only ten more years it had entered the top ten list of American cities; by the time of the Civil War its population exceeded 160 thousand. Cincinnati was notable for the speed of its growth, but it was not unique in that. The American population as a whole had risen from just over 7 million in 1810 to well over 31 million by 1860, but this rise was not evenly distributed across the states. Massachusetts, one of the original thirteen states, saw its population rise from just under .5 million in 1810 to 1.2 million in 1860, but this increase paled in comparison to the burgeoning growth of some of the new Western states: Indiana, Illinois, and Kentucky all outstripped the population of Massachusetts by 1860; states such as Pennsylvania and Ohio had twice as many inhabitants as the Bay State, although both still lagged behind New York. This rise of the West had serious implications for the stability of the Union; the West was where nineteenth-century America was heading, and as a result, it became the political battleground for the kind of society America was to become.[4]

Free white settlers were not the only inhabitants relocating in nineteenth-century America. As the nation's white population streamed across the Appalachians, another group was on the move, but not of its own volition. The slave population of the early United States had been distributed across the Union, although the bulk of it was in the South. In Virginia, South Carolina, and Georgia, the slave economy found its earliest and surest footing, but slavery did, nevertheless, exist in the Northern states. Slaves in the North were never as numerous, nor were local economies so dependent on slave labor as in the South, but they did represent an element, an increasingly embarrassing one, of Northern society. Despite this, there was no sudden rush to emancipate Northern slaves, even after Congress officially ended the slave trade in 1808. The Northern states did, however, begin the process of gradually abolishing the institution of slavery—very gradually, in some cases—after the Revolution.

While some states saw a dramatic reduction in slave numbers after 1790, others saw only a very slow decline, and, in the case of New Jersey, even a slight rise at the turn of the nineteenth century. At the same time, however, the South saw its economy transformed and slavery as an institution revived by a dramatic rise in the demand for cotton: demand produced by the growth of the textile industry in Britain and also in America—specifically, New England—itself. The invention, in 1793, of Eli Whitney's cotton gin permitted the automated separation of seed from fiber in upland (or short-staple) cotton, which was more easily cultivated than the long-staple variety. This combination of demand, technology and a more viable strain of cotton made cotton production more widespread, faster and more lucrative than before, and increasingly dependent on slave labor to harvest the crop. The South, therefore, fast became a net importer of slaves both from abroad (before 1808) and from the Northern states. As the number of slaves in the North declined, Southern states, such as Alabama, Georgia, Louisiana, and South Carolina saw massive increases in their slave populations. Between 1810 and 1860, Georgia saw a fourfold increase; in South Carolina and Kentucky the enslaved population more than doubled;

and in Alabama the increase was almost tenfold. By 1860, the Southern slave population had reached four million, so had the annual production of cotton bales. As cotton cultivation spread, so too did slavery, mainly in a southwest direction, to the new states of Alabama and Mississippi, and from Virginia into Kentucky and Tennessee. Slavery's expansion, however, came at the price of sectional harmony. With the North moving toward emancipation and the South moving in the opposite direction, it increasingly became the case that the tension between them revolved around the question of where, exactly, the slave population might be moved next.

The year of the Federal Convention and the Northwest Ordinance—1787—might be described as the year of decision; but it proved to be the year of indecision on the slavery issue. The Federal Constitution had skirted around the subject—it never, for example, used the words "slave" or "slavery"—but it condoned slavery's existence, even if it hoped to limit its future development. The *three-fifths clause*, which counted a slave as three-fifths of a person for representation and tax purposes, acknowledged that slaves existed, but the Convention's decision to permit the importation of slaves only until 1808 expressed the expectation that somehow, at some point in the future, they might not. The Northwest Ordinance, passed in 1787, prohibited slavery in the territory between the Ohio River and the Great Lakes—land that would eventually form the states of Ohio, Indiana, Illinois, Michigan, and Wisconsin. Here again, however, the intention was not specifically to abolish slavery; the Northwest Ordinance simply prevented its further expansion. That so large an area was closed to slavery, however, only exacerbated the sectional tensions that were already a feature of American political debate.

The Northwest Ordinance sought to prevent slavery's westward expansion but, in the context of the institution's gradual disappearance from the Northern states it aided in the sectional distinctiveness of slavery as a means of production and a way of life for black and white alike. In effect, the Northern states not only separated themselves from the institution physically but also distanced themselves from the problem morally. This was significant. The late colonial period had seen the Southern states shift, in historian Duncan MacLeod's phrase, from "societies with slaves into slave societies"; in the antebellum period the Northern states made a parallel shift in the opposite direction. From societies with slaves, the Northern states became not merely societies without slaves, but ostensibly free societies, apparently the polar opposite of those states in the South. That this juxtaposition of a free North against a slave South was, as Nell Painter observed, "a facile symbolic opposition" did not detract from its impact. The stage was set for a production in which the North was cast as an entirely egalitarian, forward-looking, free society even as it still held considerable numbers of slaves, while the South took on the role of a backward slave society, increasingly at odds with the rest of the growing nation. The differences between individual states, as future President James Madison realized during the Federal Convention, were less of a danger to the fledgling Union than was the growing sectional divide that arose out of slavery. He understood that the "real difference of interests lay not between the large and small" states, but between the North and South, and it was slavery that "formed the line of discrimination." Slavery had been a national issue; over time, it became a sectional one, and over that single fact the Union would come apart.[5]

Treason, Tariffs, and Territories

That slavery would eventually prove to be the catalyst for an internecine war was not, of course, apparent at the end of the eighteenth century. James Madison may have hit the nail on the head with his assessment of the North/South divide, but his words have to be placed in the context of a society still very much in the early stages of development—one in which the Southern "Cotton Kingdom" had not yet reached the size nor gained the political power that it would over the course of the next few decades. In fact, no obvious threat to the Union occurred until Madison's second term as president, in 1812. From the perspective of the late-eighteenth century, the Constitution was sufficiently ambiguous on the matter of slavery to satisfy the Southern states, and it offered some hope to slavery's opponents that, in time, the nation might actually subscribe wholeheartedly to the ideals of liberty and equality on which it had predicated its break from Great Britain. In the meantime, the slavery issue was sidelined as the new nation found its voice, and celebrated its existence via a combination of commemorative occasions, such as 4th of July festivities, and the creation—in pretty short order—of a set of national symbols suitable for the new republic. The Declaration of Independence, the Constitution, George Washington himself, the Great Seal with its classical allusion "*Incipit Novus Ordo Saeclorum*" (a new order of the ages is born), and the motto "*E Pluribus Unum*" (one out of many) soon acquired—and have retained to this day—the status of sacred national icons. The Revolution took its place alongside the foundation myths—of the arrival of the Pilgrim Fathers aboard the *Mayflower* and the "Great Migration" of the Puritans in the seventeenth century—within a fast-developing sense of historical achievement and national mythology at the center of which stood the Union, the symbol of all that America had achieved by the act of revolution. Confidence in that Union was bolstered by the speed of its growth and by the seemingly unlimited expanse of its territory. Thomas Jefferson's purchase from France (for $15 million in 1803) of the land lying between, south to north, the Gulf of Mexico and the Canadian border and, east to west, the Mississippi River and the Rocky Mountains, only reinforced this optimism. The Louisiana Purchase doubled the size of American territory at the time. A further factor, and an important one, was the new nation's almost total isolation from unwanted European interference, thanks in large part to the War of 1812 with Great Britain—sometimes called the "second war for independence"—which resulted in America being left to its own devices at a crucial time in its development.[6]

The War of 1812, (now, mostly forgotten by Europeans, who tend to remember 1812 as the year of the Battle of Borodino and Napoleon's ill-fated Russian campaign) offers some clues to the state of American nationalist sentiment in the early nineteenth century. The war, declared formally on June 18, 1812, arose not merely to protect American trade from British naval interference but was overtly expansionist in concept; the desire to acquire the territory of Florida (held by Spain) and seize Canada (held by Britain) was certainly part of the equation. Yet the war was not universally popular across America; it produced sectional as well as political dissension: the bulk of the Southern states supported it, but New York, New Jersey, and most of the New England states did not; the Republicans favored war, but the Federalists were unremittingly critical of it and of its effects on the nation, generally, and on New England trade specifically.

Daniel Webster, lawyer and future leading American statesman, entered the United States Congress on the back of his opposition to the war. In January of 1814 he rose in the House to condemn it: "Public opinion," he warned the administration, "strong and united, is not with you, in your Canada project … The acquisition of that country is not an object generally desired by the people." Webster's concerns that America would over-reach itself proved unjustified. The war ended in stalemate; neither side came out of it covered in glory. In military terms, America was wholly unprepared for war. The regular army was (as it would still be during the Civil War) too small to be effective and inadequately equipped. Its officers had seen service during the Revolution, and could not accurately be described as still being in their prime. Canada, which should have proved reasonably straightforward to conquer—its population numbered some half a million at a time when the population of the United States had already passed seven million—eluded the Americans not once, but twice. The single notable American victory in the War of 1812, that of Andrew Jackson at New Orleans in January 1815 over Sir Edward Pakenham commanding Britain's Peninsular War veterans, took place two weeks after peace terms had already been ratified via the Treaty of Ghent, formally signed on December 24, 1814. That victory at least provided America with a cause for celebration as well as a new national hero and future president in Andrew Jackson. The war introduced the world to the archetypal figure of "Uncle Sam," and produced the American national anthem, "The Star-Spangled Banner," which was composed by Francis Scott Key in response to the British attack on Baltimore. These were all valuable and emotive additions to the short supply of national icons for the new nation, but hardly worth going to war for.[7]

Above all, the War of 1812 (even though it could hardly be described as an unqualified routing of the British from American soil because the British never had any intention of even attempting to take back their former colonies) did at least drive home the point that Britain would be best advised to steer clear of American affairs in future. It was a valuable boost for the United States and a lesson for the European powers; the new nation was capable of protecting its own interests. That the war produced an upsurge of national sentiment was clear to American diplomat and Secretary of the Treasury Albert Gallatin who believed that the war had "renewed and reinstated the national feelings which the Revolution had given and which were daily lessened. The people have now more general objects of attachment with which their pride and political opinions are connected. They are more American; they feel and act more like a nation; and I hope that the permanency of the Union is thereby better secured." In offering this conclusion, however, Gallatin was sweeping under the carpet some very worrying evidence to the contrary. If the conclusion of the war had the positive effect that he described, in the midst of the conflict the picture had seemed rather different. Far from reinvigorating national feeling, the war had revealed a dangerous strain of sectional interest that threatened the Union. It came not from the South, but from the region that would come to define, in many ways, the American ideal: New England.[8]

Financial problems, as well as military ones, had hampered America's war effort. These derived from the long-running trade embargo (initially imposed by Britain but the United States had responded with one of her own) that had been one of the causes of the conflict. Problems were exacerbated when the Bank of the United States failed to get its charter, leaving the nation fiscally weakened. Gallatin, as Secretary of the Treasury, was aware of the full extent of the problem, because it fell to him to resolve it—a task he met with little success. Exacerbating matters was the fact that the New England Federalists, furious at the ruinous effect of the war on New England commerce, prevented their state militia from falling under federal control, refused the government loans, and even went so far as to lend money and sell provisions to the enemy. In December of 1814, Federalist discontent was formally expressed at a meeting in Hartford, Connecticut at which some fairly substantial Constitutional amendments were discussed. The Hartford Convention "recommended to the Legislatures of the several states represented in this Convention to adopt all such measures as may be necessary effectually to protect the citizens of said states from the operation and effects of all acts which have been or may be passed by the Congress of the United States, which shall contain provisions, subjecting the militia or other citizens to forcible drafts, conscriptions, or impressments, not authorized by the Constitution of the United States." The Convention also approved a report that made the point even more forcibly: "A severance of the Union by one or more States against the will of the rest, and especially in a time of war," it declared, "can be justified only by absolute necessity." But it could be justified; that was the point. In effect, the Convention asserted that states had the right of noncompliance with federal laws they disagreed with; in short, they could nullify them or, in a worst-case scenario, they could secede from the Union. For this reason, the Hartford Convention has been described by historian Maurice Baker as "a highlight not only of the last winter of the war but also of American political history," although it, like the war itself, ended not with a bang, but with a whimper. Commissioners were sent to Washington to present the Convention's terms to the government, but because they arrived to the news both of Jackson's victory at New Orleans and the Treaty of Ghent, their mission was in vain. As things turned out, it would be left to the hero of the Battle of New Orleans to grasp the nettle of nullification when it reared its head again, but this time in the South.[9]

The Hartford Convention had revealed a dangerous strain in New England thinking, one that boiled down to the idea that it was their way—or the highway. Yet, in the short term at least, this came to nothing. As the threat of interference from European powers faded, Americans could turn their attention once more to internal matters. Unsurprisingly, however, the removal of a foreign threat left more room for domestic disputes, and before too long the North and South were squaring off on the subject of slavery. The years following the War of 1812 were ones of territorial consolidation and political realignment. Although historians sometimes term this "the era of good feelings," the period was actually one of bitter political dispute and, within four years of the Treaty of Ghent, sectional dispute, too. Ironically, in many ways it was the desire for a stronger national cohesion that produced sectional disagreements. Keen to promote a more common feeling across the Union and to draw its component parts into a more smoothly functioning and more profitable whole, the government instigated a program of economic nationalism, designed to protect and encourage American industry. The "American System," as it came to be called, introduced tariffs as a means of achieving this, but a difficulty lay in the fact that the North and South had very different requirements, and, increasingly, no single tariff could accommodate both sections. In the beginning, support for the tariff crossed the sectional divide. In 1816, the great Southern statesman, John C. Calhoun (who would later become famous for opposing the Tariff of 1828 with his *Exposition and Protest*), was of the opinion that the tariff would give a much-needed boost to the Southern economy. But subsequent tariffs did not meet with Southern approval, and the sectional divide widened over this, as over other issues, between 1816 and 1830. Although the tariff was the immediate subject of this growing sectional antagonism, it was slavery, above all, that was the cause.

The famous "fire bell in the night," as Thomas Jefferson described it, alerting Americans to the potential dangers of the slavery issue, was the Missouri Compromise of 1820. As more territories applied for statehood, the pressure to maintain a political balance between the slave and free states became pressing. The balance had been maintained in the admission of states to the Union. Of the six newest arrivals, three were from the lands covered by the Northwest Ordinance—Ohio (1803), Indiana (1816), and Illinois (1818)—and three were in the South and were slaveholding states—Louisiana (1812), Mississippi (1817), and Alabama (1819). It was at that point of balance, in February 1819, that the territory of Missouri applied for admission. Missouri was a territory mainly settled by migrants from the South; about 10 percent of its population was enslaved. Although the balance could have been maintained between slave and free states because Maine—at that point still part of Massachusetts—was also seeking admittance that year, Northerners in Congress objected—strongly—to the idea that Missouri be admitted because it not only held slaves but was proposing to ban free blacks from entering the state.

When the bill to admit Missouri came before Congress, James Tallmadge, representative from New York, proposed gradual manumission as a condition of Missouri's admittance. The "Tallmadge Amendment" passed in the House—just—but was defeated in the Senate, with voting along clearly sectional lines. The issue was so heated, in part, because of growing moral objections to slavery, but more so because of the political implications: the North, with a far greater population than the South, dominated the House of Representatives, even with the three-fifths clause in place; in the Senate, of course, it was a different matter. There the balance relied on there being an equal number of slave and free states. This balance was maintained via the Missouri Compromise, effected in large part by Henry Clay of Kentucky, that brought Maine and Missouri, free and slave states, respectively, into the Union and, at the same time, closed to slavery all territories that were part of the Louisiana Purchase north of latitude 36°30', with the exception of Missouri itself, which formally gained admittance in 1821.

For the time being, therefore, the issue was put aside, but Jefferson, for one, was horrified by its implications. Writing to John Holmes in April of 1820, Jefferson described how "this momentous question, like a fire bell in the night, awakened and filled me with terror. I considered it at once as the knell of the Union. It is hushed, indeed, for the moment. But this is a reprieve only, not a final sentence. A geographical line, coinciding with a marked principle, moral and political, once conceived and held up to the angry passions of men, will never be obliterated." In the case of slavery, Jefferson believed that the nation had "the wolf by the ears, and we can neither hold him, nor safely let him go. Justice is in one scale, and self-preservation in the other." He concluded his letter on a bleak note:

> I regret that I am now to die in the belief, that the useless sacrifice of themselves by the generation of 1776, to acquire self-government and happiness to their country, is to be thrown away by the unwise and unworthy passions of their sons, and that my only consolation is to be, that I live not to weep over it. If they would but dispassionately weigh the blessings they will throw away, against an abstract principle more likely to be effected by union than by scission, they would pause before they would perpetrate this act of suicide on themselves, and of treason against the hopes of the world.[10]

In fact, Jefferson's countrymen did pause, but only for a decade, before returning, in 1828, to the subjects of tariffs, slavery, and disunion. By the late 1820s in the North, especially in New England, manufacturing was becoming increasingly important, as were the tariffs to support it. The South, however, had seen little benefit from earlier tariffs, and South Carolina, in particular, was not inclined to support the 1828 tariff, which soon acquired the nickname, "Tariff of Abominations"—hardly a title that tripped off the tongue, but it conveyed the sentiment well enough. South Carolina's response expressed itself most cogently in Vice President John C. Calhoun's *Exposition and Protest*, which he wrote anonymously in 1828, and in which he set out, more clearly even than the Hartford Convention had done, the right of nullification and its implications. South Carolinians, Calhoun declared, "would never desire to speak of our country ... but as one great whole, having a common interest, which all its parts ought zealously to promote," but in the wake of the Tariff of 1828, he suggested, "it will be impossible to avoid the discussion of sectional interest, and the use of sectional language." He was right.[11]

The North, the South, and Sectionalism

Alexis de Tocqueville had arrived in America just prior to what became known as the "Nullification Crisis," the attempt on the part of South Carolina to nullify a revised Tariff of Abominations that had been passed in July 1832. The timing of his arrival gave him a unique opportunity to observe the North and South in action, as it were, over this and other issues. When Tocqueville arrived in 1831, it was immediately apparent to him that "two opposite tendencies" existed in America, "like two currents flowing in contrary directions in the same channel." On the one hand, various states that made up the Union were moving closer together; on the other, there was clear evidence that some of them, at least, were moving away from the rest. "The inhabitants of the Southern states," he observed, "are, of all the Americans, those who are most interested in the maintenance of the Union; they would assuredly suffer most from being left to themselves, and yet they are the only ones who threaten to break the tie of confederation." Struggling to understand the causes of the "deep-seated uneasiness and ill-defined agitation … observable in the South," Tocqueville concluded that the "precipitate" speed of growth in America—demographic and geographic—exacerbated North/South tensions. If the changes "were gradual, so that each generation at least might have time to disappear with the order of things under which it had lived," he decided, "the danger would be less."[12]

If anything, however, the speed of growth and, with it, change increased after Tocqueville's visit. Immigration, in particular, picked up dramatically after 1830. The rise in the cotton trade meant that there were more ships sailing between Europe and America, ships able to transport passengers—and at a reduced cost. By the early 1840s, some 50,000 people a year were coming to America; between 1847 and 1854, partly as a result of the Irish famine, over 300,000 immigrants were arriving annually. The majority of migrants arrived, and remained—for a time at least—in the northeastern seaboard cities, or they moved to the upper Mississippi Valley, to Ohio, Illinois, and Pennsylvania or to the new mill towns of New England. The South, by contrast, saw little white immigration: its slave-based economy offered immigrants fewer opportunities, but it was also the case that the developing transport links tended to take people in an east-west direction. The Erie Canal, for example, completed in 1825, linked the Hudson River to Lake Erie, and so New York to the Great Lakes region; in 1852 the first rail link was established between New York and Chicago, but the railroad construction boom of the 1850s mostly passed the South by. By 1860, 71 percent of all American railroads were in the North, a crucial, although not decisive, benefit for the North when the war finally came.

Some of this frenetic activity, of course, was financed by the profits made by Northern bankers, merchants, and manufacturers on the back of the South's profitable cotton business: the South was a crucial player in the national economy, but as the arguments over the tariff demonstrated, it felt itself to be an undervalued one.

In part, the breach that prompted the Nullification Crisis arose out of personal political ambitions; in larger part, however, it arose out of the as yet unsettled issue of the extent and validity of states' rights within the federal system. Matters reached a head in one of the most revealing debates over the function and nature of the federal Union that ever took place in the United States Senate: The personal rift was between Jackson and his Vice President, John C. Calhoun, whose earlier nationalist position on the tariff had, with his *Exposition and Protest*, clearly undergone some revision. Unable to take an open stand in the Senate on the matter, Calhoun nevertheless informed the famous debate in January 1830 between Daniel Webster (by then senator for Massachusetts) and Robert Y. Hayne, of South Carolina. On the surface it was a clear-cut debate between a states' rights advocate (Hayne) and a nationalist spokesman (Webster); in fact, the Webster-Hayne debates appeared to turn into a confrontation between the North and the South, between the nation and the section, between the Northern Yankee and the Southern Cavalier. Yet it was not that simple. Although portrayed as an event in which, according to one historian, "the virtues of New England life and character were pitted against those of the South," the debate was actually a bizarre game of nationalist one-upmanship. Webster accused the South of narrow-minded selfishness and proposed that, by contrast, the North, and specifically New England, was fervently patriotic. "Our notion of things is entirely different," he declared. "We look upon the states, not as separated, but as united. We love to dwell on that Union, and on the mutual happiness which it has so much prompted ... We do not impose geographical limits to our patriotic feeling or regard." It was common in this period for notable political exchanges to be widely disseminated in pamphlet form and through the press. Even by the standards of today, Webster's gung-ho defense of the Union in the name of New England—or possibly vice versa—was a best seller, selling over 100,000 copies. Clearly, as far as the North was concerned, Webster's words had struck a chord; in the case of the South, however, they had hit a nerve.[13]

The months and years following the Webster-Hayne debates found each side entrenching; more a reconnaissance of each side's position on the issue than a concerted attempt to change minds, the debates exacerbated rather than muted sectional disagreement and, if anything, raised sectional awareness. Above all, they helped solidify Southern, specifically South Carolinian, opposition to federal policy on the tariff and its perceived attack on slavery and the whole Southern way of life. Future governor of South Carolina George McDuffie summed up the South's position with his observation "When I hear a Southern man cry 'Union' methinks I smell treason on the tainted gale; but when I hear a Northern man shout 'Union,' I think I hear the trumpet blast of a robber band." As would be the case in the secession winter of 1860–61, the voices of moderation in the South after 1830 were drowned out by the increasingly vituperative shouts of those whose stand on nullification was, with hindsight, the start of a process that would eventually push the South into a corner from which nullification's logical extension, secession, would be the only way out. Calhoun vigorously denied the suggestion that nullification, over time, might result in secession, arguing on the basis of state sovereignty within the federal system. Indeed, the tariff, the ostensible bone of contention at the center of the controversy, was all but ignored. When, however, the revised tariff was passed in 1832, Calhoun threw caution aside and resigned from the vice presidency—the better to support his state. South Carolina adopted an ordinance nullifying the tariff acts of 1828 and 1832 and, finally, made it clear that the state would secede if any force was used to ensure its compliance.[14]

President Jackson was having none of it. In a proclamation issued in December 1832, Jackson made it clear that, "the power to annul a law of the United States, assumed by one State, [is] *incompatible with the existence of the Union, contradicted expressly by the letter of the Constitution, unauthorized by its spirit, inconsistent with every principle on which it was founded, and destructive of the great object for which it was formed."* He reminded his audience that the national compact was between the people, that the states no longer held absolute sovereignty but had abrogated that right to the federal Union, and pointed out that had the doctrine of nullification "been established at an earlier day, the Union would have been dissolved in its infancy." He ended with a not-so-subtle threat on the need to uphold federal laws:

> Those who told you that you might peaceably prevent their execution, deceived you—they could not have been deceived themselves. They know that a forcible opposition could alone prevent the execution of the laws, and they know that such opposition must be repelled. Their object is disunion, but be not deceived by names; disunion, by armed force, is TREASON. Are you really ready to incur its guilt?[15]

Put like that, the people of South Carolina had little choice. They were, in any case, somewhat outnumbered. Although other Southern states were equally opposed to the tariff legislation, they were not in favor of nullification. South Carolina had long been a state apart, in many ways. In the low country, whites were heavily outnumbered by slaves, and the memory of slave rebellions—including the famous Denmark Vesey conspiracy of 1822—made South Carolinians particularly uneasy about the stability of the 'peculiar institution.' They were not alone in their concerns, but in 1832 their reaction was deemed too extreme by the rest of the South. Jackson had already sent troops to Charleston, promising to lead them himself if it came to it. South Carolina began to mobilize, but the wind had gone out of its sails. A further compromise tariff, drafted by Henry Clay, passed Congress in 1833 and was accepted by South Carolina. The Nullification Crisis, like the War of 1812, ended with both sides claiming a victory of sorts, but neither side feeling entirely easy about the implications. Jackson's strong defense of the Union established a valuable precedent for Abraham Lincoln to work from some thirty years later; but it was Calhoun's defense of the right of nullification that called up the specter of secession and disunion that, in the intervening period, was never fully laid to rest.

Both the Webster-Hayne debates and the Nullification Crisis need to be seen in the broader context of the North/South relationship before their full impact can be properly understood. Sectionalism and nationalism had been, at best, eddies in the stream of American political and cultural life up to that point. It is important to bear in mind, too, that although the South had committed itself to a slave-based economy as the North had to a free-labor one, the similarities between the two sections were as striking as their very obvious differences. As Edward Pessen pointed out, North and South were, and are, "figures of speech that distort and oversimplify a complex reality," and if the South was not entirely a land of palatial plantation splendor, no more was the North a land of opportunity for the huddled masses of the early- to mid-nineteenth century. Each section had its opportunities; each its barriers. Neither section was racially or ethnically inclusive, as we would understand the concept today, although in chattel slavery the South had refined a system that went beyond mere racism in its conception, its dehumanizing impact, and its cruelty. Agriculture was the dominant means whereby both Northerners and Southerners made their living, although the crops they grew were different: wheat in the North; cotton, rice, tobacco, and sugar in the South. Although urban growth did not occur on the same scale in the South as in the North, nevertheless Southern cities grew fast: Baltimore had been the third largest city in 1810; by 1860 it had only dropped to fourth after New York, Philadelphia, and Brooklyn (not yet a borough of New York). New Orleans was of a similar size to Boston, Cincinnati, and St. Louis. Wealth in both sections was concentrated in the hands of a few, and they tended to hang on to it; consequently, vertical mobility was similar, that is, infrequent, in both North and South. The wealthy held political power and wielded social and political influence in both sections. Although the short-lived and more radical political movements that were part of the Northern political landscape—the Liberty Party and the Free-Soil Party, both committed to the prevention of slavery's further extension—were not represented in the South, the main political parties—after the 1830s, the Whigs and the Democrats—evinced no strong sectional bias, tended to vote along party lines, and had leaders from both North and South. Yet it would have mattered little had North and South been identical twins. Separated, not at birth but certainly in early adolescence, by slavery, North and South had, by 1850, each reached a point where the stereotype—be it positive or negative—held stronger sway than the reality.[16]

Exactly when—if at all—it becomes accurate to talk of a distinct "South" will doubtless remain a matter of historical debate, but certainly by the time that Tocqueville visited America, the sense that there was already an entity that might be so termed was palpable. Webster relied on a popular understanding of the idea of "The South" in his debate with Hayne, just as Hayne, Calhoun, and many other Southern spokesmen had a fairly clear concept of what it was they were defending in the whole debate over the tariff—and it was not the individual state but a way of life, predicated on slavery, a *herrenvolk* democracy that achieved the myth of white unity in the face of racial diversity. It was not an entirely Southern construction. Northerners were equally involved in the development of the mythical entity that became "The South." In Boorstin's words, this was "the most unreal, most powerful, and most disastrous oversimplification in American history." Initially, it was not a wholly negative simplification. The more obvious pace of change, fueled in part by immigration in the North, prompted some Northerners to look at the South in a positive light, as a stable society protected in some senses from the fluctuating forces of urbanization, immigration, and (early) industrialization that seemed to cause so much upheaval in their own section. The positive image of the South was also informed as much by Northern racial attitudes as by concerns over matters such as immigration, but so, paradoxically, was the negative image. Slavery very rapidly became a fading memory in the North, and as the institution transformed from national embarrassment to Southern problem, abolitionists in the North were able to shift from the margins of Northern reform debate, where they had been seen as little more than a group of extremists, and toward the center of growing opposition, not just to slavery, but to all things Southern. At the same time, because the "Cotton Kingdom" of the South was growing in economic importance and geographic spread, Southerners were becoming increasingly defensive about slavery and the society they had structured around it.[17]

From its earlier position as a necessary and national evil, slavery after 1830 was increasingly presented, in Calhoun's words, as "a good—a positive good." This conclusion (which many found surprising in its implications, to put it mildly) was reached in 1837, and couched in the specific context of a long-running debate over the right of Congress to hear abolitionist petitions. Its broader context lay outside of Congress, and derived from events both in, and far beyond, the South. In 1829, a free-born African American from North Carolina, David Walker, published his now-famous *Appeal to the Colored Citizens of the World*, in which he advised African Americans: "If you commence, make sure work—do not trifle, for they will not trifle with you—they want us for their slaves, and think nothing of murdering us in order to subject us to that wretched condition—therefore, if there is an *attempt* made by us, kill or be killed." This was not at all what white Southerners wished to hear, and their worst fears were realized when, two years later, in August 1831 in Southampton County, Virginia, a slave named Nat Turner led an uprising that was as short-lived as it was brutal. The ripples it sent out reached far beyond Virginia, far beyond the South. The Civil War had already begun when Thomas Wentworth Higginson, colonel of one of the first black regiments, recalled the Turner affair of thirty years previously as "a memory of terror, a symbol of wild retribution." What Turner had done, in the words of future governor of Virginia James McDowell, was awaken "the suspicion eternally attached to the slave himself, the suspicion that a Nat Turner might be in every family, that the same bloody deed might be acted over at any time and in any place, that the materials for it were spread throughout the land, and were always ready for a like explosion." That William Lloyd Garrison had, in January 1831, published the first edition of his abolitionist paper, *The Liberator*, was a further irritant to Southerners, who suspected that both Walker's *Appeal* and Garrison's paper had helped foment Turner's uprising. Garrison called for the immediate emancipation of all slaves, and famously declared "I am in earnest—I will not equivocate—I will not excuse—I will not retreat a single inch—and I will be heard." He was. Although *The Liberator* had a relatively modest circulation—some 3,000 mainly African-American subscribers—its views were sufficiently irritating to Southerners to ensure it enough negative publicity that its impact belied its sales figures. Increasingly, its influence spread among the ever-widening pool of Northerners whose opposition to the radicalism of abolition was gradually being replaced by a desire to see an end to slavery in the land of the free.[18]

The fact was that slavery was already becoming an anachronism in the world of the mid-nineteenth century, and Americans were hardly oblivious to that fact. Britain had abolished the slave trade in her colonies in 1807, and the pressure to end slavery itself had been growing since the late-eighteenth century. The Congress of Vienna in 1815 saw European statesmen condemn the institution, although no effective steps were taken to end it at that point. However, when the campaign in Britain gathered momentum after 1830, Americans were well aware of it. Newspaper coverage of the British Parliamentary debate over slavery in the West Indies was widespread between 1830 and 1833, when Britain finally passed the Abolition of Slavery Act. Southerners did not, at that point, have their heads in the sand over slavery's implications; they were prepared to discuss it—up to a point. That point came in 1831, when the Virginia General Assembly decided to tackle both the subject of slavery and the status of free blacks in the state. For two weeks in January 1832, the Virginia delegates debated the question of whether or not to retain slavery, and what the alternatives might be: they found very few. In the end, the Virginia slavery debate was significant not for what it achieved, but because it was the last public, open debate in a Southern state legislature on the subject. Apart from Roderick Dew's *Review of the Debate in the Virginia Legislature of 1831–1832*, little that was tangible emerged from the debate. It did, however, throw into sharp relief the divisions within the state on the subject. With opposition to slavery coming from west of the Blue Ridge Mountains, support mostly concentrated in the Tidewater and Piedmont regions; slavery's supporters realized that the audience they needed to convince was not in the North— there was little chance of that anyway—but much closer to home. Dew's summation of proslavery thought from biblical times to his own did not reach a wider audience until the 1850s, but Southern proslavery spokesmen rehearsed its highlights in public and in private with an enthusiasm born of desperation. At the same time, and flying in the face of common sense, they sought to restrict discussion of the subject in Congress via the passage of the Gag Rule (the 21st Rule) of 1836, which required all petitions relating to slavery to be automatically tabled, that is, not discussed. If they had wanted to raise public awareness of the subject, they could not have picked a better method. In attempting to stifle debate, slavery's supporters had only succeeded in opening new avenues for opposition to their actions on the grounds that they had undermined civil liberties and restricted free speech in a supposedly free republic.[19]

When Calhoun rose in the Senate in 1837 to speak on the subject of abolitionist petitions, it was already the case (as he realized) that a "large portion of the Northern States believed slavery to be a sin," and that this view was spreading. His own arguments reiterated those of the Virginia debates five years previously, and summed up, with little deviation, the proslavery creed that would, in time, spread more widely throughout the South. For Calhoun, as for others, slavery was the solution to the eternal battle between labor and capital, and "the existing relation between the two races in the South," as they saw it, offered "the most stable and durable foundation on which to rear free and stable institutions." Yet Calhoun's confidence in the "positive good" of slavery was tempered by his awareness that the South's adherence to the institution coupled with growing Northern opposition to it contained the seeds of disunion. "By the necessary course of events, if left to themselves," he warned,

> we must become, finally, two people. It is impossible under the deadly hatred which must spring up between the two great nations, if the present causes are permitted to operate unchecked, that we should continue under the same political system. The conflicting elements would burst the Union asunder, powerful as are the links which hold it together. Abolition and the Union cannot coexist.

Calhoun's radical defense of the indefensible confirmed what Tocqueville had realized during his visit in 1831–32: slavery did "not attack the American Union directly in its interests, but indirectly in its manners." Tocqueville also concluded at that time, however, that the "civilization of the North appears to be the common standard, to which the whole nation will one day be assimilated." Calhoun's response to that observation can only be imagined.[20]

Increasingly, slavery affected almost every aspect of American political life. In a nation that was still expanding and to which people were flocking in hundreds of thousands, the need to establish the ground on which that nation would develop became ever more pressing. If the 1830s had been, in some senses, the decade of the slavery debate, the 1840s was the decade of westward expansion on a grand scale; it was the decade in which America began to consider the nature of its "Manifest Destiny." The phrase itself came into popular use after 1845, when John O'Sullivan, editor of the *Democratic Review*, used it in the context of a complaint against Great Britain that, he asserted, was attempting to impede "the fulfillment of our manifest destiny to overspread the continent allotted by Providence for the free development of our yearly multiplying millions." O'Sullivan was referring to the ongoing dispute over British interests in Oregon and California, and the admittance to the Union, that year, of Texas, all areas that were becoming increasingly attractive to American settlers. By the 1840s, American expansion was irrevocably tied to the slavery issue, and the debate over the validity of further territorial acquisition in this decade was overtly sectional in tone. Texas, at that point under Mexican jurisdiction, had attracted mainly Southern settlers, who had brought their slaves with them despite the fact that slavery had been abolished in Mexico in 1829. Attempts by Mexico to force compliance with its laws resulted in Texas declaring itself an independent republic in 1836 and seeking admission to the Union, but this move was blocked by Northern opposition to what was perceived as an attempt to extend both slaveholding territory and the political power of the South. California, another Mexican province, had very few American settlers—about 700 in 1845—but it, too, was interested in applying for admission to the Union. Oregon was a rather different proposition, being held jointly by Great Britain and the United States, but by the 1840s it, too, was seeking to formalize its relationship with America. By the mid-1840s, therefore, an enormous amount of territory appeared to be within America's grasp. The question was, if it acquired that territory, at what cost, and on what basis: slave, or free?[21]

The election of 1844 was dominated by the question of these prospective territories, with the Democrats pushing for the acquisition of Texas and Oregon and many antislavery Whigs giving their votes to the Liberty Party, which had just been formed in 1840 but in 1844 was powerful enough to influence the outcome of the election in the crucial state of New York. With a very narrow Democratic victory—James K. Polk was elected—the election revealed both that expansion was not universally popular and that antislavery was rising as a political force. The final act of the outgoing administration had been to bring Texas into the Union, and it was the controversy surrounding this that prompted O'Sullivan's analysis of the annexation issue in the *Democratic Review*. O'Sullivan was adamant that there was no truth in "the charge that Annexation is a great proslavery measure—calculated to increase and perpetuate that institution. Slavery," he asserted, "had nothing to do with it." Not everyone was convinced. The issue became more heated with the outbreak, in 1846, of war with Mexico. The Oregon dispute had been settled that year, with the 49th parallel agreed upon as the boundary between America and Canada. Further south, however, the question of Texas was raised again when Mexico proved unwilling to relinquish the territory. Mexico's intransigence, however, simply gave Polk the opportunity to go after other Mexican territories—California and New Mexico—and the resultant war proved to be the cause of yet further schism on the slavery issue in America. Many leading congressmen, Calhoun among them, saw the war as one of unjustified aggression, while large parts of the Northeast were convinced that it was a war designed to extend the influence of what was becoming known as the "Slave Power." When, in 1846, Pennsylvania representative David Wilmot proposed that slavery be prohibited in any territory resulting from the Mexican War, the battle lines were drawn. Although the Wilmot Proviso passed the House twice, each time it was defeated in the Senate. Nevertheless, it polarized opinion on the subject of slavery in the territories. Searching for a "third way" between the extreme proslavery position of Calhoun and the opposition forces gathering in the North, Senator Lewis P. Cass of

Michigan devised the concept of "popular sovereignty" as a solution to the question of whether any territory should be slave or free. On the surface, it made perfect sense; let the people of that territory decide, but reading between the lines, it was less obvious when, exactly, that decision might be made or what the political outcome might be.[22]

The 1848 election raised the stakes of antislavery politics still further with the appearance of the Free-Soil Party. Although short-lived as a political force in its own right, the appearance of the Free-Soil Party signaled the beginning of the end for the Second Party System as both politicians and their constituents began to realign along the divisions raised by slavery. The discovery of gold in California that year raised the stakes as far as territorial expansion was concerned but, again, the question was whether California, at that point a territory of some 100,000 people, would be slave or free. California's population favored a constitution prohibiting slavery, and it was on that basis that it applied for admission. New Mexico's application only a few months later on the same basis only exacerbated Southern concerns that the carefully maintained congressional balance between slave and free states would be destroyed in favor of the free states and that the national abolition of slavery would soon follow. Again, South Carolina was in the vanguard of opposition, but this time it was joined by Mississippi. With the threat of secession once more on the horizon, Henry Clay stepped in, yet again, to broker a compromise. The resultant Compromise of 1850 got through, but only by the most adept of political maneuvering on the part of democratic senator Stephen A. Douglas. Under its terms, California came into the Union as a free state, the territory gained from Mexico was divided in two—New Mexico and Utah— and the issue of slavery was left for the doctrine of popular sovereignty to resolve at some unspecified time in the future. By the end of 1850, then, the Union remained intact. The North had gained control of the Senate with California's admittance; the South's loss seemed, that year, the greater with the death of John C. Calhoun. Yet death had not really removed Calhoun from the South, nor from the sectional battles that would intensify after his passing. As Missouri senator Thomas Hart Benton put it, in refusing to eulogize Calhoun in the Senate: "He is not dead, sir—he is not dead. There may be no vitality in his body, but there is in his doctrines." It was not intended as a compliment.[23]

The Turbulent Fifties

As with previous compromises, the Compromise of 1850 was, at best, a temporary solution. For over thirty years, American politicians had succeeded in papering over the cracks caused by the growing disparity between North and South. It was becoming clear, however, that the cracks were no longer attributable to the natural settling expected in any new construction, but revealed foundational flaws in the Union. At the same time, as David Potter once stressed, it is important not to apply hindsight with too sweeping a brush. If the 1850s appears to us to be an inexorable build-up to war, from the perspective of the time the decade promised little more than business as usual: arguments about slavery in the territories; increased defensiveness in the South; and growing abolitionist agitation in the North. If anything, the absence of these familiar factors might have proved a greater cause for concern. Yet a shift had occurred in the interaction between North and South, one that did not bode well for the Union. Confidence in the nation's future, arising from the dramatic population growth and geographical expansion of the previous two decades, coexisted with a deep-rooted concern over the kind of nation America was to become. The population imbalance between North and South—the North had three times the population of the South in 1850—was a source of concern to both sections, but for different reasons. Southerners feared for their political influence and increasing isolation in a nation moving away from them, geographically, demographically and, above all, ideologically. For their part, Northerners were concerned by the rapid growth of the nation and the incorporation of non-Anglo-Saxon peoples into the polity—especially after the Mexican War—and the national implications of this; about this issue, they were perhaps more concerned than Southerners. In a sense, the South simply stuck to the script, as Calhoun had bequeathed it to them: "We of the South will not, cannot, surrender our institutions," he had bluntly stated in 1837, and for many white Southerners his words became an article of faith, a mantra that, if they just kept repeating it often enough, would keep both the North and the surely restless spirit of Nat Turner from their door.[24]

The continuous search for a workable compromise reveals how hard Americans were prepared to strive for the Union, but each compromise, in a sense, weakened it. Americans North and South had much in common: a shared history, however brief, for which migration and the Revolution formed the bedrock; shared heroes, most notably Washington and Jefferson; a shared political system, albeit one prone to change; a shared way of life, in the main; a shared belief in the merits of popular government; and a shared commitment to the ideals of liberty. Alternative interpretations of this last point, however, served only to widen the gulf between the free and slave states. "We all declare for liberty," Lincoln observed in the course of the Civil War, "but in using the same *word* we do not all mean the same *thing*. With some the word liberty may mean for each man to do as he pleases with himself, and the product of his labor; while with others the same word may mean for some men to do as they please with other men, and the product of other men's labor." Out of that fundamental difference grew fear and more than a degree of mutual hostility. Each side in the sectional standoff that was coming to typify America felt threatened by the other. In the North, the South saw a potential threat to its "peculiar institution" of slavery; in the South, the North perceived a growing political threat, the so-called Slave Power, the perceived political unity of Southern politicians within the nation generally, Congress specifically, and the executive branch of government particularly. First identified by New England minister and historian John Gorham Palfrey in 1846, this specter had all the apparent trappings of an exaggerated conspiracy theory; but it was actually a fairly realistic appraisal of the South's influence in the nation up to the 1850s. Southerners had not only held the presidency for twenty-four years, but the entire federal political structure worked in their favor. The three-fifths clause enhanced their representation at the national level, and parity in the Senate—until the admittance of California—meant that they only had to secure one Northern vote to get their way. Northerners, at least up to the election of 1848, had evinced no particular unity at regional or federal levels. This was hardly surprising, but it did leave them susceptible to the rather better organized South. The South united around slavery; that was its strength. The North did not unite around antislavery; that was its weakness—until the 1850s.[25]

One immediate bone of contention arising from the Compromise of 1850 was the revised Fugitive Slave Act that had replaced an earlier act from 1793. The new act permitted slave owners to seize their property without recourse to the law and denied those seized the right of a fair trial—of any trial, come to that. Many Northern states passed "personal liberty laws" designed to protect runaway slaves—in effect, they nullified the Fugitive Slave Act, but the furor over several high-profile slave rescues that took place in Boston and New York meant no one explored the implications of this Northern nullification movement too closely. In some senses, the matter had gone beyond debate. Exacerbating the increased sectional hostility of the 1850s was the publication in 1852 of Harriet Beecher Stowe's *Uncle Tom's Cabin*. More frequently cited than actually read these days, this sweeping and somewhat melodramatic novel about slavery and its impact took the North by storm—and caused one in the South. Still, a novel, however widely read, would have had a limited impact on events had it not been for the dramatic political realignment that took place in the 1850s. With slavery moving center-stage in the political arena, Stowe's novel spoke to the concerns of its day. The 1852 election was the last to field a Whig candidate (he did not win); the Whig Party disappeared from the political scene, not entirely overnight but with sufficient rapidity as to cause major upheaval. 1852, as it turned out, was not a good year for the Union: two of America's leading statesmen, each of whom had done a great deal to hold the Union together—Henry Clay and Daniel Webster—died that year, and with them passed the age of compromise.

The event that pushed many people into the antislavery camp was the Kansas–Nebraska Act of 1854. Conceived by democratic senator for Illinois, Stephen A. Douglas, the Kansas-Nebraska Act extended the use of the popular sovereignty approach into these newly created territories. Both of them lay within the land acquired by the Louisiana Purchase and were north of the line of latitude above which slavery was excluded; therefore, under the terms of the Missouri Compromise, should have automatically been free. In proposing popular sovereignty as the means of deciding their status, Douglas believed he was giving nothing away in practice, merely establishing a point of principle to appease the South, and viewed opposition to it as "raised by Abolitionists, and Abolitionists alone." It was no longer merely abolitionists, and abolitionists alone, however, who were opposed to the repudiation of the Missouri Compromise. Opposition to the Kansas-Nebraska Act was far more widespread than that, taking a variety of forms via a range of anti-Nebraska groups. From the Republicans to the short-lived, but influential, Nativist American "Know-Nothing Party," the groups were all opposed to the further extension of slavery and they were equally concerned about other issues, notably immigration. That the Republican Party was the one to emerge from this morass of opposition to Douglas's bill had much to do with its agenda, which went beyond simple opposition to slavery to define, ultimately, a Northern opposition to the South that was capable of transcending and incorporating a multitude of contemporary concerns. Under the slogan "Free Soil, Free Labor, Free Men," the Republicans attracted a broad constituency: radical abolitionists as well as those whose opposition to slavery was based more on its economic and political effects on the white population—former Whigs, free-soil Democrats, and Know-Nothings. The Republican slogan was not likely to attract many voters south of the Mason-Dixon line, and the Republicans did not try with any enthusiasm to attract them. Republican rhetoric built on the gradual development, over the previous few decades, of concerns over Slave Power, of a growing hostility to the South, not just to slavery as an institution, and to the stereotypical perception of the South as a region antithetical to Republican values—to American values, as the Republicans understood and presented those values. In the end, Douglas's bill was forced through, but at the cost of the Second Party System: Northern Whigs opposed it; both Southern Whigs and Democrats supported it; but Northern Democrats were split over it—44 for and 43 against. With the passage of the Kansas-Nebraska Bill, party loyalties dissolved; sectional ones solidified.[26]

Douglas's bill wreaked havoc, and not just in Washington. Popular sovereignty produced mob violence in Kansas, as both free-soil and proslavery settlers swarmed into the territory, spurred on in part by support—financial and practical—from the opposing sections, for whom Kansas had become the battleground between North and South, slave and free. The elections held in 1855 and 1856 to establish the governance of the territory were something of a joke, but there was no humor in it. Proslavery supporters from neighboring Missouri—understandably unwilling to have a free state next door—voted, illegally, in Kansas in 1855 to establish a proslavery legislature at Shawnee; antislavery voters met at Topeka to try to establish the territory on a free-soil basis, but the federal government deemed that illegal and recognized the Shawnee legislature. With two legislatures and two governors, Kansas descended into a state of mini-civil war in 1856. Proslavery supporters attacked Lawrence, and the radical abolitionist John Brown retaliated with an attack at Pottawatomie Creek, during which five people were killed. The violence in Kansas found its echo in Washington, in the halls of Congress, no less. When the radical politician Charles Sumner of Massachusetts was physically attacked in the Senate by Congressman Preston Brooks of South Carolina (Sumner had made a speech condemning the South and Brooks's relative, Andrew P. Butler), Northerners expressed both shock and a certain grim satisfaction that their worst fears about the South had been confirmed. They had some grounds for this, because the attack on Sumner was simply one of several occasions when Southerners had resorted to violence to make their point. In December 1855, William Smith, representative from Virginia, attacked the editor of the Washington *Evening Star*. Within a few months another newspaper editor, the well-known Horace Greeley of the *New York Tribune*, incurred the wrath of Albert Rust, representative from Arkansas, and in the same month—May—as Brooks's attack on Sumner, Philemon T. Herbert, representative from California, but a native of Alabama, shot and killed a waiter in a Washington hotel in an argument over, of all things, breakfast. With the twinned symbolic headlines, "Bleeding Kansas" and "Bleeding Sumner," the North/South relationship, by the middle of 1856, had never seemed worse.[27]

In the 1856 election year, the new Republican Party fielded its first presidential candidate, John C. Frémont. He did not win, but he came close, carrying all but five of the free states. Yet the new administration, headed by James Buchanan, seemed to ignore the potential implications of this near-miss for a very new and overtly sectional party; North/South tensions worsened only days after Buchanan took office in March 1857, when the Supreme Court ruled on *Dred Scott v. Sandford*. This case, brought by a slave from Missouri who had spent most of his life in the free states, blew apart the already weakened Missouri Compromise. Chief Justice Roger B. Taney denied Scott's application on two main points: first, that as a slave, he could not be a citizen; second, that under the Fifth Amendment to the Constitution no citizen could be deprived of property without due process, and that therefore any legislative attempt to deny the right of slave owners to take their property where they wished—such as the Missouri Compromise—was unconstitutional. Taney used both legal and extra-legal precedent to establish the grounds for the decision, and the prevarication of the Founding Fathers on this point rebounded on their progeny with a vengeance. "It is difficult at this day," Taney pronounced,

> to realize the state of public opinion in relation to that unfortunate race, which prevailed in the civilized and enlightened portions of the world at the time of the Declaration of Independence, and when the Constitution of the United States was framed and adopted ... They had for more than a century before been regarded as beings of an inferior order, and altogether unfit to associate with the white race, either in social or political relations; and so far inferior, that they had no rights which the white man was bound to respect.[28]

As it was in 1787, Taney concluded, so it was in 1857: slaves were not citizens, they were property; property could be taken anywhere; therefore slaves could be taken anywhere. There could be no constitutionally sanctioned division between free and slave states because, as Taney interpreted the Constitution, there could be no "free" states from which slavery was excluded. When, in 1858, a series of debates in Illinois between Senate hopefuls Abraham Lincoln and Stephen A. Douglas addressed the matter, the echo of Calhoun could be heard in Lincoln's famous declaration that "a house divided against itself cannot stand. I believe this government cannot endure, permanently half *slave* and half *free*. I do not expect the Union to be *dissolved*—I do not expect the house to *fall*—but I *do* expect it will cease to be divided. It will become *all* one thing, or *all* the other." As Lincoln and Douglas debated the issues, however, more radical figures sought to bring slavery to an end more directly, and more conclusively, than any series of political debates seemed likely to do. The following year, John Brown attacked the federal arsenal at Harpers Ferry, Virginia, hoping to foment a slave uprising. That the attempt was ill conceived and failed utterly was no real surprise, nor was the South's reaction to it. Brown's actions brought back forcibly the memory of Nat Turner and reinforced the suspicion that the entire North was arraigned against the South and its peculiar institution. John Brown himself was undoubtedly a fanatic; his actions in Kansas in 1855 suggested as much; his actions at Harpers Ferry in 1859 confirmed it, but even a stopped clock is right twice a day. Brown professed himself certain that "the crimes of this guilty land will never be purged away, but with blood," and so it proved. In contemplating the implications of Brown's actions, and their reaction to them, both North and South in 1859 might have benefited from the advice of French author Victor Hugo. The death of John Brown, he was certain, "would be an irreparable fault. It would penetrate the Union with a gaping fissure which would lead in the end to its entire disruption ... there is something more terrible than Cain slaying Abel," Hugo warned; "It is Washington slaying Spartacus."[29]

CHAPTER 2

Divisions

And the young were all elation
Hearing Sumter's cannon roar,
And they thought how tame the Nation
In the age that went before.

—Herman Melville, from "Apathy and Enthusiasm," 1860/61[1]

Although John Brown's attack on Harpers Ferry, and the decision to hang him for it, produced shock waves across the nation, it was not yet the case that Civil War between North and South appeared inevitable—far from it. Hindsight tells us the war came, but that does not mean that, in 1859, Americans saw it coming. Funeral bells rang out across the North on the day of Brown's execution, but few Americans asked for whom these bells tolled, nor would they have believed that they tolled for the Union. Certainly an influential group of Northerners had supported Brown and approved of his actions; but many Southerners had supported Brooks when he attacked Sumner (they sent him any number of replacement canes since he had broken his over Sumner's head) so as far as support for extremist behavior was concerned, the sections were pretty even. Despite the worrying escalation of violence in Washington, Kansas, and Virginia, the evidence to support the strength of the Union was still at least as strong as that suggesting its weakness; although talk of secession was becoming more common in the South, Southerners had cried wolf too often on that score, and there was no suggestion that, this time, they might mean it. By the eve of the election of 1860, North and South both thought and functioned in an increasingly sectional way. That the North was capable of sectional thinking has been less apparent to historians whose interest in the South—be it the Slave South, the Confederacy, the New South, or the Solid South of a later era—has somewhat obscured the existence of an equally potent sectional strain in Northern thinking. The Hartford Convention of 1815 had hinted at this, but the Webster-Hayne debates of 1830 established the ground on which Northern sentiment would be predicated: the North as the national norm, the South as the sectional other. With the appearance in 1848 of the Free-Soil Party, with its agenda of opposition to slavery in the territories (loosely—if at all—aligned to moral objections to the institution), it was clear that antislavery was extending its appeal beyond the abolitionist camp. Daniel Webster, for one, understood the implications: "We talk of the North," he observed, "but up to the recent session of Congress there has been no North, no geographical section of the country, in which there has been found a strong, conscientious, and *united* opposition to slavery." In the buildup to the election of 1848, however, Webster believed that "the North star is at last discovered. I think," he concluded, "there will be a North."[2]

Twelve years later, the relatively inchoate concept of a united North had acquired both form and substance in the Republican Party, which was approaching its second attempt at election in 1860. The Republican campaign articulated a critique of the South that proved to have a greater impact than the sum of its parts would initially suggest. At the Republican Convention in Chicago in May 1860, the party adopted a platform that stressed the importance of the Union, to which "this nation owes its unprecedented increase of population, its surprising development of material resources, its rapid augmentation of wealth, its happiness at home and its honor abroad" and reaffirmed the party's "abhorrence" for "all schemes for Disunion, come from whatever source they may." At the same time, however, the Republicans challenged Justice Taney's 1857 ruling in the Dred Scott case, and asserted:

> That the normal condition of all the territory of the United States is that of Freedom: That as our Republican fathers, when they had abolished slavery in all our national territory, ordained that "no person should be deprived of life, liberty, or property, without due process of law," it becomes our duty, by legislation, whenever such legislation is necessary, to maintain this provision of the Constitution, against all attempts to violate it; and we deny the authority of Congress, of a territorial legislature, or of any individuals, to give legal existence to slavery in any Territory of the United States.[3]

This was direct enough, but not in itself grounds for disunion; such statements had been made before, indeed this clause—verbatim—had been part of the Republican Party Platform of 1856, when it had been debated at length, through arguments in Congress and the courts, in pamphlets and in newspapers, and between Lincoln and Douglas, without any sign of a resolution one way or the other. In making this demand central to its platform, it was the Republican Party's intention to win the election, not precipitate yet another sectional crisis, and certainly not to dissolve the Union that they revered. They anticipated objections, of course, but the available evidence suggested that, despite Southern leaders' increasing entrenchment on the subject of slavery, the bonds of Union would always withstand the sectional forces pulling at them. Even as Southerners threatened secession in the event of a Republican victory in 1860, and even as it became obvious that the South would never accede to the idea of banning slavery from the territories, many Republicans clung to the idea that the Union was paramount, that it was rooted in mutual sacrifice (if no longer mutual esteem), and that the voices of reason would prevail. This was not so much a case of ignoring the writing on the wall as failing to recognize the face in the mirror: as a sectional party with little or no support beyond that section, the Republicans' very existence revealed that American politics, perhaps the Union itself, had entered a period of freefall.

Northern attitudes had, as Webster recognized, been hardening over the years, to the point where the South had come to define all that was wrong with the nation—as Northerners saw it. In slavery itself, many, including Abraham Lincoln, saw a moral transgression at odds with America's republican mission; in the political power accruing from the "Slave Power," many saw a threat to their own liberties; in the Southerner, many Northerners saw an aristocratic throwback to a world America had removed itself from by the act of revolution; this was a stereotype that some Southerners were not overtly displeased with. This opposition to all things Southern, however, did not automatically imply an assumption that the nation's days were numbered. Indeed, the persistent ability of some Northerners to remain optimistic about the Union's future despite mounting evidence to the contrary was revealed in a famous Senate debate in 1858. James Henry Hammond, one of the South's leading spokesmen, made what became known as his "Mudsill Speech," in which he defended slavery and the social system deriving from it by arguing that all nations, all societies, were constructed upon what he termed a "mudsill" (as in lowest level) of laboring people; the South, as he saw it, simply had the courage to call this system by its correct name. Hammond's speech was also famous for its ringing pronouncement (made after a lengthy consideration of the economic value of the South to the Union): "You dare not make war on cotton—no power on earth dares make war upon it. Cotton is King." Neatly sidestepping the gauntlet that Hammond had just thrown down, James R. Doolittle, former Democrat but now Republican senator for Wisconsin, responded that it "will never be forgotten by the American people, that the bonds of the Union were sealed with the blood of a common ancestry, with common sacrifice, heroism, and suffering." During the Revolution, he reminded his audience, North and South had been as "a band of brothers," and he reaffirmed his "confidence in the perpetuity of the Union," and in the power of "the devoted patriotism of the great mass of the American people," based as that was on "identity of language, sympathy, and interests; upon a common history, common recollections, common hopes, and a common destiny." In a similar vein, New York lawyer James A. Dorr, encouraged Northerners to remember that the citizens of the South were "our brethren—bone of our bone, flesh of our flesh, blood of our blood ... *joint tenants and heirs with us of a common inheritance.*" Slavery, he asserted, was "an evil, a wrong, and a sin" but, he stressed, "it is a *national* evil, a *national* wrong, a *national* sin." Not everyone saw it that way.[4]

By the eve of the election of 1860, even some very moderate Northerners, who eschewed violence of all kinds, were approaching the point of no return on the slavery issue. One example was the New York lawyer and future famous diarist George Templeton Strong. He was certainly no radical, and professed himself in tune with "nine-tenths of the community" in being heartily sick of the way in which John Brown had been lionized in the New York press. At the same time, Strong was running out of patience with "Southern brag," and weary of Northern attempts to persuade the South "not to commit the treason and violence it is forever threatening." A more aggressive response came from the Northern writer Lydia Maria Child. Child had abolitionist credentials; she had published *An Appeal in Favor of that Class of Americans Called Africans* in 1833, and had served as editor of the *National Anti-Slavery Standard* in the 1840s; although this labeled her a radical, she was hardly that on the subject of the Union. The violence in Washington and Kansas in the 1850s, however, produced a perceptible shift in her thinking. When John Brown was arrested in Virginia, she instigated a remarkable correspondence with the governor of the state, Henry Wise, initially requesting permission to visit Brown. Wise professed surprise that she should even feel that such permission might not be granted; "Why should you not be so allowed, Madam?" he enquired, "Virginia and Massachusetts are involved in no civil war, and the Constitution which unites them in one confederacy guarantees to you the privileges and immunities of a citizen of the United States in the State of Virginia." Child was having none of that, and she replied that "the Constitution has, in reality, been completely and systematically nullified, whenever it suited the convenience or the policy of the Slave Power." Child's gloves were off, and in her ringing conclusion to her second letter she voiced what many Northerners were now thinking:

> The people of the North had a very strong attachment to the Union; but, by your desperate measures, you have weakened it beyond all power of restoration. They are not your enemies, as you suppose, but they cannot consent to be your tools for any ignoble task you may choose to propose ... A majority of them would rejoice to have the Slave States fulfil their oft-repeated threat of withdrawal from the Union. It has ceased to be a bugbear, for we begin to despair of being able, by any other process, to give the world the example of a real republic. The moral sense of these States is outraged by being accomplices in sustaining an institution vicious in all its aspects ... If you would only make the offer of a separation in serious earnest, you would hear the hearty response of millions, "Go, gentlemen, and stand not upon the order of your going, but go at once."

The shift in Child's thinking paralleled that of many Southerners by the eve of the 1860 election. Child had for years held to the belief that persuasion would affect the removal of slavery from the land, and that such persuasion was most potent within the context of a united country. By 1859, she no longer believed this. For many Southerners, too, the belief that slavery would be better protected in the Union than out of it was giving way to the idea that only out of the Union could the South retain its peculiar institution—and all that it implied.[5]

North and South had much in common; for both, the nation's founding documents were a tangible bond, but the meaning of that bond was clearly open to interpretation. By 1860, many Northerners had arrived at a point where the Declaration of Independence represented a principle for the nation to live up to and the prevarication of the Founding Fathers on the slavery question an error to be corrected. Southerners, by contrast, had no problem with the Founding Father's position on slavery, and saw the Declaration as an insurance policy against the encroachments of centralized power. The argument that a people had the right to "alter or abolish" a government which no longer guaranteed their "safety and happiness" became more important to Southerners than the "life, liberty, and the pursuit of happiness" philosophy that the Republicans believed informed America's national doctrine. Yet separation of the sections on this issue was by no means inevitable, although leading spokesmen, both North and South, sometimes talked as if it was. By 1858, William H. Seward, senator for New York, believed that America was on the verge of "an irrepressible conflict between opposing and enduring forces," but his was an extreme view that many people discounted. Two years later, in an echo of Seward's concerns, Georgia senator Robert Toombs concluded that the "feeling of nationality, of loyalty to the State, the feeling of a common interest and a common destiny, upon which foundations alone society can securely and permanently rest, is gradually but rapidly passing away. Hostility to the compact of Union, to the tie which binds us together, animates the bosoms and finds utterance in the tongues of millions." Sectional antipathy was certainly growing, but Toombs was guilty of some exaggeration in his description of widespread opposition to the Union. The acoustics of political ambition amplified the disunion message in Congress, but beyond Washington there was little reason to suppose that the victory of the Republicans in 1860 would result in the secession, not only of South Carolina—that might have been anticipated—but of *fifteen* slave states. Indeed, at the beginning of 1860 there was no guarantee that the Republicans would win at all.[6]

The Election of 1860

The Democratic Party had no crystal ball on hand at their convention in Charleston in April 1860, but many Democrats certainly believed that the chances of Republican victory were better—far better—than they had been four years previously. This lent a somewhat unhelpful air of desperation to the proceedings. Added to this, the choice of Charleston, South Carolina was not, perhaps, ideal for a convention seeking to decide on a national policy and a national leader. As C. Vann Woodward once put it, for many years, the South had been living in "a crisis atmosphere" produced by the need to defend slavery, and its response had been "to retreat into an isolationism of spirit." Nowhere, perhaps, was this crisis atmosphere, this self-destructive spirit, more evident than in Charleston in April 1860.[7]

Long before the convention met, several Southern states had already debated what course of action to follow in the event of a Republican victory. Most of their deliberations were predicated on the Alabama Platform. Drawn up by lawyer and former congressman William Lowndes Yancey in 1848 in response to the Wilmot Proviso, the Alabama Platform called for slavery to be permitted and protected in the territories and for delegates to walk out of the 1860 Democratic Convention if this was not agreed upon. It was not, and many delegates did. This, in itself, revealed the changing temper of the times. Twelve years previously, Yancey had walked out of the Democratic Convention over precisely the same issue. Then, he had cut rather an isolated figure, but in 1860 Yancey no longer walked alone. Delegates from eight other Southern states—Mississippi, Louisiana, South Carolina, Florida, Texas, Delaware (in part), Georgia, and Arkansas—joined Yancey as he left, taking with them any hope that the Democrats might represent a cohesive and national political force to counter the sectional threat posed by the Republicans in the forthcoming election. Divided, the Democrats did not fall, but they did split their forces at a critical juncture in American political history. The move had worked for Nelson at Trafalgar; it would work for Robert E. Lee at Second Manassas and at Chancellorsville; it did not, unfortunately, work for the Democrats in the spring of 1860. Slavery and the sectional forces arising from it had finally destroyed the last national political party America had left. For some, it seemed a price worth paying. One member of the South Carolinian delegation to follow Yancey out of the convention was John S. Preston, who stuck to his belief that "Slavery is our king—slavery is our truth—slavery is our Divine Right"; had he had the gift of foresight he might have added, "slavery is our downfall," but he didn't, and it was.[8]

By the time those Democrats who had remained in the Charleston convention reconvened in Baltimore six weeks later, two more presidential candidates had entered the opposition's lists: John Bell of Tennessee, representing the newly formed Constitutional Union Party, and Abraham Lincoln of Illinois, the eventual, and perhaps surprising, choice of the Republicans. The selection of Lincoln revealed caution and an awareness of the growing sensitivities of the South. There were many more prominent politicians in the Republican camp, notably William H. Seward of New York and Salmon P. Chase of Ohio, but both were considered too radical and, consequently, possibly too dangerous to have in charge in such uncertain times. Lincoln offered the best of both worlds; sufficiently outspoken on slavery in the territories to enthuse the radicals, he was also moderate enough in his views to appeal to the broadest possible constituency in the still new, and fairly disparate, conglomerate that was the Republican Party in 1860. Lincoln, unlike Seward, was not likely to talk of an "irrepressible conflict" in his attack on slavery, and indeed he resolutely refrained from any such emotive language—then, and subsequently. Nevertheless, Lincoln's stance on slavery left the South no doubt that he was not on its side. In his Cooper Union address of February 1860, Lincoln accused the South of desiring either "to rule or ruin," and on slavery he was clear and unequivocal. Lincoln was of his age—his was not a sound-bite culture—but when he came to his point he made it succinctly. "If slavery is right," he averred,

> all words, acts, laws, and constitutions against it, are themselves wrong, and should be silenced and swept away. If it is right, we cannot justly object to its nationality—its universality; if it is wrong, they cannot justly insist upon its extension—its enlargement ... Their thinking it right, and our thinking it wrong, is the precise fact upon which depends the whole controversy.[9]

The Cooper Union speech was a significant factor in Lincoln's eventual nomination, and once he had been nominated, the battle lines were drawn. With the Democrats now split between Stephen A. Douglas, nominated by the reconvened convention, and John C. Breckinridge of Kentucky, the incumbent vice president, nominated by the breakaway group led by Yancey and pledged to stand on a variant of Yancey's Alabama Platform, the election of 1860 was as confusing as might be expected with such a lineup. As campaigning began in earnest, what began as a four-way fight turned into a two-way contest, split along sectional lines: Lincoln and Douglas battled it out in the free states, leaving Bell or Breckinridge as the options for the slave states. It was a breakdown that almost amounted to two separate elections. As historian David Potter pointed out, this had a considerable impact on the respective campaigns, and probably on the outcome. Yet Republican victory was not the product of Democratic division; had the party stayed united, they still could not have won. Lincoln received 1,838,347 votes in the free states and 26,388 in the slave states, giving him a total of 1,864,735 against a combined total 2,821,157 opposition votes. In terms of the popular vote, therefore, Lincoln received just less than 40 percent of the votes cast. However, what this translated into (under the American system the winner in each state receives the electoral college votes for that state) was a total of 180 electoral college votes for Lincoln, against 12 for Douglas, 72 for Breckinridge and 39 for Bell: in short, Lincoln would still have won had all the votes cast for his opponents been cast for a single candidate.

In the 1860 election, it was the sectional distribution of the vote that was significant. Lincoln received all—bar three—of the electoral college votes cast by the free states—the exception was New Jersey, which gave three to Douglas out of a possible seven. Lincoln and his running mate, Hannibal Hamlin of Maine, won only 2 out of a possible 996 counties across the entire South, but they nearly swept the North and Northwest. Although Douglas ran a close second in Illinois and Indiana, and Pennsylvania gave Breckinridge some serious consideration, Massachusetts, the heartland of Northern opposition to the South barely gave the Republicans the time of day. Lincoln won, therefore, because his support was sectional and concentrated in states that could give him the needed electoral college votes. Southern hostility toward Lincoln prevented him from even being on the ticket in nine of the slave states—Alabama, Arkansas, Florida, Georgia, Louisiana, Mississippi, North Carolina, Tennessee, and Texas—and South Carolina chose its electors through the state legislature not by popular vote so, needless to say, Lincoln was not an option there. This meant that for the duration of the 1860 campaign Lincoln remained for many Southerners a distant but nevertheless potent caricature of their worst fears—and his victory a confirmation of them. For Northerners, Lincoln's election had been a fait accompli since early October, and for many, voting was a matter of form; the outcome of the election was assured. The same could not be said for its long-term implications. As George Templeton Strong noted in his diary on the day of the election: "A memorable day. We do not know yet for what."[10]

What may seem remarkable with hindsight is that although moderates and radicals alike had been predicting secession in the event of a Republican victory in November, and the growing support for the party had been made apparent in the gubernatorial elections held in September and October, few grasped the seriousness of the predicament facing the Union. In part they were guilty, as historian Allan Nevins charged, of "blind optimism which took all too little account of the peril hanging over the nation." The divisions within each section were real, although the gap between extremists and moderates, and between the upper and lower South, was narrowing in the face of the Republican threat. Breckinridge was strong in the South—he carried eleven states in all—but opposition to him was also substantial; 55 percent of the slave state vote had gone against him. While this certainly indicated a secessionist spirit that was more diluted than men like Yancey would have liked, it was not, as many Republicans believed, proof of strong Unionist sentiment across the South. The true situation was clearer to Stephen A. Douglas, whose campaign for the presidency, (once he realized that the office was out of reach) became a campaign for the Union. "We must try to save the Union," he announced; "I will go South." Go South Douglas did, campaigning in states so hostile to him that his safety was compromised, his health ruined, and his presidential ambitions disintegrated; but his faith in the Union remained undiminished. Yet even the efforts of one of the few remaining statesmen to have a foot in both sections and an understanding of each could not counter Southern fears, fears that were not entirely groundless, but were, perhaps, exaggerated and, ultimately, self-defeating. As a minority president with no Republican majority in Congress behind him and a Democrat dominated and pro-Southern Supreme Court, Lincoln would have found it hard to eradicate slavery had the South itself not given him, and its own slave population, the opportunity to do so.[11]

The Birth of the Confederacy

The second session of the thirty-sixth Congress convened on Monday, December 3, 1860. In the Senate, the chaplain offered up a prayer that America's statesmen would act "not as partisans, but as brethren and patriots, seeking the highest welfare of the country and of the whole country."

There was little chance by that stage that his prayer would be answered. Senators soon got down to the business, rather more serious now, of sectional polemics. Moderate voices tried to interpose between the sectional factions, but it was not their hour. This was, of course, a lame-duck session, the last gasp of the old Democrat regime of James Buchanan, and it whiled away its last weeks with a series of increasingly bitter exchanges that not only went over old ground but established plenty of new ground on which hostility and bad feeling could be constructed. Future Confederate brigadier general Thomas Clingman, senator for North Carolina, launched into an attack on the North generally, the Republicans particularly, and Lincoln specifically on the second day of the session, while John J. Crittenden of Kentucky attempted to parry Clingman's points and introduce reason to a session from which, clearly, after one look it had fled. In response to Clingman's grim picture of sectional domination of the South by the North and his barely veiled threats about the "current of resistance" running through the South, Crittenden expressed the somewhat vain hope that there was not a senator present "who is not willing to yield and to compromise much in order to preserve the Government and the Union of the country." Crittenden did not give up easily. Showing admirable perseverance, in mid-December he introduced a bill proposing an amendment to the Constitution that, among other things, confirmed the territorial limitations of slavery set out in the Missouri Compromise and extended these to the Pacific coast. Hope concentrated around the "Crittenden Compromise" for the remainder of December and into early 1861, but the bill met with opposition from the Republicans (Lincoln especially), who were unwilling to make any further compromise on the slavery issue. Crittenden's plan, along with other compromise proposals put forward during this session of Congress, went nowhere.[12]

The immediate problem facing the Union over the secession winter of 1860–61 seemed to have a single straightforward source: the South had a cause to unravel the Union at a time when the federal government was at its weakest point, neither fully in one administration or the other. The outgoing Democrat president, James Buchanan, has often been criticized for inaction at a time when executive leadership was clearly needed, but he did at least grasp, as many Republicans seemed not to, that the danger to the Union was of the clear and present variety. In a cabinet meeting held three days after the November election, he raised the matter of the defenses at Charleston, South Carolina—fortifications constructed against a possible foreign threat but now open to an attack from an enemy closer to home. Fort Moultrie, that protected Charleston Harbor from the northeast but could be attacked by land, and Fort Sumter, positioned on an island in the center of the harbor (and, at the time, not garrisoned), were the main focus of Buchanan's concerns. Unwilling to make any overt act that might further aggravate the South, Buchanan did no more than replace the garrison commander at Fort Moultrie. He appointed a young officer who, crucially, was proslavery with Southern connections but of undoubted loyalty to the Union, Kentucky-born Major Robert Anderson. As an opening move in the game, it was a cautious one but an important one as events in the South, and especially in Charleston unfolded that winter. Buchanan's intention was to try and keep the lid on the powder keg until some form of compromise measure could be agreed on, but time was running out for his administration and for the Union.

Buchanan understood Southern fears, and perhaps even appreciated their validity, but what he could not do was offer a solution. His annual message to Congress was critical of the North, perceptive in its summation of the Southern perspective, and blunt in its predictions: "The long-continued and intemperate interference of the Northern people with the question of slavery has at last produced its natural effects," he observed. "The different sections of the Union are now arrayed against each other, and the time has arrived, so much dreaded by the Father of his Country, when hostile geographical parties have been formed." Political realignment in itself, was not the real threat; as Buchanan understood, the real threat came from agitation over slavery itself, which, he explained,

> has at length produced its malign influence on the slaves and inspired them with vague notions of freedom. Hence a sense of security no longer exists around the family altar. This feeling of peace at home has given place to apprehensions of servile insurrection. Many a matron throughout the South retires at night in dread of what may befall herself and her children before the morning. Should this apprehension of domestic danger, whether real or imaginary, extend and intensify itself until it shall pervade the masses of the Southern people, then disunion will become inevitable.[13]

The invocation of the frightened Southern mother was a cheap shot, but an accurate one. The fear of servile insurrection was what lay beneath Southern bravado on the slavery issue and fueled the growing secessionist impulse. In 1860, the South was a land haunted by the twin specters of Nat Turner and John Brown; it believed that, by leaving the Union, it could somehow lay these ghosts to rest.

Even as Buchanan and moderate politicians in both the House and the Senate struggled to find some means of holding the Union together, Southern leaders were already packing their bags. Howell Cobb of Georgia, the leading Southern spokesman in Buchanan's cabinet, resigned on the weekend following Buchanan's annual message; it was a symbolic move that showed in which direction matters were moving. Nevertheless, it remained the case that Southerners were far from united on the subject of secession, and the process of dissolving the Union should not be understood as one mad rush for the door on the part of the South. It was a process that gathered momentum gradually and with the very considerable help of proslavery ideologues and secessionist politicians, men such as Edmund Ruffin, Robert Barnwell Rhett, and Louis T. Wigfall of South Carolina, and, of course, William Lowndes Yancey of Alabama—the so-called fire-eaters—whose self-appointed task it was to awaken the whole South to the dangers of which it may have only been half aware. Yet the South was not yet united, and the North had no cause to be unduly concerned over events in Washington and further south. Outside of the rather poisonous air of Congress itself, many expected that the crisis would pass, that it was no more than the usual "gasconading from the sunny South," as George Templeton Strong put it. For him, as for others, there seemed to be "not the slightest ground for apprehension," because they believed—and not without good reason—that "the storm will blow over and die away without uprooting anything." In New York, the markets fell, then rallied, then fell again as Northerners eyed the South cautiously, aware that these were unsettled times but not yet convinced that they were dangerous ones. When it became apparent that secession was not only likely, but was liable to involve more than just South Carolina, Northerners like Strong evinced their own form of bravado. "We are generally reconciling ourselves to the prospect of secession by South Carolina, Georgia, Alabama, little Florida, and perhaps Mississippi," he wrote. "We shall be well rid of them."[14]

The apparently blasé nature of the Northern response derived from the fact, obvious to many Southerners, that the advocates of secession were not offering the South what it purportedly wanted; the right to export slavery to the territories. This could hardly be achieved by walking out of the Union. To achieve their ends, the fire-eaters had to change tack. They fed Southern fears of a possible slave uprising—as Buchanan had predicted—and asserted that there should be a separate South via a combination of legal and constitutional argument and historical precedent. Pro-secessionist spokesmen used two main lines of argument, in varying ways, to make their case: the first concerned slavery itself, and the second concerned states' rights within a federal system. On the subject of slavery, Southern spokesmen did little more than reiterate long-practiced arguments on its supposed economic, racial, and social benefits. The states' rights side of the equation was little more than a rehash of arguments made during the Nullification Crisis in the 1830s—sometimes offered by the very same men who had devised the arguments in the first place. The fact that some of the fire-eaters seemed to be reliving their political youth, proving unable to relinquish arguments they had lost thirty years previously, offers some clue to the mindset of a group of individuals who were not so much stuck in the past as trying, desperately, to remain there. In their attempt to hold back the tide of Northern antislavery agitation they were also attempting to deny that their labor system belonged to a different world, and that its day, and theirs, was passing: but not yet. Four days after Lincoln's election, South Carolina passed a bill calling for a state convention to meet on December 17; three days after that—on December 20, 1860—South Carolina's state convention passed, unanimously, an Ordinance of Secession formally dissolving "the Union now subsisting between South Carolina and other States." With this act, South Carolina had, finally, left the building.[15]

South Carolina's actions were decisive, but her sister Southern states were still not wholly behind her. That this time, in 1860–61, she managed to pull so much of the South with her derived from the erosion of the political middle ground—on which any compromise measures could be effected—and from the efforts of the fire-eaters who established an impressive network of commissioners to stump the South, setting out the case for secession. One week after South Carolina's secession, the governor of Alabama, Andrew B. Moore, appointed commissioners to travel to the other states. The correspondence between one of these, Stephen F. Hale (later to die at the Battle of Gaines Mill) and the governor of Kentucky, Beriah Magoffin, offered as clear and comprehensive an example of the secessionist argument, in all its aspects, as one can find. Hale threw everything into the mix in a detailed letter that ranged from the subject of the inalienable rights of the people to abolish any form of government not conducive to their life, liberty, and property via a sustained defense of slavery to an open attack on the Black Republicans of the North and the threat they offered the South. Hale's reasoned analysis of the nature of the federal compact and the economic value of slavery soon gave way to angry denunciations of the North, and of the "fanatical war" it had waged against the South's peculiar institution. This war, he asserted "has been waged in every way that human ingenuity, urged by fanaticism, could suggest. They attack us through their literature, in their schools, from the hustings, in their legislative halls, through the public press," and with the election of Lincoln, this war would be extended into the territories, and the rights of the slaveholder would be further eroded. For the South, Hale asserted, it was now

> a question of self-preservation. Our lives, our property, the safety of our homes and our hearthstones, all that men hold dear on earth, is involved in the issue. If we triumph, vindicate our rights, and maintain our institutions, a bright and joyous future lies before us ... If we fail, the light of our civilization goes down in blood, our wives

and our little ones will be driven from their homes ... Will the South give up the institution of slavery and consent that her citizens be stripped of their property, her civilization destroyed, the whole land laid waste by fire and sword? It is impossible. She cannot; she will not. Then why attempt longer to hold together hostile states under the stipulations of a violated Constitution? It is impossible. Disunion is inevitable.[16]

Hale's argument found its echo in countless speeches, pamphlets, and newspapers across the South in the winter of 1860–61. Under this onslaught, Union supporters in the lower Southern states found themselves politically isolated, outmaneuvered by their secessionist opponents. Within only a few weeks, many states had bowed to what the secessionists told them was the inevitable. In January and February of 1861, with the momentum of falling dominoes, six more states quickly followed South Carolina's lead: Mississippi (January 9), Florida (January 10), Alabama (January 11), Georgia (January 19), Louisiana (January 26), and Texas (February 1) all passed ordinances of secession and removed themselves from the Union.

Most of the secession ordinances specified the protection of slavery as a primary cause of Southern actions; Georgia's revealed how much to heart the state had taken the dire forebodings of the fire-eaters with its assertion that the federal government's "avowed purpose is to subvert our society and subject us not only to the loss of our property but the destruction of ourselves, our wives, and our children, and the desolation of our homes, our altars, and our firesides." Not all Southerners were convinced by such dire predictions, but, by early February, Jeremiah Clemens, former senator for Alabama and member of the state's Secession Convention, was able to report that although there "is still much discontent here at the passage of the ordinance of secession ... it is growing weaker daily, and unless something is done to stir it up anew will soon die away." It did indeed die away. On 4 February, delegates from the seceding states met in Montgomery, Alabama, adopted a constitution, and elected Jefferson Davis of Mississippi as president of the newly formed Confederate States of America. In both its preamble and in its detail, the Confederate Constitution was remarkably similar to that of the nation from which these states had recently separated, but the differences were telling. "We, the people of the Confederate States," it began, "*each State acting in its sovereign and independent character*, in order to form a permanent federal government, establish justice, insure domestic tranquillity, and secure the blessings of liberty to ourselves and our posterity invoking the favor and guidance of Almighty God do ordain and establish this Constitution for the Confederate States of America" (emphasis added). It was unashamedly decisive on the matter of slavery, and asserted that the "citizens of each State … shall have the right of transit and sojourn in any State of this Confederacy, with their slaves and other property; and the right of property in said slaves shall not be thereby impaired." Slavery and states' rights went hand in hand in the Confederacy. In late March the new Confederate vice president, Alexander H. Stephens of Georgia explained, in what became known as his "Cornerstone speech," the significance of the Confederate Constitution, which "has put at rest forever all the agitating questions relating to our peculiar institutions—African slavery as it exists among us—the proper status of the negro in our form of civilization." The Constitution of the United States was flawed, he asserted, constructed as it was "upon the assumption of the equality of races … Our new Government," he declared,

> is founded upon exactly the opposite ideas; its foundations are laid, its cornerstone rests, upon the great truth that the negro is not equal to the white man; that slavery, subordination to the superior race, is his natural and moral condition. This, our new Government, is the first, in the history of the world, based upon this great physical, philosophical, and moral truth.

By the day of Lincoln's inauguration—March 4, 1861—the new Confederacy was already an established fact: predicated on the protection of slavery couched within the context of states' rights, it offered the greatest challenge yet to the American Union. There was some irony in the fact that its political leaders, and its future military ones, were men of moderate views, opposed to secession and supportive of the Union, but caught on the horns of a dilemma when it came to choosing between their state and the Union. Davis, Stephens, Robert E. Lee, and Joseph E. Johnston at first followed the South, then came, reluctantly, to lead it. The fire-eaters, by contrast, were consumed by their own heat, and died—politically speaking—in the process of producing the Confederate nation. Yet produce it they had, and now everyone—North and South—looked to Lincoln to see how he would respond.[17]

From Secession to Sumter

When the lower Southern states moved to form a separate Confederacy, the Northern reaction was one of shock, but there was hesitation when it came to the subject of a possible military response. It was still by no means certain that all the slaveholding states would follow the lower South's lead. By early 1861, only seven of the fifteen slave states had left the Union. Parts of the upper South and the West were as yet undecided. Virginia, Missouri, and Arkansas had rejected secession through their state conventions;

North Carolina, Delaware, Maryland, Kentucky, and Tennessee had not called conventions at all, waiting to see how matters would develop. It is in this context that Northern hesitation can be understood; there was no immediate rush to the colors because there was every reason to suppose that some kind of compromise—although what form that might take was far from certain—might be achieved. Opinion, therefore, remained mixed. In response to the act of secession itself, many concurred with the *New York Tribune* that it "is really of the greatest and most enduring consequence to know whether the nation called the United States of America is a sham, a humbug, a myth, or not. It has always been supposed to be a power of stability and consequence. It is fashionable now to deride it as a fabric without strength or cohesiveness." At the same time, the views expressed in another Northern paper, the *Springfield Republican*, summed up the prevailing perspective across much of the North. The *Republican* did not yet see the necessity for military action and cautioned against any encouragement for this beyond ensuring that the volunteer militias were in a state of readiness. To do more, it argued, "to indefinitely enlarge this force; to throw open our state treasuries for the purpose of putting ourselves on a war footing, as the phrase is; to open recruiting stations in every principal town and village ... is neither a work of necessity nor mercy; it is an expensive way of saving the Union ... An excess of patriotism is not to be feared," it concluded, "but it may put on too belligerent a face, and so provoke the very evil it seeks to repress. There is nothing in present circumstances, or future probabilities, to justify it, and we are not called upon to assume a hostile attitude toward the South. We do not desire war with them, and are not likely to have it." The Southern perspective was slightly different, and some, certainly, believed that the South ought to prepare for "the breaking out of a war of vast magnitude and almost unparalleled ferocity."[18]

As events unfolded in Washington and in the South, and Northerners struggled to decide on the best course of action, Major Robert Anderson found himself stranded in the midst of what had suddenly become hostile territory. He had already moved his garrison from Fort Moultrie to Fort Sumter in late December, a decision that fell to him—although Major Don Carlos Buell (then with the adjutant general's office) concurred with it—in the face of understandable, but nonetheless frustrating, administrative vacillation in Washington. He was wise to do so, as South Carolina state troops seized Fort Moultrie the following day, and moved on several other federal sites in early January 1861, including the United States Arsenal in Charleston. Although the situation was precarious, Buchanan authorized a relief expedition for Fort Sumter, and the steamer *Star of the West* set out from New York on January 5 with supplies and fresh troops for Anderson's garrison. On its arrival in Charleston harbor a few days later, South

Carolina's shore batteries fired on it, but did little damage; the incident ended in stalemate. Anderson did not get his supplies, the *Star of the West* returned to New York, and everyone avoided the subject for a time. As the Confederacy gradually consolidated in January and February, Charleston itself came under the jurisdiction of the new government, and on March 3, Brig. Gen. P. G. T. Beauregard of Louisiana assumed command of Charleston Harbor itself. The next day—the day of Lincoln's inauguration—found the president-elect facing the established fact of a separate Confederate government on United States' soil, a potentially explosive military confrontation developing off the coast of South Carolina, and an expectant, and increasingly impatient, Northern public whose initial professions of "good riddance" to the South were gradually being replaced by a desire for the federal government to assert, and if necessary enforce, the constitutional integrity of the Union. Not everyone felt that Lincoln was the man to achieve this.

As president-elect, Lincoln had maintained a politic public silence on the matter of secession and how best to meet it. Although in his private correspondence his shock at events was palpable, his public utterances tended to downplay the seriousness of the situation, especially in those speeches he made en route to Washington for his inauguration. In Indianapolis he had mocked secessionists for viewing the Union less like "a regular marriage ... but only as a sort of free-love arrangement," but, more seriously, he asked, by "what principle of original right is it that one-fiftieth or one-ninetieth of a great nation, by calling themselves a State, have the right to break up and ruin that nation as a matter of original principle?" Lincoln denied utterly the right of the South to oppose the results of a lawful election, dismissed the doctrine of states' rights as unconstitutional, and reminded his opponents that the opportunity to remove him would arrive in only four short years. "No great harm can be done to us in that time," he suggested, "in that time there can be nobody hurt." It was not one of history's most prescient statements. His suggestion that there was "no occasion for any excitement. The crisis ... is altogether an artificial crisis" seemed shortsighted to some, but his observation that "it may be necessary to put the foot down firmly" was met with resounding cheers by the New Jersey audience to whom it was made. By the time Lincoln arrived in Washington, he had taken the measure of Northern sentiment on the matter of secession, even if many observers, North and South, American and foreign, had not yet taken the full measure of *him*.[19]

Inauguration day itself was tense—rumors of possible assassination attempts had dogged Lincoln for weeks—and the setting—a temporary platform in front of the unfinished Capitol Building—surrounded by the troops required for the new president's protection—reinforced the fragile nature of the Union that Lincoln was about to take charge of. Lincoln's first inaugural address, however, is justly famous both for the way in which it established the ground on which the Union would be defended and for the powerful invocation of those forces that he believed held the Union together. The Union, he argued, was "perpetual" and "much older than the Constitution," and remained "unbroken." As Lincoln interpreted it, secession was an act of rebellion committed in the South, but not by the South, and the actions of the few did not, and should not, overthrow the lawful government chosen by the many. "This country," he asserted, "with its institutions, belongs to the people who inhabit it." Lincoln reiterated this message on many occasions over the years of the war, and in 1861 he left his audience in no doubt of his beliefs, although he remained somewhat vague about his immediate intentions. Secession was "the essence of anarchy," and he could not accept it. Nor, however, would he instigate war. Addressing the South directly in his closing remarks, Lincoln set out his position under the Constitution as he understood it:

> In *your* hands, my dissatisfied fellow countrymen, and not in *mine*, is the momentous issue of civil war. The government will not assail *you*. You can have no conflict, without being yourselves the aggressors. *You* have no oath registered in Heaven to destroy the government, while *I* shall have the most solemn one to "preserve, protect and defend it."

Lincoln closed by stressing that North and South were "not enemies, but friends. We must not be enemies," he pleaded. "Though passion may have strained, it must not break our bonds of affection. The mystic chords of memory, stretching from every battlefield, and patriot grave, to every living heart ... will yet swell the chorus of the Union," he predicted, "when touched again ... by the better angels of our nature." By March 1861, however, the bonds of affection between North and South were, if not yet wholly severed, certainly frayed beyond repair. Lincoln had made it clear—perhaps the one thing he *had* made clear in his inaugural—that if war came, it would come through Southern aggression alone; the South, unfortunately, was fully prepared to oblige him. Before he had been twenty-four hours in office, Lincoln found himself faced with the problem of the Union forts. Forts Moultrie and Johnson had already been taken by South Carolina state troops in December 1860, as had Castle Pinckney in January 1861. Two Union forts remained in the seceded territories: Fort Sumter in Charleston, and Fort Pickens near Pensacola, Florida. Of the two, Pickens was less open to attack, but Sumter, constructed to oppose invasion from the sea rather than the land, could not easily be reinforced because, as the *Star of the West* attempt had shown, any vessels approaching it were vulnerable to

South Carolina's shore batteries. In theory, the federal government could have simply ceded these forts to the new Confederate government, but that would have meant acknowledging that there was such an entity as a valid Confederate government. Lincoln was not prepared to go that far, but the deadlock had to be broken—somehow.[20]

The symbolism of Sumter, a fort garrisoned by a few Union men in the heart of secession country, could not have been more potent. For the North, it symbolized the Union in peril; for the South it represented the unwelcome presence of federal authority (or as the secession's leaders would have it, a *foreign* authority) in its midst. Remarkably, whether the objective was aiding a Union outpost or ejecting an enemy of the state, both sides could approach the issue of Sumter as one requiring defensive, not offensive, action—not a situation that promised much progress. Again, the Lincoln administration's apparent hesitation on the matter reflected the broader concerns facing the Union, not the least of which was the sentiment of those slaveholding states that had not yet seceded and the wider strategic implications of conducting any kind of war—however limited—in the South. Lincoln was also not well served by advisors. His main military advice came from his general in chief, Winfield Scott, known as "Old Fuss and Feathers," a veteran of the War of 1812 and the Mexican War. While undoubtedly experienced, Scott was in his mid-seventies by 1861, and possibly not as sharp (although by all accounts still as grumpy) as once he had been. He did have the benefit of having been there before, as it were. The concept of invading South Carolina was hardly alien to him; he had been ready to do so during the Nullification Crisis some thirty years previously, but Lincoln was facing a problem of far greater magnitude than the nullification of an unwelcome tariff. Scott himself lacked any coherent general staff beneath him, and above him the chain of command from president—and commander in chief—to secretary of war to general in chief was far from clear; Scott also had extremely limited military resources available to him. With a regular army of 16,215 men distributed mainly along the western frontier, and with resignations and defections to the Confederacy taking place on a daily basis, the United States armed forces in early 1861 were hardly in a position to enforce federal law in the seceded states, let alone conduct a full-scale civil conflict. Given this state of affairs, it was hardly surprising that the advice Lincoln received—from Scott and from Major Anderson himself—was that evacuation of Fort Sumter was the only feasible option. Any other action, they said, would most likely precipitate war.[21]

In these tense days in March, it became clear that any concession made to the Confederacy would only produce demands for further concessions, and a concomitant move toward recognition of the Confederacy on the part of the federal government, would result. The forcible seizure of

Fort Moultrie and the federal arsenal at Charleston had already challenged federal jurisdiction, so the choice facing Lincoln over Fort Sumter was really no choice at all: to save the Union, he had to move to defend it. At the end of March he ordered relief expeditions for both Forts Sumter and Pickens, and a message was sent to Governor Francis W. Pickens of South Carolina via Robert S. Chew, a clerk in the State Department, stating: "I am directed by the President of the United States to notify you to expect an attempt will be made to supply Fort Sumter with provisions only; and that, if such attempt be not resisted, no effort to throw in men, arms, or ammunition will be made, without further notice, or in case of an attack upon the Fort." This was hardly inflammatory, but it was received as if it were. The seizure of the mail from Fort Sumter by the Southern authorities gave them sight of the increasingly desperate messages being sent to Washington, and revealed the precarious nature of the garrison there. Further, the enthusiasm with which Governor Pickens conveyed his state of readiness to meet what he insisted on calling an "attack" did not bode well for a peaceful resolution of the Sumter crisis. Pickens reported having over two thousand men already on Morris Island—the outermost island protecting Charleston's harbor—with ten more companies and two more regiments on the way. More worryingly, he had a serious amount of weaponry at his disposal, including Enfield rifles, two Dahlgren guns, and a rifled cannon just in from Liverpool, which he was clearly itching to try out. "I trust we are ready," he wrote with a degree of understatement and what sounded suspiciously like glee, "and if they come we will give them a cordial reception, such as will ring through the country." The very same day—April 9, 1861—Martin J. Crawford of Georgia, one of three commissioners sent to Washington by Jefferson Davis, sent his conclusions South: "Diplomacy has failed," he wrote, "the sword must now preserve our independence." Swords, however, are notoriously double-edged. The Confederacy's leaders might have done better in April 1861 had they recalled the words of Gouverneur Morris during the Federal Convention of 1787: "This Country must be united. If persuasion does not unite it, the sword will."[22]

Opening Shots

"It is a twice-told tale," wrote New York businessman John Murray Forbes, "that of the opening of the war." It was also a deceptively simple one. The relief expedition for Sumter set sail from New York on April 10, 1861. By that time it was clear to Major Anderson how the situation would be resolved. As he reported on the frenetic activity of Confederate forces on Morris Island—and his own dwindling supplies—he realized what the attempt at supplying the fort would mean. "We shall strive to do our duty," he wrote, "though I frankly say that my heart is not in the war which I see is to be thus commenced." The bombardment of Fort Sumter began at 4:30 a.m. on April 12 and continued through that day, all that night, and for much of the following day, for thirty-four hours in all. When it was over, amazingly, no one had been killed, although two Union soldiers died as a result of a misfire during the saluting of the flag ceremony held just before the fort was evacuated.

The South had, then, fired the first shot. Lincoln had not, as has been sometimes argued, maneuvered it to that position; he could not have known that the Confederates would not fire on the relief vessels—as they had at the *Star of the West*—but would instead bombard the fort itself. In a sense, even as Sumter fell under the Confederate barrage, neither side was definitely committed to war. Lincoln was acting, as he saw it, entirely within his rights under the Constitution; the Confederate leaders were acting partly defensively, as they saw it, to protect their territory, partly aggressively, in the hope that it would send the North a message that any attempt to force the seceded states back into the Union would be pointless. Modern psychologists might describe the actions of both as of the passive-aggressive variety, but the fall of Sumter certainly ended any passive tendencies in the North. "From the first announcement that hostilities had actually commenced in Charleston Harbor," the *New York Tribune* observed, "the feeling that has stirred the people as one man, here, and, so far as we can learn, everywhere also, was too deep, too strong, and will be too enduring, to be characterized by the term excitement. Never have we seen anything like it." "So Civil War is inaugurated at last," exulted George Templeton Strong; "God defend the right."[23]

The growing opposition to all things Southern that had been a feature of Northern sentiment since the 1840s (if not before), found both validation and an anticipated consummation in the war about to begin. With every indication of recognizing the value of something just at the point of losing it, some Northerners, such as distinguished scholar Ralph Waldo Emerson, discovered their pro-Union sympathies only in the Union's disintegration. "We are wafted into a revolution which, though at first sight a calamity of the human race, finds all men in good heart, in courage, in a generosity of mutual and patriotic support," Emerson announced, and concluded, "now we have a country again." By country, of course, Emerson meant the upsurge of patriotism that accompanied the outbreak of hostilities and the belief that the war would, in a very short time, bring the South to heel and return it to the Union on Northern terms. Northern enthusiasm for the fight was matched, unsurprisingly enough, by equally potent sentiments in the South. When the *London Times*' correspondent William Howard Russell arrived in Charleston a few days after the fall of Sumter it was to scenes of mass revelry. "Secession is the fashion here," he observed:

> Young ladies sing for it; old ladies pray for it; young men are dying to fight for it; old men are ready to demonstrate it. The founder of the school was St. Calhoun. Here his pupils carry out their teaching in thunder and fire. States' Rights are displayed after its legitimate teaching, and the Palmetto flag and the red bars of the Confederacy are its exposition. The utter contempt and loathing for the venerated Stars and Stripes, the abhorrence of the very words United States, the intense hatred of the Yankees on the part of these people, cannot be conceived by any one who has not seen them.

"I am more satisfied than ever," Russell concluded, echoing the views of many European observers, "that the Union can never be restored as it was … it has gone to pieces, never to be put together again."[24]

In the immediate aftermath of Fort Sumter, the Union disintegrated even further. When Lincoln sent out a message to all state governors requesting 75,000 militia troops to suppress the rebellion, called for a blockade of the Confederate coast, and passed resolutions for the enlargement of the army and the navy, several of the slaveholding states that had been staying their hand joined the new Confederacy. Virginia, Arkansas, Tennessee, and North Carolina all passed ordinances of secession, albeit in some cases narrowly, and in Virginia's case, not conclusively. Virginia, the Old Dominion, would eventually split into two, with West Virginia remaining with the Union—on admittedly very flimsy legal ground since it was not a properly recognized state at that point, but Union ground nevertheless. With eleven states now seceded from the Union, it was becoming clear that Lincoln's initial call for troops to serve for ninety days only might not be sufficient. The situation in the Border States—Maryland, Delaware, Kentucky, and Missouri—was especially tense, and, as they were of critical strategic value to the Union, it was imperative that they not join the Confederacy.

The precarious nature of Border State loyalties was made clear later, in April 1861, when Union troops—the 6th Massachusetts—clashed with secessionist supporters in Baltimore; the disturbances that resulted lasted several days. At the center of all this, literally and figuratively, was Washington, the national capital—dangerously close to Confederate territory. And in May it was decided that the Confederate capital would be moved from Montgomery, Alabama to Richmond, Virginia, a location that the *Richmond Dispatch* described, without any obvious sense of irony, as having "so many historical associations, and around which cluster so many National recollections." With the Union based at Washington and the Confederacy only 120 miles away at Richmond, the ground between them—ground on which the Civil War would mainly be fought—had been established by May 1861. It would take both sides several months to actually bring their armies to this ground, but the hiatus between the fall of Sumter and the first large-scale encounter between Union and Confederate troops did nothing to diminish enthusiasm for the fight to come; if anything, it gave it time to grow.[25]

Quite a different kind of ground, however, was also established in May 1861, although no one recognized its significance at the time. Benjamin Butler had been a Breckenridge supporter during the election of 1860, but with the fall of Sumter gave his full support to the Union as a brigadier general in the Massachusetts militia. Promoted to major general by Lincoln in May 1861, Butler was sent to Fort Monroe in Virginia. Very soon he found himself facing the problem of fugitive slaves who had taken the opportunity of the proximity of the Union army to flee their owners and head for protection into Union lines. As Butler advised Winfield Scott, there was every indication that the slaves who had come to Fort Monroe "were about to be taken to Carolina for the purposes of aiding the secession forces there." Butler proposed retaining them at Fort Monroe, because he was in need of manpower, and sending a receipt "as I would for any other property of a private citizen which the exigencies of the service seemed to require to be taken by me, and especially property that was designed, adapted and about to be used against the United States." The Fugitive Slave Act, Butler asserted, "did not affect a foreign country which Virginia claimed to be" and suggested that Virginia "must reckon it one of the infelicities of her position that in so far at least she was taken at her word." This was no minor issue, as Butler made clear, but "one of very serious magnitude." He well knew that the "inhabitants of Virginia are using their negroes in the batteries and are preparing to send the women and children south," and he understood the value of slave labor to the Confederate war effort. "As a military question," he suggested, "it would seem to be a measure of necessity to deprive their masters of their services," but the matter went beyond military considerations alone. "As a political question and a question of humanity," Butler asked, "can I receive the services of a father and mother and not take the children?" The secretary of war, Simon Cameron, approved Butler's decision not to return the slaves to their owners, leaving the legal intricacies of their position for the future. Yet in establishing that fugitive slaves were "contraband of war," as the phrase was, and also protecting them and their families within Union lines, Butler had set a precedent that could not be ignored. By May 1861, barely a month after the fall of Fort Sumter, two powerful forces had already met in Virginia, forces that between them would help to end the Confederacy's hopes of independence: the Union army, and the South's own slaves.[26]

CHAPTER **3**

The Road to Perdition

It is astonishing what effect the waving of a woman's handkerchief has upon a soldier. They all cheered it with deafening peals, every time they saw it; and I verily believe a woman with a handkerchief could send an entire little army to perdition.

—**Samuel Wickliffe Melton, Confederate States of America (CSA), April 25, 1861**

Mary Boykin Chesnut, the Southern socialite and diarist, expressed her amazement "that one could live such days of excitement" as those experienced in the wake of the attack on Fort Sumter. For both sides, there was a sense that this conflict had been a long time coming and that its origins lay not in the election results of 1860, but much further back in their nation's past. As the *Louisville Courier* put it, the "true irrepressible conflict lies fundamentally in the hereditary hostility, the sacred animosity, the eternal antagonism" between North and South. The fall of Fort Sumter, therefore, occasioned what military theorist Basil Liddell Hart described as "that vast human sigh of relief ... marking the outset of every conflict, down to 1914." It brought to an end what the *New York Tribune* had complained was "intolerable suspense and uncertainty," and ushered in a period of unbridled enthusiasm for the war to come. The 1861 4th of July celebrations in the North prompted the *Springfield Republican* to suggest that in the Union's disintegration lay its regeneration. The war to come between North and South would be "the decisive battle between freedom and slavery as ruling elements in the American government ... This storm of shot

53

and lightening of steel is sent to clear our political atmosphere," it exulted, "which had become too foul for honest men to breathe in." Not only did this particular 4th of July represent "a second declaration of Independence," the *Republican* was confident "that before the next national birthday dawns, we shall have a re-united country." There was a strong sense that a Rubicon had been passed and that the period of tense anticipation was about to give way to one of intense, but limited, action. When it came to contemplating that action, however, Americans in 1861, like Europeans some fifty years later, expressed more than a degree of what David Cannadine terms "patriotic *naïveté*." For both, battlefield death was regarded as "noble, heroic, splendid, romantic—and unlikely." Indeed, A. J. P. Taylor's observations on the First World War apply as easily to the Civil War: "no man in the prime of life knew what war was like ... All imagined it would be an affair of great marches and great battles, quickly decided." The sentiments of one recruit from the 2nd Michigan, who expressed his "fear that it will all be over before we have a chance to do anything," were echoed many decades later by Sir Edward Mosley, who recalled how, on the eve of the First World War, the "one great fear was that the war would be over before we got there."[1]

That in conception, the anticipated war bore a stronger resemblance to one of Walter Scott's novels than to any of the harsh campaign realities of the Napoleonic or Crimean wars is hardly surprising. Americans in 1861 were not unique in selecting only the highlights from previous conflicts with which to feed their imaginations—the noble leaders, their plucky troops, and the glorious charges by dashing cavalry. It was Wellington's victory at Waterloo, not his sober assessment of it, that inspired them—and in fact, the loser at that battle, Napoleon, impressed them even more. Americans own, most recent war—the Mexican War of 1846–48— offered prime examples of speed and decisiveness, and it was this war that had blooded several of the Civil War's leading generals, including Robert E. Lee, George B. McClellan, "Stonewall" Jackson, and Ulysses S. Grant. What was perhaps unusual was the degree to which the romantic view of war was sustained by reference to the American Revolution, hardly the most strategically decisive, and certainly not the shortest, conflict in history. By 1861, however, the Revolution, too, had been shorn of its gruesome realities. People forgot that discipline in that war had been poor, the officer corps barely competent, recruitment difficult, and morale hard to sustain—all aspects that Washington had complained of consistently. Instead they recalled that a group of untrained colonials had met, and beaten, the most professional military force of its day.

The voluntary aspect of the Revolutionary War, as well as its idealism, was at the forefront of many people's thoughts in 1861; Southerners invoked the Revolution to justify their decision to remove themselves from the Union—from a government they believed was no longer conducive to their happiness; Northerners held it up to the national gaze to remind themselves and others of the great sacrifice involved in creating the very nation the South was attempting to destroy. Both sides tried to claim it; neither side saw it clearly for what it had been—in many aspects, a civil war that pitted Americans, loyalists, and patriots against each other—but chose instead to remember it as a noble and heroic conflict from which America, nation and people, had emerged victorious. This was no elite rhetorical construction, either, but was a fundamental ingredient in Civil War soldiers' understanding and interpretation of their war; frequently, it was their inspiration for fighting it. One recruit in the 38th Georgia Infantry, Miller Wright, advised his brother to "remember them who fought in the revolution they fought with but little hope of glory … their whole military life was one of suffering & retreat of want & sickness and lingering death." With hindsight, this was somewhat grim advice to proffer in the very first summer of the war, and not suited to sustaining morale over the long haul, but both sides had grounds for believing that the war would be short and to the point.[2]

From a Union perspective, the odds seemed to be strongly in its favor. Even after the Confederacy had augmented its strength with the inclusion of Virginia, Tennessee, Arkansas, and North Carolina, it was still the case that the Union appeared better positioned, having retained what there was of the regular army, the navy, the bulk of the nation's industrial centers, and by far the greater part of its population. Granted, the army was neither big nor proximate enough to Washington be of much immediate use, and the navy had a grand total of forty-two vessels actually in commission in 1861, some of which were deployed far from America's shores; nevertheless, the Union had some material to work with, whereas the Confederacy had nothing beyond its state militias and those federal arsenals that it had seized as the states seceded.

The North's industrial capacity also far exceeded that of the South. Economic diversification had failed to flourish in the Southern political and economic climate where, as James Henry Hammond had put it, cotton was king. Cotton could well have proved a powerful military resource. Certainly Southerners believed that their economic ties with global markets (they supplied four-fifths of the cotton used in British and western European mills) would encourage if not ensure foreign recognition of their cause. As one Southerner observed to *London Times'* correspondent William Howard Russell, "a hint about cotton … will set matters right." The Confederacy's shortage of both merchant ships and naval vessels was something of a handicap in this regard, but in the post-Sumter excitement, that awkward fact was dismissed. However the war would develop, in the short-term at least, the greater industrial strength of the North was of more obvious practical value. Even a relatively small Northern state like Massachusetts could out-produce the entire South in 1860, and the bigger states of New York and Pennsylvania individually could produce over twice the value of manufactured goods that the South as a whole was capable of.[3]

When it came to sustaining the war effort, the North also held more of the cards; it produced in excess of 90 percent of the nation's pig iron, cloth, footwear and, crucially, given the situation, a decisive 97 percent of its firearms. Transporting these goods was also less problematic for the North than for the South; the latter had only 9,000 miles of the 31,000 miles of railroad in the United States in 1860, and in that year it produced only nineteen out of a total of 470 locomotives constructed. The northern railroads ran from the Atlantic seaboard to the Northwest, offering a valuable transport route for both troops and supplies. Most importantly, the North had the most people. The Southern population numbered only 8,726,644 out of a total population of 31,443,321 in 1860. Included in this number were 3,953,760 slaves. On paper at least, the North's demographic strength was impressive. During the War of 1812, Daniel Webster had warned that "there are in this country no dregs of population, fit only to supply the constant waste of war." By 1860, it was a different situation, at least for the North. Assuming that the Border States remained with the Union—although Lincoln could not assume that with any certainty in the opening months of the conflict—the North had a 4:1 advantage over the South in terms of the population it could mobilize. If, however, the Border States, with their 3.5 million people, had gone with the Confederacy, the balance would have shifted considerably in the South's favor, but even as things stood in 1861, the South was not in as weak a position as it might have seemed to observers at the time.[4]

The Confederates hoped that the apparent advantages enjoyed by the North would be offset by the logistical difficulties involved in subduing the South, an area of some 750,000 square miles. Northern troops were wholly unfamiliar with the territory, so—the theory went—Southern troops had only to wage a defensive campaign to secure victory. The topography of the South presented considerable obstacles to invasion from the North; it made Richmond, despite its proximity to Washington, a hard target to hit. The Shenandoah Valley—the "Breadbasket of the Confederacy"—runs for some 200 miles between the Blue Ridge Mountains to its east and the Allegheny mountain chain to its west. It was ideal territory from which to strike at Washington; it was less ideal for attacking Richmond, because the valley veered away from the Confederate capital. The rivers, too, were formidable barriers to any attempt the Union might wish to make on Richmond. The Rapidan and Rappahannock Rivers—that join as the Rappahannock just as the river curves around Fredericksburg—run west to east; they would stall the movement of any troops moving north to south. The James River effectively protected Richmond on its northern perimeter, while the York and the Chickahominy blocked it from the northeast. Internal waterways were not the only problem the Union would face; with 3,550 miles of coastline, any attempt by the Union to blockade the South would be problematic, even if the bulk of the Union fleet had not been out of date and out of commission in 1861. Sheer distance made blockading the Gulf coast difficult, while the Sea Islands and sandbanks off the coast of the Carolinas ensured that establishing any effective blockade on the Atlantic coast would never be plain sailing. On the Confederate side of the ledger was also the fact that the population imbalance was not as devastating as it looked on paper. As Ben Butler realized very quickly, large numbers of slaves were an important resource for the Confederacy; more of its white male population could be freed up for its armies if it were left to slaves—male and female—to do the labor required for constructing fortifications and generally maintaining the armies in the field as well as keeping the Southern economy running at home. That slaves might also represent a threat to the Confederate war effort on the battlefield was something most Southerners preferred not to dwell on too closely, although the question of slave loyalty did exercise Southerners from the start. There was, as William Howard Russell noted, "something suspicious in the constant never-ending statement that 'we are not afraid of our slaves.'" Outwardly, however, Southerners felt secure on their home ground, held fast to their faith in cotton and slaves, and were reasonably optimistic that the future would validate their decision to secede from the Union.[5]

The South's optimism was not predicated on the importance of cotton alone. Certainly, in 1861 the balance sheet of available resources—demographic, economic, and industrial—suggested that any conflict would almost certainly result in a Union victory. Southern hopes—and Northern concerns—derived from the fact that each side had different objectives. Seeking only the recognition of its independence as a separate nation, the Confederacy had no need to invade the North, acquire Northern territory, or even destroy Northern armies. All it had to do, it thought, was make it clear—via a few battles, or even a single decisive engagement—that it was not willing to return to the Union, and that further attempts to force it to do so would be fruitless. In short, it had to persuade the North that the game was not worth the candle, and it believed this could be accomplished in pretty short order, not least because the view prevailed—in the North as much as in the South—that Southerners had a far stronger military tradition than Northerners. One Southerner, so the myth ran, could whip ten

Yankees, a belief that was as persistent as the faith in it was misplaced. In part, it grew out of the Revolutionary precedent where the apparently weaker side had emerged victorious. The number of leaders the South had given the nation (in the eighteen elections held between 1789 and 1860, Americans had elected a Southerner as president no fewer than twelve times) was another ingredient. There was also an operational belief in the Cavalier origins of Southerners and their tendency, as Russell saw it, to "affect the agricultural faith and the belief of a landed gentry" with the attendant assumption that hunting and shooting game would automatically prepare one for the rather more serious sport of war. In fact, there was little of substance to the notion of Southern military superiority. At least as many Northerners as Southerners attended the military academy at West Point, and simple common sense—admittedly in short supply in 1861—should have told Southerners that a Northerner was just as likely (or unlikely) to be capable of shooting straight as a Southerner. Jefferson Davis, at least, suffered from no misconceptions on that score. Although his observation that "we are a military people" is usually read as a reference to the South, in context it is more likely that he meant Americans generally. As he told Mary Chesnut, "only fools doubted the courage of the Yankees, or their willingness to fight when they saw fit." In the spring of 1861, however, many Southerners did not believe that their desire to form a new nation was matched in intensity by either the North's desire or its ability to retain the old one intact, and they doubted whether the North had the will to fight at all.[6]

Arms and the Men

The question many Southerners asked themselves in 1861 was one that still exercises historians today: what motivation did the North have for fighting? Union sentiment was strong, but not universal. In the midst of the secession crisis, one Northern paper had warned of the dangers of "a fire in the rear" if the North took up arms against the South, and predicted opposition to armed conflict throughout the Northern states. In the immediate enthusiasm of the post-Sumter period, voices raised against a military response to secession were generally ignored in the general rush to form regiments and see some action, but they were raised, they were persistent and, in the long term, they had to be answered. In the short term, the attitude of the *Chicago Tribune* pretty much summed up the prevailing mood of the North, indeed the prevailing mood of any nation on the verge of armed conflict: "Henceforth," the paper thundered, "there are but two parties in the United States—patriots and traitors—defenders of the Constitution and assailants of the Constitution." The current crisis, it concluded, was "no place for neutrality." In secession, many Northerners saw a direct threat to "the cause of Republican government—of Free Democracy," which, according to an Illinois paper, "stands or falls with the preservation of this Union ... this nation had a sacred origin; it has had the most favorable auspices," it argued, "and if it falls to pieces, it will be because of the inherent weakness of popular government." Whether many of the volunteer troops really saw the coming struggle as a defense of popular government or more as a long-awaited opportunity to thrash the South is a moot point. Motivations doubtless varied, but the end result was the same. One of Lincoln's private secretaries, John G. Nicolay, remembered the period after the fall of Sumter as one of growing enthusiasm for the cause. "Meetings, speeches and parades voiced the public exhortation to patriotism," he recalled, as Northerners literally and figuratively waved the flag in a heady atmosphere of growing anticipation of the war to come. Donations were received from state legislatures and city councils to fund the newly organized volunteer regiments that poured into Washington in such numbers that the city soon resembled a military encampment. On his return to New York in June 1861, after a tour of the South, William Howard Russell noticed the changes that had taken place since he had left in March. With shop windows ablaze with patriotic song sheets, flags flying from the houses, and children dressed in mini-uniforms, it was obvious to him that Southern assumptions regarding Northern reticence were misplaced, even if he also thought that "Mars would die with laughter if he saw some of the abdominous, be-spectacled light infantry men who are hobbling along the pavement."[7]

War fever gripped the Confederacy, too, although enthusiasm for the fight was initially tempered with doubt when there was still some hope that war might yet be averted. South Carolinian lawyer and future district attorney of the state Samuel Wickliffe Melton watched with foreboding as the situation deteriorated in the early months of 1861 and, unlike many, he understood that the war, if it came, would be "long and heartily contested." He hesitated to enlist, but by late April he had concluded that war was inevitable and that he "ought to take some position in the struggle." His reasoning was that "nearly every other family in the State are represented in our armies," and he could not "bear the thought that ours ... should be unknown in the roll of honor." "When I reflect that every member of our staff ... is the father of a large family," he explained to his wife, "I am more content, more clearly assured that I am not doing a wrong to you and my dear children." Not everyone had the luxury of choice in the South in the spring of 1861. Increasingly, opposition to the secessionist cause was no longer tolerated, and was sometimes met with violence involving "the lasso ... tarring and feathering, head-shaving, ducking, and horseponds, deportation on rails, and similar ethical processes." Given that kind of pressure, it is hardly surprising that one Southern private from the 5th Alabama concluded that he "could not git out of the company on honerable terms so I cum to the conclusion to see it out for it shall never be said jerry was a coward & wood not fight for his country." That Southerners sometimes resorted to extreme measures to ensure enlistment revealed that they, too, were more divided than they wished to appear. As with the Union, the united front the Confederacy put up disguised some serious divisions over the wisdom of the war, divisions that would, in time, hamper the progress of that war. On his visit to the South in the spring of 1861, William Howard Russell experienced more than his share of the rhetoric of war, and noted that "if words mean anything, all the Southern people are determined to resist Mr. Lincoln's invasion so long as they have a man or a dollar." He also observed, however, that only some 15,000 men out of a possible 50,000 had mustered in from Louisiana and that the troops in one of the Tennessee regiments he encountered seemed uninspired by their general's emotive patriotic speech, but were very interested in the fact that slaves might soon be brought in to do their work. "A love of military display," he concluded astutely, "is very different indeed from a true soldierly spirit."[8]

The gaping divide between the image of war and the practical requirements of the deed itself was not unique to the Confederacy. Both sides could certainly talk a good fight, but neither was prepared to wage one. The cry in the North as spring gave way to summer in 1861 was "On to Richmond!" but with what, and how, was by no means clear. The most obvious building blocks available to each side for the construction of their armies were the state militia regiments, but in both North and South, these had become more symbolic than active. Although every able-bodied male between eighteen and forty-five was supposed to muster in for drill a couple of times per year, the practice had fallen into abeyance; in some states it had been abolished; and in some of the newer states it had never been introduced. The impact of Harpers Ferry in 1859 meant that the Southern state militias were slightly better trained, but neither side had a pool of well-drilled recruits to draw on. Within only a few weeks of the fall of Sumter, however, both the Union and the Confederacy had begun to raise armies on a scale never before seen in America, armies that by their very nature—in their size, social makeup, command structure, and organizational characteristics—would dictate the way the Civil War was fought.

Lincoln's initial call for 75,000 volunteers to serve for three months for the purposes of dealing with "combinations too powerful to be suppressed by the ordinary course of judicial proceedings, or by the power vested in the Marshals by law," drew on already existing militias in the North "in order to suppress said combinations, and cause the laws to be duly executed." Lincoln did this without congressional approval—Congress approved his actions retrospectively when it next met in special session on July 4—because time was no longer on the North's side. The individual state militias, however, did not offer a long-term solution for the Union's manpower problem; although the constitution enabled the president to call them out—as Lincoln did in April 1861 and again in 1863, when Robert E. Lee looked poised to invade the North—the militias came under state, not federal control. Federal control was needed if a large force were to be raised. Expansion of the regular army was another option for the Union, but in the heady martial atmosphere of the spring of 1861 it was easier, and quicker, to call on volunteers to meet an immediate and, many thought, temporary need. The South, even more than the North, had difficulty with the state-controlled nature of its militias, and the battle between state governors and Richmond made it necessary for the Confederacy to raise a force independent of individual state control.[9]

The answer for both sides lay in the establishment of volunteer armies on the pattern established during the Mexican War of 1846–48, but on a much larger scale. In the end, some 2,100,000 men served in the Union army and 800,000–900,000 in the Confederate army; these armies' peak strength was 1,000,000 and 600,000 respectively. The basis for the Union's mass volunteer army was laid in May of 1861, when Lincoln—still acting on his own authority as commander in chief of the army and navy—called for a further 42,000 volunteers in forty regiments to serve for three years "unless sooner discharged," and at the same time increased the size of the regular army—mainly its infantry—by nearly 23,000 men. By the start of July, however, no fewer than 208 regiments had been raised—far in excess of Lincoln's original forty—and when Congress did meet on the 4th it was to the news that over 300,000 men had enlisted for the Union. Seizing his chance to keep the momentum going, Lincoln requested a further 400,000 men, and $400 million, and Congress, matching his enthusiasm, authorized 500,000; after First Bull Run, it would authorize 500,000 more. Meeting these quotas was no problem in early 1861. Many more men rushed to enlist in the volunteer regiments than the Union could accommodate—the regular army, by contrast, could not fill its new regiments. The competition to establish patriotic credentials resulted in the raising of a variety of regiments, some based on ethnic ties or social interest—temperance, for example; there were German regiments and Irish regiments and even, in the case of the Garibaldi Guard (39th New York, the first of the New York three-year regiments), an eclectic mix of immigrants who had previously served in the revolutionary armies of Europe, some under Giuseppe Garibaldi himself. What all the various volunteer regiments did have in common in 1861, however, was that all were white: African-American volunteers were turned away and advised that this was a "white man's fight." African-American leader and spokesman Frederick Douglass expressed his anger and frustration at this succinctly:

> Colored men were good enough to fight under Washington. They are not good enough to fight under McClellan. They were good enough to fight under Andrew Jackson. They are not good enough to fight under Gen. Halleck. They were good enough to help win American independence but they are not good enough to help preserve that independence against treason and rebellion. They were good enough to defend New Orleans but not good enough to defend our poor beleaguered Capital.

Douglass recognized that the issue of arming free blacks was linked to that of freeing the slaves; until both issues were addressed, the Union stood little chance of success. Until "they shall make the cause of their country the cause of freedom," he asserted, "until they shall strike down slavery, the source and center of this gigantic rebellion, they don't deserve the support of a single sable arm, nor will it succeed in crushing the cause of our present troubles." This was more information than the federal government wanted in the war's early stages. It was not until late-1862 that pressing demand caused the federal government to enlist African-American troops.[10]

The initial raising of the Union's volunteer force could be described, at best, as organized chaos: within states, private individuals sometimes raised their own regiments, as Ben Butler did in Massachusetts, much to the irritation of Governor Andrew. Andrew himself delivered almost treble his assigned quota of six regiments by sending seventeen to Washington, all of which had to be sustained and supported by a federal government that was, quite literally, surrounded by more troops than it could easily accommodate in the environs of Washington. Some of these state regiments were housed in temporary barracks within the Congress Building itself. In time, the system was more controlled, but in its early stages it was susceptible to both corruption and inefficiency, some of it the fault of then Secretary of War Simon Cameron (replaced by Edwin Stanton in 1862). The disorganization and corruption established some unhelpful precedents for the future. It undermined the development of any effective command structure because officers were divided in their loyalties between the state governors who had initially assigned them and the senior federal government officers who assigned all officers above the rank of colonel; worse, many—although by no means all—of these state-appointed officers lacked military experience and/or aptitude for command. Most damaging of all, however, was the regimental one-battalion structure—the new regular regiments had three—that sent the volunteer regiments off to war in their entirety rather than retaining one battalion in the rear from which fresh recruits could be drawn. When these regiments suffered the inevitable losses, rather than being reinforced with fresh recruits they were left to their own dwindling devices; new recruits were assigned to new regiments, with new officers; so the valuable opportunity to learn from more experienced soldiers at the regimental level was lost. What was gained were strong bonds within regiments, but they rarely extended beyond the regiment, leaving the larger units—which in any case were subject to almost constant reorganization throughout the war as troops became fatigued— comparatively weak.[11]

Civil War volunteer regiments were grouped into companies and grouped together into larger units: brigades, divisions, army corps, and finally, into groups as large field armies, the most famous of which, on the Union side, was the Army of the Potomac (originally called the Army of Northeastern Virginia), created in 1861. Regiments were commanded by colonels, and the larger units by brigadiers, major generals, or lieutenant generals, the latter being the norm for Confederate forces but only Ulysses S. Grant held that rank in the Union. Confusingly, both North and South initially had an Army of the Potomac; Beauregard's army fought under that name at First Bull Run in July 1861, but when Robert E. Lee assumed command in June 1862, its name was changed to the Army of Northern Virginia—the Confederacy's most famous army. The naming of Civil War field armies roughly followed the convention whereby the Union named their armies after rivers, the Confederacy after states; a similar convention, by and large, held for the naming of actual engagements. So the Union had an Army of the Mississippi (in fact it had two), an Army of the Tennessee, an Army of the Cumberland, of the Ohio, and of the James, whereas the Confederacy had, for example, the Army of Tennessee and the Army of Northern Virginia but also, confusingly, an Army of the Mississippi that fought at Shiloh; First Bull Run was named by the Union for a nearby creek; the Confederacy named it for the closest settlement, Manassas. The speed with which both North and South managed to pull together their armies was in many ways a triumph of organization, but raising them was one thing; using them effectively was another. On the battlefield Civil War armies proved cumbersome; hard to maneuver, they were equally hard to destroy. Described by one historian as "like a dinosaur, a killing machine with powerful muscles and a tiny brain," the typical Civil War field army was capable of delivering and sustaining a great deal of damage, but unable to produce the kind of conclusive outcome that both the Union and the Confederacy were expecting at the start of the war.[12]

Like the Union, the Confederacy initially had more volunteers than it could deal with, and it certainly had more than it could arm. In March of 1861, Jefferson Davis called for 100,000 troops to serve for a twelve-month period. In May, the Confederate Congress authorized the raising of additional troops to serve for a three-year period; by August of 1861, the Confederacy had 200,000 men in the field and was looking to raise 400,000 more. The actual raising of Confederate regiments followed the Union pattern, with individuals in each state, not always the governors, organizing the enlistment and equipping of troops. As in the Union, the local loyalties that raised the regiments sometimes limited their combat effectiveness. Even more so than was the case in the North, Southern state governors demanded authority over the regiments from their state; some even went as far as to withhold vital supplies, including arms, from the Confederacy, thereby retaining a measure of control that, in military terms, would have been more effective had it been deployed centrally. Confederate soldiers were to suffer from this detrimental side to localism in the years to come, but in 1861 they, like their Union counterparts, entered military service reasonably well equipped and, initially, well supplied. One Confederate officer from the 4th Tennessee reported home enthusiastically, describing in some detail the very good living standards he was enjoying in June of 1861, although the luxury he experienced did not originate with the Confederate government: "We had roast-Beef, fried chicken, Irish potatoes, Green peas, snaps, Coffee, fine biscuits and other things such as high livers have for dinner, including buttermilk and finished off with nice custard with nutmeg and good sweet milk. The reason we have been living so well," he explained, was that "we have been stationed between two plantations on each of which there are from 100 to 150 negroes. At one of them is a splendid cook, and by each of us paying her 25 c each can get every thing cooked we want." Just under a year later, however, this same officer was exclaiming: "*Confound this war.* I despise the whole business and if I ever get into another I want somebody to have me put in the lunatic asylum. I often wish I was a negro with a good master. We keep nearly starved, and get nothing but biscuit, and occasionally some fresh beef." For him, and many like him in the Confederacy, it only got worse.[13]

"Johnny Reb," unlike "Billy Yank," could not rely on the efficiency of his government when it came to basic requirements such as food, even at the start of the war. This mainly stemmed from distribution difficulties rather than neglect. Americans North and South had devoted more time and energy in the previous few years to averting war than planning for any large-scale mobilization, so it was hardly surprising that many of the basic support services—taken for granted by any modern military unit—were simply not in place in 1861. Both the Union and Confederate quartermaster generals found themselves having to become masters of invention, quickly familiarizing themselves with the operations of mills or the methods of food distribution, and all on a scale never anticipated. At the start of 1861, the federal quartermaster general's office employed only thirteen clerks who were responsible for an annual budget of some $5 million; three years later, by which time Quartermaster General Montgomery Meigs had organized a new and expanded quartermaster's bureau, annual expenditure had reached some $285 million and required hundreds of civilian staff to ensure the distribution of goods, supplies, and transport, which was done mainly by horse and wagon.

This new bureau had to be constructed from the ground up, and the Union was fortunate in having a man like Meigs to do it. Meigs had more military experience than most, but this had not prepared him for the tasks he had to face during the Civil War—tasks such as finding ways to provide support for all the troops, even when, in the four months after the fall of Sumter, the number of troops multiplied twenty-seven times. To place this in some perspective, during the First World War, American military forces trebled; during the Second they quadrupled in a single year, but both those increases were as nothing compared to the sudden increase produced by the Civil War. Meigs's success in supporting the Union was a considerable factor in the war's final outcome. As early as 1862, he was able to provide George B. McClellan's Army of the Potomac with over twice the level of support that Napoleon's troops had enjoyed; by 1864 he had almost trebled this, and when William Sherman's troops arrived in Savannah after their famous "March to the Sea" that year, Meigs had fresh uniforms and supplies waiting for them—both there and at Beaufort, North Carolina. By the war's end, Meigs had transformed the business of supplying and supporting the American armed forces at war; at its start, however, he had his work more than cut out for him.[14]

Despite Meigs's efforts, Union soldiers had it only slightly better than the Confederate troops. Such food as was supplied to the Confederate soldiers was grim and limited: cornbread and salted pork or beef. Union troops fared marginally better; at least their hardtack (solid flour and water biscuits) and pork was often supplemented by tinned vegetables; and sutlers (private traders) were on hand to provide—at a price—better fare than basic army rations. Developing distinctive uniforms took time for each side; a certain degree of confusion arose at First Bull Run because the respective armies not only shared a name but also looked pretty similar to one another. This remained a problem for some time. Just prior to the Battle of Shiloh, in April 1862, William T. Sherman was concerned that his men "went out in gray flannel shirts, which at a distance of 100 yards resemble the secession uniform"; he ordered that "Commanders of regiments never leave their camps for action unless their men wear the blue coat, jacket, or blouse." The uniforms themselves were not well designed for battle in the hot Southern summer, and a general shortage of all supplies—tents and blankets as well as uniforms and, especially, footwear—gave Civil War armies less of a coherent appearance than most European armies of the same period. Again, the speed at which these armies were raised had much to do with their disorganized nature. Although several months elapsed between the fall of Sumter and First Bull Run/Manassas, it was hardly enough time to transform groups of volunteers into a professional fighting forces. The Northerners needed time to adjust to the high temperature and humidity in Maryland and Virginia, and troops on both sides needed time to get used to all the unfamiliar routines and requirements of camp life, military drill, and discipline. Drill, indeed, was a main feature of camp life in the initial few months of the conflict, and it was about all that the new recruits received as their military training. There was little in the way of tactical exercises to hone their skills, and even less of target practice that would have familiarized them with their weapons and improved their ability to use them.[15]

A great deal has been written about Civil War weaponry and its ability to transform the battlefield by undermining—if not entirely obliterating— the efficacy of the frontal assault. In popular history, the war is sometimes seen to hinge on the Springfield rifle and the Minié ball: the latter, devised by Captain Claude Etienne Minié for use by the French army, this conical bullet had a hollow base smaller than the gun's barrel, allowing it to be loaded with ease, but it expanded on firing to engage with the barrel's rifled grooves; this increased the rifle's range by making the bullet emerge at a faster speed and in a straighter trajectory, which made it more accurate. Its impact on infantry firepower was certainly understood by the time of the Civil War, because several of the engagements in the Crimea—notably the battles of the Alma and Inkermann in 1854—had revealed the superior firepower afforded by the rifled musket. The "Minié is the king of weapons—Inkermann proved it," the *New York Times* reported in 1854: "The regiments of the fourth division and the marines armed with the old and much belauded Brown Bess, could do nothing with their thin line of fire against the massive multitudes of the Muscovite infantry, but the volleys of the Minié rifle cleft them like the hand of the destroying angel, and they fell like leaves in Autumn before them." This was fairly conclusive, but Americans—and indeed Europeans—were slow to learn the lesson, and the proven efficacy of this new weaponry did not automatically translate into its distribution to Civil War troops. A bewildering array of weaponry, some old, some new, much of it broken, was available and employed in the course of the Civil War, with varying degrees of success depending on the specific conditions of the engagement concerned.[16]

The majority of small arms available in 1861 consisted of old smooth-bore muskets of Napoleonic-era design but updated by the replacement of the flintlock with a percussion cap ignition system (first developed in the 1820s). Many of these muskets, however, no longer functioned, and more modern weaponry was simply not available in the numbers required. In 1861 there were only about 40,000 rifled muskets spread across the U.S. armories and state arsenals, some of which had already been seized by the Confederacy, so neither side was adequately armed at the war's outset and both had to send agents abroad to purchase weapons in order to make up for the shortfall. The Union favored the purchase of Enfield rifles, and had acquired over 700,000 of these by the end of 1862. By that time, home production had gathered momentum, and after 1862, American armories, such as those at Springfield, Massachusetts and at Harpers Ferry, together with private companies such as Colt Firearms managed to keep pace with demand. The Springfield armory alone was able to produce some 200,000 rifled muskets per year—this represented a tenfold increase from pre-war production levels. Over one and a half million Model 1861 Springfield rifled muskets (an improved version of the Model 1855) had been produced by the end of the war; not all of them in Springfield itself—as might be expected, the South copied the improved design. The Confederacy was in a more precarious position because the Union blockade, however imper-fectly applied, made shipping arms difficult. Nevertheless, by the end of 1862 the Confederacy had managed to acquire 50,000 rifled muskets, but some were of dubious quality. This was not a problem confined to the Con-federacy in the early period of the war. The Union purchased a variety of weaponry from the European powers, not pausing to consider why, in some cases, said powers were so keen to sell them. In December of 1861, Laurens Wolcott, a sergeant in the 52nd Illinois Volunteer Infantry described the "defective arms" that his regiment had been issued: "the ones which came from Geneva were not fit to shoot gophers," he complained, "in fact they were, many of them, not bored out so that they were incapable of being dis-charged at all & many of the bayonets were so limber that you could take them in your hands and bend them double." Wolcott was able to report that he had, within a few months, been issued a better weapon, a Belgian rifled musket, which he described as very good indeed, but not all soldiers were so lucky, and it was well into the second year of the war before the majority of Civil War regiments had reliable rifles. Until then, troops went into battle with whatever they could lay their hands on; sometimes this was Revolutionary-era flintlocks or even Bowie knives, in the absence of functioning firearms.[17]

The new rifled weapons, when available, were an improvement on previous weaponry. Prior to the Civil War, the six-foot-long (two meter) smoothbore musket was the most common weapon, but it was cumbersome and accurate only up to about 50 yards (46 meters). The Springfield rifled musket, by contrast, although still a muzzle loader, was easier to handle and accurate up to about 500 yards (although it was sighted to either 900 or 1000 yards (830 or 923 meters), it was not reliable at that range.) The M1855 Springfield was the first American rifle to use the Minié ball, but it was very expensive to produce at about $25 a unit. The M1861 that replaced it was simpler in design, half the price to produce (and consequently more popular), and equally accurate—so accurate, indeed, that it is estimated that it was responsible for some four-fifths of battlefield casualties. Conveniently for both sides, the ammunition for the .58 Springfield (the .58 is the size of the bullet and the rifles were known as .58 Springfields or .577 Enfields, the latter taking a slightly smaller bullet) worked as well in the Confederacy's favored weapon, the .577 Enfield. It was the Springfield that many of the new Union volunteer regiments were issued—eventually. Breech-loading and repeating rifles were also available, but they used up ammunition at a faster rate than the Springfield—and, because a soldier was expected to carry all his own ammunition, they weren't very popular. Nevertheless, repeating models such as the Sharps and the Colt Military Rifles, the Henry Rifle and the Spencer Repeating Rifle, along with a great many others, made their way onto the battlefield, sometimes for the specific use of the cavalry or by sharpshooters.

The Colt (breech-loading) rifles, in particular, had a few teething problems in the way of gas leaks and simultaneous firing on all chambers that made them, at best, unreliable, and, at worst, a liability. Nevertheless, the breech-loading rifle was the more effective weapon, but never, in the Civil War, the most common infantry one. Civil War soldiers had an equally broad variety of smaller arms at their disposal, many brought their own private guns, while others relied on army-issue sidearms. As with rifles, these varied from the famous and relatively modern Colt revolver to the type of flintlock pistol carried by Washington's Continental Army, some of which were still being produced as late as 1861. Edged weapons were more for show than for action, and only a small percentage of battlefield wounds in the Civil War could be ascribed to the sword or the bayonet. The latter was very much a weapon of last resort, which is not to say that it was never resorted to: Joshua Lawrence Chamberlain of the 20th Maine famously led a bayonet charge down Little Round Top at Gettysburg on July 2, 1863, and other regiments, such as the 17th Wisconsin at Corinth in 1862, executed successful bayonet attacks in the course of the war.[18]

Another example of rifled weaponry, artillery weaponry, was also at a transition stage by the time of the Civil War. Here, too, the rifled barrel was becoming more common, but both sides continued to use a combination of rifled and smooth-barreled cannon throughout the war. Montgomery Meigs stressed the importance of effective artillery long before First Bull Run. In general, he argued, with "new troops, such as must be employed in this contest, a full supply of field artillery is of even greater importance than with veterans." The Napoleon 12-pounder was the mainstay artillery weapons of the war; a smoothbore muzzle-loaded cannon, it was easier to load and to use, and had a greater impact than some of the rifled models, could fire a wide variety of shot (from round or solid to spherical case/shrapnel shell), and had a range of between 200 yards or 185 meters (with grape and canister shot) and 1600 yards or 1480 meters (with round shot). The new rifled cannon was better at long-range fire, but the lower weight of its projectiles reduced its value as an artillery piece generally. The best use of the artillery during the war was at close range against the infantry regiments. This made the artillery better at defense than attack, and this, too, had an impact on the structure as well as the outcome of many Civil War engagements. As was the case with infantry weapons, the Civil War represented the cusp between the muzzle- and breech-loading artillery weapon, but both the breech-loading and the rifled cannon had too many teething problems, mainly with their fuses, to render them reliable weapons in 1861–65. As far as the industrial, technological, and military developments of the period's weaponry were concerned, the Civil War was more of a testing ground than a full-fledged exploitation of these marvels' potential on the battlefield.[19]

Had America been engaged, as many of the European powers had been, in almost continuous warfare in the decades prior to 1860, then both its military and civilian leaders would have had a better grasp of what was available on the military market and how best to deploy it. As it was, developments in weaponry, together with the growth of the railroad and the invention of the telegraph, pointed the way toward a new kind of warfare. America in 1861 was at the start of the road that would lead to the entrenched battlefields of the First World War; it was the Civil War that first saw the decline of the frontal assault and the mobilization of troops on the massive scale required by the wars of the later nineteenth and twentieth centuries.

For both the Union and the Confederacy, the war's outcome depended—on the battlefield at least—on their volunteer troops, not the weapons these were issued or the strategic and tactical rethinking that some of the new weaponry forced upon their military leaders. Both sides were looking for the decisive engagement at a time when decisiveness was harder to come by on the battlefield, when attrition—not the glorious charge—and administration—not individual innovation—proved to be deciding factors. The Union was better equipped; the Confederacy seemed, from the perspective of 1861, better motivated. But for both sides, it was less a case of what they had than what they did with it. The American Civil War remained very much an infantryman's war; it was the first large-scale war of the modern age, but this did not make it, in its totality, as it is sometimes described, the first modern war.[20]

On to Richmond

Having raised their respective armies and armed them (up to a point), the pressure on both sides was to figure out what to do with them. There had been a few minor skirmishes in the spring and early summer of 1861—enough to boost the Union's confidence, but insufficient in scope to give any hint of what was to come. Union forces in western Virginia met, and defeated, a small Confederate occupation force at Philippi in early June, an engagement that arguably had the honor of being the first land battle in the Eastern Theater (although a minor skirmish had taken place two days previously at the Fairfax Court House). Philippi was a victory of which the Union was inordinately proud. William Howard Russell caustically observed that "Napoleon scarcely expended so much ink over Austerlitz as is absorbed on this glory in the sensation headings of the New York papers."

From the Union's perspective in 1861, it had two main theaters of operation: in the first extreme caution was needed, in the second, decisiveness. The first was the political arena. With the Border States perched on the fence—Kentucky in particular was attempting to remain neutral—it was essential that nothing be said or done in early–mid-1861 that might push the Border States into the Confederacy—or Kentucky off the fence in the wrong direction. The second arena was the military arena. On that front, with the South having fired the first shot, it fell to the North to fire the next one: popular opinion, momentum within the volunteer regiments (bearing in mind that some regiments had only signed up for three months), and the apparent numerical advantage enjoyed by the North made it likely that the opening move would come from that direction, and sooner rather than later. The *New York Tribune* was loudest in its exhortation "On to Richmond!," but military thinking, in the form of General in Chief Winfield Scott's strategic plan, was initially that the long way round might prove the better shortcut to a decisive outcome. The recognition that the new volunteer regiments lacked training, together with his own preference for the enveloping maneuver, prompted Scott to argue against any precipitate moves in Virginia; instead, he wanted the Union to concentrate on the Mississippi basin, from which it could affect an envelopment of the Confederacy's forces and seize strategic strongholds on the rivers and at railway junctions. Together with the blockade on the Atlantic and Gulf coasts that, in theory, would cut the Confederacy off from European supplies, Scott planned to destroy the Confederate field armies by separating them, the better to wear them down. This gradualist policy of divide and conquer was roundly mocked by the press, who dubbed it the "Anaconda Plan"; it did not reflect the thinking of most of the other military leaders, nor did it satisfy the impatience of the Northern public, who believed that a bold strike at the Confederate capital was not only necessary, but feasible. And public opinion could not be ignored in a war involving volunteer troops, as Lincoln well realized. "The enthusiastic uprising of the people in our cause, is our great reliance," he asserted, "and we cannot safely give it any check, even though it overflows, and runs in channels not laid down in any chart."[21]

The situation facing the Union in the early summer of 1861 was one in which the Confederate capital looked tantalizingly close but was, for all practical purposes, about as far out of reach as it was possible to get. The geography of the area below the Ohio and Potomac Rivers naturally divided the fighting ground into three main theaters of war: the Eastern Theater, between the Atlantic and the Appalachians; the Western Theater, between the western side of the Appalachians and the Mississippi; and the trans-Mississippi Theater, from the river westward to the Pacific. In 1861, the focus of attention was—as it has been for many historians since—the Eastern Theater, specifically Virginia. Both the Union and the Confederacy had arranged their main forces in the area south of Washington, with support on their flanks in the Shenandoah Valley (west) and on the Virginia coast (east). By the start of July, the Union had about 35,000 men across the Potomac from Washington, commanded by Major General Irvin McDowell, supported in the west by Robert Patterson (like Scott, a veteran of the War of 1812 and almost of an age with him) with 18,000 troops, and in the east by Ben Butler at Fort Monroe with 15,000 men. The main Confederate force, numbering about 22,000 men commanded by General P. G. T. Beauregard, was stationed at Manassas Junction, with a reserve brigade under Brigadier General Theophilus H. Holmes at Aquia Creek to the south of the main force. Beauregard was supported by generals John B. Magruder and Benjamin Huger in the east and by Joseph E. Johnston in the Shenandoah Valley. Most of these commanders had regular army backgrounds, but they now found themselves in command of a very different kind of army indeed—one ill prepared for combat, unused to discipline, spoiling for a fight but having little, if any, idea of what an actual battle might entail. The general lack of cohesion was not restricted to the new recruits but was also reflected at the command level. On the Confederate side, neither Beauregard nor Johnston enjoyed a good relationship with Jefferson Davis and both were sufficiently ambitious to ensure that their relationship with one another was also sometimes strained. On the Union side, Patterson was rather long in the tooth, Butler, a political general, was a bit of a loose cannon (with a very short fuse), while McDowell, although a solid enough officer, was inexperienced in field command and daunted by the rawness of many of the troops under his command. Lincoln famously sought to reassure him with the observation "You are green, it is true, but they are green, also; you are all green alike." Whether or not McDowell took comfort from Lincoln's words, he was right to be concerned.[22]

"Chaotic" is the best way to describe the first significant encounter between Union and Confederate forces at Bull Run/Manassas on July 21, 1861, but that might have been expected given the previous month's events. At Big Bethel, Virginia on June 10, 1861, Union and Confederate forces met in an engagement that ended in Union defeat, not least because Union troops managed to fire on each other. Further apparently random and inconclusive skirmishing took place throughout the rest of June, none of it suggesting coherence at either the command or regimental level. Nevertheless, the orders from Washington were for McDowell to move on to Richmond, and to this end he conceived a plan whereby his troops would advance on Manassas in mid-July as Patterson engaged Johnston in the Shenandoah Valley, thereby preventing Johnston from coming to Beauregard's aid. As a plan it had merit enough, but it was complicated, too complicated, as it turned out, for the inadequately trained volunteer troops involved. It was also blighted from the outset by delay, by the weather—it was extremely hot, even for Virginia in July—and by the general inability of McDowell's troops to keep hold of either rations or equipment en route or, in some cases, sight of their regiments.

McDowell was entering unknown territory (in every sense of the phrase), and it took two full days to move his forces from the banks of the Potomac to Centreville. Matters were not helped by developments in the Shenandoah Valley; Patterson failed utterly to restrain Johnston and the latter was able to move three brigades—by rail—to a position near Manassas by July 21. Beauregard knew in advance that McDowell was on his way, thanks to the efforts of Confederate spies in Washington, and he had arranged his troops along the south side of Bull Run Creek, concentrating them at the fords to block crossing attempts, for a distance of over four miles, stretching between the Stone Bridge on the Warrenton Turnpike in the north to Union Mills Ford on the Orange and Alexandria railway line to the south. Beauregard's preparations would have made less of a difference had McDowell been able to move faster than he did and had Patterson succeeded in pinning down Johnston's Army of the Shenandoah. Further, McDowell had purposely delayed his arrival in Centreville, partly in order to gain time to acquire supplies for his exhausted troops, partly to plan his next move. Minor skirmishing on July 18 at Blackburn's Ford on Bull Run Creek between Union troops—the 12th New York—and Brigadier General James Longstreet's men resulted in a disorganized retreat by the Union forces, forcing McDowell to reconsider his options; this he did for the entirety of the following day; in the meantime Johnston's troops were moving closer.[23]

At 2:30 on the morning of July 21, McDowell began to move his troops toward the Stone Bridge, taking the Confederates somewhat by surprise: Beauregard had been expecting them on his right, and their appearance on his left caused some confusion and ensured that the initial stages of the first battle of Bull Run/Manassas went the Union's way. As Beauregard struggled that morning to reassess the situation and regain some momentum for his forces, picnickers and sightseers from Washington arrived— politicians, journalists, women, and even children—eager to witness what they anticipated would be the sole military engagement of the war and, they expected, a resounding Union victory. It was not to be. By mid-afternoon the center of the battle was concentrated on Henry House Hill, where Beauregard and Johnston both arrived in time to witness the battle shift in the Confederacy's favor. One of the brigade commanders from Johnston's Army of the Shenandoah, Thomas J. Jackson, rallied his troops, prompting the famous comment made by another of Johnston's commanders, Brigadier General Barnard E. Bee, to encourage his men: "There stands Jackson like a stone wall,"—and "Stonewall" Jackson was born. Jackson was not the only notable Civil War commander to see his first major action at Bull Run: William T. Sherman, Ambrose Burnside, J. E. B. Stuart, James Longstreet, Jubal Early, and Richard S. Ewell were all there at the start: most of them were still there at the end of the war, but with the events of July 21 the end they had expected was no longer clearly in sight. "It needed but *morale* among the troops to hold the battle-ground," observed Lincoln's private secretary John Nicolay. "Unfortunately the Union army had lost its *morale*. The mere disorder of the final repulse was slight; but the demoralization and loss of discipline had been growing during the whole afternoon, until, of a sudden, the army was half dissolved."[24]

When Confederate reinforcements arrived the Union attack faltered, swiftly becoming a withdrawal and then a full-blown, panic-stricken retreat that shocked commanders and immediate onlookers alike, many of whom became entangled in the mad rush back toward Washington. McDowell reported that his "men could not be rallied," and that confusion had broken out. Haversacks and other equipment had been discarded in the heat of battle, the Union had run out of artillery ammunition, and the troops themselves had become "a confused mob, entirely demoralized," and desperate to leave the field. "The news," William Howard Russell reported the following morning, "seemed incredible, But there, before my eyes, were the jaded, dispirited, broken remnants of regiments passing onwards ... and it was evident enough that the mass of the grand army of the Potomac was placing that river between it and the enemy as rapidly as possible." In the immediate aftermath of Bull Run, Northerners anticipated an attack on Washington, and they waited nervously. "Why Beauregard does not come I know not," Russell wrote, "I have been expecting every hour since noon to hear his cannon. Here is a golden opportunity. If the Confederates do not grasp that which will never come again on such terms, it stamps them with mediocrity."[25]

The Confederates did not come. Jefferson Davis, who had arrived at Manassas, certainly wanted his armies to push on to Washington, but his field commanders persuaded him against it; the weather had turned, the rain poured down on the "steady stream of men covered with mud, soaked through ... who were pouring irregularly, without any semblance of order, up Pennsylvania Avenue," and the Confederates did not pursue them. Neither Beauregard nor Johnston believed that in the rain and general confusion any such pursuit would succeed, and although the road to Washington lay apparently open, it was the road not taken in July 1861. In the end, the Confederate victory at Bull Run failed to produce the single decisive blow for Southern independence that so many had anticipated, but it certainly put paid to Northern assumptions that the South could be brought back into the Union before the year was out. An important outcome of Bull Run was the hint it offered, for those able to see it, of the scale of the conflict to come and the resources—morale and determination as much as matériel—that would be necessary to decide its final outcome. The omens for the Confederacy were not promising, despite its resounding victory on that July day. Joseph E. Johnston, for one, believed that the "Confederate army was more disorganized by victory than that of the United States by defeat." He recalled how the

> Southern volunteers believed that the objects of the war had been accomplished by their victory, and that they had achieved all that their country required of them. Many, therefore, in ignorance of their military obligations, left the army, not to return. Some hastened home to exhibit the trophies picked up on the field; others left their regiments without ceremony to attend to wounded friends, frequently accompanying them to hospitals in distant towns ...

Exaggerated ideas of victory prevailing among our own troops cost us more men than the Federal army lost by defeat.

The weeks following First Bull Run were therefore something of an anticlimax, but also a wake-up call to a North finally forced to recognize not merely the possibility, but the harsh reality of defeat. After Bull Run, Nicolay believed, "the North reconciled itself to the painful prospect of a tedious civil war all the more readily because of the necessity of bending every energy to immediate preparation on a widely extended scale." With the Confederate victory in July 1861, both sides had taken their first steps on a road to a war more brutal, more destructive, and certainly of far longer duration than anyone had conceived of in the spring of 1861. "The lesson is learned," observed the *Springfield Republican* three days after the battle. "It is a costly one; but we may have need of it by-and-by."[26]

CHAPTER 4

All Quiet Along the Potomac

All quiet along the Potomac to-night,
Where the soldiers lie peacefully dreaming,
Their tents in the rays of the clear autumn moon,
And the light of their watch-fires are gleaming.
A tremulous sigh, as the gentle night wind
Through the forest leaves softly is creeping,
While the stars up above, with their glittery eyes,
Keep guard, for the army is sleeping.

**—Ethel Lynn Beers, "The Picket Guard," *Harper's Weekly*,
November 30, 1861**

The Confederacy may have missed an opportunity at First Bull Run, but Union commanders and the troops on the front line swiftly began to take stock of what had occurred on July 21, 1861 and searched for ways to prevent it from ever happening again. Everyone had their own perspective on the defeat, but that of Union soldier Charles Haydon, of the Kalamazoo Light Guard (Company I, 2nd Michigan) was as perceptive as any. "The next attack," he suggested, "needs to be made with more care, with better preparation for a retreat if necessary. We should not have retreated on Sunday farther than Centreville. We need more good skirmishers & sharp shooters & all the men need better guns." Bull Run, he concluded, showed the Union's "want of a more perfect military establishment," and, in particular, it showed the weakness of the Union's officers. This last was a failing the Union moved quickly to rectify. The day after the battle,

George B. McClellan replaced McDowell. "Circumstances make your presence here necessary," ran the telegram to McClellan from Washington, "come hither without delay." McClellan's minor victory at Rich Mountain in West Virginia ten days before the Union's defeat at Bull Run positioned him as the man of the Union's very pressing hour. The press lauded him as "the Napoleon of the Present War," and as a man with "a future before him."McClellan himself concurred with both sentiments. Writing to his wife to report on his promotion, McClellan observed that he appeared "to have become *the* power of the land ... Who would have thought," he added, "that I should so soon be called upon to save my country?"[1]

As the "North's first battlefield hero," McClellan certainly seemed the commander most likely to succeed in pulling the demoralized Union troops together into a properly functioning field army. Although William Howard Russell pointed out that all McClellan had actually done at that point was "had some skirmishes with bands of Confederates in Western Virginia," he acknowledged that even this, "at such a time is quite enough to elevate any man to the highest command." Indeed it was. Initially given command of the Union forces around Washington (the Division of the Potomac), within a few months McClellan had succeeded General Scott as general in chief of the Union armies. Even by that stage, however, both his (over) attention to detail and his fatal hesitation were evident. "Day follows day and resembles its predecessor," Russell observed. "McClellan is still reviewing, and the North are still waiting." The opening line of a popular song that first appeared in *Harper's Weekly* toward the end of the year: "All Quiet Along the Potomac To-Night," became imbued with a wholly appropriate but far less reverential sentiment as 1861 gave way to 1862. The Army of the Potomac was clearly shaping up to be a powerful fighting force, but one stuck on the banks of the Potomac, which was not where it was needed.[2]

As McClellan set about sorting out the disorganization that was the Union army in Washington with obvious enthusiasm, Southerners were reveling in their recent success. For Savannah lawyer Charles Colcock Jones, Manassas represented "a victory without parallel in the history of this western world, an engagement continental in its magnitude, a success whose influence must be felt and acknowledged not only within the limits of our own Confederacy and of the United States but also throughout the civilized world. Surely," he concluded, "the God of Battles is with us." Jefferson Davis did not share Jones's enthusiasm. In Richmond, recriminations flew thick and fast between Davis and Beauregard over the failure to capitalize on the victory at Manassas, and the two continued to bicker for the remainder of 1861 and into 1862. Much of the debate revolved around strategy, defined by Henry W. Halleck—author of one of America's

standard textbooks on the science and art of warfare—as "the art of directing masses on decisive points, or the hostile movement of armies beyond
the range of each other's cannon." As a West Point graduate and former
Secretary of War, Davis not only had a firm grasp of the resources at the
Union's disposal—and a concomitant understanding of the Confederacy's
relative weakness—but he held informed, and fairly fixed, opinions on the
way in which the war should be conducted.[3]

Hoping to duplicate George Washington's approach with the numerically challenged Continental Army during the Revolutionary War, Davis
sought a policy of aggressive defense, or the "offensive–defensive" as it was
known. This was a logical response to the disparity in numbers between the
Union and Confederate armies, and would allow the Confederacy to concentrate its troops at strategic points rather than stringing them out over
a wide area that could not possibly be defended. Politically, however, this
idea was a nonstarter, because the various states looked to Richmond for
support, preventing Davis from ignoring—as Washington had done—the
coastal areas in favor of troop concentration in the interior. Distributing
troops along the Confederacy's borders, however, risked an overextension
of resources, leaving the Confederate line so thin as to be obviously susceptible to attack. Davis's idea, therefore, was to combine an essentially defensive strategy with one that more aggressively seized the initiative, to force
battle on the Union at several strategic points. One of these, which Davis
felt Beauregard had failed to exploit to its full potential, was Manassas. In
essence, Davis's approach was straight from Halleck's textbook: "The main
object in *defensive* war is, to protect the menaced territory, to retard the
enemy's progress, to multiply obstacles in his way, to guard the vital points
of the country, and—at the favorable moment, when the enemy becomes
enfeebled by detachments, losses, privations, and fatigue—to assume the
offensive, and drive him from the country." It all sounded quite simple on
paper, although it must be remembered that the Union was using a similar
approach. In the short term, therefore, Davis had a clear idea of where the
enemy was coming from, both literally and figuratively. In the long term,
theory did not translate from page to field so smoothly.[4]

As Bull Run had made clear, both Union and Confederate strategy in
1861 was traditionally Napoleonic in outlook, influence, and execution.
The writings of Antoine Henri Jomini, the foremost military theoretician
of the early nineteenth century, represented the cornerstone of West Point
strategic studies, such as they were at the time; Henry Halleck's study of
the *Elements of Military Art* (1846) was largely a translation of Jomini's
Précis de l'art de guerre (1838). With its emphasis on the offensive, the need
to control interior lines of communication, and the concentration of force
on a decisive point, this traditional approach caused Union commanders

some concern when they contemplated the vast and varied geographical barriers between the free and slave states. Even had there not been popular demand to seize Richmond, Union commanders would still have focused their attention on it first as that was where their military education had taught them to look, at the enemy's capital. Yet this focus on Richmond was, in hindsight, a mistake. It confined much of the energy of both North and South into a relatively small area, roughly triangular in shape, with its point aimed at Washington. On the right was the Potomac, on the left were the Blue Ridge Mountains and the Shenandoah Valley, and the base of the triangle lay between the James and Appomattox Rivers, with Richmond at the midpoint between the Chesapeake Bay and the Blue Ridge/Shenandoah boundary. The focus of much of the fighting for the following three years was in the center of this triangle and along its left and right sides, but such a concentration of force did not achieve the Union's objective. The Federal army would have to force its way through the base and induce the Confederacy to fight outside of it.

To secure a position from which to attack, the Union had to gain control of several strategic centers—especially the railroad depots at Nashville, Chattanooga, and Atlanta as well as the interior waterways—the Mississippi above all. But to reach the Mississippi they first had to secure the Cumberland and Tennessee Rivers from the north, and New Orleans from the south. The achievement of this lay in the future, and it was trial and error, rather than the development and execution of a single strategic plan that forced the Union to expand its thinking beyond the initial concentration on Richmond. Lincoln had grasped the problem as early as 1862, but the solution proved more elusive. "I state my general idea of this war to be," he advised Don Carlos Buell,

> that we have the *greater* numbers, and the enemy has the *greater* facility of concentrating forces upon points of collision; that we must fail, unless we can find some way of making *our* advantage an overmatch for *his*; and that this can only be done by menacing him with superior forces at *different* points, at the *same* time.

Confederate commanders could read the numbers as well as Lincoln, of course. Stonewall Jackson, for one, had a clear idea from the war's outset of what it would take to defeat the Federal armies. "Always mystify, mislead, and surprise the enemy, if possible," he advised, "and when you strike and overcome him, never let up in the pursuit so long as your men have strength to follow." More importantly, Jackson stressed, "never fight against heavy odds, if by any possible manoeuvring you can hurl your own force on only a part, and that the weakest part, of your enemy and crush it." "Such tactics," he asserted, "will win every time." The Confederacy did not always heed Jackson's advice, but when it did, it reaped the benefits. It would be many years before the Union made its greater numbers effective in the way Lincoln proposed, and in the intervening period there were many lessons to be learned. Bull Run, however, had already taught both sides perhaps the most important lesson of all: the American Civil War was not a war of the Napoleonic age. The railroad, not a resource available to Napoleon, was what had allowed Johnston to bring his troops to Beauregard's aid. It was the modern equivalent of a coach and horses, and it ran straight through Jominian theories on the art of war. But long before the Springfield rifle altered (or, unfortunately for the troops involved, sometimes did not alter) battlefield tactics and the strategy behind these, a much more basic development made its impact felt on nineteenth-century warfare: steamships.[5]

Inlets, Ironclads, and (Diplomatic) Deep Water

In the immediate aftermath of Bull Run, the Union turned its attention to the coast, and to the implementation of an effective blockade along the Atlantic seaboard. This was done under the direction of Secretary of the Navy Gideon B. Welles and Assistant Secretary Gustavus V. Fox, who together, in 1861, had to scrabble around for any and all available vessels. Initial blockades of Richmond itself and Norfolk, Virginia, were readily avoided by the Confederacy because the Pamlico and Albermale sounds in North Carolina offered alternate access for its ships. Looking to block this route, toward the end of August 1861, Benjamin Butler joined Flag Officer Silas H. Stringham of the Atlantic Blockading Squadron to launch an attack on Hatteras Inlet. On August 26, the fleet—comprising the flagship *Minnesota* plus the steamers *Wabash*, *Monticello*, *Pawnee*, and *Harriet Lane* along with some chartered steamers and transport vessels—set out for the Carolina coast. As at Bull Run, delay caused by inexperienced troops proved a hindrance. Butler's troops, as yet unused to war let alone landing on a beach in high weather, had a bad time of it, but the attack on the forts—Clark and Hatteras—proved effective. This was due, in large part, to the ability of the steamships to maneuver out of the reach of the forts' batteries while maintaining fire on them. Fort Clark fell first, lying as it did within range of the deep-draft vessels; firing on the fort began at ten in the morning on August 28, and by midday the battle was over. Fort Hatteras proved a tougher nut to crack, and the Union fleet was forced to haul off for the night. On the following day, however, the *Susquehanna*, soon joined by the *Harriet Lane*, opened fire on the fort at eight in the morning; in just over three hours the fort had surrendered.[6]

The taking of Hatteras Inlet was a great morale boost for the Union, even though William Howard Russell thought the reaction to it one of exuberance over common sense. "Here they are," he observed,

> as rampant because they have succeeded with an overwhelming fleet in shelling out the defenders of some poor unfinished earthworks, on a spit of sand on the coast of North Carolina, as if they had already crushed the Southern rebellion. They affect to consider this achievement a counterpoise to Bull Run ... it no more adds to their chances of crushing the Confederacy, than shooting off the end of an elephant's tail contributes to the hunter's capture of the animal.

Russell was both right and wrong. Other than its outcome, Hatteras Inlet had many similarities to Bull Run, similarities that revealed the lack of, as the modern phrase has it, joined-up military thinking. Rather than following up on his victory, Commodore Stringham took the Confederate prisoners north, a decision that backfired on him in both the press and in Washington, especially because the Union blockade was being openly and frequently flouted by Confederate vessels. The success or failure of the blockade was no minor matter, especially at this stage in the war. The U.S. consul in London wrote frequently to Secretary of State William H. Seward, advising him of Confederate-owned and British vessels setting off for the South loaded with the latest military equipment. The steamer *Bermuda*, for example, sailed from Hartlepool in mid-August—under English colors—but she was carrying rifled cannon and ammunition destined for the South. That same month the British government was in negotiation with Southern agents for the purchase of some 10,000 Minié rifles. What made it worse was that, as the Union was moving to establish a blockade on the Atlantic coast, further out in the ocean it was running into potentially deep water with the British government over the legality of blockades of any kind. In part this stemmed from confusion—in Washington as much as abroad—over the nature of the Civil War that had just begun. Lincoln's firm insistence that it was a rebellion within the nation rather than a conflict between two belligerent nations contained contradictory elements, especially over the matter of a blockade. If there was no such thing as the Confederacy, then there could be no blockade of its coast. A nation cannot blockade itself, but that was what America was attempting to do in 1861, at least within the context of international maritime law.

The matter was exacerbated by America's previous reluctance to enforce some aspects of maritime law, specifically the 1856 Declaration of Paris that stipulated, among other things, that to be legal a blockade had to be effective (a bit of a chicken and egg situation, but presumably it made sense to the lawyers) and that privateering (engaged in under Letters of Marque) not be condoned. It also placed restrictions on the extent to which neutral nations could aid "a belligerent" by ferrying goods to it under a neutral flag. Britain had declared her neutrality on May 13, 1861, but recognized the belligerent status—although not the legal national existence—of the Confederacy, so furnishing the South with munitions was, from the British perspective, perfectly legal. From the Union's perspective, of course, it was a disaster, and hostility toward the British grew in the opening months of the war, tempered by the awareness that if Britain returned the hostility and officially recognized the Confederacy, the Union cause would be seriously undermined. Matters reached a head in November of 1861. Union officer Charles Wilkes provoked a diplomatic incident when his ship, the *San Jacinto*, fired at the British mail packet *Trent* that was en route from Havana to St. Thomas in the West Indies. The *Trent* carried James Mason and John Slidell, Confederate commissioners bound for Europe, and Wilkes promptly removed these gentlemen to his ship and returned them to America. The hero's welcome Wilkes received from the public and Congress soon gave way to a sober assessment of his actions, and concern grew over Britain's response to this apparent violation of the rights of a neutral nation. The British reaction was predictable: fury. Fury at American presumption "with their dwarf fleet and shapeless mass of incoherent squads which they call an army, to fancy themselves the equals of France by land and Great Britain by sea," as one London paper put it, and fury at interference with one of its ships. The *Trent* affair eventually blew over; Mason and Slidell were permitted to return to Britain, and diplomatic oil succeeded in soothing the troubled waters of American/British relations in the Atlantic in 1861. The persistent need to keep foreign powers out of America's conflict and the legal complexities of the blockade made it all the more crucial that any blockade was seen to be effective—and legal (so far as anyone understood the matter)—and did not contravene neutral rights on the high seas. In this context, Flag Officer Stringham's departure from the Carolina coast—thereby weakening the blockade—was not at all what Washington expected. The resultant criticism of Stringham was so persistent that, he resigned in mid-September, dismayed at the lack of appreciation shown for his "labors in behalf of my Government." The price of defeat, as Irvin McDowell had learned, was high; the price of a victory only half-secured, Stringham found, was higher still.[7]

Although international sensitivities helped to sink Stringham's naval career, Hatteras Inlet had been a victory, and it would be a mistake to dismiss, as Russell did, the impact this admittedly minor success had on the Union. What the success at Hatteras Inlet had done was overturn forever the traditional assumption that coastal defenses were likely to withstand attack from the sea; the greater maneuverability offered by steam, combined with the longer range of the shell gun, as naval historian William Fowler noted, upset the "historic balance between ship and shore," and offered the Union some chance of effecting a blockade that, however imperfectly applied, would hamper the Confederate war effort. Hatteras Inlet was no fluke, as the subsequent battle at Port Royal Sound in November 1861 made clear. Port Royal, off the coast of South Carolina between Charleston and Savannah, was potentially an important base for the Union. It offered not just a large harbor from which to organize the blockade but, crucially, secured access—via control of the coast—to internal waterways from Edisto Island all the way down to the St. Johns River by Cape Canaveral in Florida. After the departure of Stringham, Secretary of the Navy Welles divided the Atlantic Blockading Squadron into two, and in early November 1861, Flag Officer Samuel Francis du Pont of the South Atlantic Blockading Squadron launched an attack on the forts protecting Port Royal Sound—Fort Walker on Hilton Head and Fort Beauregard on Bay Point Island. The ability of the Union fleet—led by the *Wabash*—to maneuver in an elliptical pattern that kept them out of the reach of the shore batteries proved to be the decisive factor. Seeing the danger, Jefferson Davis had recalled his advisor, Robert E. Lee, from the interior, but when Lee arrived on November 7 all he could do was pull the Confederate troops back from the coast, out of the reach of the Union navy. This time, it was the turn of the Secretary of the Confederate Navy, Stephen R. Mallory, to be criticized—for his failure to anticipate, never mind counter, the Union threat. Mallory however, had a plan. Had it not been for the fact that the Union had exactly the same plan, it would have been a good one: deploying ironclads.[8]

By early 1862, in the Eastern Theater McClellan was preparing to embark on what became known as the Peninsula Campaign. The dramatic events at the Union naval base in Hampton Roads, Virginia, in early March were a part of that campaign, but they were also sufficiently unusual as to be regarded as a distinct aspect of the Civil War, a foretaste of the future in a conflict still very much rooted in the past. The idea of wrought iron plating on ships was not conceived during the Civil War, but the decision on the part of both the Union and the Confederacy to experiment with this technology was part of the desperate scramble both were engaged in: on the Union side, to consolidate the American fleet and produce a viable and effective navy; on the Confederate side, just to produce any kind of navy at all. The Union's retention of the bulk of the American fleet in 1861 was of no immediate benefit to it, because the American navy was in serious need of an overhaul to bring it up to date. Although the efficiency of their respective navies was something of a preoccupation for the European powers in the first half of the nineteenth century, America's pre-war navy was small and hardly a military or political priority in a nation protected by some three thousand miles of ocean in a time of, for America, relative peace. As a result, America was largely out of step and out of touch with developments in naval warfare when the Civil War came. The new shell guns that had done so much damage to the Turkish fleet during the Crimean War were not unknown to the Americans, but the ironclad vessels constructed to withstand such shells were not a development that America had paid much heed to—until it became a matter of urgency. Mallory started exploring the potential of the ironclad within weeks of the fall of Sumter; Welles took slightly longer to come round to the idea—he was held back by the scepticism of many of America's senior naval commanders—but by the summer of 1861 Welles, too, was looking closely at what the ironclad might have to offer. The result of both sides' deliberations met at Hampton Roads on March 9, 1862: the Confederate ironclad *Virginia* (previously the USS *Merrimack*: a name which has nevertheless stuck), and the USS *Monitor*.

At first it seemed as if the Confederates had the edge over the Union. When the *Virginia* sailed into Hampton Roads on March 8, 1862, the panic induced—as much by the bizarre physical appearance of the ship as its capabilities—was all that the South could have wished for. Looking, in the words of the *New York Times*, "like a submerged house, with the roof only above water," this floating death knell for the age of sail wreaked the havoc she was built for. As fire from the Union batteries (mostly) bounced off her hull, the *Virginia* headed for the USS *Cumberland*, an impressive but dated, sailing frigate, sinking her without much ceremony, and then moved on to the *Congress* and the *Minnesota*, grounding both before retiring, damaged but unbowed, to fight another day. The next day, however, saw the appearance of the Union's answer to this Confederate contraption: the *Monitor*. Smaller than the *Virginia*, and even less visible above the waterline, the *Monitor* had been en route from New York to Washington when she heard the guns at Hampton Roads. A change of course brought her to the scene just in time, and for much of March 9 the two vessels slugged it out; evenly matched. The encounter was inconclusive. Neither ship could do much damage to the other: the *Virginia* retired at the day's end and did not return. As an encounter between Federal and Confederate forces it was dramatic, but it advanced neither side one whit. Ironclads would be the future, but their time had not yet come. Their design problems undermined what efficacy they had as engines of war; too unstable to maneuver safely in deep water, and too prone to keeling over even in calm conditions, their impact on the Civil War was limited. Other ironclads were constructed in the course of the war, but both the *Monitor* and the *Merrimack* survived Hampton Roads for only a brief period. The *Virginia/Merrimack* was a casualty—one of the few, some observers might have said—of McClellan's Peninsula Campaign, sunk by the South in the evacuation of the Confederate naval base at Norfolk; the *Monitor* sank in a storm later that year. As with the changes in infantry weaponry, the battle of the ironclads in 1862 demonstrated the transition stage in warfare that America's Civil War represented: both sides explored the possibilities of the new technologies, but neither was able to exploit them to their full potential. If the impact of Hampton Roads on the Civil War's outcome was minimal, its implications for the future were undeniable. Herman Melville made the point succinctly in his poem inspired by the encounter at Hampton Roads: "Trafalgar is over now," he wrote, "O, Titan Temeraire,/Your stern-lights fade away;/Your bulwarks to the years must yield,/And hearts-of-oak decay … The rivets clinch the iron-clads,/Men learn a deadlier lore … O, the navies old and oaken,/O, the Temeraire no more."[9]

Into the Valley(s)

As the first anniversary of the fall of Fort Sumter approached, the Confederacy's initial success on land at Manassas had been somewhat soured by a string of defeats on water, both in the Atlantic and on the inland rivers. The Confederacy was stalled in the Eastern Theater, where Joseph E. Johnston, with an army of some 50,000 troops, had been waiting for the anticipated attack across the Potomac that never came; meanwhile, in the Western Theater, Albert Sidney Johnston, with only some 40,000 troops scattered across several locations, was trying to work out how to defend a three-hundred-mile front—from the Cumberland Gap (the "doorway to the West" where the borders of Kentucky, Virginia, and Tennessee meet), to Columbus in western Kentucky (on the Mississippi, near where it meets the Ohio). Columbus was strategically vital; it was where the Mobile and Ohio Railroad terminated as well as being a location that granted control of the Mississippi itself—which was the focus of a great deal of Union attention in late 1861 and early 1862. It was part of the Union's strategy—insofar as it had a coherent strategy in early 1862—to blockade the South along the coasts and to take control of the interior railroads and waterways, notably the Mississippi and its tributaries. Sometimes referred to as the Mississippi Valley Campaign or, more usually, the Mississippi River Expedition, the intention was for the Union to work its way down the Mississippi from the north to the Gulf of Mexico where they would meet up with their blockading squadron. Command in the West was divided between Brig. Gen. Don Carlos Buell with some 45,000 troops at Louisville, Kentucky and Maj. Gen. Henry Halleck in St. Louis, Missouri with 91,000. The idea was that these two commanders would work together, but their persistent inability to do so undermined the execution of any coherent Union campaign in the West.

The future general in chief of Union forces, Ulysses S. Grant, first came to public notice when he failed to take Columbus at the Battle of Belmont in November 1861. He had been driven off by, among other things, the "Lady Polk," a 6.4 inch Columbiad rifled cannon, named—presumably with complimentary intent—for the wife of the "Fighting Bishop," Confederate commander General Leonidas S. Polk, the former bishop of Louisiana. Grant's reputation, however, was recovered in the opening months of 1862, when two forts—Fort Henry on the Tennessee River and Fort Donelson on the Cumberland—fell to the combined forces of Grant and Flag Officer Andrew Foote. The victory gave Grant his nickname, "Unconditional Surrender" Grant, when he resolutely rejected the proposal of an armistice from one of the Confederate commanders at Fort Donelson, his pre-war friend Simon Bolivar Buckner: "No terms except unconditional and immediate surrender can be accepted," Grant advised him, a response that Buckner described as both "ungenerous and unchivalrous," but he had no choice but to comply. The fall of Forts Henry and Donelson broke the defensive line held by Albert S. Johnston, leaving Nashville vulnerable (it was evacuated just over a week later) and opened the Tennessee and the Cumberland to Union vessels, finally forcing the evacuation of Columbus. It only got worse for the Confederacy after that. Roanoke Island, off North Carolina, fell to Union troops in February—taken by Flag Officer Louis M. Goldsborough, commander of the North Atlantic Blockading Squadron, and General Ambrose E. Burnside as Grant was in the process of moving his troops between Fort Henry and Fort Donelson. Within a few short weeks the Union had taken control of Nashville—the first Confederate state capital to fall—and a long stretch of the Mississippi. In those opening months of 1862, not the least of the Confederacy's problems was the distance between their armies. Johnston was based at Murfreesboro, in central Tennessee; Beauregard was at Corinth, Mississippi, near the Tennessee border; and Braxton Bragg was in Mobile, Alabama, with the Army of Pensacola. Pooling these powerful but geographically disparate resources became a priority.[10]

Union momentum in the West, however, also stalled in the early part of 1862. Henry Halleck, now in charge of the Department of the West, sought to consolidate the Union's strength and ordered Grant to remain with the Union Army of West Tennessee (soon renamed the Army of the Tennessee) at Pittsburg Landing on the Tennessee River and await the arrival of Don Carlos Buell and the Army of the Ohio, then en route from Nashville. Halleck's plan was for the two armies to launch a joint attack on the Memphis and Charleston Railroad, a vital supply route for the Confederacy. Johnston and Beauregard, seeing an opportunity in Halleck's delay, and sensibly unwilling to fight two armies when one was just sitting there, decided to move on Grant's forces before Buell could join him. Beauregard had already called for Leonidas Polk's troops (8,000) from Columbus and they, together with Braxton Bragg's army from Mobile (10,000), Daniel Ruggles's troops (5,000) from Memphis, and Johnston's main force of some 17,000 men, gave the Confederates a combined force of over 40,000 at Corinth; it was this force that Johnston planned to use against Grant's Army of the Tennessee at the start of April, 1862. The Battle of Shiloh (The Battle of Pittsburg Landing) took place over April 6 and 7, 1862, when the newly organized Confederate Army of the Mississippi met the Army of the Tennessee and, as it turned out, the Army of the Ohio who arrived in time for the second day of the battle.[11]

Grant was, famously, caught unaware at Shiloh (Hebrew for "place of peace") when his army of some 49,000 men was attacked by the Confederates on the morning of April 6. Not anticipating an assault, his brigades were strung out in no particular defensive pattern, with only a few pickets in place to keep an eye on Confederate activity (and this despite some skirmishing that had taken place two days previously). Grant was distracted by his suspicion that the Confederates were planning an attack on Lewis Wallace's division, which was encamped at Crump's Landing. William T. Sherman, too, was convinced that no immediate threat was in the offing. Clearly, neither Grant nor Sherman had any idea of the size of the force gathered at Corinth, with estimates from their scouts varying wildly between 80,000 and 200,000 men. Johnston, on the other hand, had prepared his forces for the attack with a rousing pre-battle address:

> I have put you in motion to offer battle to the invaders of your country. With the resolution and disciplined valor becoming fighting men, as you are, for all worth living or dying for, you can but march to a decisive victory over the agrarian mercenaries sent to subjugate and despoil you of your liberties, property, and honor. Remember the precious stake involved; remember the dependence of your mothers, your wives, your sisters, and your children on the result; remember the fair, broad, abounding land, the happy homes, and the ties that would be desolated by your defeat.

"The eyes and the hopes of eight millions of people rest upon you," Johnston concluded, which was stretching the truth a bit because a large proportion of the eight million referred to were slaves, whose hopes probably did not rest on Johnston's men. Suitably inspired, the Confederates advanced on the Union army at Pittsburg Landing. The battlefield itself, between Snake Creek on its northern perimeter and one of its branches, Owl Creek, on the northwest, was swampy and crisscrossed by small streams, swollen by recent rains. Johnston's plan had been for his forces to attack on the left, driving the Union army away from Snake Creek and the Tennessee River—its obvious route of retreat—and toward Owl Creek on the opposite side of the base of the triangle that was the battlefield. The Confederate line of battle—comprising William J. Hardee's and Braxton Bragg's divisions and stretching some seven miles—was however, overextended, preventing the necessary concentration on one point. Nevertheless, the Confederate assault that began at 5:15 a.m. on April 6 when a Federal patrol first encountered the Confederates had the element of surprise on its side, and the battle seemed, initially, to be over almost before it had begun. It did not take long, however, for Hardee's and Braxton's line to become confused, and in the meantime the Union generals had taken stock of the situation and were preparing a defense. Leaving Beauregard in charge, Johnston himself went forward to lead his men, and the fighting against Sherman's division that morning was intense and costly. Grant himself did not arrive until about two hours into the battle. He immediately began sending urgent messages for reinforcements. "The attack on my forces has been very spirited," he advised the commanding officer of Buell's advance force that was still making its way from Nashville. "The appearance of fresh troops in the field now would have a powerful effect," he wrote, while to Brig. Gen. T. J. Wood he urged "move your command with the utmost dispatch to the river … where steamboats will be waiting to transport you to Pittsburg." His message to General Nelson was even more blunt: "Hurry up your command as fast as possible."[12]

Johnston's attack had been blocked in a part of the battlefield that became known as the "Hornet's Nest," near the center of the action, and here the Union's left flank took their stand against the Confederates— against twelve charges in all—for much of the afternoon. Leading one of these charges, and at the cost of his own life, was Johnston: struck in the knee, he did not seek medical aid immediately, and he bled to death. By the end of the day, the Confederates had not only lost their commander, but they had been unable to shift Grant away from the Tennessee River. Although bloodied, the Union was not yet bowed; it was somewhat farther back than it had been at the start of the battle, but it had maintained the front it had before Pittsburg Landing. Nevertheless, Beauregard still advised Richmond that the day was his (as clear a case of counting chickens as there ever was), but the battle the next day put paid to Beauregard's overconfidence. On the evening of April 6, Lewis Wallace's troops had, finally, and after some confusion over orders and direction, arrived from Crump's Landing; by dawn of the following day 25,000 troops from Buell's Army of the Ohio had made it across the river to support the Army of the Tennessee. Together, Grant and Buell launched a counterattack on the Confederate forces. Now it was Beauregard's turn to be surprised, but he managed to rally enough of a defense that the second day of Shiloh was no cakewalk for the Federals. In the end, however, he was forced to call a retreat; by late afternoon, the by now very bloody field of Shiloh belonged to the Union.

Shiloh had been a shock to commanders and troops alike. Years later, in his memoirs, Grant described the battle as one "of Southern dash against Northern pluck," but he also recalled the intensity of the fighting all that first day, when there "was no hour … when there was not heavy firing and generally hard fighting at some point on the line." At Shiloh the greenness of the troops showed. "Many of them had arrived but a day or two before," Grant observed, "and were hardly able to load their muskets according to the manual." Shiloh, he concluded,

> was the severest battle fought at the West during the war, and few in the East equaled it for hard, determined fighting. I saw an open field … over which the Confederates had made repeated charges the day before, so covered with dead that it would have been possible to walk across the clearing, in any direction, stepping on dead bodies, without a foot touching the ground.[13]

Confederate dispatches in the aftermath of Shiloh told their own grim side of the story. "Our condition is horrible," Braxton Bragg advised Beauregard the day after the battle. "Troops utterly disorganized and demoralized." Losses on both sides were high, high enough, indeed, to make First Bull Run seem what many observers had anticipated its being—a picnic. Union casualties numbered 1,754 killed outright, 8,084 wounded, and 2,885 missing; Confederate numbers were similar, with 1,728 dead, 8,012 wounded, and 959 missing. Aggregate losses for each side numbered 13,047 for the Union, 10,699 for the Confederacy, a casualty rate comparable to that of the Battle of Waterloo in 1815.[14]

The death rate from wounds in the Civil War should be borne in mind when looking at casualty figures, especially the number of wounded. In this conflict, disease—some of it derived from wounds or from the treatment of same—accounted for two-thirds of total deaths; "wounded" did not carry the expectation of the addendum "but alive" that it would in future wars. Civil War-era medical care was, at best, primitive; surviving the battlefield wounded all too often meant a slower death in unhygienic and disorganized hospitals. In the aftermath of Bull Run, Confederate congressman Augustus Wright described the dreadful "stench from the wounds" and the protracted "suffering & dying" that so many of the wounded experienced. Northern nurse Cornelia Hancock was describing the aftermath of Gettysburg when she recalled the sight of a field hospital and the atmosphere produced by the dead and dying, an atmosphere, she wrote, "which robbed the battlefield of its glory, the survivors of their victory, and the wounded of what little chance of life was left to them." The "gruesome spectacle" of a wagonload of amputated limbs horrified her, but it was one that was repeated after every engagement, from Bull Run to the Wilderness. Similar sights in the aftermath of Shiloh produced an equally stunned reaction: "We had *expected* to find dead and mangled bodies," wrote one soldier, "but we were not prepared to come in sudden contact with that naked and ghastly mass of human flesh." Grant himself found the sight of the field hospital at Shiloh (one of the first in the Civil War, and a factor in reducing the death rate at that particular battle) as "more unendurable than encountering the enemy's fire," and retreated quickly from it. The lesson that both sides learned from Shiloh went beyond the relative weaknesses of strategy and tactics and to the heart of what a civil war, any civil war, is about. Shiloh made clear to both sides the full horror of what they had unleashed, and for Union generals Grant and Sherman, in particular, it gave some inkling of what it would take to defeat the South. "Up to the battle of Shiloh," wrote Grant, "I, as well as thousands of other citizens, believed that the rebellion against the Government would collapse suddenly and soon." After it, he "gave up all idea of saving the Union except by complete conquest." For anyone still harboring the belief that the Civil War would be both brief and relatively bloodless, Shiloh was a wake-up call. For many soldiers, Shiloh was not what they had anticipated—and it was more than they wished to experience: "I have all ways wanted to see one battle field," one soldier advised his mother, "and now I have seen it I never want to see a nother one." "What like a bullet can undeceive!" exclaimed Herman Melville in his "requiem" inspired by this battle that entered American legend as the bloodiest single day of the Civil War; a dubious honor that, in any case, it held for less than six months.[15]

Shiloh was the most violent clash between the Union and the Confederacy in early 1862, but hardly the only one. The Union was making progress at several points across the West in this period, and it achieved some important—if minor—victories such as that at Pea Ridge/Elkhorn Tavern one month prior to Shiloh in the trans-Mississippi West, and later, the much more significant success at New Orleans. The victory of Union general Samuel R. Curtis at Pea Ridge in northwest Arkansas over Earl Van Dorn, the new Confederate commander in the trans-Mississippi region, stymied Van Dorn's ambitious plan to attack the Union advance in the West from the rear—via Arkansas and Missouri, and it consolidated the Federal position in that area. The fall of New Orleans in April to Flag Officer David Glasgow Farragut was a further boost for the Union. New Orleans was the most important port of the South; positioned on the Mississippi, the nation's most important river, the city was an obvious target for a Union that enjoyed the additional benefit of having in former midshipman Gustavus Fox, its assistant secretary of the navy, a man long familiar with the waters of the Gulf. Most of New Orleans's defenses faced northward; its main protection from the direction of the Gulf came from two forts positioned near one another on a bend in the Mississippi about sixty miles south of the city itself: Fort Jackson (south bank) and Fort St. Philip (north bank). A further twenty miles south of these forts the river subdivided into several channels, only one of which was deep enough to permit larger vessels to gain access to the river itself. So, in many ways the decision of where to launch the attack on New Orleans was made by a combination of nature and the limitations of Confederate defensive preparations which left the Gulf entry point relatively undefended. Since events at both Hatteras Inlet and Port Royal had suggested that the forts themselves, although heavily armed, would not necessarily present an insurmountable difficulty, a Union fleet began to move toward the Gulf coast in the opening months of 1862.

The planned operation to take New Orleans was a combined one, with Ben Butler in charge of the Army of the Gulf for the land assault at Fort St. Philip and Admiral David Dixon Porter commanding the mortar fleet that would fire on the forts. On April 18 the mortar fleet began its bombardment, and kept it up for six full days, launching some 7,500 shells at the two forts, many of which either exploded too soon or landed in mud. Because that particular approach was proving slow and not obviously effective, Farragut decided to begin his push past the forts, which he did on April 24. It was a daunting and dangerous journey: the Confederacy brought one of its ironclads, the *Manassas*, into play; but it was eventually disabled, and Farragut made it past the forts, leaving them for Ben Butler to attack from the land (or more accurately, the swamp) that surrounded Fort St. Philip. When Farragut reached New Orleans on April 25, the panicked citizens tried to destroy everything of value, loading ships with cotton and setting them ablaze. The "destruction of property was awful," Farragut reported, and the "levee of New Orleans was one scene of desolation; ships, steamers, cotton, coal, etc., were all in one common blaze." Within only a few days, however, Farragut was able to advise Gideon Welles, "that our flag waves over both Forts Jackson and St. Philip, and at New Orleans over the custom-house." New Orleans had been taken back into the Union. It was a conclusive victory on several counts, not least because it opened up the Mississippi and allowed Union forces to attack their Confederate opponents from the south as well as the north. "The way is clear," wired Captain Theodorus Bailey of the Union gunboat *Cayuga*, "and the rebel defenses destroyed from the Gulf to Baton Rouge and probably to Memphis." Mary Chesnut, too, saw the implications clearly: "New Orleans is gone, and with it the Confederacy!" she exclaimed. "Are we not cut in two? The Mississippi ruins us if it is lost." With the fall of New Orleans, opportunity beckoned for the Union; it only had to seize it.[16]

Unfortunately, First Bull Run seemed to have set something of a precedent for early Civil War engagements—for both sides. In the case of New Orleans, the Mississippi lay open, but this time it was the Union's turn not to follow up on victory; no reinforcements were sent, and the chance slipped away. Somewhat left to his own devices, Farragut pushed on upriver, taking Baton Rouge and then Natchez, but he was blocked at Vicksburg, which remained in Confederate hands until July 4, 1863. Naval success in the Atlantic and in the Gulf was neither matched by Union victories in the Eastern Theater nor followed up on in the West. In the aftermath of Shiloh, Halleck was focused on Corinth, seemingly oblivious to the fact that an equally promising, perhaps even better, opportunity to undermine the Confederacy had just presented itself with the fall of New Orleans. Instead, Halleck devoted a large part of May to inching toward Corinth—certainly strategically crucial given that it was where the Memphis and Charleston Railroads crossed the Mobile and Ohio line. The force by then included some 100,000 troops: the Army of the Tennessee under Grant (before command was passed to George H. Thomas); the Army of the Ohio under Don Carlos Buell; and the Army of the Mississippi under John Pope. Defending Corinth was the Confederate Army of the Mississippi under Beauregard and the Army of the West under Earl Van Dorn.

Halleck's progress was painfully slow, peppered with minor skirmishes en route, but there were no major confrontations. On arrival at Corinth, Halleck prepared for a siege operation, but Beauregard decided not to wait for the inevitable bombardment and moved his troops some fifty miles south, to Tupelo. By the end of May, Corinth was in Union hands, but since Halleck had prepared for a siege rather than for movement, the momentum had almost entirely gone from the Union's Western campaign. Halleck's successes in the West were enough to have him summoned to Washington to replace McClellan as general in chief of the Union armies, but as spring gave way to summer the Western initiative passed to the Confederacy and to Stonewall Jackson, who was playing merry havoc with Federal forces in the Shenandoah Valley.[17]

Jackson's Shenandoah Valley Campaign of May–June 1862 paralleled, and was designed to stymie, McClellan's push on the James Peninsula in the Eastern Theater. Conceived by Robert E. Lee—at that point Jefferson Davis's advisor in Richmond—as a diversion that would slow the Union advance on Richmond, the operation was a complete success. In Stonewall Jackson the Confederacy had a remarkable military mind, even if some parts of that mind held unusual notions about the health benefits of sucking lemons and the dangers of pepper on one's constitution. A religious fanatic and a teetotaler, Jackson was a force that the Union proved wholly unable to reckon with as he ranged up and down the Shenandoah Valley, striking at the Union in engagements such as Cross Keys (June 8) and Port Republic (June 9). With only some 15,000 troops to deploy, Jackson succeeded in unsettling the three much larger Union armies ranged against him: Nathaniel P. Banks in the Valley, Irvin McDowell in the east, and John C. Frémont in the west. Part of Jackson's objective was to prevent Banks and Frémont from joining forces, but the overarching objective was to take McDowell's troops away from Richmond and engage them, and Banks, in the Valley, leaving Robert E. Lee, who had on June 1 taken over command of the Army of Northern Virginia, the opportunity to strike at McClellan on the Peninsula. The Valley Campaign was brief, aggressive, and to the point. It achieved its objectives—it kept McDowell from the Peninsula—and it secured Jackson's reputation as one of the Confederacy's most decisive and capable generals. It set the stage for the emergence of the last best hope for the Confederacy in the East: Robert E. Lee; but its impact on the Union's equivalent, George B. McClellan, was less positive. As Lee and Jackson both went up in Confederate—and indeed Union—estimation for their fighting prowess, McClellan fell—and hard.

The Peninsula Campaign

McClellan had never enjoyed a good relationship with Lincoln; he was as impatient with what he perceived to be the president's shortcomings and his interference with military affairs as Lincoln came to be with McClellan's own shortcoming: his inability to take action. That they were on opposite sides of the political fence did not help. In fact, McClellan would run against Lincoln for the presidency in 1864, but for a would-be president, McClellan's political instincts were remarkably blunt, and he appeared to have little grasp of the political pressure Lincoln was under to get the Army of the Potomac moving. As the months passed and McClellan's frequent drilling of the Army became something of a joke in Washington, it became apparent to Lincoln and to others that the Union's foremost general had commitment issues as far as his army was concerned; he simply didn't want to commit it to any serious engagement with the enemy. This was, in some ways, a perfectly sensible approach given the situation in 1861 and the rawness of the Union's recruits. McClellan had an overall strategic plan to attack Richmond indirectly from the east, thereby drawing Johnston's troops away from Washington. It was a complex plan, involving support from the Union navy as well as the mass movement of his own men southward; its successful execution required a trained and disciplined army, by his own estimation it would take some 273,000 troops with 100,000 in reserve. McClellan was understandably cautious about sending an ill-prepared army into the field. Yet McClellan's plan was, with hindsight, a triumph of optimism (or perhaps ambition) over reality. On taking command of the Union armies, McClellan had famously declared—in response to Lincoln's suggestion that McClellan was possibly taking on too much—"I can do it all," and his intention both to take Richmond and destroy the Confederate armies certainly suggested that he might have to. Not that everyone was fully aware of the scope of McClellan's plans. Not the least problematic aspect of his generalship was his unwillingness to confide in the president or any other military advisor. In keeping his thoughts to himself, McClellan weakened his own position, and undermined a plan that, for all its flaws, at least arose from a grand vision of how the Confederacy might be defeated with minimum loss of life on each side.[18]

Matters came to a head at the start of 1862 when McClellan contracted typhoid fever. In desperation, Lincoln called a series of meetings with members of his cabinet—Salmon P. Chase, Montgomery Blair, Assistant Secretary of War Thomas A. Scott and William Seward—and Generals McDowell, Montgomery Meigs and William B. Franklin and, at the final meeting, McClellan himself—to assess the situation and, hopefully, decide on a plan of action. The final outcome—which did not emerge until the end of the month and even then had to be revised several times—was a plan to move the Union forces from the environs of Washington to Urbanna on the Rappahannock in the lower Chesapeake, from which position, McClellan believed, he could better attack the Confederate forces under Joe Johnston, then massed south of Manassas. In reaching this conclusion, McClellan was at odds with Lincoln, not least because Lincoln believed—as he had told Don Carlos Buell—that the Union's strength was superior numbers. McClellan did not concur. Although he actually outnumbered Johnston two to one, McClellan believed that his army was the weaker of the two, and it was on this erroneous belief that much of his strategic thinking was predicated. His error in regard to Confederate numbers was made painfully clear within a few weeks, when he arrived at Manassas only to discover that Johnston had withdrawn South, close to Urbanna, leaving behind him clear evidence (including logs painted to resemble guns) that the Confederate army was nothing near the overwhelming force that McClellan had described. This was embarrassing enough, but it got worse. Lincoln decided to remove McClellan from his position as general in chief, the rank he had been promoted to after the Union disaster at Bull Run, so that he could concentrate on the Army of the Potomac. Lincoln meant this as a positive move, but it was not appreciated by a man who believed he could do it all, but was having serious problems even getting started.[19]

Because the Confederate army had moved too close to McClellan's planned base of operations on the Rappahannock, a change of plan proved necessary. McClellan's new idea was to take his army to the tip of the James Peninsula (between the York and James Rivers) and to move rapidly—too rapidly, he hoped, for Johnston to stop them—on Richmond. His plan took advantage of Union strength on the Atlantic coast, and moving his 100,000 troops by water down the Chesapeake Bay promised to be both faster and safer than attempting an overland march. Having selected Fort Monroe as the best starting point for an advance up the James Peninsula, McClellan began the lengthy process of actually getting his army there in mid-March 1862. The weather was warm when the troops boarded the vessels that would take them down the Potomac and south to the Virginian Peninsula. Many of the Union ships were decorated with flags and the general mood of the army was buoyant, prompting Union soldier Elisha Hunt Rhodes to describe the scene as "more like a pleasure excursion than an army looking for the enemy." Rhodes was a part of the largest movement of men and matériel ever seen in America, and it was with some degree of understatement that William Howard Russell observed that the "Federal armies are not handled easily." They were, he noted, "luxurious in the matter of baggage, and canteens, and private stores; and this is just the sort of war in which the general who moves lightly and rapidly, striking blows unexpectedly and deranging communications, will obtain great results."[20]

The Peninsula Campaign, the final outcome of so much delay and forced compromise, was over-engineered from the outset and hampered by setbacks beyond McClellan's control. Not only had Johnston moved out of immediate range, but the Confederate ironclad *Virginia/Merrimack* remained at Norfolk, on the other side of Hampton Roads from Fort Monroe, blocking Union access to the James and, to top it all, Lincoln had held back a significant part of McClellan's forces in order to defend Washington: the 30,000 men of Irvin McDowell's corps (who were later sent to the Shenandoah). On the plus side, when McClellan arrived at the Peninsula in April, the Confederate forces opposing him comprised only some 10,000 troops under John Bankhead Magruder. Yet McClellan failed to take advantage of the opportunity this afforded him, despite Lincoln's increasingly impatient messages advising him to engage. Instead, McClellan worried about numbers and the Army of the Potomac's overall preparedness to such an extent that Lincoln advised the general that his constant "complaining" pained him "very much." "By delay," the president cautioned the commander, "the enemy will relatively gain upon you—that is, he will gain faster, by *fortifications* and *re-inforcements*, than you can by re-inforcements alone." It "is indispensable to *you* that you strike a blow," Lincoln urged, "*I* am powerless to help this," and he warned McClellan that the "country will not fail to note—is now noting—that the present hesitation to move upon an intrenched enemy, is but the story of Manassas repeated ... *you must act.*" McClellan did not act; indeed, he found Lincoln's advise intrusive and continued to fret from a standstill. As April wore on, it became "very plain" to Confederate general Daniel H. Hill "that with our defective artillery and munitions we cannot contend with the enemy ... they certainly outnumber us now two to one." He reminded Secretary of War George Randolph that the Union army "can bring up ten guns to our one, and his guns will be infinitely superior." Confederate ordnance, by contrast, was woefully lacking; guns and cannons both proved unreliable to such a degree that Hill suspected sabotage, although Randolph put it down to the "scarcity of metal" in Southern foundries. What was clear to Hill, however, was entirely opaque to McClellan, and rather than taking advantage of Confederate weakness with a quick and decisive engagement, McClellan settled down to besiege Yorktown while he contemplated the carefully planned assault that, he believed, would terminate the conflict. It was a remarkable decision given the relative strengths of Union and Confederate forces in Virginia in late April 1862. "No one but McClellan," Joe Johnston advised Lee, "could have hesitated to attack."[21]

For much of April everyone was impatient for some action on the Peninsula. Lincoln waited for McClellan to move; McClellan waited for his heavy artillery. The Confederates were as anxious for battle as Lincoln was, believing that only an open fight would offer them any chance of success against the superior Union forces gathering against them. The soldiers in the Army of the Potomac grew restive, worn out by a series of minor skirmishes and the attention of Confederate snipers in place of the anticipated conclusive battle, while in New York the populace "gathered in knots at corners, from which one is sure to hear in passing the words *Merrimac* or *Monitor*," George Templeton Strong reported. He, in common with many others, announced himself "tired of this state of tension, which has now lasted a year." The tension might have been broken sooner had Confederate general Joe Johnston had his way: realizing, as McClellan clearly did not, that the Confederate forces were outgunned, he had advised a swift retreat from the Peninsula, but both Jefferson Davis and Robert E. Lee ordered him to Magruder's aid.[22]

Every day of delay, while it bought time for the Confederacy to move its troops into position, also brought more misery for these troops. Less comfortably provisioned than their Union counterparts, disease, sickness, and unreliable weaponry all worked to wear them down. Problems that would plague the Confederacy throughout the war became apparent on the Virginia Peninsula in April of 1862, as commanders struggled with inadequate supplies and, already, a shortage of men. "Our sick list is fearfully increasing," Daniel Hill reported. "Two thirds of our men have no tents. Exposure, fatigue, loss of sleep, and hard work are sending hundreds to the rear every day." The initial enthusiasm that had taken both Northerners and Southerners into their respective armies was diminishing; in time, both sides would be forced to introduce conscription to maintain the war effort, but for the Confederacy the issue was pressing as early as the spring of 1862. Hill, for one, was concerned at the depletion of his forces, dismayed that conscription had been delayed, and worried that the Confederacy was spreading itself too thin. "If the men are not called out sooner," he cautioned, "I fear that we will be beaten. The policy of trying to hold every point leaves us always weaker than the enemy at the vital point. We are committing the mistake of the Austrians in Napoleon's first Italian campaign." Joe Johnston too, was convinced that the Confederacy was "engaged in a species of warfare at which we can never win. It is plain," he advised Lee, "that General McClellan will adhere to the system adopted by him last summer, and depend for success upon artillery and engineering. We can compete with him in neither."[23]

Johnston's previous call to retreat from the Peninsula—the better to defend Richmond—was reiterated at the end of April. The fall of Yorktown was inevitable, he believed, and he advocated open battle as the only possible hope for an army so weak in artillery support as his was. "Our troops have always wished for the offensive," he wrote Lee, "and so does the country.... We can have no success," he stressed, "while McClellan is allowed, as he is by our defensive, to choose his mode of warfare." Johnston firmly believed that a "concentration of all our available forces may enable us to fight successfully." At any rate, he concluded, "Let us try." Seeking the best position from which to engage McClellan, the Confederate army began a tactical retreat—a slow backward movement up the Peninsula—just at the point when, with every siege gun in place, McClellan was finally ready to launch his attack at the start of May. McClellan was therefore forced to follow Johnston up the Peninsula until, by the end of the month, both armies had arrived on the outskirts of Richmond. At that point, the situation looked promising for the Union. Norfolk had been evacuated and the *Virginia* scuttled in the process, leaving the James open to Union vessels. As so often in war, however, the weather (this time, rain) influenced events. The fine March weather enjoyed by the Union army as they left the banks of the Potomac for those of the James soon gave way to heavy spring showers, cold and persistent, turning roads to mud and placid rivers into torrents that hampered any movement, especially that of the heavy artillery that had to come by rail. For the Union this had serious consequences. By the end of May, McClellan was camped at White House on the Pamunkey River awaiting—as was becoming usual—the arrival of his siege artillery.

Between him and Richmond flowed the Chickahominy River, unusually swollen by the rains and across which the Union army was divided, with two corps separated from the bulk of the army. In this division of McClellan's forces Johnston saw an opportunity, and attempted to seize it at the battle of Fair Oaks (or Seven Pines) on May 31–June 1, 1862.[24]

Johnston's attack on the Union army at the end of May proved timely for another reason. Siege artillery was not all that McClellan was waiting for. He was also expecting—indeed, relying on—the arrival of Irvin McDowell and his men from Washington. It was something of a shock, therefore, when he received a telegram from Lincoln advising him that the president had been "compelled to suspend Gen. McDowell's movement to join you. The enemy are making a desperate push upon Harper's Ferry," Lincoln explained, "and we are trying to throw Frémont's force and part of McDowell's in their rear." It was bad enough to learn that McDowell would not be coming after all, that he had, in fact, been sent to the Shenandoah to try and counter the threat offered by Stonewall Jackson, but worse still was the message sent the following day: the enemy was moving north in force, Lincoln advised McClellan, "I think the movement is a general and concerted one, such as could not be if he was acting upon the purpose of a very desperate defence of Richmond. I think the time is near," Lincoln declared, "when you must either attack Richmond or give up the job and come to the defence of Washington." Later that same day Lincoln sought to reassure his by now furious general that the decision to send McDowell to the Shenandoah derived from "no unwillingness to sustain you ... Please understand this," Lincoln pleaded, "and do the best you can with the force you have." It was, therefore, with rather less of an advantage and rather more pressure than he had anticipated that McClellan, one week later, sought to carry out Lincoln's command to "hold all your ground, or yield only, inch by inch and in good order." With the weather worsening, the Chickahominy rising, and McClellan himself incapacitated by typhoid, Johnston's attack on the Federals at Fair Oaks seemed to offer an ideal opportunity to improve Confederate fortunes.[25]

Despite a promising start, the Confederate attack stumbled at the battle of Fair Oaks, in large part due to the degree of confusion and disorganization exhibited by the South's commanders as they attempted a complex maneuver that required organization above all else—the simultaneous advance of several columns who could not see each other. Johnston himself is usually assigned the bulk of the blame, but the actions of other commanders, such as James B. Longstreet who, unusually for him, got lost and took his army in the wrong direction, did not help. More a series of uncoordinated skirmishes than a concerted attack, Fair Oaks ended in stalemate, with serious casualties, especially among the senior command, on both sides. McClellan, rising from his sick bed to review the final outcome—a Confederate retreat—regarded this bloody but ultimately inconclusive battle as the beginning of the end for the Confederacy. The rousing address he gave to his troops the day after the battle ended promised them glory, and assured them that the "final and decisive battle is at hand. Unless you belie your past history," he insisted, "the result cannot be for a moment doubted ... wherever you have met the enemy you have beaten him ... I ask of you now one last crowning effort. The enemy has staked his all on the issue of the coming battle. Let us meet and crush him here in the very center of the rebellion." But it was not to be. Fair Oaks proved something of a turning point for the Confederacy in an unanticipated way. One of the casualties of the battle was Johnston himself, hit by a musket ball in the shoulder. Robert E. Lee, a Winfield Scott protégé (to whom Scott had offered command of the Union armies at the start of the war, but who had elected to follow his state out of the Union), was swiftly removed from his desk job to replace Johnston as the theoretically temporary commander of what, under his leadership, became the Army of Northern Virginia. At that point it seemed as if the Confederacy was at a disadvantage. Expectations of Davis's former advisor were not high. Nicknamed the "King of Spades" for having his troops dig entrenchments outside Richmond, Southern hopes focused instead on Stonewall Jackson. "Unless we can reinforce Stonewall," Mary Chesnut bemoaned, "the game is up," a dismissal of Lee with which his detractors concurred. McClellan professed himself unconcerned at this change in Confederate leadership, little realizing (like the Confederates themselves) that in Lee the South had its best hope for victory.[26]

The Seven Days Battles

Lee's far more aggressive—and organized—style of leadership was apparent at once. Lee had a plan by which, he believed, the South could gain its independence. He realized that remaining on the defensive to fend off successive attacks by the Federals was only going to wear the South down. Whatever McClellan imagined, Lee knew that that the numbers stacked up on the Union side. At that point, Lee had about 65,000 troops against McClellan's 100,000. McClellan was sending for—indeed, consistently demanding—reinforcements, and Lee knew these would come. The South's sole hope was to seize the initiative before McClellan got his heavy guns into place and his reinforcements into line. It needed, in short, to implement Jefferson Davis's preferred "offensive-defensive" strategy. Lee concurred with Davis but, thrown in at the deep end as he was in June 1862, the emphasis had first to be on the offensive side of the equation. McClellan left Lee plenty of room to maneuver and develop and set in motion a Confederate counter-attack to the Union offensive at Fair Oaks: remaining on the outskirts of Richmond in the aftermath of Fair Oaks, McClellan grew increasingly confident to the point of apparent complacency. Not that McClellan was actually complacent: he was simply reluctant to move until every detail was, in his view, right. "I dare not rush this army," he explained, "on which I feel the fate of the nation depends." McClellan delayed, however, far beyond the point where decisive action was required and might have been effective, thereby ensuring that by the time the Army of the Potomac was sent into action, it was against the newly organized Army of Northern Virginia, an army powerful enough, at that point, to match his own. In effect, McClellan had allowed Lee the time he needed to make real a force that, prior to June 1862, had only existed in McClellan's mind.[27]

McClellan realized none of this, of course. As both the weather and his health improved (the former only temporarily), he assured Washington that he was fully prepared for any Confederate assault, while Washington—in the person of Lincoln and many members of his cabinet—waited in vain for McClellan to initiate the action. "I could better dispose of things," wrote Lincoln in frustration, "if I could know about what day you can attack Richmond, and would be glad to be informed." His general, however, seemed content to wait for the battle to come to him and, as he advised Lincoln, "await only a favorable condition of the earth and sky and the completion of some necessary preliminaries." As McClellan dallied, hoping for the heavens and the earth to come into propitious alignment so that he might deliver the final decisive blow to Southern hopes, Lee busied himself by drawing as much of the South's forces as he could to his position and moved them north of Richmond. His commanders, meanwhile, prepared their men for what they, like McClellan, believed would be the decisive engagement that would decide the conflict. Confederate General James Longstreet invoked the horror of servile insurrection as well as the many evils perpetrated on Southern civilians by the Union army in order to get his troops in the right frame of mind for meeting the Yankees. In case that was not sufficient inspiration, he advised them, disingenuously, that "though the fiery noise of battle is indeed most terrifying, and seems to threaten universal ruin, it is not so destructive as it seems, and few soldiers after all are slain." It was a dubious argument, but in any case moot unless Lee could find the Army of the Potomac's Achilles' heel—some point at which he could attack unexpectedly, with force, and to maximum effect. Thanks to cavalry commander J. E. B. (Jeb) Stuart's dramatic circuit of McClellan's entire force in mid-June, Lee found the Union's weak point: it was on the north bank of the Chickahominy, on the Union's right flank. Stuart's achievement made him a hero; it made the sole casualty of his daring exercise, William Latané, a martyr, *the* symbolic martyr, indeed, of the Lost Cause after the war; but above all it gave Lee the valuable information he needed to engage, and hopefully defeat, McClellan at the gates of Richmond.[28]

Having delayed so long, on June 25, 1862 McClellan finally, and somewhat cautiously, moved on Oak Grove, close to the battlefield of Fair Oaks, thereby instigating the first of what became known as the "Seven Days Battles." The following day Lee initiated the Confederate counteroffensive, supported by Stonewall Jackson, whom he had recalled from the Shenandoah. In summoning Jackson to his aid, Lee made it clear that concentration of force against McClellan was essential. "Unless McClellan can be driven out of his entrenchments," Lee advised Jackson, "he will move by positions under cover of his heavy guns within shelling distance of Richmond." By the early morning of the 26th, however, when Lee had planned for the attack against McClellan's right to commence, Jackson had not yet arrived, leaving Lee short of men and of the comander he trusted above all others. The second of the Seven Days battles, at Mechanicsville (Beaver Dam Creek), instigated by Confederate General A. P. Hill, was a hard-fought Union victory. McClellan was ecstatic. On the evening of the 26th he assured Secretary of War Edwin M. Stanton that "this army will do all that the country expects of it," and he later reported "Victory of to-day complete and against great odds. I almost begin to think," he enthused, "that we are invincible."[29]

Yet McClellan's exuberance disguised his growing conviction that the odds he was facing were insurmountable and that taking Richmond was impracticable. Even before Lee had launched his counterattack, McClellan had advised Secretary of War Edwin Stanton, somewhat melodramatically, that if the Army of the Potomac were "destroyed by overwhelming numbers" then he would "at least die with it and share its fate." Here McClellan revealed a dangerous degree of pessimism, indeed fatalism, which even battlefield success could not eradicate. His main fear—an attack on his right by Jackson—had not materialized at Mechanicsville in the way he expected (and Lee hoped), but even this did not encourage him. Rather than spurring him on to the offensive, his immediate response to his victory at Mechanicsville was a defensive one: he moved one corps—Major General Fitz John Porter's—out of range of a possible flanking maneuver back to the more secure position offered by Gaines Mill.[30]

The contradictory combination of the previous day's success with a commander who, rather than scenting victory was instead gearing himself up for defeat, left the Army of the Potomac ill-prepared for the following day's engagement at Gaines Mill (First Cold Harbor), a battle that saw some of the worst fighting yet experienced by either side. Described by historian Stephen Sears as "a bloody slugging match," Gaines Mill was something of a fiasco as far as Lee's grand strategy was concerned, but in the short term the Confederacy's tactical success was achieved in spite of the persistent ineptitude shown by the very general in whom so much hope had been placed, Stonewall Jackson. Indeed, the Confederates were aided more by McClellan's inability to grasp what was happening on the field than they were by some of their own generals. Although the bulk of the Union's forces were being held down by the diversionary tactics of John Magruder on the other side of the Chickahominy, McClellan believed that he was being attacked "by superior numbers in all directions," and warned Secretary of War Stanton that he might "be forced to give up my position," while, again, requesting reinforcements. "Had I 20,000 fresh and good troops we would be sure of a splendid victory to-morrow," he promised. In the meantime, McClellan began to pull back, shifting his base of operations to the James River. Even more dramatically, he pulled the entire Army of the Potomac back with him. In calling for support from the Union navy for this movement, McClellan reported the "severe repulse" suffered by his army at Gaines Mill, and reiterated his belief in the "greatly superior numbers" fielded by his opponents, a belief that justified, to his satisfaction, if to no one else's, his complete abandonment of the plan to take Richmond.[31]

Gaines Mill proved a crucial engagement in convincing McClellan that Richmond was beyond his reach. It was significant most of all, however, for seriously unhinging the general, prompting him to an outburst that could have ended his career then and there. In his famous Savage Station dispatch to Stanton, composed in the early hours of June 28, he reported that the "loss on both sides is terrible. I believe," he wrote, "it will be the most desperate battle of the war." Certainly the casualty rate at Gaines Mill was high: for the Union the reported number killed, wounded, and missing was 6,837, while Confederate losses amounted to 8,751. McClellan found this hard to bear, which in part explains the intemperate nature of his missive, which went on:

> I have lost this battle because my force was too small. I again repeat that I am not responsible for this, and I say it with the earnestness of a general who feels in his heart the loss of every brave man who has been needlessly sacrificed to-day … You must send me very large re-enforcements, and send them at once … I know that a few thousand more men would have changed this battle from a defeat to a victory … I have seen too many dead and wounded comrades to feel otherwise than that the Government has not sustained this army. If you do not do so now the game is lost. If I save this army now, I tell you plainly that I owe no thanks to you or to any other persons in Washington. You have done your best to sacrifice this army.[32]

The final two, potentially damning, sentences of the message were removed by Edward Sanford, the military telegraph supervisor, before the message was delivered. Sanford thereby saved McClellan from the probable consequences that such a blunt accusation could have had, but back on the Peninsula, all that concerned McClellan was the logistics of the retreat back to the James and holding off Lee's forces who, although not overwhelming in the way McClellan described, were nevertheless in a good position to attack. That they did not do so at once was due to the simple fact that McClellan's retreat took Lee by surprise, not just the scale of it but also its direction. Anticipating a move back down the Peninsula on McClellan's part, Lee had prepared his troops for pursuit, and was initially nonplused at the move south to the James. Lee's confusion secured the Union time in which to undertake the laborious process of shifting south en masse, but Lee did not stay confused for long.

By the time the Union's advance regiments reached Charles City Crossroads on Sunday, June 29 they were, as one soldier recorded, suffering from lack of food and were "tired almost to death," although able to deal with the Confederate forces they encountered. The Union's rearguard regiments, meanwhile, engaged Lee's troops at Savage Station and then at White Oak Swamp in two successive days of fighting that advanced neither side to any great degree. McClellan's telegrams to Stanton became increasingly desperate: "I shall do my best to save the army," he advised him. "Send more gunboats." Stanton for his part, tried to steady McClellan's clearly faltering nerve, advising him that troops from McDowell's corps, and others, were on the way. "Hold your ground," he advised, "and you will be in Richmond before the month is over." Stanton's advice came too late. McClellan was already committed—mentally since early June and now, at the start of July, in practical terms too—to abandoning the Peninsula. Before he could do so, however, he had to face Lee's Army of Northern Virginia. By the start of July 1862, both generals had arrived at a point—Lee by seeking it, McClellan by trying to avoid it—where a head-on clash between their respective armies could, and did, occur. That point was Malvern Hill.[33]

"O the horrors of this day's work," exclaimed Union soldier Elisha Hunt Rhodes in the aftermath of Malvern Hill, "but at last we have stopped the Rebel advance." Casualty rates at Malvern Hill, as at Gaines Mill, were high—3,124 on the Union side and 5,355 on the Confederate—but for the Confederacy it was wasted life, as Malvern Hill was a terrible defeat. Lee probably should not have attacked the Union at Malvern Hill. It was a strong defensive position, and the Army of the Potomac was well entrenched by the time Lee's troops arrived. Expecting a demoralized army in the retreating Union forces, Lee, in fact, encountered McClellan's troops at their best and most committed. That there was nowhere for either side to go doubtless helped the Union repulse of the series of Confederate infantry assaults upon their position. The failure of Confederate heavy artillery to function in any kind of coordinated manner allowed the Union to demolish it piecemeal. This time it was Confederate general John Magruder who arrived late, ensuring that, yet again, Lee's careful planning fell apart at the execution stage, as it would do on several occasions in the next few years. McClellan, too, played true to form: with the Confederates in retreat by the day's end, the opportunity was there—indeed it was staring him in the face—to marshal his forces for a decisive counterattack. Of course he did no such thing. In the face of probable victory, McClellan saw only possible defeat.[34]

The Union retreat kept to schedule. McClellan continued to promise Washington that "Richmond shall yet be taken if I am properly supported," but it was becoming clear to Lincoln and to others that Richmond would never be taken by McClellan. McClellan was undoubtedly successful at creating a better organized, reinvigorated, and cohesive Army of the Potomac, but, in the long term, he proved more adept at administration than at action. He persistently hesitated in committing his troops, and finally prompted Lincoln to suggest that if McClellan was not willing to use the Army perhaps Lincoln could borrow it, "provided he could see how it could be made to do something." None of this had been apparent in the immediate aftermath of Bull Run. At that point there was an obvious job that needed doing, and McClellan seemed the best man to do it. By the conclusion of the Seven Days Battles it was a different story. The first of these battles, Oak Grove, was a grim but inconclusive engagement, but it presaged a series of encounters that are often described as the turning point of the war. As the climax of McClellan's Peninsula Campaign, the fate not just of Richmond but also of each side's respective cause hung in the balance in that week of hard fighting and missed opportunities, at the conclusion of which neither side had achieved their goal and the end of the war seemed—and indeed was—further off than ever. At the end of the Seven Days Battles, both armies had seen their ranks seriously depleted: total Union losses amounted to some 16,000; total Confederate casualties reached 20,000, and the end result was stalemate. For the rest of July until early August, the Army of the Potomac remained encamped near Harrison's Landing on the James River until, at the start of August, McClellan began the process of withdrawing from the Peninsula. He had taken his troops from the Potomac to the Peninsula, only to bring them back again with very little—except serious and sobering losses—to show for it. "I wonder what our next move will be," mused Elisha Hunt Rhodes. "I hope it will be more successful than our last."[35]

CHAPTER 5

Battle Cry of Freedom

If the North had but dared to take for its battle cry the grand pre-amble of the Declaration of Independence: "We hold these truths to be self-evident, that all men are created equal; that they are endowed by their Creator with certain inalienable rights; that amongst these are life, liberty, and the pursuit of happiness"; then it might have appealed to the world for sympathy in a manner it cannot now ... The North still ignores the principles contained in its great charter of freedom, but it does not repudiate them like the South ... If the war continues, it must continue as a war for emancipation. This is a fact it is useless ignoring.

—Edward Dicey, *Spectator of America,* **1863**

With no obvious sense of irony, Richmond resident Sallie Brock Putnam described the Union's retreat from her city as "one of the most masterly retreats in the records of military history." She had little time to dwell on it, however. For her, as for thousands of Richmond residents, the human cost of the Seven Days Battles preoccupied them for weeks and months to come. Morale among Lee's remaining troops may have been high, despite the setback of that final repulse at Malvern Hill, but the residents of Rich-mond had to deal with the many soldiers from the Army of Northern Vir-ginia who had been wounded and killed in the defense of the city. It was a grim business. Death, Sallie Putnam recalled, "held a carnival in our city" in the summer of 1862, "and every house was a house of mourning or a private hospital." In the midsummer heat, "gangrene and erysipelas attacked the wounded, and those who might have been cured of their wounds were cut down by these diseases." In an atmosphere made fetid by sickness and death, in which each day brought the sight of yet another soldier's funeral procession, Richmond remained a city under siege, but it was not the Army of the Potomac at the gates. In the midst of such misery, Sallie Putnam found grounds for optimism, as she looked forward to the eventual recognition of the Confederacy by the European powers, the just reward, she believed, of the sacrifices made by the Army of Northern Virginia. Writing with the benefit of hindsight, of course, she knew that no such recognition ever came.[1]

As Sallie Putnam struggled to maintain some sense of normality in the grief-stricken Richmond of July 1862, a parallel misery was the lot of the residents of many Northern cities. Morale in the North was not high. In New York, George Templeton Strong sarcastically remarked that "McClellan has gloriously evacuated Harrison's Landing and got safe back to where he was months ago. Magnificent strategy. Pity it has lost so many thousand men and dollars." Beneath such dismay, however, other sentiments were stirring. English journalist Edward Dicey, who visited America in the opening years of the conflict, was in Boston in the aftermath of Jackson's Shenandoah Valley Campaign. Even by that early stage in the war, he found many of the city's residents both hardened to its realities and challenged by its implications. "I used to see the funerals of soldiers who had died in the campaign, passing by on their way to the cemetery," he recalled. "Nobody, I noticed, paid any heed to the occurrence." He also detected a renewed resolve among those Bostonians he encountered, people for whom "the conviction that the Union could not be preserved consistently with slavery, was beginning to make way rapidly." The North, he noted,

> had become so accustomed, at this time, to the idea of victory, so wedded to the conviction that the downfall of the rebellion was close at hand, that the intelligence of a Federal army having been disastrously defeated fell like a thunderbolt on the Northern States ... the manner in which this intelligence was received gave me a stronger impression of the resolution and power of the North than anything I had yet witnessed ... Within a week, a hundred thousand volunteers had enlisted.[2]

Dicey was an astute observer. In the short time that he had been in America, he had witnessed a significant shift in Northern outlook. From relative equanimity toward the South, predicated in part on the misplaced certainty of the Union's military success, and in part on the belief that Union sentiment remained strong there, Northerners increasingly became more hostile to a South that, they gradually realized, was more tightly wedded to the Confederate cause than they had initially thought. Each military setback dispelled the illusion of easy victory and prompted a revised assessment of what the war was being fought for. As the death toll increased, so too did the belief that the war was about more than the simple restoration of the Union; that, fundamentally, it arose out of slavery, and that at some point—and soon—the future of slavery in America would have to be factored into the Northern military and moral equation.

The Contraband Question

In his first inaugural address in March 1861, Abraham Lincoln had advised Southerners that there "has never been any reasonable cause for such apprehension" as they felt on the slavery issue. "I have no purpose, directly or indirectly, to interfere with the institution of slavery in the States where it exists," he reminded them. This had been a consistent theme in Lincoln's speeches up to his election. "I believe I have no lawful right to do so, and I have no inclination to do so." Almost exactly a year later, however, Lincoln recommended to Congress a resolution offering financial support to "any state which may adopt gradual abolishment of slavery," reminding Congress that there was a risk that those slave states still in the Union might, at some point, decide to join with the Confederacy. This was no *volte-face* on Lincoln's part, but neither was it exactly a promise to maintain the status quo: he still adhered to the belief that as a rebellion *in* and not *of* the South, the Constitution, and all that it implied in the way of property rights, still applied to those states that had seceded. The certainty that the war could be fought, and won, without factoring in the slavery issue at all was giving way to the realization that the nettle of slavery had to be grasped. In the early months of the conflict the *National Intelligencer* had echoed the then common view that the war "has no direct relation to slavery. It is a war for the restoration of the Union under the existing constitution." Yet under the pressures of war it became increasingly difficult to maintain such a limited policy. As Dicey realized, by the summer of 1862, there was a "growing earnestness" in the North "to make the war for the restoration of the Union a war also for the abolition of slavery."[3]

Events in the field, in any case, ran ahead of the moral debate raging in the North. The slaves themselves were hardly concerned with, nor prepared to wait for, the finer points of this discussion to be resolved, but frequently took matters into their own hands. Union generals were very quickly faced with a growing number of slaves who, dislocated by the war or simply seizing the opportunity of the proximity of Union forces, were making their way through to Union lines. While the federal government prevaricated on the question of arming blacks for a variety of political and military reasons, the Union generals found themselves faced with a growing problem that required more immediate resolution. Consequently, the first moves both toward arming blacks and freeing slaves during the American Civil War came not from Washington but from the front line. Ben Butler's precedent in May of 1861 in declaring escaped slaves "contraband of war" had a limited impact on northern attitudes, but it did reinforce the views of African-American leaders such as Frederick Douglass, who felt that slavery was of great military use to the Confederacy—and therefore damaging to the Union—and who realized that the Civil War was likely to turn into a war for freedom if it lasted any length of time at all.

Butler's actions did find favor among the troops and in some departments in Washington, although frequently for different reasons. George Tillotson, serving in Company H (the Dickinson Guards) of the 89th New York Volunteers felt that it would relieve white troops were the army simply to "enlist and arm the contrabands," because all those he had spoken to had said "they would like to fight for the north." Taking a more radical line, the Joint Committee on the Conduct of the War (founded in December of 1861) strongly supported both emancipation and the arming of blacks as a matter of urgency. In the spring of 1862, one of its members, Indiana Republican George Julian, described the South's rebellion "as a gigantic conspiracy against the rights of human nature and the brotherhood of our race," and looked forward to the day when the "defenders of slavery and its despicable apologists will be nailed to the world's pillory." That day had not yet come, however, and because it was not part of official federal policy, many of the early attempts either to attend to the needs of fleeing slaves or incorporate African Americans into the war effort were ill-conceived, clumsy at best, and—in the long term—damaging.[4]

Where the Union army was most active, the problem was most acute, for obvious reasons. As slaves fled to what they hoped would be the security of Union lines, they were met with a variety of responses, ranging from the welcoming to the overtly hostile and, sometimes, violent. The contraband camps that sprung up in the vicinity of the Union army at various points across the South were, in effect, refugee centers, comparable with the worst examples of these in our own day in their unhealthy, unsanitary, and generally inadequate conditions. Northern nurse Cornelia Hancock described the hospital at one such camp near Washington in terms graphic enough, she hoped, to elicit some aid from the North. "If I were to describe this hospital it would not be believed," she wrote:

> North of Washington, in an open muddy mire, are gathered all the colored people who have been made free by the progress of our Army. Sickness is inevitable, and to meet it these rude hospitals, only rough

wooden barracks, are in use ... We average here one birth a day, and have no baby clothes except as we wrap them up in a piece of old muslin, *that* even being scarce. Now the Army is advancing it is not uncommon to see from 40 to 50 arrivals in one day.[5]

As Hancock's description made clear, contrabands were frequently women and children, for whom the desperation to escape from slavery made worthwhile an exhausting, dangerous, and frequently life-threatening journey away from their owners, with no guarantee of finding refuge. Because they were mainly responsible for the care of the young and the elderly, the pressure on slave women to support (often, extended) families in the confusion wrought by the war was acute. Increasingly, after 1863, many women followed as their husbands joined the Union army, but their reception by the white troops was, at best, mixed. Branded—as indeed were many white women who followed their men to war—as either prostitutes or "idle, lazy vagrants," freedwomen frequently found the Union army less than welcoming and there were cases reported of flagrant and sadistic sexual abuse by Union troops whose attitude toward black women expressed, in an overt and brutal way, the most negative gender and racial assumptions of the nineteenth century. In contrast to black men, whose value to the Union was usually accepted, even if only in a non-military capacity in the early years of the war, black women were more often regarded as a hindrance and a drain on crucial federal military resources—an attitude that showed all too clearly that the Union was not prepared for the practicalities of waging a war on a slaveholding society.[6]

As the war progressed and Union forces penetrated deeper into the South, black women's responsibilities only increased. While proximity to Union lines made flight an option, it also increased the likelihood of their partners joining Union forces, leaving the women to either to endure the anger of their white owners or face the challenge of leading their families out of slavery and into the extremely uncertain short-term future of the contraband camps. Lacking adequate clothing, frequently in poor health, and bearing the physical and mental marks of slavery, the condition of these women and children horrified Hancock, as it did many Northerners. Governmental and individual insensitivity to the escaped slaves' needs horrified them even more, however. Hancock described one woman as having "carried her child in her arms and dragged two by her side," to reach the halfway house between freedom and slavery that these camps had come to represent. "Judge of the condition of that woman when she arrives," Hancock demanded. "Should not some comfortable quarters await her weary body?"[7]

The Union army, unsurprisingly, found dealing with male escapees (especially when unencumbered by families) a more straightforward proposition. That did not always mean that it treated such men well, or fairly, however. With the best intentions, the Union frequently handled the issue clumsily. In Missouri, John C. Frémont, then commander of the Department of the West, unilaterally declared martial law in August, 1861, and freed all slaves owned by Confederate sympathizers. Embarrassed by the Constitutional implications of Frémont's pronouncement, Lincoln forced him to modify his policy and bring it in line with the 1861 Confiscation Act, which authorized the removal of slaves only from owners actively engaged in hostilities against the Union. The following year, a similar situation arose in the Deep South when Major General David Hunter assumed control of the Department of the South from Sherman. In March of 1862 he, too, declared martial law, emancipated all slaves held in Georgia, South Carolina, and Florida. He then forced as many escaped male slaves as he could find into military service. Hunter's actions, although intended as a positive step, proved problematic, and the aggressive manner in which he recruited blacks for the Union army served only to alienate the very people he was attempting to help; his inability to pay the black soldiers only made matters worse. Thomas Wentworth Higginson, the white officer in charge of what became the 1st South Carolina Volunteers (and later the 33rd U.S. Colored Infantry), was irritated by Hunter's rashness, and reported that although his troops were good fighters who seemed "fully to understand the importance of the contest, and of their role in it," they nevertheless remained suspicious of the federal government. Higginson put this down to the "legacy of bitter distrust bequeathed by the abortive regiment of General Hunter—into which they were driven like cattle, kept for several months in camp, and then turned off without a shilling, by order of the War Department." Former U.S. senator, Brigadier General Jim Lane had more luck in Kansas, simply by ignoring the War Department altogether. He raised the 1st Kansas Colored Volunteers in 1862, and the regiment was officially recognized the following year, but by that point it had already gone into action against the Confederacy.[8]

There was no consistent policy among military commanders because no policy existed at the federal level. It fell to individuals, therefore, to make the call, and not everyone was sensitive to, or sympathetic toward, the plight of escaped slaves. General Halleck, for one, was opposed to the presence of contrabands within Union lines; in November 1861, he issued orders specifically excluding them on the grounds that they hindered military operations. The Union navy was more welcoming of contrabands, and Secretary of the Navy Gideon Welles seized the opportunity to recruit them into Union service; he had a blockade to maintain, and contrabands offered one very obvious means to strengthen it. The legal basis for Welles's decision remained moot. It was by no means clear whether these contrabands were free people or simply no longer enslaved property. Whereas in the South the legal status of a slave had depended on the status of the mother, under the First Confiscation Act a slave's status depended on the status of the owner, because only the slaves of rebels could be freed. The slaves of pro-Union Southerners, or slaves from the Border States, were, in theory, not covered by the act; in practice—as might be expected—the applicability of the Confiscation Act was frequently hard to determine. Welles left the finer points of this bizarre legal twist for others to debate. He simply recruited escaped slaves, put them to work, and paid them; it was not an ideal situation, but as a response to the problem it was certainly better than returning them as contraband to their former owners.

Military commanders and politicians in Washington became at first uncomfortable with, and then openly critical of those who adhered too rigorously to the 1850 Fugitive Slave Act. At the end of March 1862, it was made illegal for army or naval officers to send contrabands back. Not everyone approved of this decision, nor implemented it. "It is with deep regret," reported one Union officer, "that the general commanding ... has received several reports against officers for returning fugitive slaves ... It will hardly be believed," he continued, "when it is announced that a New England colonel is to-day ... in arrest for having been engaged in the manly task of turning over a young woman, whose skin was almost as white as his own, to the cruel lash of her rebel master." Finally, in August 1862, the War Department sanctioned the limited recruitment of African Americans when General Rufus Saxton, the military commander in charge of the Sea Islands off South Carolina, requested, and was granted, the right to "enroll and organize ... colored persons of African descent for volunteer laborers to a number not exceeding 5,000, and muster them into the service of the United States." Much more significantly, by the same orders Saxton was authorized "to arm, uniform, equip, and receive into the service of the United States such number of volunteers of African descent as you may deem expedient, not exceeding 5,000, and may detail officers to instruct them in military drill, discipline, and duty, and to command them." The official recruitment of black regiments was still some way off, but the first crucial step had been taken. The challenge facing the federal government in the summer of 1862 was how to take the next one.[9]

Saxton's request had been informed by a combination of moral and practical imperatives, but he was clear that the arming of contrabands was an opportunity for all concerned: the men and women involved, their families, and the Union war effort. In requesting that the (male) contrabands be armed, he explained:

Along the entire coast occupied by our forces ... the people suffer greatly from fear of attack by their rebel masters, in the event of which they expect no mercy at their hands ... The rebellion would be very greatly weakened by the escape of thousands of slaves with their families from active rebel masters if they had such additional security against recapture as these men ... would afford them.

Saxton was asking for little more than a formalization and extension of a process that was already half begun, but which was open to abuse in its semi-formed state. He reminded Secretary of War Stanton that there were several contraband communities along the South Carolina coast and on the Sea Islands, many of which were self-sustaining "without any expense to the Government," but these were under attack by Confederate troops. It was the case, too, that many contrabands had been conscripted without pay into Union service, and in some cases even hired from their masters, whose agents received "high rates" for their services. "All these abuses," he argued, "would be speedily corrected" if contrabands could be officially employed by the Union, a move that Saxton believed would "increase a little at least the efficiency of our noble Army in its mighty struggles for the integrity of our bleeding country."[10]

Lincoln, of course, was not oblivious to the need to maintain the integrity of his bleeding country, but as far as the contraband issue was concerned he was caught between a rock and a hard place. Saxton's proposition was acceded to in large part because it offered a way to ensure the continuation of agricultural production in the South. By protecting the contrabands and enabling them to support themselves on the land, the Union would be keeping one small part of the South's economy functioning. As part of the nation—in Lincoln's view—it was hardly desirable that the economy of the South be altogether destroyed by war. It would be overly cynical to suggest that such practical issues were the sole motivating factor behind the early attempts to protect the black communities in the South, but they were a factor. In the face of an immediate and pressing need, the Constitutional barriers to interference with slavery could be circumvented, and sometimes entirely vaulted over, in the early years of the conflict. Yet there were limitations to how far Lincoln could go in regard to slavery in 1862, circumscribed as he was by the need to adhere to the Constitutional integrity—as he understood it—of slavery in the nation, not just in the South but, crucially, in the loyal but slaveholding Border States. On the other side of the equation, of course, there was the matter of the European powers to consider, especially Britain, to whom the Confederacy looked not just for physical ammunition, but moral ammunition in the form of recognition of its cause and, indeed, its very existence as a distinct and valid nation.

Bemused by the war but sensing opportunity in America's division, Britain could find little in the federal government's policies with which to sympathize. It was entirely unclear to many British observers what, precisely, the North was fighting for. When British Chancellor of the Exchequer William E. Gladstone announced in October 1862 that "there is no doubt that Jefferson Davis and other leaders of the South have made an army; they are making, it appears, a navy; and they have made what is more than either, they have made a nation," he was reflecting a fairly widespread view that the separation of North and South was inevitable. Gladstone's speech earned him a sharp rebuke from Foreign Secretary Lord John (Earl) Russell: "I think you went beyond the latitude which all speakers must be allowed when you say that Jefferson Davis had made a nation." Russell continued, "Recognition would seem to follow, and for that step I think the Cabinet is not prepared."[11]

Journalists like Edward Dicey attempted to explain to the British public the complexities of the federal government's Constitutional obligations, but to England, a nation that had for so long openly and loudly campaigned against slavery and the slave trade, the persistence of the institution in America was dismaying. Slavery was a barrier to the recognition of the Confederacy that the South craved, the Union's lack of any overt stand against slavery was equally a sticking point for the British. Not that it was ever in Britain's interests to come off the fence. There would have been risks in recognizing the Confederacy, even if there had also been some trade benefits to doing so. Britain was more inclined to support the Union—from a distance—and shared its view that the war was no more than an internal rebellion. Yet when the Union requested that Britain cease supplying the Confederacy with munitions, British diplomats and politicians prevaricated. The continuing existence of slavery in the Union was a stumbling block in the diplomatic relations between America and Britain in 1862, and Lincoln was well aware of this. Although he believed he had no right to eradicate slavery, he nevertheless hoped he could persuade pro-Union slaveholders to start to dismantle the institution of their own accord. In July of 1862 he made an appeal to representatives from the Border States on the subject of gradual and compensated emancipation in which he suggested that had they supported such a policy in 1861 "the war would now be substantially ended." He warned them:

> The incidents of the war cannot be avoided. If the war continues long, as it must ... the institution in your states will be extinguished by mere friction and abrasion—by the mere incidents of the war. It will be gone, and you will have nothing valuable in lieu of it. Much of its value is gone already. How much better for you, and for your

people, to take the step which, at once, shortens the war, and secures substantial compensation for that which is sure to be wholly lost in any other event.[12]

His arguments had little impact in the Border States, whose slaveholding population seemed oblivious to the very obvious truth of Lincoln's argument and the fact that it was being borne out in the field. At the same time, Lincoln himself was coming under attack from Northern radicals who believed that he was moving too slowly on the slavery issue. One of the most famous attacks came the following month via the pages of the *New York Tribune*, under the heading "The Prayer of Twenty Millions," which accused Lincoln of taking account of "timid counsels" on the slavery question. Lincoln's carefully crafted response—mindful that it was a very public response—gave nothing away:

My paramount object in this struggle *is* to save the Union, and it is *not* either to save or destroy slavery. If I could save the Union without freeing *any* slave I would do it, and if I could save it by freeing *all* the slaves I would do it; and if I could save it by freeing some and leaving others alone I would also do that."

Too frequently taken as evidence of a lack of concern for the slave, Lincoln's concluding comment was more revealing: "I have here stated my purpose according to my view of *official* duty; and I intend no modification of my oft-expressed *personal* wish that all men every where could be free."[13]

Whatever Lincoln's personal wishes were, and however he interpreted his official duty, both were irrelevant without the available power to act; for that, Lincoln needed military victories. With victory, he had options; without it, he had nothing. When a delegation from Chicago presented him with a resolution in favor of emancipation, Lincoln asked them frankly:

What *good* would a proclamation of emancipation from me do, especially as we are now situated? I do not want to issue a document that the whole world will see must necessarily be inoperative, like the Pope's bull against the comet! Would *my word* free the slaves, when I cannot even enforce the Constitution in the rebel States?

Lincoln also drew the delegation's attention to the fact that there were "fifty thousand bayonets in the Union armies from the Border Slave States. It would be a serious matter," he stressed, "if, in consequence of a proclamation such as you desire, they should go over to the rebels." The issue of emancipation, he assured them, was never far from his mind, but Lincoln was waiting for the opportune moment, for some indication that the war was going the Union's way, which, in the late summer of 1862, it clearly was not. When Lincoln decided to visit the Army of the Potomac at Harrison's Landing in the aftermath of the abortive Peninsula Campaign in order to assess the situation for himself, he knew very well what was at stake. Within less than a week, he would draft the Emancipation Proclamation; the difficulties he was having with General McClellan were hardly the only things on his mind.[14]

The War Changes Direction

Lincoln was certainly not short of advice in 1862; indeed, it was being proffered from all directions. When he visited the Army of the Potomac in July, McClellan took the opportunity to hand-deliver a letter detailing his views on the future direction of the war. "The time has come," he advised the President, "when the government must determine upon a civil and military policy covering the whole ground of our national trouble … This rebellion has assumed the character of war," McClellan asserted, and he had clear, if rather traditional, ideas of how such a war should be conducted. It should, he stated,

> be conducted upon the highest principles known to Christian civilization. It should not be a war looking to the subjugation of the people of any State … It should not be at all a war upon population, but against armed forces and political organization. Neither confiscation of property, political executions of persons, territorial organization of States, or forcible abolition of slavery should be contemplated for a moment.[15]

Noble though McClellan's notion of war was, events had overtaken him, especially as far as slavery was concerned. The war had moved on but McClellan had failed, in several senses, to do so: his errors may have been in the execution of his plans, rather than in the plans themselves, but by failing to bring them to fruition he not only prolonged a conflict that he found personally distasteful but ensured that, in the future, it would of necessity be a harder and more ambitious war. Others saw the probable consequences of McClellan's actions more clearly than he did, and they did not hesitate to warn Lincoln. Erasmus Keyes, a former brigadier general promoted to major general immediately prior to the Peninsula Campaign, held strong views on the nature of the war and on the best method of waging it. While McClellan continued to promise the earth—or at least that part of it that was the Confederate capital—if he had just a few thousand more troops, Keyes was of the opinion that remaining at Harrison's Landing much longer was suicide, and that the Army of the Potomac should pull back to Washington. "When a large army reaches, or is placed in, a position where it cannot hold the enemy in check nor operate effectively against him," he advised, "it is a military axiom to move that army without delay." Lincoln clearly concurred, much to McClellan's dismay and what was more, he appointed Henry Halleck general in chief of the Union armies—to McClellan's further disgust. It was Halleck's opinion, too, that removing the Army of the Potomac from the Peninsula was a better option than reinforcing it further, and he issued orders to that effect at the start of August 1862, orders that McClellan reluctantly, and with all the speed for which he was famous, carried out.[16]

Halleck's accession to the post of general in chief, vacant since McClellan's removal from that post in March, was only one of several changes the Union army underwent in the summer of 1862. In late June, the forces in the Shenandoah Valley and West Virginia were brought together with Irvin McDowell's corps and reinforced with veteran troops from the Army of the Potomac. This new force was designated the Army of Virginia, and had John Pope—an aggressive and effective military comander—in overall charge. Confederate forces also underwent a reshuffle when Lee divided the Army of Northern Virginia into two corps under Stonewall Jackson and James Longstreet, respectively. Throughout July and August, as both sides retreated, regrouped, and reconsidered their options; as a result both the Union and the Confederacy reconfigured their forces for what everyone now realized would be a long and costly war. On balance, the Confederacy was in the stronger position. By the summer of 1862, as a result of both Jackson's Shenandoah Valley Campaign and the Union's failure on the Peninsula, the Confederacy was poised to strike in every theater of the war. It would never be so well placed again. Braxton Bragg and Kirby Smith were, between them, positioned to move in east Tennessee, ideally en route to Virginia, while Robert E. Lee, although still in the vicinity of Richmond, was in a position to move north and threaten Washington. The aim was not battlefield victory alone. The South also hoped to achieve diplomatic recognition from abroad, which might end the Union blockade. In addition, and more realistically, Confederate policy was aimed at encouraging opposition to the war in the North to such an extent that Lincoln would find the war effort impossible to sustain. For that reason, the Confederacy had to move soon.

For Lee specifically, there was some pressure to prevent McClellan's Army of the Potomac and John Pope's new Army of Virginia from joining forces against him (not that this was very likely, given the two Union general's personalities and their mutual loathing). Pope's weaker army seemed the more promising target. Lee, partly in response to the disaster at Malvern Hill but mostly because of the disparity in numbers, decided to use a series of turning maneuvers, thereby avoiding any head-on frontal assault. As Lee advised Jefferson Davis: "My desire has been to avoid a general engagement, being the weaker force." Lee hoped he could maneuver round and attack the Union indirectly. The opportunity to implement this strategy presented itself during McClellan's reluctant retreat from the James River, because Union forces were so disorganized: strung out between Harrison's Landing on the James River, Aquia Creek (a tributary of the Potomac), and Alexandria, just south of Washington, the logistics of moving troops and supplies up the coast and overland preoccupied commanders and troops alike for much of August. A shortage of both transport and supplies caused problems, and nerves became frayed. "Our animals are dying in their harness for want of forage," reported one brigade quartermaster to Montgomery Meigs; trains ran slowly, supplies and artillery were not where they were supposed to be, nor, indeed, were the troops. The general chaos prompted Union Colonel (later, general) Herman Haupt, a former railway engineer in charge of transportation, to complain that the soldiers on arrival at Alexandria "scatter all over the country, and I cannot ascertain the location of any particular regiment, as no report is made to me on their arrival." Meanwhile Halleck and McClellan sniped away at each other in a series of ill-tempered missives, until Halleck terminated the exchange by advising McClellan: "As you must be aware, more than three-quarters of my time is taken up with the raising of new troops and matters in the West. I have no time for details. You will, therefore, as ranking general in the field, direct as you deem best."[17]

It was a pity that Halleck had "no time for details," because the far from minor detail that Lee's forces, under Jackson, were approaching Pope's position near Manassas Junction was not one to overlook. Jackson, with 25,000 troops, succeeded in flanking Pope by taking the long way round and approaching through Thoroughfare Gap on August 26. Having destroyed both railroad and telegraph links in Virginia, temporarily cutting the Union troops' links with Washington, Jackson's troops moved on the Union supply depot at Manassas and destroyed what they could not remove. The North responded with shock, but also with anger. The North was forced to endure reports of "these brilliant, dashing, successful raids or forays of rebel cavalry within our lines," complained George Templeton Strong. "They have penetrated to Manassas, destroying supply trains and capturing guns, taking us by surprise. Are our generals traitors or imbeciles? Why does the Rebellion enjoy the monopoly of audacity and enterprise?" There were no obvious answers, because in this instance the Confederates clearly had the upper hand, not just in audacity and enterprise, but also in organization and strategic effectiveness. Pope tried to gather his forces—and his thoughts—to counter the attack, but the Union army was simply too disorganized even to find Jackson and, while it looked, Lee came up through Thoroughfare Gap with reinforcements. The Second Battle of Bull Run/Manassas on August 29 and 30, 1862, fought over the same ground as the first just over a year before, was an even more comprehensive Union defeat, and the Confederate repulse, led by James Longstreet, of Pope's counterattack was conclusive. Although the *New York Times* initially reported victory, the terrible truth of Second Manassas soon became known. Pope led the army, as Strong disdainfully recorded, "back to its old burrows around Washington. It will probably hibernate there … after all this waste of life and money and material," he scorned, "we are at best where we were a year ago." Unlike a year previously, however, this latest defeat, coming on the back of the Union's failure on the Peninsula, took a heavier toll. "It is hard," remarked Elisha Hunt Rhodes, "to have reached the point we started from last March, and Richmond is still the Rebel Capital." As Pope observed disconsolately to Halleck, morale among the men was at an all-time low: "Unless something can be done to restore tone to this army," he warned, "it will melt away before you know it."[18]

The aftershock of Second Manassas went on and on, far beyond the battlefield. It reverberated through the army, through Washington, and through the North. Pope and Halleck both blamed McClellan for the defeat at Second Manassas, a charge that was not wholly off the mark. McClellan had hardly strained every nerve to aid Pope, and had even gone so far as to suggest to Lincoln that one option at Second Manassas was simply "to leave Pope to get out of this scrape," a proposal that horrified the president. The fault, however, was not McClellan's, nor was it Corps Commander Fitz John Porter's, who later found himself court-martialed for what Halleck believed were failings at Second Manassas. Fundamentally, Pope had been both outmaneuvered and outgeneraled by Lee, and for that he paid an even higher price than Irvin McDowell had after First Bull Run: he was assigned a command in Minnesota, as far from the scene of the Union's latest disaster as possible. The question facing Lincoln was how to replace him—and with whom. In the context of the autumn of 1862, with Lee threatening Washington and the Union armies so seriously demoralized, there was only one choice to make, and Lincoln did not hesitate to make it—nor, it must be noted, did he discuss it with his cabinet, knowing full well what the reaction would be. McClellan was the sole general capable of pulling the army together; he had done so before, and that aspect of his abilities was beyond doubt. In the aftermath of Second Manassas, therefore, McClellan was put back in charge and the Army of Virginia disbanded, its troops sent to swell the ranks of the Army of the Potomac, now defending Washington. There were objections, of course, but as George Templeton Strong remarked of McClellan, the "army believes in him … that is a material fact."[19]

A Telling Fray

Morale among the troops of the Army of the Potomac may have received a boost from McClellan's reinstatement, but the rest of the North was holding its breath in September 1862. The Confederacy felt more confidence in Lee, whose star was riding high. Second Manassas had gone better than he had anticipated, but in overall terms neither the Union nor the Confederacy had seen much actual progress in the first year of fighting: in the space of six months the Confederates had been driven from Washington back to Richmond, and now the Union, in turn, had been driven back from Richmond to Washington. This push-me/pull-you type of warfare supposedly prompted the Prussian General Helmuth von Moltke to describe the Civil War as little more than "two armed mobs chasing each other round the country," although William Sherman, who met Moltke ten years later, did not think that "he was such an ass as to say that." Either way, there was some truth in the observation, however dismissive it was and whoever actually made it. Lee's task in September 1862 was to break the pattern, because the Confederacy could ill-afford to sustain such indecisive action for long. Although morale was high in the Army of Northern Virginia, its losses at Second Manassas had run to some 19 percent—for the Union it was about 13 percent—preventing it from taking immediate advantage of its victory. Like the Army of the Potomac, the Army of Northern Virginia was, frankly, exhausted. It needed time to recover and, having done so, Lee and Jefferson Davis concluded, it had to go on the offensive. "The present seems to be the most propitious time since the commencement of the war for the Confederate Army to enter Maryland," Lee advised Davis. Not that Lee was unaware of the problems. As he reported to the Confederate president:

> The army is not properly equipped for an invasion of an enemy's territory. It lacks much of the material of war, is feeble in transportation ... and the men are poorly provided with clothes, and in thousands of instances are destitute of shoes. Still, we cannot afford to be idle, and though weaker than our opponents in men and military equipments, must endeavor to harass if we cannot destroy them.[20]

For Lee, Maryland beckoned, not merely as a strategic military consideration, but as a possible lever to foreign recognition and, perhaps, support within Maryland itself for the Confederate cause, if he could secure victory there.[21]

Time was not, however, on Lee's side, and his troops barely got a few days to recover from Second Manassas before they were off again. At the end of the first week of September, Lee crossed the Potomac and camped at Frederick, Maryland. He lost a great many troops in the process, men too drained by the sustained campaigning they had experienced since Lee had begun to drive McClellan back from Richmond in early July. Both sides experienced a degree of desertion (not always permanent) in the aftermath of Second Manassas, but combined with the general lack of enthusiasm Lee encountered in Maryland at his arrival, the lack of support was a disappointment to him. "Notwithstanding individual expressions of kindness that have been given, and the general sympathy in the success of the Confederate States," Lee reported, "situated as Maryland is, I do not anticipate any general rising of the people in our behalf." Straggling was more of a problem—it eventually diminished Lee's forces by a quarter—and Lee was unsympathetic to stragglers, whom he viewed as little more than "cowards" despite recognizing that the cause was often "the forced marches and hard service" of recent months. Despite these problems, Lee remained confident that Maryland offered the best opportunity to press home the advantage of Second Manassas. As at that battle, Lee divided his army on arrival in Maryland, sending Jackson to attack the now isolated federal garrison at Harpers Ferry (the Confederate advance in Virginia had separated it from Washington and from any help from the Army of the Potomac), which was a potential source of much-needed supplies for his men, while he crossed over South Mountain in the direction of Hagerstown.[22]

In contrast to the Army of Northern Virginia's rather cool reception in Maryland, the Army of the Potomac found a surprising degree of support from the inhabitants. Moving out from Washington on September 7 to meet Lee's forces, morale was not high, but within a few days the welcome the Union troops received had, in the words of one private, "aroused our patriotism which was becoming dormant." A further boost to both McClellan's and his army's morale came in mid-September when a copy of Lee's operational plan for the Harpers Ferry raid, detailing the four-way division of his forces and their respective objectives, was discovered wrapped around cigars in an abandoned camp. McClellan was exuberant, and telegraphed Lincoln with the news:

> I have the whole rebel force in front of me, but am confident, and no time shall be lost ... I think Lee has made a gross mistake, and that he will be severely punished for it ... I have all the plans of the rebels, and will catch them in their own trap if my men are equal to the emergency. I now feel I can count on them as of old ... Will send you trophies.[23]

As McClellan's enthusiasm grew, the Army of Northern Virginia was losing momentum. Although Lee did not yet realize that McClellan had seen his plans, the operation against Harpers Ferry took longer than expected. The plan had been for Jackson to attack Harpers Ferry from the west; Lafayette McLaws and John G. Walker were to seize Maryland and Loudon Heights that overlooked it from the east, while Lee and Longstreet would remain at Hagerstown, protecting the passes through South Mountain. Anticipating that Harpers Ferry would be evacuated of Union troops—there were still over 10,000 garrisoned there—Lee was faced with a potential problem when this did not happen; so, for that matter, was McClellan, who had been hoping, as usual, for reinforcements. Poor command on the Union side ensured, however, that Harpers Ferry, which was vulnerable to any army in command of the surrounding heights, did fall to the Confederates. By the time it fell, Lee had realized, via Jeb Stuart, that McClellan knew of his intentions. This was not the disaster it might have been for Lee, because, despite having in his possession the best means yet to defeat the Confederacy, McClellan saw no need for urgency; he did move faster than was his norm, but he still did not move fast enough.

When Union troops reached the routes through South Mountain, they found the routes heavily defended. In the ensuing series of battles on September 14 the Union gained the upper hand, and McClellan's overconfident reaction to these victories stood in contrast to Lee's almost total despair at what seemed to be the end of his attempt to invade Maryland. According to McClellan, Lee "stated publicly that he must admit they had been shockingly whipped," and McClellan enthused about the great Union victory, announcing that the "*morale* of our men is now restored." His enthusiasm was sufficiently contagious that Lincoln felt it "safe to say that Gen. McClellan has gained a great victory over the great rebel army in Maryland between Fredericktown and Hagerstown. He is now pursuing the flying foe." To McClellan he simply said "God bless you, and all with you. Destroy the rebel army if possible." Secretary of the Navy Gideon Welles was less convinced, hearing in McClellan's bombast only the same old song: a "tale like this from Pope would have been classed as one of his lies," he noted. Welles was right to be suspicious. McClellan's foe flew neither far nor for long, and so it turned out that McClellan's pronouncements were both exaggerated and premature. Lee's initial response to the defeat was to accept it. "The day has gone against us," he advised McLaws, "and this army will go by Sharpsburg and cross the river. It is necessary for you to abandon your position to-night." At Sharpsburg, however, on the banks of Antietam Creek, Lee finally received word that Harpers Ferry had fallen. It was more than just another victory. Its spoils provided him with valuable reinforcements that would enable him to attempt the Holy Grail for almost all Civil War commanders: the decisive battle. At Antietam, Lee finally saw his chance to achieve it.[24]

When McClellan encountered Lee's army lined up against him at Antietam Creek on September 15, his immediate reaction was, unsurprisingly, to pause. Despite knowing of Lee's plan, and therefore knowing that Jackson, along with the bulk of Lee's forces, was probably some seventeen miles away at Harpers Ferry, McClellan failed to believe what was in front of him: only a part of Lee's men—15,000 at most—faced him. Jackson was still many miles away, and if there was ever an opportunity to make use of superior Union numbers, this was it. McClellan knew full well that Jackson and Longstreet were on the way. Andrew Curtin, Governor of Pennsylvania, had advised him of that. "Look out for Jackson's column from Harper's Ferry … also for Longstreet's column which moved from Boonsborough last night … It is thought that both will combine with Lee to give you another heavy battle," Curtin warned. How quickly McClellan expected Jackson and Longstreet to march is not clear, but as he hovered on the banks of Antietam Creek and on the verge of action, Lee's reinforcements had plenty of time to get there; by the time McClellan did engage, on September 17, his delay had—yet again—created a situation in which Lee's full army was opposing him. The Battle of Antietam (Sharpsburg) earned its place in history almost instantly for its ferocity and its casualty rate. It was the bloodiest day of the Civil War, indeed the worst day of fighting yet experienced by American troops at any time. With a total of 25,000 killed, wounded, and missing, it bears comparison with British casualties on the first day of the Somme. Modern historians recognize Antietam as one of the war's turning points—because it opened the way for Lincoln's Emancipation Proclamation. Of course, at dawn on September 17, 1862, no one involved realized that they were, as James McPherson's describes it, at the "crossroads of freedom." Yet on the outcome of Antietam much more depended, as it turned out, than Lee's success or failure to take Maryland. Antietam, as Herman Melville described it, was indeed "a telling fray."[25]

To describe Antietam as a missed opportunity for the Union is something of an understatement. As so often before, McClellan had a solid enough plan; it simply fell apart in execution. Far from being a coordinated attack, McClellan deployed his divisions individually, thereby diminishing the undoubted numerical superiority of his army—he had some 75,000 troops available against some 36,000 on the Confederate side. He also kept his cavalry in reserve, planning a final and dramatic cavalry assault on what he imagined would be fleeing Confederate forces; it was a decision that prevented him from receiving both the valuable reconnaissance information and needed support on his flanks. The battle itself began with Union general "Fighting Joe" Hooker's artillery attacking Stonewall Jackson's men in a cornfield (the Miller Cornfield) just to the north of the village of Sharpsburg. The fighting was of such intensity that Hooker, in his report on the battle, recalled the speed with which "every stalk of corn in the Northern and greater part of the field was cut as closely as could have been done with a knife, and the slain lay in rows precisely as they had stood in their ranks a few moments before. It was never my fortune," he wrote, "to witness a more bloody, dismal battle-field." Hooker himself was wounded in this initial exchange, and described with some degree of sangfroid how he had been removed from his saddle "in the act of falling out of it from loss of blood." In a condolence note sent after the battle, McClellan expressed the view that had Hooker not been wounded, the result would have been "the entire destruction of the rebel army," which may have made Hooker feel better, or possibly, depending on how he read it, worse. Confederate reinforcements enabled Jackson to push the Federals back some, then a Union counterattack regained some of the ground, but the losses on both sides were severe even well before mid-morning. In the West Wood and on the Sunken Road, Union and Confederate troops slugged it out— in the Sunken Road for nearly four hours—until both sides were too worn down and depleted to continue. By early afternoon, McClellan was sufficiently apprised of the scale of the slaughter then taking place around him to advise Halleck that he was "in the midst of the most terrible battle of the war—perhaps of history."[26]

As the battle tailed off in the center of the field—around the Sunken Road—by early afternoon, it picked up southeast of the village (the Union's left flank) where Union General Ambrose E. Burnside had been trying for much of the day to cross the Rohrbach Bridge over Antietam Creek itself, but had been held back by some 400 Confederate sharpshooters. Burnside, with some 13,000 troops at his disposal, finally made it across the bridge and started across the hills toward Sharpsburg. With barely 4,000 men to pit against Burnside, Lee might have been in trouble but for the timely arrival from Harpers Ferry of A. P. Hill's division in the late afternoon, a development that McClellan, having failed to deploy his cavalry, was at first unaware of. When he realized what was happening, and when Burnside requested reinforcements, McClellan failed to provide them; he had on hand his reserve division (Fitz John Porter's 5th corps) but he did not send it to Burnside's aid. In fact, in this most crucial of battles between the Army of Northern Virginia and the Army of the Potomac, one third of the latter was never deployed at all. As Burnside, left to his own devices, fell back almost to the bridge he had taken so long to cross earlier in the day, the battle drew to a close, an indecisive end to the worst day of fighting many soldiers had seen and, for some of the new recruits—there were many such in the Union ranks—a baptism of fire with a vengeance. With losses at some 12,000 for the Union and some 13,000 for the Confederacy, Antietam seemed like a zero-sum game, but with fewer men to draw on in the first place, the Confederacy could not easily bear such losses. The Union could not sustain such high losses indefinitely, either. However, if the momentum for the prosecution of the war was maintained on the home front, and men were still prepared to join up, then the North at least had the option to replenish its depleted ranks; the Confederacy did not.

The locations of the hardest fighting at Antietam—especially the Cornfield, Sunken Road (Bloody Lane), and Burnside's Bridge—soon acquired mythic status, as a testament to the severity of the engagements that took place there, but also because their aftermath was recorded for posterity—and a horrified Northern public—by Civil War photographers Alexander Gardner and Matthew Brady. Of Brady's exhibition in New York, "The Dead of Antietam," which opened a month after the battle, the *New York Times* said: "If he has not brought bodies and laid them in our door-yards and along the streets he has done something very like it," and concluded that Brady's shocking images had "done something to bring home to us the terrible reality and earnestness of war." For those viewing the destruction firsthand, the horrors of Antietam left their mark for years to come. "The excitement of battle comes in the day of it," wrote one Union soldier, "but the horrors of it two or three days after." Another observed: "No tongue can tell, no mind conceive, no pen portray the horrible sights I witnessed." Until his death in 1935, Oliver Wendell Holmes, Jr., future Supreme Court justice, but during the war an officer in the 20th Massachusetts, toasted each anniversary of Antietam, the battle where he had nearly lost his own life; for him, as for many others, Antietam was a grim reality check, and for some of them, worse was to come. What made Antietam especially bitter, however, was the Union's failure to follow up on its admittedly partial victory. Despite his terrible losses, Lee did not flee; he remained on the banks of Antietam Creek, considering a possible counterattack, but his army, he realized, was simply too damaged. While McClellan watched and did nothing all through the following day, Lee finally accepted that it was over, and retreated back across the Potomac. McClellan let him go, as he had let the battle go: unsure of what action to take, he chose to take none at all. He felt he had done enough. On September 19 he reported to Halleck: "Last night the enemy abandoned his position, leaving his dead and wounded on the field ... We may safely claim a complete victory." Three days later he was lecturing Halleck on the impossibility of pursuing Lee, and on the pressing need to reorganize the Army of the Potomac. He was probably right about the latter, but at a time when action was most required, all McClellan seemed to have to offer was administrative advice.[27]

A War for Freedom

Antietam was not the resounding victory McClellan described, but it was victory enough for Lincoln, who had been preparing to issue a general proclamation of emancipation for some months, if only the military situation would improve. On September 22, as McClellan composed his advice for Halleck regarding the future of the Army of the Potomac, Lincoln issued his Preliminary Emancipation Proclamation, which dealt with the somewhat larger matter of the future of the nation. Although Lincoln stressed that "hereafter, as heretofore, the war will be prosecuted for the object of practically restoring the constitutional relationship between the United States," and also reiterated his support for gradual, compensated manumission in those slave states that had remained in the Union, he set in motion a process that would change the nature of the war when he declared:

> That on the first day of January in the year of our Lord, one thousand eight hundred and sixty-three, all persons held as slaves within any state, or any part of a state, the people whereof shall then be in rebellion against the United States shall be then, thenceforward, and forever free.[28]

It was one of the most carefully phrased, radical documents of the era. At the time—and indeed since—Lincoln was criticized for, in effect, freeing the slaves in those parts of the nation over which he had no control and leaving the states he did have authority over to retain slavery. The Preliminary Proclamation was like a stone dropped into a lake: the ever-widening circles it produced would affect slavery in all parts of the nation—as Lincoln knew, and astute observers understood. Historians of slavery such as Ira Berlin have rightly stressed that the "beginning of the Civil War marked the beginning of the end of slavery in the American South." It was, however, more than merely a matter of time and attrition for emancipation to be effected. The institution of slavery was already being undermined by the slaves the slaves themselves, the free black population North and South, the Union army (once it fully came round to the idea) and now, in 1862, by the federal government. Slavery's demise was clearly imminent, but it was not going to be a quick or easy death. Frederick Douglass, for one, certainly understood the effort it would take, and he fully grasped the implications of Lincoln's actions: three days before the Emancipation Proclamation proper came into effect, he exulted that "the cause of human freedom and the cause of our common country ... must stand or fall together ... This sacred Sunday ... is the last which will witness the existence of legal slavery in all the Rebel slaveholding States of America." Douglass held few illusions about the effort it would take to eradicate not just slavery but the white supremacist mindset that had produced and sustained it, but he was confident that "Law and the sword can and will, in the end abolish slavery."[29]

Not everyone thought that Lincoln's proclamation would have much effect; indeed, some believed its impact on Union morale would be detrimental. Lincoln was, it must be remembered, taking a huge political risk in announcing emancipation, especially with the mid-term elections approaching in the North. The large Democratic constituency in the Union was not likely to support Lincoln's decision, and in the Union army, too, not everyone agreed with it. Some of the Union's foremost generals—Halleck and McClellan among them—had little sympathy for slaves, and considered that the Emancipation Proclamation was little more than a distraction from the war effort, if it did not actually hamper it. The troops were, as might be expected, mixed in their views, which ranged from the strongly abolitionist to the vituperatively racist. But a great many stood on moderate middle ground, where agnosticism on the issue of slavery prevailed. One Rhode Island private expressed his disapproval of Lincoln's decision with racist vitriol when he announced that he "did not want to se enny more fighting done for the niggers … the Northern fanaticks," in his harsh opinion, "do not care a dam for the union or country if they can but carrey the day and have a free nigger thrown in, if they had kept that word nigger out of congress, this rebellion would have ben settled much sooner." Even those troops who were generally supportive of emancipation believed that Lincoln's proclamation would extend the war. When George Tillotson, a private in the Army of the Potomac, told his wife that the army had "just got news that the president has issued a proclamation freeing all the slaves on the first of January," he remarked: "It may be for the best but still my hopes (if I had any) of a speedy termination of the war is thereby nocked in head for I know enough of the Southern spirit so that I think that they will fight for the institution of slavery even to extermination." Not all African Americans were convinced, either, of the benefit of suddenly having the opportunity to fight for the Union, which they realized was the next logical step after emancipation had been announced. As one New Yorker argued, the race had "nothing to gain, and everything to lose, by entering the lists as combatants." To respond to the Union's call for troops, he asserted, would be simply to repeat the errors of previous generations of blacks, who had "put confidence in the words of the whites only to feel the dagger of slavery driven deeper." Given the virulent racism of the North, he concluded, free blacks were in "no condition to fight under the flag which gives us no protection."[30]

Whatever individual opinions suggested, the process of abolishing—or at the very least weakening—slavery was already underway in the Confederate states by 1862 as slaves there, whenever they could, were already either fleeing from their owners or taking direct action against the Confederacy by aiding the Union. Contrabands provided valuable information to the advancing Union armies, but there were limits, obviously, to how much could be achieved by an unarmed and geographically disparate population in a world of armed, aggressive, and increasingly nervous white southerners. In an environment suddenly awash with weaponry, the thought that their slaves might get hold of some of it was never far from slaveholders' minds. This was, of course, slaveholders' worst nightmare, however much they denied it and however strongly they professed faith in the loyalty of their slaves. The most famous expressions of disquiet on the subject of what she termed the South's "sacred property" came from southern diarist Mary Chesnut. Chesnut drew a comparison between the lot of slaves and that of women in the South in her exclamation "Poor women, poor slaves," but her view of slavery, and of African Americans, was less sisterly than that remark suggests. Her professions of faith in the loyalty of the South's slaves need to be juxtaposed with her awareness of reports of slaves murdering their owners and the nervous response of one of her friends to her slave's proposition to sleep in her bedroom, the better to protect her in the absence of her husband. "Is this to protect me or to murder me?" her friend had wondered.[31]

Chesnut's diary makes clear the ambivalence across the South in the face of slavery's disintegration, and the gradual hardening of attitudes toward African Americans as a whole as the institution crumbled. There was more than a degree of irony in her observation, made toward the end of the war, that the "fidelity of the Negroes is the principal topic everywhere. There seems not a single case of a Negro who betrayed his master." Irony was wholly absent, however, from the writings of the Colcock Jones family of Georgia, whose naivety on the feelings of their "sacred property" left them ill-prepared for their slaves' reaction to the war. Mary Jones confided to her journal that her "people are all idle on the plantations," and although many of what she termed her "servants" remained loyal, others were "false and rebellious." Her daughter-in-law, Eva, was similarly less than thrilled when, shortly after the war, she discovered that her savings had been stolen by one of the freedwomen to pay for a wedding. Anticipating continued loyalty, her amazement at her former slave's behavior revealed the self-delusion at the heart of the South's peculiar institution.[32]

The South was hardly unique in being guilty of self-delusion on the subject of race, however, and the Emancipation Proclamation, although a document specifically relating to slavery in the Confederacy, could not fail to have an impact in the North, too, where African Americans were free, but hardly equal. Frederick Douglass was persistent in his condemnation of the federal government for refusing to allow the raising of black regiments, or the inclusion of African-American troops in white regiments. "The Washington Government wants men for its army," he observed, but thus far, it has not had the boldness to recognize the manhood of the race to which I belong. It only sees in the slave an article of commerce—a contraband … I owe it to my race … to affirm that, in denying them the privilege to fight for their country, they have been most deeply and grievously wronged. Neither in the Revolution, nor in the last war, did any such narrow and contemptible policy obtain … Is McClellan better than Washington? Is Halleck better than Jackson?[33]

Although the Preliminary Emancipation Proclamation made no reference to the arming of free blacks—or escaped slaves—the final proclamation as it was delivered on January 1, 1863 not only made such reference, it went further than that. As announced on January 1, 1863, the Emancipation Proclamation not only freed slaves in the Confederate states, "a fit and necessary war measure for suppressing the rebellion," Lincoln stressed, but opened the door for freed slaves to be "received into the armed service of the United States to garrison forts, positions, stations, and other places, and to man vessels of all sorts in said service." Again, it was a move toward formal acceptance of a process already under way. The legal basis for raising black regiments had been established in both the Second Confiscation Act of July 1862 and the Militia Act of the same month, and Rufus Saxton had already been granted the authority to enlist contraband in the summer of that year. As a result, the 1st Regiment of the Louisiana Native Guards had already been mustered in for service in the Union Army in September, with a 2nd and then a 3rd regiment following in October and November. Jim Lane's 1st Kansas Colored Volunteers (they became the 79th U.S. Colored Infantry) had already fought the Confederacy, to some acclaim, in October at Island Mound, Missouri. Their standing was formalized in January of 1863, along with that of the 1st South Carolina Colored Volunteers.[34]

The emancipation of slaves in the Confederacy did not, however, automatically translate into the raising of African-American regiments either in the North or the South, and it would be a mistake to see January 1, 1863 as the date when the African American world changed instantly. Frederick Douglass saw rhetorical advantage in portraying it as the "Day of Jubilee," but the reality was that the federal government still balked at the thought of widespread black involvement in the war. In March 1863, Secretary of War Edwin Stanton concluded that the matter required investigation, at least as far as freed slaves were concerned, and to that end established the American Freedmen's Inquiry Commission. Its remit was:

to investigate the condition of the colored population emancipated by acts of Congress and the president's proclamation of January 1, 1863, and to report what measures will best contribute to their protection and improvement so that they may defend and support themselves; and also how they can be most usefully employed in the service of the Government for the suppression of the rebellion.[35]

The Commission's initial report noted the valuable service freed slaves performed for the Union as military laborers, noting, too, that demand was far in excess of supply; Burnside, for example, had a "standing requisition" for 5,000 such laborers, but never managed to engage more than 2,000. Therefore, the Commission argued, there was scope for many more freed slaves to be employed in that capacity. Indeed, given that in the Army of the Potomac alone some 10,000 troops were regularly unavailable for combat due to fatigue and support duties, the Commission suggested that the need for labor was pressing. There was also a larger issue, and that was how the Union might incorporate African Americans not merely as valuable labor at a time of need, but as full-fledged American citizens, with all the rights that status implied. Little thought had been given to this side of the equation. Almost in passing, the Freedmen's Commission remarked that the employment of freed slaves "as military laborers ... with badges around their hats labelled 'U.S. service' ... has been found in practice to have an excellent effect. It tends to inspire them with self-reliance." African Americans, however, did not just want badges on their hats; they also wanted them on their sleeves. As Frederick Douglass famously argued, "once let the black man get upon his person the brass letters U.S., let him get an eagle on his button, and a musket on his shoulder and bullets in his pocket, and there is no power on earth which can deny that he has earned the right to citizenship in the United States."[36]

The Freedmen's Inquiry Commission reached a similar conclusion, and expressed its "conviction that if the Government can, before the end of the present year, bring 200,000 or more colored troops into the field ... the result will be alike advantageous to the cause of the Union and the race to which these troops belong." It argued:

> If the placing in the field ... of 200,000 efficient black troops ... should ultimately prove to be one of the chief agencies to prevent the restoration of slavery in the insurrectionary States ... The slave States will have been doomed themselves to forge a weapon to destroy that system, for the existence and extension of which, taking up arms, they have deluged a continent with blood.[37]

The evidence in support of their argument came from the field. Although some had queried whether African Americans would fight at all, by the time the Commission made its report on June 30, 1863, it was clear that they could—because they had. Even before its official recognition by the War Department, Jim Lane's black regiment had performed well in Missouri, prompting one journalist to write that it was "useless to talk any more about negro courage. The men fought like tigers, each and every one of them." Skirmishes between Thomas Wentworth Higginson's 1st South Carolina and the rebels, and between Benjamin Butler's 2nd Louisiana Native Guards (later the 74th U.S. Colored Infantry) and Confederate cavalry and infantry regiments were equally decisive in terms of proving that the black troops could and would fight. The first major engagement for the black regiments came in the spring of 1863, with an assault on Port Hudson on the Mississippi in Louisiana. The assault itself was misconceived, and the Union army suffered a defeat. For the black troops who had fought there, however, Port Hudson proved a turning point in their acceptance by previously cynical whites. This was recognized by some white troops as well as by black. Before the actual assault, white private Henry T. Johns expressed his belief that the black regiments would perform well, and that consequently whites would "give them a share in *our* nationality, if God has no separate nationality in store for them." In the aftermath of the battle, Johns's optimism seemed justified. One lieutenant reported that his company had fought bravely, adding "they are mostly contrabands, and I must say I entertained some fears as to their pluck. But I have none now." The *New York Times* was similarly impressed by the ability of these "comparatively raw troops," who "were yet subjected to the most awful ordeal than even veterans ever have to experience—the charging upon fortifications through the crash of belching batteries. The men, white or black, who will not flinch from that," it remarked, "will flinch from nothing."[38]

If further proof were required that the black soldier had potential, it was given in one of the Civil War's most bloody engagements, the battle of Milliken's Bend in June 1863, which came shortly after the Port Hudson defeat. Here, too, raw black recruits found themselves facing substantial Confederate forces. In the black units engaged, casualties ran to 35 percent and for the 9th Louisiana Infantry (later the 5th U.S. Colored Heavy Artillery) alone casualties reached 45 percent. The cost was clearly high but, as at Port Hudson, white commanders declared themselves impressed with the courage of the black troops under fire. Charles A. Dana, the assistant secretary of war, believed that "the sentiment in regard to the employment of negro troops has been revolutionized by the bravery of the blacks in the recent Battle of Milliken's Bend. Prominent officers, who used in private to sneer at the idea, are now heartily in favor of it." The federal government, too, finally showed itself fully in favor of black regiments, and in May 1863 it established the Bureau of Colored Troops, headed by C. W. Foster, giving it the remit of organizing the training and administration of the new black regiments, all of which (with the exception of the Connecticut and two of the Massachusetts regiments) came under the designation "United States Colored Troops" (USCT), whether they were Infantry (USCI), Cavalry (USCC), or Heavy Artillery (USCHA). Massachusetts, Connecticut, and Rhode Island were the first Northern states to raise black regiments, but others soon followed, and the Union began a process of active recruitment among the free black population of the North.[39]

The rationale behind the decision to raise black regiments may not have derived wholly from the belief that slavery was a moral wrong, but Lincoln's justification for his actions has to be interpreted in context. The emphasis on the decision as a necessary war measure can be read as a reluctant response to the crisis or, equally plausibly, as the best explanation available to a government seeking to implement a policy that was far from universally popular. Certainly the belief that slavery underpinned the Confederate war effort persuaded some Northerners of the need to remove this support from the South, and the fact that the decision to allow blacks to join the Union army coincided with the first draft in the North ensured support for the measure from even the most extreme racist elements in northern society. One soldier observed, with some irony, that "just in proportion as the certainty of a draft increased, did the prejudice against Negro soldiers decrease. It was discovered that Negroes were not only loyal persons and good mule drivers, but exceedingly competent to bear arms." Such attitudes were summed up in a piece of racist doggerel—that nevertheless made its point—written by Lt. Col. Charles Halpine, under the pen name of "Private Miles O'Reilly." Entitled "Sambo's Right to Be Kilt," that ran: "The men who object to Sambo/Should take his place an' fight/And it's better to have a naygur's hue/Than a liver that's wake an' white … So hear me all, boys, darlings,/Don't think I tippin' you chaff,/The right to be kilt I'll divide wid him,/And give him the largest half!"[40]

Abraham Lincoln was fully aware that such attitudes existed, and he was not oblivious to the negative mindset they reflected, even as they aided the enlistment of African Americans in the Union cause. His Annual Message to Congress in December 1862, however, sought to place a rather different slant on the subject of emancipation, one that emphasized its significance for the nation's future. "Without slavery," he argued, "the rebellion could never have existed; without slavery it could not continue." Although he acknowledged the "great diversity, of sentiment and of policy, in regard to slavery, and the African race amongst us," Lincoln nevertheless made clear his case for emancipation, not as a temporary war measure, but "as permanent constitutional law." In his famous conclusion to his message, he reminded his audience:

Fellow-citizens, *we* cannot escape history. We of this Congress and this administration, will be remembered in spite of ourselves ... The fiery trial through which we pass, will light us down, in honor or dishonor, to the latest generation ... We—even *we here*—hold the power, and bear the responsibility. In *giving* freedom to the *slave*, we *assure* freedom to the *free*—honorable alike in what we give, and what we preserve. We shall nobly save, or meanly lose, the last best, hope of earth.[41]

Lincoln reinforced this message in his equally famous letter to James Conkling, in which he defended his emancipation decision in the face of criticism that he was changing the nature of the war. "You say you will not fight to free negroes. Some of them seem willing to fight for you," Lincoln noted. There "will be some black men who can remember that, with silent tongue and clenched teeth, and steady eye, and well-poised bayonet, they have helped mankind on to this great consummation," he pointedly observed, "while, I fear, there will be some white ones unable to forget that, with malignant heart, and deceitful speech, they have strove to hinder it."[42]

By the end of 1863 the Union army had recruited some 50,000 African Americans, both free blacks and former slaves. By the end of the war this number had risen to some 186,000, of which 134,111 were recruited in the slave states. African-American troops comprised 10 percent of the total Union fighting force, and some 3,000 of them died on the battlefield and many more in prisoner of war camps. Toward the end of 1863, Henry S. Harmon, a soldier in the 3rd USCI, felt confident enough to declare that "you can say of the colored man, we too have borne our share of the burden. We too have suffered and died in defence of that starry banner which floats only over free men ... I feel assured that the name of the colored soldier will stand out in bold relief among the heroes of this war." Yet despite the fact that blacks had shown that they could fight, they still suffered from racial prejudice in the Union army, a problem compounded by the practical conditions of a war fought by volunteer troops of any color. By the time the African-American regiments were raised and sent into the field, the Civil War had been going on for almost two years. Fresh recruits, therefore, both black and white, found themselves facing a Confederate army that had much more combat experience. At Milliken's Bend, for example, the most experienced Union officers had been in uniform for less than a month. Even worse, some of the black troops received little in the way of military training prior to going into battle. When the 29th USCT arrived at Camp Casey in 1864, for example, they were issued the .58 Springfield Rifled Musket. They were not, however, given any training in how to use these beyond basic parade (or display) evolutions. In such circumstances it was unsurprising that the troops struggled under battlefield conditions.[44]

Deliberately prejudicial policies compounded the more general problems that the African-American regiments faced after 1863. Most obviously, blacks were neither paid nor promoted on a par with whites. Initially, there was no indication that the War Department intended to pay black troops less than white troops. When Governor Andrew was granted permission to raise the Massachusetts 54th, for example, he was instructed to offer $13 per month plus rations and clothing, along with a bounty of $50 for signing up and $100 on mustering out. In 1863, the army paymaster actually gave the 33rd Colored Infantry the standard pay. In June, however, the War Department decided that black troops were entitled to only $10 per month, of which $3 should be deducted for clothing. The reasoning was that the raising of black regiments came under the Militia Act of 1862, which specified the lower rate of pay on the grounds that it had not anticipated combatant blacks. Even before this, however, the promised $50 bounty was slow in coming, and in some cases never came at all. Promotion followed the same dismal course. Benjamin Butler, in mustering in the Louisiana regiments, had created a mixed officer class. Jim Lane in Kansas did likewise, and because he was acting against orders anyway he never troubled himself to defend his actions. However, when Governor Andrew sought to appoint black officers to the 54th and 55th Massachusetts, he was told that only white officers would be accepted. Similarly, when Jim Lane's Kansas regiments were officially recognized, its black officers were not. Nathaniel P. Banks, on taking over from Butler in the Department of the South promptly set about removing all the black officers, usually by forcing them to resign. By 1865 only one in 2,000 black troops had achieved officer rank, mostly as chaplains or physicians.

African-American regiments also received a greater proportion of fatigue duty than many of the white regiments. Medical care for the black regiments was equally discriminatory, and it was a particular problem given the high rate of combat casualties in these regiments. Many of the black troops, being relatively new to the field, had little immunity to the diseases that infected the camps, and the problem was compounded by a widespread assumption that blacks were not as susceptible to disease as whites. Finding surgeons to work with black troops was also difficult; by 1863 there was a general shortage of physicians in the Union army, and those that could put up with the rigors of camp life had long ago been employed by regiments formed earlier in the war. By far the worst aspect of the black Civil War, however, was their treatment by some Confederates. Perhaps unsurprisingly, a greater proportion of wartime atrocities were directed at the colored regiments. The most notorious incident occurred on April 14, 1864, at Fort Pillow, north of Memphis. A force of some 1,500 Confederates, under the command of Major General Nathan Bedford Forrest (an early leader of the Ku Klux Klan) demanded the surrender of the fort, which was manned by about 500 Union troops, half of them black. In the fighting that ensued some 66 percent of the black troops were killed and some 33 percent of the whites. The Joint Committee on the Conduct of the War investigated the incident; its report makes for gruesome reading, even to a modern audience familiar with, if not inured to, the atrocities of twentieth- and twenty-first-century conflicts. That it stands out because it was unusual in the degree and the extent of violence in no way diminishes the tragedy that was Fort Pillow.

The atrocities committed at Fort Pillow, the Joint Committee concluded, "were not the result of passions excited by the heat of conflict, but were the results of a policy deliberately decided upon and unhesitatingly announced." It found that most of the black troops killed had been murdered after the fort had surrendered, but that was just the most overt example of the "cruelty and murder without parallel in civilized warfare" at Fort Pillow. From the many testimonies it solicited, the Joint Committee pieced together a day of

> indiscriminate slaughter, sparing neither age nor sex, white or black, soldier or civilian. The officers and men seemed to vie with each other in the devlish work; men, women, and even children ... were deliberately shot down, beaten, and hacked with sabres; some of the children not more than ten years old were forced to stand up and face their murderers while being shot; the sick and the wounded were butchered without mercy, the rebels even entering the hospital building and dragging them out to be shot, or killing them as they lay there unable to offer the least resistance.[44]

When Union troops were able to retrieve the dead, they found even more gruesome evidence of what had occurred at Fort Pillow, including living persons having been thrown into hastily constructed graves, and the dead only partially, and irreverently, buried. Northern public opinion rallied to black troops in the wake of Fort Pillow, but for those concerned, it was a high price to pay for the recognition of valor. The whole issue of emancipation, the raising of African-American regiments, and the incorporation of blacks into the national polity went to the heart not just of what the Civil War was about, but what America as a nation stood for. Lincoln invoked the better angels of human nature in his defense of emancipation and his determination to secure a nation worth fighting for, one in which no one was a slave, but Fort Pillow served as a cruel reminder of the increasing desperation that lay at the heart of the South on the eve of the final big Union push into Virginia and Georgia in the spring of 1864. Emancipation represented the highest ideals to which the mid-nineteenth-century nation aspired; Fort Pillow offered a terrifying glimpse of what it would cost to achieve them.

CHAPTER **6**

Into the West

Then it was that I saw the power of one man, born to command, over a multitude of men then almost routed and demoralized. I saw and felt that he was not fighting for glory, but that he was fighting for his country because he loved that country, and he was willing to give his life for his country and the success of our cause.

—Sam Watkins, CSA, *Co. Aytch: A Confederate Memoir of the Civil War,* **1881**

The 1st Arkansas Infantry (African descent), later the 46th U.S. Colored Troops, was mustered in to Union service on May 1, 1863, and assigned to the Department of Tennessee. Reportedly, the regiment marched into battle singing, to the tune of "John Brown's Body" (the "Battle Hymn of the Republic"):

> We have done with hoeing cotton,
> we have done with hoeing corn,
> We are colored Yankee soldiers, now,
> as sure as you are born;
> When the masters hear us yelling,
> they'll think it's Gabriel's horn,
> As it went sounding on.[1]

Their optimism that the war had taken on a new and positive meaning in the spring of 1863 was understandable, but in the broader context of the Union position, somewhat misplaced. At least they were able to express their antislavery sentiments. In the Army of the Potomac, McClellan had banned his troops from singing "John Brown's Body," and he would hardly have approved of the 1st Arkansas's version. For McClellan, the post-Antietam lull—a self-induced one—brought several unwelcome surprises, not the least of which was the Preliminary Emancipation Proclamation, but Lincoln's temporary suspension of *habeas corpus* upset him almost as much; both were done in the name of strengthening the Union war effort but, in McClellan's opinion, they were radical and dangerous developments, and productive of the same end: emancipation of the slaves. The suspension of *habeas corpus*, in his view, threatened to produce "servile war, emancipating the slaves, & at one stroke of the pen changing our free institutions into a despotism—for such I regard as the natural effect of the last Proclamation suspending the Habeas Corpus throughout the land." As summer gave way to autumn, and a depressing silence fell once more on the Potomac, Lincoln's impatience with McClellan's apparently too-patient attitude to the war grew. The general remained of the opinion that the Army of the Potomac was in no state to mount another campaign, but Lincoln could not afford to wait until McClellan felt ready—because it didn't look like he ever would be. In October, Lincoln again visited the Army of the Potomac, to see if some action could not be instigated. On that occasion Lincoln reportedly inquired what force he was looking at. On being told it was the Army of the Potomac, Lincoln retorted: "So it is called, but that is a mistake, it is only McClellan's bodyguard."[2]

By failing to attack the enemy, McClellan had made too many personal enemies to remain much longer in command of the North's foremost army. Lincoln wanted McClellan to get back across the Potomac and engage with Lee, but, as delay followed delay, the frustration of both the president and the senior command reached breaking point. In mid-October, Lincoln wrote to McClellan, in one of the longest communications he ever sent to his general, setting out the situation as he saw it. He pointed out that "you are now nearer Richmond than the enemy is by the route that you *can*, and he *must* take. Why can you not reach there before him … His route is the arc of a circle, while yours is the chord. The roads are as good on yours as on his … If we cannot beat the enemy where he is now," Lincoln warned, "we never can." It was to no avail. Toward the end of the month, Lincoln's patience was clearly running out. In response to yet another complaint from McClellan about the parlous state of the Army of the Potomac, Lincoln snapped: "I have just read your despatch about sore tongued and fatigued horses. Will you pardon me for asking what the horses of your army have done since the battle of Antietam to fatigue anything?" By the end of October, Halleck professed himself "sick, tired and disgusted with the condition of military affairs here in the East, and wish myself back in the Western army. With all my efforts," he complained, "I can get nothing done. There is an immobility here that exceeds all that any man can conceive of. It requires the lever of Archimedes to move this inert mass." On November 5, Lincoln, finally, and with some reluctance, advised Halleck that McClellan should be removed from command and replaced by Ambrose Burnside; Fitz John Porter, too, was removed from the command of his corps (the 5th Corps), and replaced by "Fighting Joe" Hooker. Two days later, McClellan addressed the Army of the Potomac for the last time:

> As an army, you have grown up under my care ... The battles you have fought under my command will proudly live in our nation's history. The glory you have achieved, our mutual perils and fatigues, the graves of our comrades fallen in battle and by disease, the broken forms of those whom wounds and sickness have disabled—the strongest associations which can exist among men—unite us still by an indissoluble tie.

Yet the tie had, finally, been dissolved. "This has been a sad day for the Army of the Potomac," Elisha Hunt Rhodes confided to his dairy, "Gen. McClellan has been relieved from command and has left us ... This change produces much bitter feeling." But the change Rhodes observed, also produced hope, at least in Washington, if not yet on the banks on the Potomac.[3]

The Western Front

As Lincoln began what would turn out to be a frustrating—although ultimately successful—search for a general to break the deadlock in the Eastern Theater, the as yet undiscovered general in question, Ulysses S. Grant was helping to hold the Union line against the Confederate counteroffensive in the West. The actions of the Union Armies of the Ohio and the Cumberland and those of the Confederate Armies of Tennessee and Kentucky in the West have, traditionally, received less attention than those of the Army of the Potomac and the Army of Northern Virginia in the East. This is, in some ways, hard to comprehend. The West was as important—arguably more important—than the East in the defeat of the Confederacy. From the start, those Union armies operating west of the Appalachian mountain chain had two main objectives: control of the Mississippi and splitting the Confederacy by controlling the railroads in Tennessee and Georgia. However, the Western states were also critical to the Confederate war effort. Historian Thomas Connelly highlighted the importance of Tennessee— and the army named for it—when he entitled the first volume of his study of the Army of Tennessee—*Army of the Heartland*. Tennessee, he pointed out, was the "Confederacy's geographical heart but, more importantly, its logistical and communications heart as well." It was in Tennessee that the Confederacy manufactured its munitions and its supplies, had its main supply depots, ordnance works, and foundries; and through Tennessee ran the rail links that enabled the movement of troops and supplies both east–west and north–south. These links were critical to the Confederate prosecution of the war in the West. Despite this, Connelly argues, the Army of Tennessee consistently "received second-class treatment" from the government at Richmond, which did not understand the difficulties of fighting in the West. Yet, in the end, the relative neglect of the West—at the time and by historians since then—derived from one man's reputation: that man was Robert E. Lee.[4]

The lion's share of attention went to the Eastern Theater because that was where Robert E. Lee was fighting. Lee was the great hope of the South and the great fear of the North; both the hope and the fear were based on the same thing: Lee was the acceptable face not just of Southern chivalry but of the American military machine, the cavalier *sans peur et sans reproche*. To defeat Lee was to defeat the best that the South, possibly the nation as a whole, had to offer. Although he was initially a reluctant conscript, Lee became not only wholly committed to the Confederate cause, but the South's first and last best hope for victory—and he was a consistent presence. In contrast to the ever-shifting Union command (after late 1862), in Lee the Confederacy had its man, and the longer he remained so, the greater (and more daunting, for the Union) his reputation became. In the Confederate pantheon, Lee was first among equals. There were others in whom the hopes of the South rested between 1861 and 1865. The group comprising James Longstreet, Stonewall Jackson, Jeb Stuart, and Lee achieved battlefield success in the Virginia Theater and through that secured fame for themselves and their armies. The commanders of the Western armies were never as famous. In part, this was because as soon as any commander—on the Union side at least—looked halfway competent in the West, he was promptly whisked over the mountains to see if he could work his magic in the crucial Virginia Theater. That was the case with McClellan and with Halleck, and it would be the case with Grant, in the end. Yet, obscured from the persistent and critical gaze of Washington reporters and isolated by distance from (and therefore daily interference by) the Washington and Richmond governments), the armies that fought beyond the Appalachians were equally—if not more—significant to the outcome of the war.

Following the Confederate evacuation of Corinth in May 1862, General Halleck had moved the Union forces eastward, following the Memphis and Charleston Railroad. At the same time, Don Carlos Buell, commander of the Army of the Ohio and in overall charge of the District of the Ohio, had been directed east with his 30,000 troops, the idea being, as Halleck advised him, that by "moving on Chattanooga you prevent a junction between Smith and Beauregard and are on the direct line to Atlanta." To Secretary of War Stanton, Halleck expanded on his plan. Reports suggested—quite rightly—that the Confederate army was in some disarray, and if, as Halleck hoped, "the enemy should have evacuated East Tennessee and Cumberland Gap ... Buell will probably move on Atlanta." Halleck noted, almost in passing, that it "will probably take some time to clean out the guerrilla parties in West Tennessee and North Mississippi ... They are already giving much annoyance in burning bridges, houses, and cotton," he noted. This was no minor matter. John Hunt Morgan's raids in Kentucky, for example, were sufficiently extensive and destructive (in just under a month, Morgan had covered over 1,000 miles, wreaking havoc over most of them) that Lincoln felt prompted to raise the matter with Halleck. "They are having a stampede in Kentucky," he advised the general. "Please look to it." If the Confederacy's Western generals failed to gain prominence for their actions, some of the South's guerrilla raiders certainly did—unfairly in some respects, because their mission was by its nature a high-profile, hit-and-run operation aimed at supplies and transport links, not troops, and it required little in the way of extended logistical planning. Men such as Nathan Bedford Forrest, John Hunt Morgan, and Joseph Wheeler gained fame and a degree of notoriety—in Forrest's case, more than a degree—from their dashing cavalry raids across Kentucky and Tennessee, whereas Stonewall Jackson, of course, was by mid-1862 already a legend because of his Valley Campaign that had so hampered McClellan on the Peninsula. An offensive strategy as old as warfare itself—raiding—historian Archer Jones notes, played "a far larger role in the Civil War than in wars fought in western Europe during the previous two centuries." In the context of the Western Theater it proved to be an extremely effective strategy. Forrest and Morgan slowed Buell down considerably and hampered his operations, most notably when Forrest seized the supply depot at Murfreesboro in July; this bought the Confederacy sufficient time to plan a fresh campaign, this one to be headed by the new commander of the Western Department who had replaced Beauregard, Braxton Bragg.[5]

Bragg didn't take long to swing into action. In the summer of 1862, as Lee prepared to invade Maryland, his movements were paralleled in the West by Bragg's invasion of Kentucky, another campaign intended, or so it was hoped, to garner support for the Confederacy in that state, and ideally bring it into the Confederate fold. "The feeling in Middle Tennessee and Kentucky is represented by Forrest and Morgan to have become intensely hostile to the enemy," Bragg reported, "and nothing is wanted but arms and support to bring the people into our ranks, for they have found that neutrality has afforded them no protection." The parallels between East and West did not end there. In Bragg, the Confederacy had its own, rather diluted, version of McClellan. Like McClellan, Bragg was an adept administrator whose organizational abilities did not translate into battlefield decisiveness. One of his brigade commanders said of him that "there was no man in either of the contending armies who was General Bragg's superior as an organizer and a disciplinarian, but when he was in the presence of an enemy he lost his head." Unlike McClellan, Bragg never boasted that he could do it all; as in McClellan's case, however, people rather expected him to. And whereas McClellan created misery for himself by seeing conspiracies against him where none existed, Bragg genuinely suffered from the vagaries of a Confederate command structure that seemed, at times, more intent on undermining the South's cause by protracted and petty infighting than in engaging the enemy. In the West, there was no need for the Union to attempt a policy of divide and conquer; the Confederates proved more than capable of dividing themselves.[6]

The August 1862 Confederate invasion of Kentucky did not go as planned, nor did it achieve all that Bragg had hoped for. As was the case for Lee in Maryland, Bragg did not encounter the waves of Confederate support he had anticipated, and he wasted valuable time in trying to stir some up when he took a detour to Frankfort to attend the publicity stunt that was the installation ceremony of the state's Confederate governor. In the battle for hearts and minds in Kentucky and Tennessee in late 1862, Confederate commanders talked a good talk, but the general sympathy this elicited in their audience did not translate into practical support. In trying to rally the people of East Tennessee to the cause, Confederate General Sam Jones told them, with some exaggeration that Kentuckians were "flocking by thousands to our standard," but the reality was rather different—to Bragg's dismay. An even bigger problem than public and tactical support lay in the lack of coordination between Bragg, moving north from Chattanooga in an attempt to engage Buell, and Kirby Smith, moving into Kentucky from his base at Knoxville, East Tennessee. Bragg had announced his belief that his "campaign must be won by marching, not fighting," and Buell certainly seemed determined to fulfill his opponent's expectations in that regard. The main Union force managed to stay out of reach of the Confederates for several weeks, first retreating north to Nashville—as Buell initially thought that Nashville was where Bragg was headed—and from there to Bowling Green, Kentucky. Bragg finally caught up with Buell's rearguard forces at Munfordville in mid-September, only to have them move out of reach again, this time all the way to Louisville on the Ohio, where Buell acquired reinforcements. By this point, Confederate forces were too small and too strung out to be effective, and supply problems exacerbated an already faltering campaign. Finally, at the start of October, Buell brought the Army of the Ohio to meet Bragg's Army of Tennessee, which by that point was in the process of joining with Smith's Army of Kentucky. This was exactly the maneuver that Buell had been hoping to forestall. But it was not the crisis it could have been for the Union, because at Perryville (Chaplin Hills) only a part of the Confederate force was actually in position on the morning of October 8, 1862; Smith's forces and one of Bragg's divisions remained out of reach at Frankfort, where the governor's installation ceremony had taken place. The numbers, therefore, more than stacked up on the Union side, with 60,000 federal troops facing a total of some 35,000 Confederates. Numbers, however, did not necessarily translate into an effective fighting force.[7]

By the time the Army of the Ohio encountered Bragg at Perryville, it was a disillusioned force: indeed, according to its foremost historian, it was no force at all, but "a fragmented collection of regimental communities." In part this derived from its leadership. Bragg and McClellan were not the only Civil War commanders to suffer from a few leadership issues. Don Carlos Buell's biggest problem was that he lacked McClellan's charisma. He was almost as fixated on the fictional numerical superiority of the Confederate forces as McClellan was, and he was just as touchy—and just about as indecisive. These traits were even worse for Buell because he lacked whatever leadership qualities McClellan did possess; above all, he lacked McClellan's ability to get the troops' support, or inculcate corps' cohesion. In the particular case of Perryville, he was absent altogether, which hardly helped matters. Buell was, bizarrely, unaware that the Battle of Perryville was even underway on October 8. As a result of an "acoustic shadow" (a rare phenomenon produced by a combination of terrain and weather conditions that prevents sound from carrying), what was in fact a major engagement sounded to Buell and the people at the Army of the Ohio's headquarters like random artillery shots. Being absent from the battlefield meant Buell could not really be held responsible for the fact that his three corps failed to act in unison, which meant that the Army of the Ohio, although victorious, suffered a higher cost in lives than should have been necessary—and possibly only achieved their victory because the Confederates were not up to full strength.[8]

Buell pursued Bragg as he retreated in the days following Perryville, but not with any urgency, and he soon fell back. Bragg marched initially to Harrodsburg, where he finally joined with Smith's troops, and then all the way back through Cumberland Gap to Chattanooga. Lincoln could not tolerate yet another Confederate general slipping away. Just over a week before the decision was made to remove McClellan in the East, Buell was relieved of his command in the West, and replaced by William S. Rosecrans. Partly in recognition of the fact that morale in the Army of the Ohio was low, a former name was resurrected for Rosecrans' force—the Army of the Cumberland—and the troops in the field designated, somewhat unimaginatively, the 14th Army Corps.

In the Confederacy, Bragg was on safer ground because Jefferson Davis trusted him, but his enemies were gathering and the ground was shifting. In all, his Kentucky campaign had been a failure, not so much in military or strategic terms but as a recruitment drive. The expected, and much needed, reinforcements from the populations of Kentucky and East Tennessee failed to materialize, casting doubt on the future of the Confederate cause there. The Union had no more reason to be cheerful in the autumn of 1862. Minor battles in Mississippi in mid-September, at Iuka, and early October, at Corinth, hardly advanced matters, and Grant's forces were weakened by the fact that Halleck had reinforced Buell so heavily from Grant's troops. Grant's advance toward Vicksburg in the last two months of the year was not, therefore, proving a success. In both the Eastern and Western Theaters, both North and South were, in effect, back to square one after a year of hard fighting, with little but losses to show for it. In the Eastern Theater, however, the Union situation still had time to get worse— much worse—before the year was finally out.

The Great Triumvirate: Fredericksburg, Chancellorsville, and Gettysburg

"Patriotism and the exercise of my every energy in the direction of this army," Ambrose Burnside told the Army of the Potomac, "aided by the full and hearty co-operation of its officers and men, will, I hope … insure its success." Burnside's first act on taking command was to reject the advice offered by both Halleck and Lincoln and move the Army to the east, toward the Rappahannock River and the town of Fredericksburg. His plan, he advised Washington, was to implement a feinting maneuver, to "impress upon the enemy a belief that we are to attack Culpeper or Gordonsville … and then make a rapid movement upon Richmond." In an attempt to convince an uncertain Lincoln that his circuitous attack on Richmond would succeed, and just as if he were viewing his planned campaign like a chess game, Burnside set out eventualities for each possible alternate route. At all points, Burnside assured Lincoln, the Army of the Potomac would "be nearer to Washington than the enemy, and we will all the time be on the shortest route to Richmond, the taking of which … should be the great object of the campaign." Moving this particular Union army, however, had always been a slow and cumbersome process and now, when speed was most required, it was not forthcoming; much of the second half of November was spent just getting into position. While Burnside fretted at Falmouth on the opposite bank of the Rappahannock to Fredericksburg, Lee moved into position on the outskirts of the town. New York lawyer George Templeton Strong experienced "a dim foreboding" that the war would all too soon become "a terrible crushing, personal calamity to every one of us ... The logic of history," he believed, "requires that we suffer for our sins far more than we yet have suffered." As treasurer of the Sanitary Commission, a civilian support organization for the Union, Strong had already visited the Army of the Potomac, and so he knew from firsthand experience just how much the war had cost in human misery so far. In the South, Joseph Jones, recently appointed a surgeon in the Confederate Army, also quickly arrived at the realization that the South's population as yet knew "but little of war," the reality of which lay not on "the battle field covered with glory, and rendered attractive by deeds of valor," but in the hospitals where the "victories of disease exceed ten fold those of the sword."[9]

For non-combatants like Strong, the war was a distant tragedy that impacted on them, in a physical sense, only indirectly. Northern citizens became familiar with the sight of coffins being delivered to families fortunate enough to be able to repatriate their dead. The war could never be far from anyone's thoughts; it was front-page news in every paper, every day. Even if—and this became increasingly unlikely as the war continued—someone were not related to, or personally acquainted with, a soldier, a nurse, or a member of the Sanitary Commission, it was still impossible to avoid the war, even on the streets of New York. Yet, although Matthew Brady's photographs had brought the image of death to New York's doorstep, its horrific reality was many miles away, on the battlefields of Virginia and Tennessee. For Southern civilians, the war had more immediate impact, as they were often driven from their homes in the face of Union advances, refugees from a constantly moving war front that destroyed their homes, their possessions, and their way of life. Slaves were frequently forcibly shifted away from the approaching Union armies as their owners tried desperately to cling to what they viewed as their private property and the institution of slavery itself. Separation from families and communities was a common and devastating experience for African Americans across the Confederacy, but also in the loyal slaveholding states such as Kentucky and Missouri. The story of Mattie Jackson who fled to Union lines only to be returned to her owners in Missouri then kidnapped and sold for an inflated price in Kentucky is one dramatic example of the ways in which some individuals exploited the upheaval of war that even in the midst of the misery wrought by conflict they sought to extract a profit out of the last days of slavery.[10]

Mattie was in her late teens during the war, but even for younger children growing up in those years of war, the memories of that time were frequently of hardship and loss, even as some aspects of life continued as normal—a bizarre counterpoint to the devastation going on around them. Céline Frémaux, a twelve-year-old living in Baton Rouge, recalled how the citizens of that city had dug trenches in which to avoid the Union bombardment of the city in the summer of 1862, pits that in the bombardment's aftermath were filled with the decomposing bodies of the dead. "When a pit was filled up," she recalled, "an army blanket was stretched atop, the corners held down with bricks, and there ended the disposition of the dead." Such were the sights that the young girl passed on her way to school each day because, as she explained, "I had to cross the heart of the city," a city that had, in large part, been destroyed by the federal attack. In the end, Céline and her family became refugees, moving first to Port Hudson and, when that was evacuated in early July 1863, to Jackson, Louisiana. They hid from Union troops when they had to and attended school when they could. As Burnside and the Union army moved toward Fredericksburg in November 1862, many of its citizens were about to share Céline's terrible experiences in Baton Rouge.[11]

When Burnside reached Fredericksburg his advance was temporarily blocked. As so often before, the Union army found itself in the position of having to wait while the Confederates got themselves sorted out, not out of any sense of politeness, but out of frustration—as the Union's carefully laid plans went awry. When Burnside arrived at the point where he wanted to cross the Rappahannock, the Confederate force opposing him was weak. Longstreet was still in the Shenandoah Valley and in his absence Lee feared he might have to pull his own forces back from the town. The Army of the Potomac was unable to take advantage of this fact, however, because it was stuck, unable to cross the river until the arrival of the pontoons that were, at that point, some 25 miles to the rear of the army. By the time the pontoons arrived at the end of November and Burnside was finally able to move his troops, Longstreet's forces had returned from the Shenandoah; the chance for an unopposed crossing was gone. By that time Lee had his army up to strength and in a strong position, and sharpshooters had been sent ahead into Fredericksburg itself. Outside the town, Lee's infantry divisions were ready, in front of the artillery arranged on Marye's Heights, waiting to open fire on the Union advance. As it became clear that a battle was about to take place at Fredericksburg, its population was advised to abandon the town, and streams of refugees, mainly women, children, and slaves, tried to flee on trains and by foot, a confused and chaotic process that took place over several weeks. Many refused to leave, however, and, in the days before the battle began in earnest, had to run for cover in their cellars as skirmishing between Union troops and Lee's sharpshooters broke out in the streets and fires ignited in several buildings. From his position on the riverbank, Union soldier Charles Haydon remarked that a "very dense black cloud of smoke concealed the town & I think a considerable portion of it is burned." When, on the following day, he made it into Fredericksburg he saw for himself that it was, in fact, "partially burned & terribly riddled. Several dead Rebels lay in the streets as we passed along," he observed, but the town was, by that point, "mostly deserted."[12]

For the Battle of Fredericksburg on December 13—the first to be fought partly within a town—Burnside had divided the Army of the Potomac into three main "Grand Divisions," commanded by Edwin V. Sumner (Right), Joseph Hooker (Center), and William B. Franklin (Left), but this did not produce a more controlled battlefront. Lee still operated with his two main corps under James Longstreet and Stonewall Jackson. Burnside's plan of battle was, in historian David Eicher's phrase, "a tactical nightmare," which, even with the huge numerical superiority of the Union—some 120,000 to the Confederacy's 75,000—was unlikely to produce a Union victory. It began in fog, with a Union frontal assault on the center of Lee's line, held by Longstreet's corps, which repulsed the attack. At this point Joseph Hooker's division was deployed (as it would be again before the day was out) against the bottom of Marye's Heights in a desperate, and futile, attempt to shift the Confederate troops from position. The attacks showed, to anyone able to see in the combination of smoke and icy winter fog that blurred the field, that the day of the massed infantry assault against rifled muskets was surely over. Protected at the base of Marye's Heights by a sunken road running behind a stone wall, Confederate troops were able simply to rake the advancing enemy with rifle fire, and they did so time and again. The stone wall at Fredericksburg became the grim symbol of that battle, proximity to it the measure of a regiment's bravery on the field and, in the case of the Irish Brigade, proof of the futility not only of Fredericksburg, but of the war as a whole. It was at Fredericksburg that Lee, witnessing Confederate General John Bell Hood's attack on the Union, made his famous observation that "it is as well that war is so terrible, or we should grow too fond if it."[13]

Despite the impossibility of breaking the Confederate line, no fewer than six serious attempts were made on it directly, with many other minor assaults both on the main field and in the town itself proving equally futile. Union telegrams told the tale succinctly enough as the day progressed. "We do not seem to advance much," one aide-de-camp warned Burnside by the middle of the afternoon. General William Franklin reported "my left is in danger of being turned. What hope is there of getting reinforcements across the river?" Reports of serious fighting, of troops stalled in the face of overwhelming enemy fire or enemy skirmishers, and sharpshooters pinning the men down came in from all parts of the field. The most eloquent message came from General Darius Couch: "I am losing. Send two rifle batteries." Toward the end of the day, Charles Haydon recalled seeing the final assault made by E. P. Alexander's artillery battalion on the Union troops:

> After dark I saw from the hill above a terrible contest on the right. There were two long lines of Infantry very near each other. I could not hear the guns but could see the flash & the wavering of the lines. Sometimes there was a solid sheet of flame but for the most part twinkle, twinkle, twinkle like sparks when the fire is stirred, rapid as thought. About 20 pieces of artillery poured an enfilading fire into our ranks. The shells burst right among them. There was some reply from our side. ... The conflict finally died away on the same ground where it opened.

By the time the battle tailed off after dusk, the dead and wounded littered a field eerily lit by an aurora. As the temperature fell to below freezing, many of the wounded froze to death, while the living bivouacked as best they could over that cold and miserable night, fully expecting that, the next day, the battle would resume.[14]

Although Burnside did indeed intend to try again on the following day, his division commanders persuaded him that any such attempt would be folly. Union losses were simply too appalling, the dead too numerous, the wounded too damaged, the living too disillusioned—and the Confederates too secure—to make another assault viable. The Battle of Fredericksburg was as complete a Confederate victory as it was possible to achieve—and it was had from a purely defensive position. At Fredericksburg, Lee had made a stand, and it paid off. The Confederates had little room for maneuvering on December 13 so they did not attempt any concerted counterattack. They didn't need to. Their position was so strong that all they had to do was absorb each successive Union infantry assault. In the process, they sustained far fewer casualties than their opponents, although Confederate losses were bad enough; several prominent men fell at Fredericksburg, including Thomas Cobb and Maxcy Gregg. In total, the South sustained some 5,300 casualties, but Union losses exceeded 12,600. It was with very good reason that one Union officer observed that the horrors of that "long, bloody and disastrous day exceeds any description of which my pen is capable." This was surely war at its worst, but it was not enough for Confederate victory, and Lee knew it. The Union was down after Fredericksburg, but not out. It would take more than a single victory in Virginia to achieve southern independence. Reporting his victory to Confederate Secretary of War James Seddon, Lee expressed the "hope that there will be no relaxation in making every preparation for the contest which will have to be renewed, but at what point I cannot say." Musing on the aftermath of Fredericksburg, Elisha Hunt Rhodes considered that the Army of the Potomac had "met with a severe loss, and I fear little has been gained." As 1862 drew to a close, he confessed himself "bewildered when I think of the hundreds of miles I have tramped, the thousands of dead and wounded I have seen, and the many strange sights that I have witnessed." What the next year would bring in the Eastern Theater was, as yet, anyone's guess.[15]

Chancellorsville

On New Year's Day, 1863, Ambrose Burnside visited Lincoln in the White House. Given the demoralized state of the Army of the Potomac, Burnside's appearance was hardly an auspicious start to the year. On that day, too, the Emancipation Proclamation came into effect, and Lincoln must have realized that its impact could not fail to be diminished if future battles went the way of Fredericksburg. The meetings between the President and his military commanders—Halleck was also under some scrutiny in light of the disaster at Fredericksburg—were tense but cordial, and Lincoln refused to accept the resignation letter that Burnside, as form demanded, offered him. So Burnside set off in early January to salvage what he could of his plans to take Richmond, restore what was left of morale in the Army of the Potomac and, hopefully, give Lincoln a victory sufficient to maintain Burnside's own job and the Union war effort. Quite quickly, however, Burnside became bogged down, literally, when, in late January he set off further up the Rappahannock in weather sufficiently bad to turn the roads to mud to such a degree that the advance could not proceed. This famous "Mud March," coming so close on the heels of Fredericksburg, was a disaster for Burnside, whose officers and men, already disenchanted with him, were now openly furious. There were few choices left now, either for the general or the President, and when Burnside again offered his resignation on January 25, Lincoln accepted it.

Two days after Burnside had resigned, Lincoln appointed Joseph "Fighting Joe" Hooker as commander of what historian John Hennessy summed up as "perhaps the saddest, angriest, most grumbly army that ever marched under America's postrevolutionary flag." Hooker was famous as a fighter—the clue was in the nickname—but he was also famous as an adept political manipulator, who did not restrict himself to the enemy when it came to backstabbing. Lincoln was well aware of this side of Hooker, and it prompted one of the President's most astute, if biting, letters to a general. He warned

Hooker that he knew of his ambition, that he believed he had undermined both Burnside and the Union cause through it, and he added:

> I have heard, in such a way as to believe it, of your recently saying that both the Army and the Government needed a dictator. Of course it was not for this, but in spite of it, that I have given you command. Only those generals who gain successes, can set up dictators. What I ask of you is military success, and I will risk the dictatorship.

Whether chastened by Lincoln's astute assessment of his character or not, Hooker certainly quickly made significant improvements in the Army of the Potomac, dealing first with its physical health, providing better medical treatment, food, and sanitation and then ensuring that soldiers' pay arrived on time and in full, that furloughs were granted, and that whiskey rations were distributed. He also introduced corps badges as a means of establishing some *esprit* in that regard, and he did away with Burnside's "Grand Divisions" in pretty short order. This last may not have been the best move: although the impact was positive on the cavalry, who were melded into a single corps, the overall effect of having eight corps proved, as has been argued, unmanageable on the battlefield. From the perspective of early 1863, however, Hooker's restructuring was part of an overall package through which a seriously demoralized force found the strength to fight another day. The only remaining question was how successfully it would do so.[16]

In April 1863 the Army of the Potomac was still on the banks of the Rappahannock, but it was a very different army than it had been a few months before. It was up to full strength, with over 130,000 troops (some of them new conscripts but many were returned absentees) making it the largest Civil War army in the field, with twice the forces then available to Lee because Longstreet's troops were at Suffolk. Hooker's plan of action was less obviously suicidal than Burnside's; rather than heading straight for Lee, he proposed a diversion by part of the army while the main body moved around Lee's left flank. The sole problem with the plan—and it was the same problem that McClellan's plans had suffered from—was that there was little flexibility in it. In the first two years of the war, Union generals showed themselves to be adept at devising excellent plans, and equally prone to floundering when their plans failed to come together. The initial stages of Hooker's plan, however, worked well, and by the end of April he had the bulk of his forces at Chancellorsville on the edge of "the Wilderness" in Virginia. Although Hooker had prevented the usual newspaper coverage of what the Army of the Potomac was up to, which would have given away his initial movements, Lee soon received word of what was afoot.

Intelligence was a serious matter during the war, and to modern minds the idea that the media would publish not only details of troop movements but maps, for the better instruction of both the Northern public and the Confederate army seems remarkable. It seemed pretty remarkable to Hooker at the time, and he issued general orders that sought to curb the "frequent transmission of false intelligence and the betrayal of the movements of the army to the enemy, by the publication of injudicious correspondence" in the press. He ordered that, in the future, all correspondents should publish over their own names—the better to identify and stop the guilty parties—but it proved a persistent problem, and sometimes it came from within the army itself. Secretary of War Stanton was forced to complain to Hooker when one of his staff sent a personal letter detailing the army's position on the eve of Chancellorsville: "We cannot control intelligence in relation to your movements while your generals write letters giving details," he pointed out. "Can't you give his sword something to do, so that he will have less time for the pen?"[17]

Fully aware that Lee knew of his intentions, Hooker began to move his troops at the start of May, but on encountering Lee's advance guard he lost his nerve and retreated back to his original position. Lee was suffering from no such hesitation; indeed, Lee was buoyant, and devised a more ambitious and offensive response to the Union threat than he had offered at Fredericksburg. Dividing his troops, Lee left some 17,000 of them to face Hooker directly, while Stonewall Jackson took the remaining 26,000 on a ten-mile trek around the Union's right flank, intending to achieve exactly what Hooker had hoped the Army of the Potomac might implement against Lee, an attack from the rear. Confused by what he was witnessing—he initially thought it was a Confederate retreat—Hooker took no steps to meet the threat from Jackson. Fog, and then wind, prevented Hooker's sending up the reconnaissance balloons, which limited his perspective, as did the absence of his cavalry that he had sent off on reconnaissance, so he was dangerously unprepared when on May 2 Jackson attacked. It was a costly attack, for the Confederacy more than the Union, because as dusk fell and visibility with it, Jackson himself was wounded by his own troops as he returned from a reconnaissance. As was the case for so many Civil War soldiers, his wound did not kill him instantly, but the combination of the amputation of his arm with poor medical treatment (being dropped on the ground after being helped from his horse certainly did not help) did not bode well. On learning of Jackson's condition, Lee assured him that could "I have directed events, I should have chosen for the good of the country to be disabled in your stead." When he later received word that Jackson had died, Lee—indeed, the South—was devastated. "A great national calamity has befallen us," Jefferson Davis wrote to Lee, "and I sympathize with the sorrow you feel and the embarrassment you must experience." Although Chancellorsville was a resounding victory for the South, Jackson's death was the greatest loss to Lee, one from which, arguably, he never recovered.[18]

As is the case with Fredericksburg, although the actual Battle of Chancellorsville on May 3, 1863 is regarded as a single, almost decisive one-day battle, it was really only the final clash in a longer maneuver of troops and munitions, skirmishing, and minor engagements. Reports from the Union line on May 3 soon advised that a "most terribly bloody conflict" was in progress. "Carnage is fearful," the chief quartermaster reported, but he remained confident that "our victory will be certain." Yet by mid-afternoon, Hooker was reporting to Lincoln on "the desperate fight yesterday and today, which has resulted in no success to us." The faint echo of McClellan could, unfortunately, be heard in Hooker's commendation of his troops and his observation that no "general ever commanded a more devoted army," but it was an army in serious need of a more decisive, general. It was hardly a surprise, therefore, when the following day's engagement saw the Union fall back—after another terrible night and a day full of horrors. Many of the wounded had frozen to death on the field at Fredericksburg; at Chancellorsville a brush fire that broke out in the woods on the battlefield the following day condemned many of the wounded from that battle to an even more gruesome end. "I never saw such a distressing sight before," wrote one Confederate soldier when he encountered the burned and contorted corpses on the field, "and hope I may never see such another." On May 5, Hooker began the retreat back to the Rappahannock, a sad conclusion for the Union of a battle that had shown Lee at his best, even as it showed war at its worst.[19]

Chancellorsville was a major—perhaps *the* major—success for Lee. Even with a serious shortage of troops at his disposal, he had succeeded in routing the Army of the Potomac comprehensively and unexpectedly, but at a terrible cost to both sides. From the Union's perspective, however, Chancellorsville was not the long-term disaster it could have been. In the absence of Longstreet, Lee's ability to consolidate the victory was limited and, although it did not distract him from his longer-term strategy to attempt an invasion of Union territory, Chancellorsville had an undeniable impact on his ability to implement that strategy. Here numbers came into play. Confederate casualties at Chancellorsville amounted to some 12,700; Union casualties exceeded 17,000. These were devastating losses for each side, but Lee could afford them less. Since he had taken command of the Army of Northern Virginia, Lee frequently had cause to request, plead for, and demand more troops, but recruitment problems across the Confederacy hampered him. In the summer of 1863, Lee expressed his concerns over the position of the Army of Northern Virginia to Jefferson Davis:

> We should not ... conceal from ourselves that our resources in men are constantly diminishing, and the disproportion in this respect between us and our enemies ... is steadily augmenting. The decrease of the aggregate of this army as disclosed by the returns affords an illustration of the fact. Its effective strength varies from time to time, but the falling off in its aggregate shows that its ranks are growing weaker and that its losses are not supplied by recruits.[20]

Lee's recruitment difficulties, ironically—in part at least—derived directly from the second way in which Chancellorsville affected Lee's ability to achieve victory for the South. This battle, as historian Gary Gallagher notes, "cemented a bond" between Lee and his army "unrivalled on either side during the Civil War." With Lee at its head, the Army of Northern Virginia felt invincible, and so did the South. Lee's victory over a Union army twice the size of his own led to the erroneous belief that what Lee had done at Chancellorsville he could, and would, do again. Just as Joe Johnston had noted with dismay the premature optimism expressed by the Southern troops after First Bull Run—that enough had been done, that no more effort need be expended—so, too, in the aftermath of Chancellorsville, there emerged "a growing impression among white Southerners that the future of their incipient nation lay with Lee and his men in Virginia." It had been bad enough for the Union when McClellan declared his belief that he could do it all; it was worse for the Confederacy when it started to believe that Lee was, in fact, the man with that ability.[21]

The High Water Mark of the Confederacy: Gettysburg

In the immediate aftermath of Chancellorsville, Lee returned to his plan to invade the Union states, and Lincoln, yet again, contemplated the fast-diminishing pool of senior commanders from which he might draw someone—anyone—with the ability to take on and defeat this Confederate master tactician. The immediate problems facing the South were a shortage of troops and resources to cover all the theaters of the war and finding a way to counter the growing Union control of the coasts, which was causing increasing hardship to southern civilians. Shortages of food and supplies affected the cities especially, a problem exacerbated by the arrival of refugees from areas held by the Union or from towns such as Fredericksburg. The situation was sufficiently desperate by April 1863 that some of the women of Richmond—almost a thousand in all—simply removed food and goods from the shops, forced into this extreme act not just by wartime shortages but by inadequate levels of relief available to women whose partners were fighting for the cause. This was just one example of the so-called bread riots or female raids that broke out in cities across the Confederacy as women became increasingly unable to feed their families or pay the exorbitant prices being charged for food. Although elite southern women sometimes referred to such actions as "disgraceful," as Richmond resident Sallie Brock Putnam did, and blamed the riots on the actions of "a heterogeneous crowd of Dutch, Irish, and free negroes … armed with pistols, knives, hammers, hatchets, axes, and every other weapon which could be made useful," whose sole purpose was theft; these events represented both desperation and a real social breakdown at the heart of the Confederacy. Doubtless, straightforward theft was the aim of some, but even Sallie Putnam had to concede that "*want of bread* was at this time too fatally true." Whereas the Union needed to achieve a victory before northern morale reached such a low that the war would no longer be viable, the Confederacy faced a more pressing requirement: to win the war before men, material, and women's patience ran out altogether.[22]

In such an atmosphere of tension and mounting anger, there was growing pressure on Richmond from the generals in the field—but, crucially, not from Lee—to concentrate Confederate forces in the West, either by reinforcing Braxton Bragg from the Army of Northern Virginia or sending Lee himself to spearhead a push on the Army of the Cumberland that might finally bring Kentucky and Tennessee into the Confederacy and draw Grant away from Vicksburg. Lee opposed the idea. Because Grant was not yet besieging Vicksburg, Lee believed that matters in the West would resolve themselves. He trusted the summer temperatures in Tennessee to slow the Union troops down, and he argued for a continuation of the offensive in the Eastern Theater. To lose the initiative in the East was to lose the war, Lee argued. Few at the time would have dared oppose the hero of Chancellorsville. So Lee went off to prepare for an invasion that would take him to the battle that above all others has come to represent the American Civil War: Gettysburg. With hindsight, we know that Gettysburg was a battle too far for Lee, but hindsight frequently hampers our assessment of the perspective of May–July 1863 and the decisions made then. Indeed hindsight, and the sheer number of books devoted to this single battle alone, has all but removed Gettysburg from the broader context of the Civil War, from Lee's evolving—and ultimately frustrated—plan to take the war to the North in order to undermine Union morale on the home front, and from events in the Western Theater that would prove so crucial to the war's outcome.

As Lee made his plans in Virginia, in Washington, Lincoln was coming to the realization that the focus on the seemingly unattainable Confederate capital was proving detrimental to the Union war effort. Although Hooker had done so much to restore the morale of the Army of the Potomac, Chancellorsville was in danger of undoing all that he had achieved in that regard. Barely a week after the battle, Lincoln advised Hooker that he had had "some painful intimations that some of your corps and Division Commanders are not giving you their entire confidence. This would be ruinous," the President warned him. It was clear to Lincoln that the Union had its eyes on the wrong prize. "I think *Lee's* Army, and not *Richmond*, is your true objective point," he advised Hooker in mid-June. "Fight him when opportunity offers." For Hooker, however, that opportunity never came. By early June, Lee was on the move. He had reorganized his army into three corps, commanded by James Longstreet, A. P. Hill, and Richard S. Ewell; increased its strength to some 75,000 troops; and was gradually taking it westward toward the Shenandoah Valley. He delegated to Hill the task of keeping Hooker distracted on the Rappahannock while Ewell and Longstreet crossed the Potomac in mid-June, heading north. Hooker was unsure of what action to take, and his various proposals—to attack Lee's rear, or to march again on Richmond—were dismissed by Lincoln and Halleck, and to make matters worse, relations between Hooker and Halleck were starting to sour. The main problem was that neither Hooker nor Halleck understood the chain of command. Even when Lincoln made clear to Hooker that Halleck's was the final word—"I shall direct him to give you orders and you to obey them,"—Halleck then assured Hooker that he "was in command of the Army of the Potomac, and will make the particular dispositions as you deem proper." In such circumstances it was perhaps unsurprising that Hooker did not know "whether I am standing on my head or feet," but if there were ever a time and place for this kind of status struggle, the Rappahannock in June 1863 was not it. When Hooker complained that he was being asked to do too much and asked to "be relieved from the position I occupy" it was as good as done.[23]

It was, therefore, the new commander of the Army of the Potomac, George C. Meade (formerly head of its 5th Corps) who faced Lee at Gettysburg in July 1863, less than a week after he had been appointed. It would be an understatement to say that Meade had to hit the ground running because when he took command, the Army of the Potomac was on the move, following Lee's movements up into Pennsylvania. By now, most of the troops and commanders on both sides were seasoned veterans who understood a battlefield and how to deploy on it. Some, such as Jeb Stuart, still favored the dramatic gesture, but Stuart's decision to ride around the Union army at the end of June, 1863 did Lee more harm than good, because at a crucial point in Lee's invasion of Pennsylvania he was left without adequate reconnaissance concerning the Army of the Potomac's movements. By the time Stuart found his army again, it was already the second day of Gettysburg, and his cavalry had little impact on it. Lee was unaware that by the time Meade took command of Union forces they were already north of the Potomac, and Stuart's absence kept him blind as he made his way toward Gettysburg. Even after Confederate troops, in search of shoes for their footsore forces, had been driven out of Gettysburg itself by Union cavalry on June 30, Lee still believed that the main body of the Army of the Potomac was many miles away. It was not.

When the Confederates returned to Gettysburg in greater force the next day—July 1—the initial skirmishing west of the town itself soon became a major engagement between Union cavalry (dismounted) under John Buford and Confederate troops under Harry Heth. As more troops were deployed, the Union's 1st Corps under John Reynolds fought with Buford to hold the Confederates off, but as the day progressed Union forces faltered and, when the Union's 11th Corps under Oliver Howard came in, they were repulsed by a strong Confederate assault. On the first day of the battle, the Confederates were undoubtedly in a better position: they had superior numbers, and the timing—unplanned—of reinforcements arriving at the scene worked in their favor. Toward the end of the first day's fighting, Richard Ewell's troops arrived and pushed the Union forces back to Cemetery Hill, but additional Union troops were arriving in force, and continued to do so over the night of July 1 to July 2. By the start of the second day of battle, both Lee and Meade had arrived on the field, and a more organized engagement opened between the two armies.

For two days, July 2 and 3, the Army of the Potomac and the Army of Northern Virginia battled over ground now familiar in its nomenclature if not its actual topography. The now famous "fish hook" of the Union line centered on Cemetery Hill, ran along Cemetery Ridge to the south and terminated at two rocky outcrops, Round Top and Little Round Top; to the east, the line ended in the woods at Culp's Hill. The Confederate line was arranged along Seminary Ridge, curved around through Gettysburg itself and wound around to face Cemetery Hill and Culp's Hill. The Confederacy was the more strung out of the two armies, and the Union, with more men, was actually covering less ground and was fighting on interior lines. This made the movement of Union forces more manageable but also restricted much of the fiercest fighting to the area between the Round Tops and Longstreet's forces—the Devil's Den, the Wheat Field, and the Peach Orchard—at the southernmost tip of the Union line, in its center—where George Pickett's division made its famous charge—opposite Meade's headquarters, and at the base of Cemetery Hill and Culp's Hill, where Ewell's attack came. To visualize the structure and main engagements of the battle, it is easiest to imagine a larger and looser Confederate fishhook some five miles (eight kilometers) in length parallel to the Union line. The main points of contest occurred from the southernmost end to about a third of the way up (Longstreet); at the center (Hill); and at the northeastern end (Ewell).

The arrangement of the opposing armies at Gettysburg was, for an unplanned battle, relatively ordered, but the engagements themselves were not. Lee had anticipated Longstreet attacking northward up the Emmitsburg Road that ran between the opposing armies toward the left of the Union line. Longstreet, however, discovered that Union general Dan Sickles had moved his troops out from the line toward the road and the Peach Orchard, in effect creating an exposed salient. This was not absolutely the smartest move Sickles could have made, but it paid off. Longstreet's attack became a full-on assault on the sides of Sickles's salient rather than a deft flanking maneuver, and Sickles's forces held out. Once the Union realized that it had left its southernmost end—at Little Round Top—exposed, the race was on to reach it, because it was an ideal position for artillery. The race was won by the Union, and the subsequent battle for Little Round Top, particularly Joshua Lawrence Chamberlain's famous bayonet charge down it to repulse the attacking Confederate troops became the stuff of legend.

The defining moment at Gettysburg came on the third day of the battle, when Lee ordered Pickett's division to attack the center of the Union line. Despite the fact that Longstreet had engaged his troops to the point of exhaustion against Sickles's forces the previous day (without making much headway), and Ewell had not succeeded in destroying the Union's left, Lee's decision was, he later wrote, predicated on "the belief that with proper concert of action, and with the increased support that the positions gained on the right would enable the artillery to render the assaulting columns, we should ultimately succeed, and it was accordingly determined to continue the attack." On the morning of the third day, Confederate artillery moved into position facing Cemetery Ridge, and the bombardment of the Union position began at 1:00 p.m. Half an hour into it, the artillery commander, Porter (E.P.) Alexander, advised Pickett that now was the best time to begin his attack. "For God's sake come quick," he urged. "Come quick or I cannot support you." Some of the Union guns had fallen silent, and it was assumed, or hoped, that the artillery barrage had done its work. The silence from the Union, however, was not what it seemed. Slowing their rate of fire to save ammunition, the Union forces still had some to spare when Pickett's assault began, but the Confederates did not. When Pickett's division began its assault on Cemetery Ridge on July 3 it had inadequate artillery support and was moving toward an enemy weakened, certainly, but not to the extent that Confederate forces believed.[24]

With a line extending over a mile, the Confederates began to move up what is, in fact, a gentle gradient toward the Union line, presenting a perfect target for, first, the Union artillery and, when they got closer—because they kept on coming regardless—for the rifled guns of the infantry, for whom the opportunity to replay Fredericksburg their way was suddenly, and amazingly, before them. Given the casualty rate, it is amazing that the Confederates did break through the Union line at "the Angle," but they did so only briefly, and veteran reserve troops waiting in the rear soon pushed them back by dint of some fairly brutal hand-to-hand fighting. This was, as it turned out, the physical "High Water Mark of the Confederacy." After that, it was all over. Lee waited for a time for a counterattack that never came, and then began to move his troops out of Pennsylvania. Shock and exuberance intermingled in Elisha Hunt Rhodes's reaction to Gettysburg. "Oh the dead and dying on this bloody field," he mourned but, the following day, he was ecstatic at the news that Lee had pulled back. "Was ever the Nation's Birthday celebrated in such a way before," he exclaimed, even though the news of Vicksburg's surrender did not reach the Army of the Potomac until the following day. Lee's retreat was recompense enough for Rhodes, who hoped that "Gettysburg will cure the Rebels of any desire to invade the North again."[25]

Why Lee had chosen to order such a suicidal frontal assault, given his experiences at Malvern Hill and at Fredericksburg, will doubtless continue to be the subject of detailed speculation among historians and psychoanalysts alike. The potential for a Confederate victory was certainly present at Gettysburg, and the generals who fought (and historians since) have devoted many hundreds of thousands of words to explaining why the Confederates did not win. From the perspective of the day, however, it was by no means obvious, for example, that Richard Ewell's troops, who succeeded only in pushing the Union back to a strong defensive position on Cemetery Hill at the end of the first day's fighting could have forestalled that move on the part of the Union. Lee had, after all, ordered Ewell to take the hill only "if practicable, but to avoid a general engagement until the arrival of the other divisions of the army," and Union troops were hardly likely to let Ewell get around them easily. The danger here is confusing an army that frequently lost with a losing army; the Army of the Potomac was a considerable force, but unlucky in leadership. At Gettysburg, it had better leadership. The signs were there, had Lee looked for them, that Malvern Hill might have been about to repeat itself as the Union troops began fixing their position on Cemetery Hill. From the perspective of the day itself, however, it is no mystery why Lee missed this: he believed the Confederate attack would succeed. Only in the context of what came later did Lee's optimism at Gettysburg become dangerous mismanagement on a grander scale than even the casualty list for that battle—the losses on each side exceeded 23,000—suggested. In any case, as historian Carol Reardon has highlighted, Gettysburg was as much a Union victory as a Confederate defeat. Lee's failure was not entirely self-inflicted; Pickett's division was not lost in a vacuum but rather, as he himself remarked, "the Union army had something to do with it." Even if Gettysburg was a Confederate defeat, on July 3, 1863 it was not yet *the* Confederate defeat. It only acquired that dubious honor in the light of events very far from Gettysburg, in Tennessee, in fact, when on the following day—Independence Day—Vicksburg finally surrendered to the forces of Ulysses S. Grant. The battle that came to define the war was fought in the East, but only parallel events in the West assured it its final stature and confirmed its place in history as the beginning of the end of the Confederacy.[26]

The Western Catalyst: Stones River and Vicksburg

As the Army of the Potomac and the Army of Northern Virginia battled it out at various points in the Eastern Theater in 1862 and 1863, the Army of the Cumberland, under William Rosecrans; the Army of Tennessee, under Ulysses S. Grant; and the Army of Tennessee, under Bragg were strung out across Tennessee and on the Mississippi: Bragg was in Murfreesboro; Rosecrans was at Nashville on the Cumberland River, and Grant still had his sights set on Vicksburg but was, as yet, nowhere near gaining that objective. Attacked by Confederate cavalry under Nathan Bedford Forrest and Earl Van Dorn, Grant's progress down the Mississippi Central Railroad line was faltering; in late December, he withdrew northward. Grant's planned assault on Vicksburg relied on the support of William T. Sherman, but he, too, was facing obstacles, and suffered a defeat north of Vicksburg, at Chickasaw Bluffs, at the end of December. By the end of 1862, for the Union at least, it was too much a case of 'all quiet on the Mississippi' although further inland Confederate raiders were keeping themselves warm in those winter months by rampaging up and down Kentucky and Tennessee and harassing the Union wherever they could—with a great deal of success. It was not, however, all over yet for the Western forces. Bragg may have been planning to settle in for the winter, but Rosecrans, only recently appointed in the wake of Don Carlos Buell's hesitation after Perryville, did not have that luxury. Lincoln expected action, and so at the end of December, Rosecrans had to oblige. Christmas Day 1862 was a flurry of activity as Rosecrans's troops made their final preparations to move south, with the intention of occupying East Tennessee and continuing on to Chattanooga. Moving out on the following day, they very soon encountered the enemy, at Murfreesboro, about thirty miles south of Nashville, lined up on the Northern banks of Stones River.[27]

Both Bragg and Rosecrans devised the same plan of attack at Stones River—an assault on their opponent's right—which made for an interesting situation when battle commenced. Unaware of this, on the eve of the first day of the battle, Rosecrans was in aggressive form. He commended his troops for their conduct so far, and urged them:

> Soldiers, the eyes of the whole nation are upon you; the very fate of the nation may be to hang on the issue of this day's battle ... Be cool! I need not ask you to be brave. Keep ranks. Do not throw away your fire. Fire slowly, deliberately; above all, fire low, and be always sure of your aim. Close steadily in upon the enemy, and, when you get within charging distance, rush on him with the bayonet. Do this, and the victory will certainly be yours.[28]

Rosecrans's injunction to fire low was standard advice for the time, as Civil War guns fired in a pronounced arc (as all guns do, but Civil War-era weaponry was far more extreme in this regard than modern). The advice to "fire low" covered most eventualities: moving targets, possibly inexperienced troops, and sights that may not have been perfectly calibrated. Not that the Union troops had much opportunity to implement Rosecrans's simple if brutal injunction, because the Confederates moved first, taking them by surprise. There was at least one of the Union's immediate opponents who would not have needed Rosecrans's advice on weaponry: William J. Hardee, commander of Bragg's II Corps, was the author of *Rifle and Light Infantry Tactics*, the standard reference work of the day. Hardee's divisions, together with those of Leonidas Polk went hard up against the Union forces under Alexander McCook at dawn on December 31. The Union right very quickly collapsed into its center, ultimately ending up battling a brutal defensive action, especially in the area of the Round Forest or "Hell's Half Acre" as it came to be known by Union Colonel William B. Hazen's men who fought there, at the northeastern edge of the battlefield. When the day's fighting ended at dusk neither side had a clear advantage, and no one felt like celebrating New Year's Eve.

As the new year dawned, only skirmishing took place between the two armies. The second day of the Battle of Stones River commenced on January 2, somewhat to Bragg's surprise, as he had assumed Rosecrans would withdraw. At first the battle went Bragg's way. His forces drove the Union off the high ground north of Murfreesboro and pursued them toward the river, to a crossing point at McFadden's Ford. There, unfortunately for Bragg, they encountered Union artillery that immediately opened fire as the Confederate charge appeared, causing massive casualties. By the day's end, Bragg withdrew through the town and Rosecrans did not follow. In some ways a stalemate, Stones River was an important encounter if only because it revealed the extent of the punishment the Union could take without breaking. For a relatively minor engagement fought over two days, the casualty rates at Stones River were appalling, with each side having 13,000 killed, wounded, or missing. Stones River, however, was more significant than its frequent dismissal as a tactical stalemate suggests. On the eve of the implementation of the Emancipation Proclamation and in the wake of the terrible defeat at Fredericksburg, the North needed Stones River, and it claimed it as a victory even though neither side, really, could assert that on January 3. It was with genuine relief that Lincoln replied to Rosecrans's telegram advising the President that the Union had held the field. "God bless you, and all with you!" Lincoln wrote back. "Please tender to all, and accept for yourself, the Nation's gratitude for yours, and their, skill, endurance, and dauntless courage." Lincoln had continuing cause to be grateful to Rosecrans. Many months later, after Gettysburg, after Vicksburg, after the dramatic—and successful— attack by the Union's most famous black regiment, the Massachusetts 54th, on Fort Wagner, when Union fortunes, in short, looked far brighter than they had in January, Lincoln's thoughts turned to Stones River again. "I can never forget," he told Rosecrans, that "you gave us a hard earned victory which, had there been a defeat instead, the nation could scarcely have lived over. Neither can I forget the check you so opportunely gave to a dangerous sentiment which was spreading in the North." After all, as Rosecrans had said on December 31, 1862, the fate of the nation did hang, in large part, on the outcome of that bloody stalemate in Tennessee in January 1863.[29]

Enemy Country: the Siege of Vicksburg

By the time Lincoln wrote to Rosecrans in August 1863, the war in the West had taken a dramatic turn for the better as far as the Union was concerned. At the start of the year, Grant, now in overall command of the Department of the Tennessee, had abandoned his attempt to reach Vicksburg overland, and had decided to take charge of the operations on the Mississippi himself, with a view to approaching the city from the north and west. As the Union command consolidated, however, the Confederates were all over the place, fielding three armies and three commanders with no clear command structure to guide their movements or ensure that they worked together. Joe Johnston had been placed in overall charge of the Confederacy's Western front, comprising the armies of Bragg (Army of Tennessee); John C. Pemberton (Army of Mississippi, in charge of the defenses at Vicksburg); and Theophilus C. Holmes and, later, Kirby Smith (Army of the Trans-Mississippi). He had his work cut out for him, and no effective means of getting the various armies to pull together because he had no authority beyond the Mississippi itself. Compounding Johnston's problems was the fact that, by 1863, the Confederacy simply could not protect both of its defensive lines: the Tennessee line and the Vicksburg line (which protected the Mississippi). But Richmond wanted Johnston to give priority to both. Left to make the decision himself, Johnston chose Tennessee, but in fact all went quiet in that part of the front in the aftermath of Stones River. Bragg was busy fretting about his leadership abilities and Rosecrans was giving him no opportunity to put them to the test again. In the East, Hooker was in the process of building up the Army of the Potomac and Lee was doing the same for the Army of Northern Virginia. In the opening months of 1863, the only active general—the only one actually getting a campaign underway—was Ulysses S. Grant.

Grant's new chosen route to Vicksburg had more than its share of obstacles, not least the very strong Confederate defenses against any assault from either the north or west. From his position at Milliken's Bend, about fifteen miles from Vicksburg, Grant devoted his attentions to probing these defenses, looking for a way in or around them, a process that worried Washington as much as it confounded Pemberton; neither knew what Grant was up to, and the suspicion was that he did not know himself. In fact, Grant knew what he was doing very well; as he later recalled, it was from that point that "the real work of the campaign and siege of Vicksburg ... began." By the end of March he had formulated a plan. It was a complex operation in which his troops would march south, down the west bank of the river, while the Union navy came north past Vicksburg's batteries to meet him at a point where his troops could be moved to the east bank; the assault on the city would, in the end, come from the south and the East.[30]

As Grant's troops, under John McClernand, traveled south in April, Admiral Porter made it past Vicksburg's guns, taking heavy fire but surviving to make the rendezvous with Grant at Bruinsburg at the end of the month. When this part of the plan was accomplished, Grant breathed a sigh "of relief scarcely ever equaled since." All had not gone as anticipated. The planned crossing site at Grand Gulf had to be abandoned in the face of Confederate opposition, causing the loss of several vessels. The landing at Bruinsburg was a hastily chosen alternative, but at least Grant was there. As he recalled the day in his memoirs, he observed:

> Vicksburg was not yet taken it is true ... I was now in the enemy's country, with a vast river and the stronghold of Vicksburg between me and my base of supplies. But I was on dry ground on the same side of the river with the enemy. All the campaigns, labours, hardships and exposures from the month of December previous to this

time that had been made and endured, were for the accomplishment of this one object.[31]

As Grant was disembarking at Bruinsburg, William T. Sherman was keeping Pemberton distracted north of Vicksburg, while the Union cavalry, under Benjamin Grierson kept him busy by destroying railroads, bridges, and supplies across the state of Mississippi before they joined up with Union general Nathaniel Prentiss Banks's forces at Baton Rouge at the start of May. At that point, Grant did something unusual. It was a move that would have repercussions not just for his assault on Vicksburg but also for the future course of the war.

In December of 1862, when Grant was bogged down on the Northern approach to Vicksburg, his supply base at Holly Springs, Mississippi had been destroyed by Confederate cavalry under Van Dorn. The locals, unsurprisingly, expressed "intense joy," Grant recalled, over this misfortune, and asked him how he was feeding his army. He advised them that his troops had simply foraged, and acquired enough food from the surrounding countryside. "Countenances soon changed," Grant wryly observed, but the unhelpful residents of Oxford, Mississippi were not the only ones to learn a lesson that day. Grant realized that he need not be encumbered by the familiar long train of supply wagons on which Civil War armies relied but which slowed them considerably, that he could—because he had to—operate without these, that the land through which he passed would support his troops, and free them to operate more flexibly, more efficiently and, in 1864, to devastating effect at the very heart of the rebellion. Of course troops had foraged before, but it was not official policy in a conflict in which the rules of engagement were circumscribed by the Constitution, a Constitution that still held, Lincoln believed, in the South. Both sides—Lee as much as any northern general—forbade the harassment of citizens or their property. Naturally these rules were frequently ignored by angry or hungry troops, but foraging was not official policy, not until the spring of 1863. Then, Grant took the first steps toward this new style of campaigning when he struck out inland, taking his army but leaving his supply line behind, looking not just for a way into Vicksburg, but a new approach to winning the war in a campaign later described by Lincoln as "one of the most brilliant in the world." When Pemberton moved to cut Grant's supply line, it was only to discover that there was none. By that time, however, Grant was past him and heading for Jackson, Mississippi; he was also past Joe Johnston's forces, which had retreated when faced with this wholly unexpected and rapid Union movement. Grant, barely pausing, turned toward Vicksburg itself. By mid-May, Grant's troops had traveled over two hundred miles, defeated several Confederate divisions who had crossed their path and had reached their objective: Vicksburg. The siege had begun.[32]

The fall of Vicksburg, Grant believed, was a just matter of time. "As long as we could hold our position," Grant explained, "the enemy was limited in supplies of food, men and munitions of war to what they had on hand. These could not last always." Pemberton initially held Grant off from seizing the city, but its inhabitants were then forced to endure a slow process of starvation and suffering as the summer temperatures rose in Tennessee. When the surrender came, as it did on July 4, 1863, it seemed an omen for the Union cause, but the choice of day was probably no coincidence. Writing afterward, Pemberton claimed that he had selected that day because "I believed that upon that day I should obtain better terms." Given Grant's reputation—summed up in his 'unconditional surrender' nickname—there are grounds for doubting Pemberton's explanation, and certainly Grant did not believe it. He believed that Pemberton's decision was made to avoid an assault on the city on that most significant national holiday. Neither, in any case, knew yet of the outcome of Gettysburg. It was the deadly combination of that battle with the fall of Vicksburg that made July 1863 so critical to the future direction and eventual outcome of the war—not just in tactical terms, but also in terms of personnel. After Vicksburg, Grant was promoted to major general in the regular army, and in a short time took overall command of the Union's Western armies. A few months later, in March 1864, he was appointed lieutenant general (general in chief) of the Union armies, and the Grant/Lee confrontation that was the final and most devastating year of the war began. In the West, Lincoln had finally found the general whom Lee did not understand, the general who might win the war for the Union. "The fate of the Confederacy was sealed when Vicksburg fell," Grant recalled, although there remained a lot of "hard fighting to be done ... and many precious lives were to be sacrificed ... the *morale* was with the supporters of the Union ever after." On this last point, memory failed Grant. In the summer of 1863, the morale of the North was far from high. Paradoxically, the Union's twin triumphs in the summer of 1863 were met by a war-weariness in the North more threatening to its cause than any defeat had so far produced. But in the South, defeat created, if anything, a renewed determination to continue fighting for a cause that, many Southerners still firmly believed, was not yet lost.[33]

CHAPTER 7

The People Embodied

The truth is, sir, that party support is not the kind of support necessary to sustain the country through a long, expensive, and bloody
contest … The cause, to be successful, must be upheld by other sentiments, and higher motives. It must draw to itself the sober approba-
tion of the great mass of the people. It must enlist, not their temporary
or party feelings, but their steady patriotism, and their constant zeal.
Unlike the old nations of Europe, there are in this country no dregs
of population, fit only to supply the constant waste of war, and out of
which an army can be raised, for hire, at any time, and for any purpose. Armies of any magnitude can here be nothing but the people
embodied—and if the object be one for which the people will not
embody, there can be no armies.

—Daniel Webster, January 14, 1814[1]

Daniel Webster, speaking during the War of 1812, was describing a very
different war but not a very different nation from that of Civil War America half a century later, one committed to republican government derived
from the very will of the people themselves. His point, therefore, remains
apposite to our understanding of a Civil War fought, not by a regular army,
but by mainly volunteer troops. The Civil War was, as Lincoln described
it, "a People's contest," in all senses of the term; the people fought it, and
neither the Union nor the Confederacy could afford to ignore the role that
their people played in sustaining, challenging, and directing it. As the initial enthusiasm to join the colors paled in the actual face of battle, both the

Union and the Confederacy were faced with the problem of how to maintain their armies and persuade the noncombatant populations on each side that their respective causes were worth fighting for. For the Confederacy, the cause remained fairly constant. For the Union, the war changed its meaning and purpose in January 1863, and not everyone was comfortable with the idea that a war to save the Union had become a war to free the slaves, not least the loyal slaveholders of the Border States and within the South itself. For this category of slaveholder, Lincoln's Emancipation Proclamation, however hedged by qualifications that protected slavery within the Union, was clearly a promissory note for a very different future for the nation—if the Union won the war. For white slaveholding Southerners, the proclamation was confirmation of what they had long suspected; the "Black Republicans," as they pejoratively termed the party, were seeking to remove their slave "property" from them; for nonslaveholders, the proclamation did not threaten their property, but it did threaten what their lives were predicated on—in social, economic, political, and racial terms. For black southerners, the proclamation did not instantly usher in the day of jubilee, but it did give official weight to a process already underway, the collapse of the peculiar institution of the South and all its attendant restrictions, traditions, and assumptions. Some African Americans, North and South, reacted to Lincoln's announcement with enthusiasm, others with cynicism, but no one could seriously imagine that the nation, if saved as a single nation, would much resemble its antebellum structure as far as race relations were concerned.[2]

For the Union, the controversy over emancipation carried a double danger; not only might it dissuade individuals from supporting the war, it might backfire on the republican administration. Emancipation could survive as an ideal (and become a nationwide legal reality) only if those who advocated it remained in power. The continuance of the two-party system in the North throughout the war was, in this sense at least, a double-edged sword: on the one hand, it muffled any hostility to Lincoln from within his own party on this, as on other issues; on the other hand, it ensured a continuous political challenge to the Lincoln administration from the Democrats, some of whom—and George B. McClellan was among them—were openly hostile to emancipation, and, by 1863, were advocating a negotiated peace with the Confederacy. It was just this kind of "dangerous sentiment" that Lincoln believed Rosecrans had helped to counteract at Stones River, but one battle did not a moral victory make nor, in 1864, an election secure.

The outcome of the war, English journalist Edward Dicey understood, "will be decided, not by any single defeat or victory, but by the relative power of the two combatants ... The one doubt is, whether the South may not be superior to the North in resolution, in readiness to make sacrifices, and in unity of action. If it is so, the chances are in favor of the South; but there is no proof yet that this is the case." Nor was there much evidence by late 1862 that the North was united: quite the opposite. From the announcement of the preliminary emancipation in the wake of Antietam until the end of the war, the North had to address itself to the growing problem of maintaining Union morale in the political and social arenas.[3]

The Union disaster at Fredericksburg came only weeks after the important mid-term elections in the North, which, prior to election day, had been closely watched because the balance and composition of the House of Representatives would be decided. The Republicans knew that war-weariness was taking its toll, and no one was surprised—though they were concerned—by the marked swing away from the Republicans. To New York Republican George Templeton Strong it was already quite clear in late October "that unless we gain decisive success before the November election, this state will range itself against the Administration. If it does, a dishonorable peace and permanent disunion are not unlikely." The Republicans did not do that badly in 1862, but for Strong they did badly enough. When the returns were announced on November 4, 1862, he described it as "a national calamity." It was, he despaired, "like a great, sweeping revolution of public sentiment, like a general abandonment of the loyal, generous spirit of patriotism that broke out so nobly and unexpectedly in April, 1861." Strong was not yet totally disheartened. He saw the swing toward the Democrats as the natural response of a population "suffering from the necessary evils of war and from irritation at our slow progress." He still feared, however, that the Northern populace was on the verge of committing "national suicide." But no victory came to buoy up the Republicans. Instead, the following month saw the Union disaster at Fredericksburg and Sherman's defeat at Chickasaw Bluffs, and there were no signs of matters improving on the military front. When the outcome of Fredericksburg became known, radicals in Lincoln's cabinet lost patience and demanded a more overt abolitionist policy be pursued, oblivious to the fact that such a policy was itself only feasible with military victory to back it up. Not that Lincoln faced a continuous and persistent challenge from a "radical bloc" as such; his party comprised too many disparate personalities, too often at odds with each other, to ever cohere around a single issue, even one as apparently clear-cut as emancipation. In December 1862, however, the challenge was serious enough to require all Lincoln's political skill to defuse the threat, which had a great deal more to do with the clashing ambitions of Secretary of State William H. Seward and Secretary of the Treasury Samuel P. Chase than with the war, which was being prosecuted about as vigorously as the armies could manage, just not yet very successfully.[4]

Copperheads and Conscripts

For Lincoln, the personality issues within his cabinet were less problematic than the challenges posed by the opposition party. The Democrats, of course, were themselves in an awkward situation, being politically bound to offer an alternative to the Republicans but having to tread a very careful line between loyal opposition and outright treason during the war. At first, there was little disagreement between the parties on the war aims of the North. The democratic slogan (attributed to radical Ohio Peace Democrat Clement Laird Vallandigham): "The Constitution as it is, and the Union as it was," seemed to reflect the sentiments of a broad constituency in the North, although the *Chicago Tribune* was less than impressed when Lincoln used the phrase "Union as it was." The paper sniffed, "such a Union loyal men do not want to see restored ... They prefer a Union *as it ought to be*." In the wake of Antietam, of course, everything changed, and the more ambitious, almost overtly abolitionist, aims of the Republican administration clashed with the Democratic view of what the war was about. In its attack on Southern "property," the Emancipation Proclamation seemed a dangerous deviation from the Constitutional strictures that, many Democrats believed, protected the American republican experiment. What was worse, however, was Lincoln's assumption of an increasing range of "war powers" at the start of 1863, notably the militia draft and, above all, the suspension of *habeas corpus*. In this last issue, the Democrats saw a genuine threat to civil liberties. "Conservatism is our only chance of safety," some Democrats argued. "Conservatism of our own American institutions ... Liberty of speech, liberty of the press, liberty of the person." Unfortunately, to that list many Democrats might have added "liberty to own slaves," because for them it was all too often a case of "the Constitution as it is, the Union as it was," and the slaves precisely where they were—in bondage and in the South. Theirs was not a vision of a racially harmonious republic of equals; it was informed by a fear that the North would be suddenly inundated with freed slaves. Democratic propaganda played on Northern racial antagonisms quite blatantly throughout the war and most intensively in the buildup to the election of 1864 when George B. McClellan stood against Lincoln. In 1863, however, it was Vallandigham who was giving Lincoln the most trouble.[5]

Vallandigham, a Democrat representative from Ohio, skirted close to, and eventually overstepped, that thin line between loyal opposition and treason. Known as a Copperhead—the pejorative title, referring to a venomous snake, given to Peace Democrats by the newspapers at the time—Vallandigham was consistently opposed to Lincoln's prosecution of the war, and he was apoplectic when emancipation entered the equation. In

January 1863, he rose in the House to condemn the republican administration in general, and Lincoln in particular:

> Defeat, debt, taxation, sepulchres, these are your trophies ... The war for the Union is, in your hands, a most bloody and costly failure ... War for the Union was abandoned; war for the negro openly begun ... With what success? Let the dead at Fredericksburg and Vicksburg answer.[6]

Vallandigham was the extreme voice of the Peace Democrat faction within the party, but too extreme for the party as a whole. Failing in his bid for the Ohio governorship in 1862, he later engineered his own arrest by deliberately flouting Ambrose Burnside's orders of April 1863 that sought to curb "the habit of declaring sympathy for the enemy" by delivering a speech in Columbus, Ohio, very much along the lines of that he had delivered in the House a few months before. Arrested in early May, Vallandigham was eventually—through Lincoln's intervention—spared a jail sentence, but he was banished to the Confederacy, to Tennessee. This assured him the support of those horrified by such apparently high-handed treatment of a civilian by military authorities, and he did eventually return to Ohio to help—or perhaps not—McClellan in his bid for the presidency in 1864. Yet although Vallandigham achieved notoriety for an opposition to Lincoln that went beyond the bounds of loyal opposition (and possibly reason), his was not a lone voice crying in the wilderness. After 1863, for example, the *Chicago Times* altered what had been its fairly moderate line on Lincoln and denounced the Emancipation Proclamation as "the most wicked, atrocious, and revolting deed recorded in the annals of civilization," and a month later the paper was advocating peace at any price.[7]

Union supporters were swift to respond to such attacks. One of their most tangible methods was the establishment of "Union" or "Loyal Leagues" across the North, whose purpose was to stimulate support for the Union cause via meetings, rallies, and publications, all aimed at shoring up the morale of the North at an especially bleak juncture in the war. In the first few months of 1863, a range of such associations sprang into existence, literally within days of each other. February saw the creation of the Loyal Publication Society in Philadelphia; it was soon joined by the Union League of Philadelphia, and in the following month the New England Loyal Publication Society and the Union Club of Boston were founded. These were not all of a piece: the Leagues were the more popular forums for expressions of loyalty to the Union; the Clubs, the elite face, and interpretation of patriotism. Boston's Union Club was so named to distinguish it from the various Union Leagues, but the differences were not always obvious from the names alone. The first club was the Union League Club of Philadelphia, founded at the end of 1862. New York's Union League Club retained its name despite the existence of other more populist loyal leagues across the state. These elite clubs, historian Melinda Lawson has shown, were determined to create "a Union as it ought to be," and their ambitions were more multi-layered and complex that the encouragement of simple patriotic flag-waving among the Northern populace. Devoted "to transforming Americans' contractual notions of patriotism and nation into unquestioning, even organic, ideas of loyalty and national identity," such clubs sought not just to create a new nationalism but also to channel it, partly toward their own social and economic ends. George Templeton Strong, one of the founders of the New York club, saw it as an association of

> influential New Yorkians who desire to sustain government against Southern rebellion and Northern sectionalism, and strengthen Northern loyalty to the nation, and stimulate property-holders and educated men to assert their right to a voice in the conduct of public affairs, national, state, and municipal, and do a little something toward suppressing the filthy horde of professed politicians that is now living on us and draining our national life by parasitical suction.

Strong was encouraged by the club's inaugural on May 12—he approved of the "nice people" who attended—but he was concerned that it did not meet with universal admiration among the wealthy and well connected of the city. This was unsurprising. The club may have set itself the task of inculcating a Northern "people embodied," but it was certainly not interested in embodying too many of them too closely. As the election year of 1864 drew nearer, the Lincoln administration needed more than the good will of a few visionary, but elitist, individuals to stay in power and to win the war.[8]

The whole issue of loyalty to the Union cause did, of course, have a partisan bias that condemned the Democrats to an awkward political limbo in which they were damned as traitors if they opposed the Republican prosecution of the war too vehemently, and damned if they did not offer an alternative to it. The available options between peace and war, however, left them little room in which to maneuver. In the election of 1864, the Democrats were frequently portrayed as the party of "Dixie, Davis, and the devil," but that did not automatically place the Republicans on the side of the angels, nor assure Lincoln the wholehearted support of his own party. Much depended on events on the battlefield. When the war was going badly, the political landscape of the North was similarly churned up by the shot and shell of the debate over loyalty and disloyalty to the Union, the future of the nation, and the very meaning of America's republican experiment itself. Paradoxically, however, the intensity of this debate, and the fact that it had to be entered into time and again during the course of the war, provided Lincoln with both the imperative and the opportunity to reiterate his understanding of the Union's purpose. In defending his suspension of *habeas corpus*, especially as it related to the Vallandigham case, Lincoln combined careful legal argument with more emotional justification for the actions he was taking. "Ours is a case of Rebellion," he insisted, "a clear, flagrant, and gigantic case of Rebellion," and the Constitution allowed for the suspension of *habeas corpus* "when in cases of Rebellion or Invasion, the public Safety may require it." There was a practical side to the situation, too. "Must I shoot a simple-minded soldier boy who deserts," Lincoln asked, "while I must not touch a hair of a wiley agitator who induces him to desert? ... I think that in such a case, to silence the agitator and save the boy, is not only constitutional but, withal, a great mercy." By transforming the political into the personal, Lincoln sent a clear message about the value and importance of the individual soldier to the Union war effort—at a time when the war was going badly and the need for conscription had, for the first time, been mooted. His message was a crucial prop to flagging morale. Lincoln never allowed either his detractors or the Northern populace to lose sight of the main object of the war: to restore the Union and eradicate slavery. And neither did he ever allow them to underestimate what that would involve as the war moved toward its bloodiest and darkest period.[9]

For Jefferson Davis and the Confederacy, the war was going well in late 1862. Behind the scenes in Richmond, however, the political situation was unstable. Although Confederate one-party politics was apparently straightforward in comparison to the battles taking place in the Northern political arena, the very lack of opposition proved detrimental to the South's cause. Lincoln possessed sufficient political skill to maneuver around the political challenges he faced; Jefferson Davis, on the other hand, was presented with a whole different ball game, one for which his political skill proved wholly insufficient. States' rights did not sink the Confederacy on its own, but whereas the structure of the two-party system in the North directed political opposition through party channels, toward party ends, and could be both charted and—up to a point—controlled, in the South it was more of a free-for-all. This proved frustrating for Davis and problematic for the Confederate cause. Lincoln knew he could take nothing for granted as far as the Union war effort was concerned. In the absence of any overt official challenge to the Confederate cause, Jefferson Davis perhaps too readily did assume that all would be well, despite all evidence to the contrary.

Many of the organizational difficulties that the Confederate armies experienced were reflected in the Confederate political arena. Each fed off and reflected the other to a great extent. Confederate military telegrams and dispatches were too often concerned not merely with the minutiae of detail that are essential to the smooth functioning of armies in the field, but with questions of honor, of hierarchy, and of the writer's place in the great Confederate military machine. From the perspective of a Confederate soldier in the ranks, the South's "generals were scrambling for 'Who ranked,'" while the "private soldier fought and starved and died for naught." Joe Johnston could not get the armies of the West to work in concert; no more could Jefferson Davis get his various state governors, let alone his cabinet members, to keep their respective eyes on the main prize—an independent Confederate nation. Instead, Davis faced a situation where individual attentions were too readily diverted elsewhere, to the detriment of the cause. In part, this derived from the antebellum political environment, where for so long Southern politicians had functioned as if they were fighting a rearguard action against persistent attacks on the peculiar institution. Certainly, they were adept at the political maneuver, but not at using it toward especially constructive ends. When it became necessary to pull together, many of them pulled each other apart instead. The problems facing the Confederate government are highlighted by the lack of consistency in Davis's cabinet; he went through, for example, no fewer than five secretaries of war between 1861 and 1865. The last of these, John C. Breckinridge, the 1860 presidential candidate and former vice president of the United States (the only vice president, to date, to have taken up arms against the nation) was appointed in 1865. By that point, Breckinridge realized, even if Davis did not, that the war was over. A debilitating rate of staff turnover, combined with a lack of common purpose, was a feature of the Confederate Congress and at the state level; too often, the Confederacy's leaders wrangled while the cities burned, the people were displaced, and the armies routed. The violence that Northern politicians had seen but a glimpse of in the National Congress after 1856 was sometimes given freer expression in the Confederate Assembly. On one occasion in 1863, senate members had to duck out of the way of a projectile (an inkstand) which Benjamin Hill hurled, with some accuracy, at William Lowndes Yancey, and which would have been followed by a chair had colleagues not intervened. This was Southern honor turned in on itself, an understandable response to the tension of the times, but unhelpful nonetheless.[10]

While interpersonal rivalry in the Confederate Congress was unpleasant enough, local loyalties proved a far more damaging phenomenon for the South. In part a simple reflection of the decentralized nature of Southern society, the too vigorous defense of individual state's rights nevertheless proved a formidable barrier to the successful prosecution of the war from Richmond. Davis found that he could not rely on the unquestioning support of state governors such as Zebulon B. Vance of North Carolina or Joseph E. Brown of Georgia, whose undoubted—in the case of Vance passionate—enthusiasm for the Confederate cause existed alongside an equal, if not greater, enthusiasm for the well-being of their respective states. The issue that drove the biggest wedge between Richmond and these states was conscription, a far from minor matter since the war's outset, and a very serious one by the end of 1863. As in the North, the initial enthusiasm for war paled soon enough and, despite the efforts of some state governors to rally their populations to the cause in April 1862, the Confederacy was forced to introduce conscription. This act of necessity transformed both the war and the popular attitude toward it. Popular reluctance to meet Richmond's call for troops was evident in politicians' increasingly desperate pleas. "The enemy is raising an immense force to overwhelm us if possible," Virginia's governor proclaimed:

> We must meet him with adequate resistance. While the Confederate Government is exerting its energy for the general defense it becomes Virginia not only to contribute her quota for that object, but to put forth her special exertion to free her population and their homes from the desecration of an unscrupulous foe. I therefore once more call upon the people promptly to obey the orders which have been issued.[11]

The pressure was intensified by the increasing absentee rates in the Confederate armies. This was not always indicative of permanent desertion but it was damaging enough, nonetheless. "It is with deep mortification," Confederate General D. H. Hill advised Secretary of War George Randolph in May, "that I report that several thousand soldiers and many individuals with commissions have fled to Richmond under pretext of sickness. They have even thrown away their arms that their flight might not be impeded." Joe Johnston was in no doubt as to the cause of this. As he advised Lee, the "troops, in addition to the lax discipline of volunteers, are partially discontented at the conscription act and demoralized by their recent elections."[12]

Writing years after the war, Sam Watkins recalled the impact that conscription had on many Confederate soldiers who had been looking forward to returning home in the aftermath of Shiloh, satisfied that they "had done their duty faithfully and well … War had become a reality," he realized, and "they were tired of it." Conscription changed everything, however:

> From this time on till the end of the war, a soldier was simply a machine, a conscript. It was mighty rough on rebels. We cursed the war, we cursed Bragg, we cursed the Southern Confederacy. All our pride and valor had gone, and we were sick of war and the Southern confederacy.

Not the least of the soldiers' grievances was the fact that conscription was not equally applied. As would be the case in the North, too, there were ways to avoid it. In the South, the possession of twenty or more slaves was enough to keep a man out of the army, but failing that, he could provide a substitute, at a price. That "gave us the blues," Sam Watkins remembered, "and there was raised the howl of 'rich man's war, poor man's fight.' The glory of the war, the glory of the South, the glory and the pride of our volunteers had no charms for the conscript." In the end, the Confederate government closed the substitution loophole. The twenty-slave exemption, however, remained, as did a twenty-pupil exemption, which led to a sudden flurry of schools appearing across the South as men discovered a sudden fascination with the education of children and rushed into the teaching profession. As the war progressed, and losses mounted, the Confederate conscription system came under so much strain it became virtually ineffective, and by the very end, in a final ironic twist given what that the original volunteers had signed up for, the Confederate government had began to make plans to arm the South's slaves in a last-ditch, desperate attempt to stave off defeat.[13]

The North did not have the states' rights philosophy to contend with, but conscription, when it was introduced in March 1863, was equally unwelcome among some sections of the North. In the army itself, reactions were more positive. William Sherman declared the Union draft to be

> the first real step toward war ... if Mr. Lincoln will now use the power thus conferred, ignore popular clamor, and do as right as he can, we may at last have an army somewhat approximating the vast undertaking which was begun in utter blind, wilful ignorance of the difficulties and dangers that we were forced to encounter.[14]

There was, however, a fair amount of clamor over the issue of conscription in the North, and not just from the Copperheads. Desertion, absenteeism, illness, and rising casualty rates forced the Union toward conscription, too, albeit a year later than the Confederacy. The Union arranged its draft rather differently from the Confederacy. In April 1862, Confederate law had simply stipulated that all men between eighteen and thirty-five years of age were automatically part of the Confederate army; in September the range widened to cover those up to forty-five; and by the start of 1864 it had widened again to cover all those between seventeen and fifty. Union legislation, by contrast, enrolled all men between twenty and forty-five into local militia units, thereby making them available for national service if called up. In the North, then, it came down to a matter of luck and money. The actual drafting process was left to individual states, each of which was assigned a quota to fill. The numbers drafted therefore depended on the number of volunteers from that state: more volunteers, fewer draftees, and vice versa. States, keen to avoid the stigma of having to draft men to the Union cause, raised bounties and offered other inducements to persuade men to sign up, but, as in the South, the system leaked like the proverbial sieve. Not only was "bounty jumping" a fairly widespread problem—whereby an individual would enlist, receive the bounty, desert, enlist elsewhere and so on—but substitutions could be bought in the Union, too. For $300 a man might be commuted from serving, or he could furnish a substitute for himself, either directly or through a broker, at the going market rate, which of course went up with every week that passed. In the Union, as in the Confederacy, the accusation that the Civil War was a rich man's war but a poor man's fight was an understandable one, although many very wealthy men fought, and died, on each side. In addition, only some 6 percent of Union forces were raised through the draft, which proved to be the least effective way to raise recruits for the armies. African Americans were exempt from the draft on the grounds that they were not citizens, but the raising of African-American regiments produced almost as many men as the first Union draft did in 1863. This made the eruption of violence in New York that summer—a mere ten days after the Union's victory at Gettysburg—violence that became predominantly a race riot—all the more bitter for the African-American community.[15]

The Draft Riots of July 1863 showed the North at its worst. Although the riots revealed a widespread unease with the implications of the draft and the Emancipation Proclamation, they derived much more from broader class, racial, and ethnic tensions in New York, tensions that the draft crystallized, but certainly did not cause. Above all, they revealed the dangerous strain of racial hatred that lay not far from the surface of the North's most prominent city, even as its soldiers were committed to risking their lives for the eradication of slavery in the Southern states. At first, as George Templeton Strong recorded on July 13, "there was nothing to indicate serious trouble," but that soon changed and the rioters became "masters of the situation and of the city." The New York mob aimed their anger initially at government buildings, but soon moved on to attack the African-American community, at first by cruelly ransacking and setting fire to the Colored Orphan Asylum on Fifth Avenue. Although the rioters held back from actually assaulting the children themselves, many African Americans were brutally attacked in the four days of rioting that took place, as were whites known for working with blacks, or supporting the abolitionist cause. The eleven lynchings of black men such as William Jones and Abraham Franklin were only the most horrific part of an outpouring of racial hatred that convinced many foreign onlookers, and Americans themselves, that the North could never be committed to racial equality, whatever the long-term prognosis for Lincoln's Emancipation Proclamation might suggest. Indeed, the grisly symbolism of the murder and mutilation of black bodies evinced a dehumanizing—for both victim and perpetrator—impulse so visceral and basic in its violence as to defy rational explanation. Such violence cannot readily be ascribed to the draft alone; it was more of a primeval scream of fear in the face of a very different battle, one that had little to do with the war raging in the South. Strong was shocked by, and especially ashamed of, the violence perpetrated against African Americans: "the outrages they have suffered during this week are less excusable—are founded on worse pretext and less provocation—than St. Bartholomew's or the Jew-hunting of the Middle Ages," he exclaimed. "This is a nice town to call itself a centre of civilization!" It was little wonder, therefore, that many African Americans in the North felt less than enthusiastic about the Union cause.[16]

What They Fought for

Behind the issue of emancipation lay a fundamental question that exercised Lincoln, Union troops, the Confederacy, bemused foreign powers of the day, and many historians since: what was the North fighting for? Lincoln had frequent opportunity to set out his understanding of Northern war aims, but he was fully aware that his views were not universal and that emancipation had complicated the matter. In any civil war, he observed, "there always is a main question; but in this case that question is a perplexing compound—Union and Slavery." Consequently, Lincoln realized it was

> a question not of two sides merely, but of at least four sides, even among those who are for the Union, saying nothing of those who are against it. Thus, those who are for the Union *with*, but not *without* slavery—those for it *without*, but not *with*—those for it *with* or *without*, but prefer it *with*—and those for it *with* or *without*, but prefer it *without*.[17]

"It is easy," Lincoln observed, "to conceive that all these shades of opinion, and even more, may be sincerely entertained," and within the Union army itself that was certainly the case. Like his Confederate counterpart, the Union soldier was an individual who fought for a variety of reasons—cause, comrades, country, God, freedom—but at the very least had some motive for fighting beyond the pecuniary. For some, volunteering was preferable to conscription, for reasons of pride as well as money, although many soldiers were driven to the battlefield by financial considerations even if higher motives induced them to remain there. Union bounties were relatively high, and for farmers or unskilled workers these offered a quick, if risky, means to security for themselves and their families. Others, no doubt, craved excitement and experiences beyond the perhaps dull domesticity that they were used to. For many, North and

South, peer-group pressure was a decisive factor: although Southern soldiers called it "honor" more often than their Northern counterparts did,
their meanings were the same.[18]

Plenty of Union troops were initially enthused by the war, and for some
the enthusiasm persisted. Robert Gould Shaw, the white colonel of the Massachusetts 54th who died during the assault of Fort Wagner in July 1863,
acknowledged that the war had made him "look at the stars and stripes
with new emotions," a sentiment echoed by Union soldier William Haines
Lytle who declared "God help the old flag! In no nobler or holier cause can
a man's life be offered up." For Lytle, the Civil War was "the great war for
Union and Liberty," but it was not the same for all. "Volunteering has about
ceased. I don't hear of any volunteers for the Old Regiments," one father
advised his son in August 1862. Despite "as much as seventy five dollars
offered over and above the ninety dollars Bounty, to any who would volunteer ... they did not receive a man, it is thought now we will have to stand a
Draft of near 40,000 men to fill up the Old Regiments in the State." In one
extreme case, at least, almost an entire regiment, or rather, what was left
of it, decided that it had seen more than enough after the first major battle.
The 1st Minnesota Volunteers suffered horrific casualties at First Bull Run,
far in excess of any other federal regiment that day. Afterward, some of the
survivors attempted to have their enlistments nullified via *United States
v. Colonel Gorman*. The soldiers lost, but their actions revealed that, even
at the start of the war, unbridled enthusiasm was not the sole response to
secession, that some, indeed, had little desire to fight at all.[19]

As the war dragged on, even previously enthusiastic soldiers lost
momentum. "I don't know why it is so, but I don't feel as *patriotic* as I did,"
Union soldier George Tillotson told his wife:

Maybe, because I have lost confidence in most of the head officers,
for I don't believe they *want* the war to end, and further, in the way
things are going it will never end, by fighting. I am not alone in this
opinion, for it is generally, and openly, expressed throughout the
ranks, except, by some of the new troops, who have not forgotten
the old home idea, that the South is a going to be scared to death
by a presidential proclamation or a call for a few hundred thousand
more men, but by the time they have *fully* seen the *elephant*, the idea
of *scare*, like that of *starve*, and nothing to *fight with*, with, will "*play
out*." I had rather see the Union divided rather than have the war last
the remainder of my term of enlistment.[20]

Tillotson was not opposed to the raising of African-American regiments;
that played no part in his growing sense of frustration, but even he, a committed Union soldier writing before the terrible defeat at Fredericksburg,

was beginning to wonder what it was all for. Fredericksburg, obviously, did little to boost his confidence. "It is not the *rebels* at the North that trouble *us*," he told his wife, "but the rebels here … You at the North, read our Northern papers, and believe them probably when they say the rebel army is nothing but a mob, without discipline, patriotism, or hope of success but *we here know* that they *lie*, and we have good reason for believing that the rebels are as *patriotic* and *concientious* in the *justness* of their cause and are as *determined* to *defend* it as the *patriots* of the *Revolution* were *theirs*." The Confederacy, Tillotson realized, would "fight to the last," and he harbored no illusions about the bloodshed that lay ahead if the Union was ever to be victorious.[21]

Among those less than enthusiastic about the war by 1863 were many African Americans, who were, at best, ambivalent about the opportunity suddenly being offered to fight and possibly die in the name of a Union that had, until that point, forcibly rejected them. Even when the Lincoln administration did open the door to the raising of black regiments, the process was a haphazard one, and it revealed the extent of the difficulty surrounding the issue, especially in the loyal slave states. In Kentucky there was pressure not to raise black regiments at all, on the grounds that it would "revolutionize the State and do infinite and inconceivable harm." Ambrose Burnside concurred; he believed that the raising of black regiments in Kentucky "would not add materially to our strength, and … would cause much trouble." Where African-American regiments *were* raised, it was not on an equal footing with white ones. In June 1863, David Tod, the governor of Ohio, wrote to advise Secretary of War Stanton that the organization of one of the African-American regiments in the state was "progressing handsomely. They are expecting the usual pay and bounty allowed white soldiers," he observed. "Will they get it?" Almost inevitably, the answer was no, and many black soldiers reacted angrily to the news that they would not receive the same remuneration as white soldiers. As James Henry Gooding of the Massachusetts 54th pointed out, "colored men generally, as a class, have nothing to depend upon but their daily labor; so, consequently, when they leave their labors and take up arms in defense of their country, their homes are left destitute of those little necessities which their families must enjoy as well as those of white men." Another black soldier thought it "strange … that we do not receive the same pay and rations as the white soldiers. Do we not fill the same ranks? Do we not cover the same space of ground? Do we not take up the same length of ground in a grave-yard that others do? The ball does not miss the black man and strike the white, nor the white and strike the black."[22]

Such blatant discrimination did little for morale, as Thomas Freeman of the Massachusetts 54th described:

there is men here in the regiment that have been in Enlisted 13 Months and have never received one cent But there bounty ... we are not Soldiers but Labourers working for Uncle Sam for nothing but our board and clothes ... we never can be Elevated in this country while such rascality is Performed Slavery with all its horrors can not Equalise this for it is nothing but work from morning till night Building Batteries Hauling Guns Cleaning Bricks clearing up land for other Regiments to settle on ... now do you call this Equality if so God help such Equality.[23]

One of Freeman's fellow volunteers, George Stephens, concurred. "After we have endured a slavery of two hundred and fifty years we are to pay for the privilege to fight and die to enable the North to conquer the South," he exclaimed, "what an idea! To pay for the privilege to fight for that tardy and at best doubtful freedom vouchsafed to us by the government. For what," Stephens raged, "are we to be grateful?"[24]

When Lincoln described the Civil War as a "People's contest" his audience's assumption would be that the phrase referred to the idea of "we, the people of the United States" as invoked in the preamble to the Constitution generally, and to the body politic specifically, but that body excluded blacks, and it excluded women. The Union war effort, by late 1863, needed the people to be embodied in the way Daniel Webster had indicated in 1814 more than ever, but when the idea of the "people" itself proved so exclusionary, how was the war effort to be understood by those on the margins of the nation? African-American spokesmen like Stephens saw the Civil War very much as a war for emancipation long before the Northern public came round to that view, not that it ever fully did. For him the matter was a simple one, and he stated it starkly: "Our destiny is united with that of the country—with its triumph we rise, with its defeat we fall." Frederick Douglass was of the same opinion, and he reminded his predominantly white audience that "the destiny of the colored American, however this mighty war shall terminate, is the destiny of America." This message was reiterated time and again in the course of the conflict. James Henry Gooding declared that the "American people, as a nation, knew not what they were fighting for" until Lincoln announced the Emancipation Proclamation, and in the aftermath of the New York City draft riots, Stephens seized the opportunity to remind white Americans that "even while your mobfiends upheld the assassin knife, and brandished the incendiary torch over the heads of our wives and children and to burn their homes, we were doing our utmost to sustain the honor of our country's flag, to perpetuate, if possible, those civil, social, and political liberties, they, who so malignantly hate us, have so fully enjoyed." That African Americans were not only showing dedication to the nation's ideals but articulating these ideals more clearly than many whites in the midst of the Civil War was a discomfiting fact for those who understood America only in white terms. Although many African Americans fought for the Union on the grounds that, as Stephens put it, "Who would be free, themselves must strike the blow," in fact, the assumption that by so doing they would "win by their valor the esteem of all loyal men and women" proved to be overly optimistic, in the long-term at least. Although black and white troops fought side by side in the last years of the war, white America took a long time to rise to the challenge offered by African-American soldiers: to make their actions fit the words of those ideals that the Union purported to be fighting for.[25]

The Female Face of Battle

If the Civil War was seen by some as a "white man's war," it was even more popularly understood as a "brothers' war"—sisters, mothers, wives, and daughters need not apply. African-American patriotism, even in the face of extreme provocation, proved equal to the task of sustaining the Union war effort and was, however grudgingly, acknowledged, if not fully appreciated. Women's patriotism, by—contrast, was either ignored altogether or, worse, taken for granted. That women might be patriotic in their own right, rather than in support of, or through the agency of, the most proximate male was simply not a familiar concept to Civil War America. As Henry Ward Beecher—father of Harriet Beecher Stowe—forcibly exclaimed, "manhood,—*manhood*,—MANHOOD ... has made this nation." The traditional perspective on women in the war has tended to support Beecher's assertion, juxtaposing the masculine environment of the battlefield against the feminine sphere of the home front; until recently, historians have assumed that there was little crossover between the two. Of course, it was never that clear-cut. Quite how the government of either side was expected to raise, equip, and retain regiments in the field without the full cooperation of half the population is something of a mystery, but hardly one unique to the American Civil War. Historian Linda Kerber notes that the popular image of the Revolutionary era, too, is one in which "women's work has been treated as service to men," despite the fact that "patriot and tory forces could recruit men not because cheerful women waved them off to war, but because those same women bravely stayed on alone, keeping family farms and mills in operation, fending off squatters, and protecting the family property by their heavy labor, often at grave physical risk."[26]

Civil War women, similarly, took a larger role in the mid-nineteenth century conflict than the limited one allotted to them by the conventions of the day. Although excluded from the political sphere, Union wife Mattie

Blanchard recognized that although politics "never much interested me before … they seem to matter now." Her sentiments found an echo on the Confederate side in Louisa McCord's observation that "even a Woman has the right to wake up when revolution is afoot, and when our Sons (even boys) throw aside their Greek, Latin and mathematics to practice rifles and study military tactics." "We all have views now, men, women and little boys," asserted Jane Stewart Woolsey. Many women expressed their wish to take a more active role, even though they knew that they were the wrong gender to do so. Louisa May Alcott famously wrote "I long to be a man; but as I can't fight, I will content myself with working for those who can," and her sentiments were repeated across both the Union and the Confederacy.[27]

Most women, of course, did not act on their expressed desire to be a man by donning male attire and joining a regiment, but some women did precisely that. Exactly how many did so remains difficult to state conclusively. Civil War nurse Mary Ashton Livermore, who worked for the Western Sanitary Commission, noted that a figure of about four hundred was circulated at the time, but she estimated that to be on the low side. Historian Elizabeth Leonard proposes a figure of between five hundred and a thousand. To put this in some perspective: some twenty thousand white women served the Union as nurses or general support staff, many thousands of black women fulfilled the same function in the army camps and behind the lines, and over three thousand nurses were official employees—as opposed to voluntary workers—of the Union army. Statistically, therefore, women's combatant experience was neither extensive relative to women's work for the Union in other capacities nor militarily decisive, but it did nevertheless exist. This fact was more apparent to contemporaries, for obvious reasons, than it was to later generations, for less obvious ones.[28]

So long as a woman's motives were deemed acceptable—that is, patriotic and/or romantic as opposed to financial—few expressed much concern. Historian LeeAnn Whites even highlights a couple of—admittedly rare—examples of Confederate women warriors whose behavior attracted esteem rather than censure. It was understandably a cause for comment when a comrade one had assumed to be male turned out to be female. Usually such discoveries were made when the soldier was wounded and required closer medical attention than the military's medical entrance examination had provided. Death in combat, on the other hand, given the exigencies of the time and the need for hasty burial, would not necessarily reveal the gender of a soldier. Such evidence would be buried with her, in most cases, although among the dead at Gettysburg the remains of one "female (private) in rebel uniform" were noted. On some occasions, female soldiers announced their gender in the most conclusive way possible: by going into labor. This, again for obvious reasons, caused the most comment. One Union soldier in the 107th Pennsylvania wrote to his wife to tell her that one of the corporals had given birth. "What use have we for women," he enquired, "if soldiers in the army can give birth to children?" This was not the sole such occurrence in the Army of the Potomac in the winter of 1862–63. In the Confederate ranks, too, at least one "father" gave birth to a "bouncing boy." Such events were sources of both amazement and gossip, but not always. Union general William Rosecrans exhibited a markedly restrained—but recognizably military—sensibility when he expressed no more than his "flagrant outrage" on the occasion of one of his sergeants giving birth, an act which, he observed, "is in violation of all military law and of the army regulations."[29]

The experiences of individual women who fought in the war have been painstakingly resurrected and recreated by historians in recent years. The Civil War activities of such women as Sarah Emma Edmonds, Jennie Hodgers, and Sarah Rosetta Wakeman were, by and large, the same as those of men in the Civil War armies. So long as women were not discovered to be women, their camp and combat experience did not differ from that of their male colleagues. So long as their gender remained undetected, they offered no overt challenge to nineteenth-century gender norms so that differentiating "their" Civil War from that of their male counterparts is impossible. It is only with hindsight, and the knowledge that they were women, that their experiences take on a more challenging slant for the historian. For those women who may have fought as women, the situation was, and is, rather different. Women were a visible part of camp life, but they were not expected to be part of the battlefield experience, and their presence at the front was not always welcome. Much depended on what role the woman played. Camp followers—by which is frequently meant prostitutes—were a reality near any Civil War army; escaped slaves looking for employment were common, especially in the Army of the Potomac; nurses were obviously present in reasonably large numbers, and usually quite close to—and sometimes on—the battlefield; and, of course, women also lived in the towns, cities, and plantations that the armies passed near, through or— in cases such as Fredericksburg—fought in. In the aftermath of a major battle, female civilians as well as male arrived to search for their relatives, or to help care for the wounded, or to look for trophies of war to take home. The Civil War soldier was not wholly deprived of female company, but the problems began when that company was a soldier's wife. Civil War armies had enough trouble keeping men in the field; reminders from home in the form of letters were incentive enough, in some cases, for a soldier to contemplate leaving, even if he did not do so. The physical presence of a wife was another matter, as George Tillotson observed. "It seems to be a bad thing for soldiers to fetch their wives to war," he commented, "since both of our company that done so have deserted." Female soldiers did not usually have wives to worry about, so that was not a danger to the regiment concerned. However, as women in the male world of the nineteenth-century military, their position was an awkward one.[30]

Some women straddled the gender divide, either physically—by adopting both male and female personas—or by their actions. The dramatic exploits of Confederate female spies such as Rose Greenbow or Belle Boyd, however, hardly represented the norm for Southern women any more than those of Harriet Tubman, escaped slave, leading African-American spokeswoman, nurse, and Union spy did for Northern women. Loreta Velazquez, the Cuban woman who was both female spy and male soldier, Harry T. Buford, fascinates those searching for challenges to conventional norms. Her autobiographical story, with all its ambiguities, may reveal an individual capable of transcending both gender and race—and the identities predicated on these apparent fixtures—but she remains as elusive a figure to historians as she must have been to her contemporaries. Velazquez's reminiscences may have been exaggerated for dramatic effect, and may have owed more to the romantic sensibilities of the age than to the reality of the woman's combat experience. In 1879, the British writer Ellen Clayton observed with some skepticism that if "we may believe Transatlantic newspapers, the Civil War in America was more productive of female warriors than almost any conflict since the days of the Amazon." In some cases, her skepticism was justified. Mary Livermore, for example, singled out the actions of two women, Nadine Turchin and Annie Etheridge, of the 19th Illinois and 3rd Michigan, respectively, in her "story of the war." Turchin, according to Livermore, took over command of the regiment when her husband, John, fell ill. She "was not one whit behind her husband in courage or military skill," Livermore asserted, and "led the troops into action, facing the hottest fire, and fought bravely at their head," before dutifully returning "to the care of the sick and wounded" once her husband had recovered. "Throughout the whole fours years of the war," Livermore also reported, Annie Etheridge "was found in the field, often in the thickest of the fight, always inspiring the men to deeds of valor, always respected for her correctness of life." Whether the reality matched Livermore's recollections, however, is less certain. Annie Etheridge had accompanied her husband, James, to war, but when he deserted she did not, becoming instead the "daughter" of the 3rd Michigan, transferring, along with the troops, to the 5th Michigan later in the war. Her presence on the battlefield is not in doubt, but she was there in a nursing capacity, not as a combatant. As a daughter of the regiment, Etheridge encouraged the soldiers and helped to maintain their morale for the fight, as well as providing nursing, cooking, and other general support duties, in recognition of which she was accorded the unprecedented honor of being buried in Arlington National Cemetery.[31]

The case of Nadine Turchin is a more complex one, if only because it highlights the mixed experiences of Civil War women in relation to the armies. Turchin was a woman who challenged the gender norms of her place and time, in particular the fate of women, in her words, "to be everything but intelligent beings authorized to enjoy the rights guaranteed to *ALL!* by the American constitution: freedom, equality, and the pursuit of happiness." Historian Elizabeth Leonard has probed Turchin's story and concluded that it was extremely improbable that she ever assumed overall command of the 19th Illinois (8th Brigade). Evidence from Turchin's diary suggests that she did not, although it is the case that when her husband, John Basil Turchin (Russian émigré Ivan Vasilovitch Turchinoff, veteran of the Crimea) was court-martialed in 1862, one of the charges was that he had violated military orders and permitted his wife to be on the battlefield. This was a minor offense compared to the main accusation he faced, that he had allowed his troops to plunder Athens, Alabama in May 1862. In the course of the assault in Athens, Turchin's troops had, it was reported, not only destroyed and removed private property but had threatened one woman with sufficient aggression as to cause a miscarriage that resulted in her death, assaulted several slaves, and violently raped a young African-American girl. Found guilty of neglecting his duty to the detriment of military discipline, Turchin received a dishonorable discharge, but was later—after pressure from his wife—reinstated by Lincoln, and served the Union until 1864. Alongside Livermore's portrayal—possibly exaggerated—of Nadine Turchin, the resourceful and brave Civil War warrior-wife, were the individual stories of women for whom the Civil War brought no opportunity to assert their agency and storm the barricades of the gender divide. Instead, the war brought them destruction, misery, and death. For every Harry Buford or Nadine Turchin, it must be remembered that there were countless women whose encounters with the armies included the type of violence and violation experienced by the residents of Athens, Alabama in May 1862. In the modern historiography, both of the African American and the women's Civil War, no one is allowed to be a victim: in the actual history many, unfortunately, were exactly that.[32]

Beyond the Battlefield

Writing in *Harper's New Monthly Magazine* in 1864, when the Civil War was in its fourth and bloodiest year, Belle Spencer recalled her reaction to her husband's departure for the battlefield over two years previously:

I had seen much before, and borne a great deal, yet it seemed but little comparatively when I came to take leave of my husband … True, I had expected this, was prepared for it in a measure; yet a strange and overpowering sense of my position came over me that I had not felt before, when I stood by the window to catch a last glimpse of a beloved form. He was standing upon the deck of a large boat, with hundreds of others around him; yet I seemed to see him only, his sad face turned to me in mute farewell as the bell clanged and the ponderous vessel swept slowly out into the stream, and turned her prow toward the mouth of the Tennessee.[33]

Belle Spencer was not the type of woman content to weep at home, however. As she herself put it, "with three hospitals in sight of my window," the direction her war-work would take was obvious, and indeed commenced soon after her husband left. Initially welcomed by the doctor to whom she applied, her horror at the conditions she encountered soon set her at odds with the hospital authorities. Undeterred, she struggled to bring comfort to the men she encountered, noting their "rapid improvement" under her care. Her response to the news that her husband had been killed at Shiloh was to set off in search of him—or his body. Finding him wounded but alive, she took him home to nurse him back to health, in time, she noted, "for the Fall campaign."[34]

Belle Spencer's story is, in many ways, typical of our image of women during the Civil War. Its publication some two years after the events described in it also suggests that it was published with the specific intention of reinforcing morale on the Northern home front in an important election year. It did not dwell on Belle Spencer's difficulties with the hospital authorities, although it did hint that these did not abate. Instead, the central thrust of the article was the wife's willingness to support her husband and, through him, the Union cause. At the article's conclusion, it is made clear that Belle has nursed her husband back to health, not for herself, but for the benefit of the Union army. In her selfless devotion to the cause, in her work to support it through nursing the troops, and especially in her willingness to give up the man she loved, Belle Spencer was the ideal of the Union soldier's wife. Although critical of male authority within the medical environment, she never directly challenged it; although devastated by the risk of personal loss, she never flinched from it.

Beyond the battlefield, in the gendered world of the nineteenth century, the prescribed norms for a woman were inflexible in terms of the kind of support she was expected to provide for her country in times of war. Despite the need for the people to pull together in a time of war, men frequently resisted any attempts at power sharing, and insisted on a rigid separation of responsibilities on both home and battlefront. Belle Spencer did not seek to adopt male dress or usurp the male combatant role. Yet nurses like her, and those who served in a more official capacity under Dorothea "Dragon" Dix, the superintendent of female nurses in the Union, faced opposition to their attempts to take a more active role in the support of the soldiers. Dix achieved her nickname, in part, by strictly refusing to employ any woman under thirty-five who was not plain in appearance, but she was only attempting to forestall the kind of criticism that women who left the confines of the domestic sphere were prone to at that time. Women who abandoned the home in favor of the battlefront not only entered a violent world deemed unsuitable to their natures, but in the process relinquished the security and protection that the home environment provided, and were therefore prey to both suspicion and censure. Even in a time of war—perhaps especially in a time of war—women were expected to be all things to all men: independent yet dependent, strong yet weak. It was a circle women could not hope to square.

For Southern women as for Northern, the male medical world proved as unwelcoming as it was disorganized. Confederate nurse Mary Johnstone's report to Alexander H. Stephens, the vice president of the Confederacy, dismissed most surgeons as "drunken political appointees unfit to run hospitals." The patients themselves sometimes proved less than grateful, too. Frederick Law Olmsted, the general secretary of the United States Sanitary Commission (USSC), the largest civilian volunteer organization during the war, recognized that there were problems connected to the presence of female nurses. "There is not a woman in all the hospitals of Washington," he noted in the autumn of 1861, "who is not constantly watched for evidences of favor to individuals and for grounds of scandalous suspicion and talked of & probably talked to, with a double meaning." He was particularly dismayed by the experience of one woman who "had come, bringing her child with her, to look after a husband who had been near dying, the behavior of the men to her," he complained, "& their talk about her, was as if she had been a convicted strumpet."[35]

If nurses encountered personal hostility, female doctors faced official censure. One of the most famous examples is that of Mary Edwards Walker, a doctor who sought to aid the Union—and eventually did so, serving with the Army of the Cumberland, although not at the same rate of pay or with the same level of prestige accorded male surgeons at the time. Initially, her medical training was disparaged both by a medical profession who did not consider it appropriate for a woman to practice medicine and by a military machine that seemed equally determined to reject much-needed medical aid if the individual offering it were not a man. Even on the subject of nursing care, men like Olmsted thought that women could not—and should not—be left to their own devices. Although the Sanitary Commission itself grew out of a female-led organization—the New York-based Women's Central Association of Relief for the Sick and Wounded of the Army—once it had been established, women's organizational role was assumed by men The "care of the sick & wounded in war is not a feminine business," Olmsted asserted. "It must have a masculine discipline, or as a system ... it must have a bad tendency." But, in distinguishing between feminine and masculine in the way he did, Olmsted's intention was not to disparage women's work for the Union. In the course of the Union's ill-fated Peninsula Campaign, when the wounded were transported in railroad cars "dead and alive together, in the same close box, many with awful wounds festering and alive with maggots," Olmsted sang the praises of such "noble women" as Eliza Newton Woolsey Howland, her sister Georgeanna Muir Woolsey, and Amy Morris Bradley, three of the most prominent nursing superintendents working for the Sanitary Commission, who "were always ready and eager, and almost always the first, to press into these places of Horror" to provide nursing care.[36]

The fact was, for the Sanitary Commission much more was at stake than simply the care of the wounded. What it sought to inculcate was nothing less than "a new consciousness, a new national culture"; and female benevolence and supposedly disinterested patriotism was a means to that end. The Sanitary Commission was happy enough to channel women's philanthropic impulses—and, in the case of nurses, even ensure that they received remuneration for their endeavors—but resolute in its belief that a rigorous "masculine discipline" was necessary overall if aid to the troops was to be delivered effectively. Consequently, as the war dragged on, the Sanitary Commission increasingly conflicted with women who did not share its view of how their benevolence should be directed or what forms it should take. By challenging the centralizing and nationalizing tendencies of the USSC via a range of local initiatives—notably the Sanitary Fairs that took place in towns across the North—Northern women challenged the power of men to direct the ways in which the people should be embodied in the pursuit of a united nation, thereby establishing some of the ground for the post-war female activism that began in the later nineteenth century.[37]

Confederate women did not have an ambitious civilian relief agency to contend with, and in some respects they fared better than their Union counterparts. They, at least achieved official recognition with the 1862 Hospital Bill, which openly acknowledged their presence in, and work for, the state. But Southern women were unwilling to volunteer in the numbers required—which in many ways paralleled the problems Robert E. Lee encountered with military recruitment. This was a source of frustration to dedicated southern nurses such as Kate Cumming who perceived such reluctance as a major factor in Confederate defeat. As disillusion with the Confederate cause set in, Confederate women began to construct for themselves, a narrative of resilience in the face of defeat. Some historians suggest that this may have even contributed to that defeat. George Rable recounts the story of a dead-letter bag in a post office in Richmond, in which almost all the letters from wives to their soldier husbands advised desertion. Although this story is doubtless anecdotal, Rable reminds us that "women *had* contributed to the decline of Confederate military power," and that from the outset they had "both sustained and undermined the war effort." Although the Confederate cause was not lost through the action—or inaction—of its women, for them, as for many white male Southerners, a stronger commitment to the cause was produced in the war's final stages than at its midpoint. If the victories of Fredericksburg and Chancellorsville produced overconfidence, the defeat at Gettysburg stiffened resolve across the South. It has been argued that by the time Sherman marched back from the sea through the Carolinas in February 1865, Confederate women were more fully behind the Confederacy than ever. As far as the war effort was concerned, this was a case of too little too late. For the post-war period, however, the female resilience in the face of defeat narrative proved fundamental to the development of that controversial phenomenon, Confederate nationalism.[38]

By mid-1863, defeat—or the prospect of defeat—unified the white South more successfully than any victory yet had or would be likely to do. Whether such a thing as Southern nationalism existed prior to the war will continue to be the subject of debate, but it is worth noting that no such political or social entity as "The South" seceded from the Union in 1861. A piecemeal conglomeration of Southern states stormed (or in some cases, sidled) out of the Union in 1860–61; by 1864–65, however, there was "a Confederacy" to surrender at Appomattox. Except on paper, this Confederacy was not created in the legislative chambers of the South, but on the battlefields and home front of the South at war, and it was not primarily created by its politicians, but by the people of the South, male and female, although not—and herein lay its unavoidable weakness—black and white. The nationalism that emerged during the war, on both sides, helped prolong that conflict; indeed, the war would have been impossible to sustain without that nationalism. The citizen armies of Europe had, at the turn of the nineteenth century, revealed but a glimpse of what war could be once national sentiment had been created and invoked. "Popular emotions," military historian Russell Weigley once observed, "rallied in defense of the national destiny could not so abruptly be turned off." So it proved for both sides by the final year of the war, but for the Confederacy, in particular, these public emotions explain the determination to continue fighting even when it became obvious that the cause was probably lost. The hope of European recognition had not yet faded by late 1863, but it did seem more like a dream than ever; the armies were depleted; and resources were running out. Yet through the determination of its armies and the support of its women, the South still had a few last stands to make before the end finally came.[39]

CHAPTER **8**

"Lee's Miserables"

I would banish all minor questions and assert the broad doctrine, that as a nation the United States has the right, and also the physical power, to penetrate to every part of the national domain, and that we will do it; that we will do it in our own time, and in our own way ... that we will remove every obstacle—if need be, take every life, every acre of land, every particle of property ... that we will not cease until the end is attained.

—William T. Sherman to Henry Halleck, September 17, 1863[1]

For Union general William T. Sherman (still with the Army of the Tennessee in July 1863) the fall of Vicksburg and the capitulation of Port Hudson represented "as pretty a page in the history of war and of our country as ever you could ask my name to be identified with." Port Hudson in Louisiana had been the last Confederate defense of the river, and when it fell, the Mississippi was opened to the Union advance. In Lincoln's famous phrase, "The Father of Waters again goes unvexed to the sea." When Lincoln made that pronouncement, he took the opportunity to highlight the role that African-American troops had taken at Port Hudson. "The job was a great national one," he observed, "and let none be banned who bore an honorable part in it." From the perspective of the summer of 1863, Lincoln believed that peace did "not seem so distant as it did" previously, but he warned against complacency and against any assumption "of a speedy final triumph." The Union had the means to win the war; conscription and the raising of black regiments had strengthened its armies—although not quite in the way Sherman had wished—and it was now well positioned via the Mississippi to strike at the heart of the Confederacy.[2]

As summer gave way to autumn, however, it became clear that the Confederacy's heart was still beating strongly, at least in the West. Devastated by Lee's defeat at Gettysburg, by Grant's victory at Vicksburg, and by the fall of Port Hudson, Richmond had finally—and possibly too late—come to realize the importance of the Western Theater. Gettysburg may have stiffened Southern civilian morale in the longer term, but the Southern armies' immediate response to Lee's failure to invade Pennsylvania was a negative one. Recalling the events of 1863, the Confederate General Daniel H. Hill mused on opportunities lost in the decision to accord the Western Theater second place to Lee's assault on the Union in the East, and on the fatal outcome of that decision:

> Vicksburg and Port Hudson had fallen, and Federal gun-boats were now plying up and down the Mississippi, cutting our communications between the east and west. The Confederacy was cut in two, and the South could readily be beaten in detail by the concentration of Federal forces, first on one side of the Mississippi and then on the other ... The drums that beat for the advance into Pennsylvania seemed to many of us to be beating the funeral march of the dead Confederacy.[3]

As the generals grimly contemplated the Confederacy's next move, many soldiers in the Army of Northern Virginia simply left their regiments and drifted home. In the West, in the autumn of 1863, however, there was still some hope. In Tennessee the last major front remained, but since Confederate general Braxton Bragg's withdrawal following Stones River/Murfreesboro, things had gone so quiet there that Tennessee was all but forgotten. Bragg was playing a defensive waiting game. He was able to do so, in part, because of the frequent forays of John Hunt Morgan's cavalry that ranged through Ohio and Indiana. But Hunt Morgan's cavalry was captured in July after one of their raids took them too far into enemy territory across the Ohio River. By then, Union General William Rosecrans had finally run out of reasons to delay an advance any longer, and had begun to move against Bragg and the Army of Tennessee, pushing the Confederates back toward Chattanooga on the Tennessee River.

Chickamauga and Chattanooga

Chattanooga, on the border of Georgia, was a critical target for the Union because it provided an entrance into that state as well as a route through the surrounding Appalachian Mountains, a route that would enable the Union to seize control of East Tennessee, the Unionist part of the state that had been cut off from army support. Plans were already in place to raise a National Guard of East Tennessee in order to aid the Union advance, and arms for this purpose had been provided. First, however, the Union had to gain control of Chattanooga. Set in a natural depression between the mountainous landscape to the north, Lookout Mountain to the South, and Missionary Ridge on the east, Chattanooga was not an easy target. As Union general Ambrose Burnside approached East Tennessee from Kentucky through the Cumberland Gap, Rosecrans moved his troops across the Tennessee River with the intention of advancing directly on Chattanooga. In the face of this advance, Bragg initially retreated from the town, moving toward Lafayette in Georgia, with Rosecrans in pursuit. The tables could have been swiftly turned, however, because Rosecrans's troops were spread out over too wide a distance—three corps with some twenty miles between them—to support each other were Bragg to attack any single corps. This was, in fact, Bragg's intention but, unable to get his own army to act in any coordinated fashion, his plan failed to come off. The end result was that Rosecrans managed to pull his troops together so that, by mid-September, the Army of the Cumberland faced the Army of Tennessee some twelve miles to the south of Chattanooga itself, on the banks of Chickamauga Creek in Georgia. For once, the Confederates were fielding a (slightly) larger army than the Union: some 66,000 to the Union's 58,000. Reinforcements for the Army of Tennessee had been sent from all over the South, most notably from the Army of Northern Virginia, from which James Longstreet's veteran corps had been selected to come to reinforce Bragg's army.[4]

As the opposing armies prepared for battle, D. H. Hill's thoughts turned to the past, to the first time he had met his commander, Braxton Bragg just before the Mexican War of 1846–48 when he, together with George H. Thomas and John F. Reynolds had been Bragg's lieutenants. Two of the four men, Reynolds and Thomas, had gone with the Union, two with the Confederacy. Only Thomas—"the strongest and most pronounced Southerner of the four," Hill recalled—stood opposite him now; Reynolds was already dead, killed by a sharpshooter at Gettysburg. "It was a strange casting of lots," Hill reminisced, "that three messmates ... should meet under such changed circumstances at Chickamauga." Hill was also worried about his commander, finding him "silent and reserved ... gloomy and despondent" and aged beyond his years. With a degree of understatement, Hill recorded that Bragg's "relations with his next in command [General Polk] and some others of his subordinates were known not to be pleasant." This, Hill ascribed to Bragg's too frequent retreats, which "had alienated the rank and file from him." In fact, Bragg's subordinates were, frankly, insubordinate, and were pushing Richmond for his removal. Bragg knew all of this, which did not make for a happy or confident general, let alone one who could effect a concerted plan of attack. On the eve of the battle, Hill drew an unfavorable comparison between the "want of information at General Bragg's headquarters" and the "minute knowledge General Lee always had of every operation in his front ... I was most painfully impressed," he stated, possibly with more hindsight than foresight, "with the feeling that it was to be a hap-hazard campaign on our part." So it proved, but Hill was writing about the "great battle in the West" well after the event itself, when he and his former messmates were, once again, on the same side.[5]

Bragg attacked the Union with precipitate haste on September 19— before Longstreet's troops had all arrived. When, on the first day of the battle, Union troops met the famed Nathan Bedford Forrest's cavalry (dismounted), it was only an introduction to a series of determined, but inconclusive, assaults that, together, made for a day of heavy fighting—and heavier losses. For both sides there was a general lack of coordination along their lines. In the afternoon of that first day, a Union infantry retreat was turned around by John Basil Turchin, now back in the Union army and a brigadier general (his actions at Athens, Alabama the previous year all but forgotten—except, of course, by the residents of that unfortunate town). Instead of a retreat, he led his troops in a charge against the Confederate line. Looking back on such confusion, Hill thought again about the differences between Bragg and Lee. Of Bragg he wrote:

> He seems to have had no well-organized system of independent scouts, such as Lee had, and such as proved of inestimable service to the Germans in the Franco-Prussian war. For information in regard to the enemy, apparently he trusted alone to his very efficient cavalry. But the Federal cavalry moved with infantry supports, which could not be brushed aside by our cavalry. So General Bragg only learned that he was encircled by foes, without knowing who they were, what was their strength, and what were their plans. His enemy had a great advantage over him in this respect.[6]

Even with such an advantage, however, the Army of the Cumberland faltered at Chickamauga. Burnside decided to strengthen the Union's left flank, which was a sensible move as that was where the Confederates attacked the following day, although without any obvious sense of urgency. Indeed, for a Civil War battle, the second day at Chickamauga got off to a very slow and late mid-morning start. Bragg attacked in oblique order (from right to left along the line) and his forces initially engaged Thomas's troops. Toward midday, Thomas requested additional reinforcements, not realizing that the troops he requested were at that point in the main line of the Union battle and unavailable. Confusion over who was where and doing what, combined with a muddle over orders, resulted in a gap appearing in the Union line—a gap that Longstreet, preparing to attack the Union center, did not hesitate to leap into, thereby dividing Rosecrans's forces in a devastating and, for once, successful frontal assault. Union troops panicked but—what was worse—so did their commander. Longstreet's bold attack was enough to drive Rosecrans himself from the field, leaving George Thomas, the "most pronounced Southerner" (who was, thankfully, on the Union side that day), to hold Horseshoe Ridge on the Union left against successive, but ultimately futile—for both sides—Confederate assaults throughout the afternoon. It was a feat that earned Thomas the nickname "Rock of Chickamauga." But it was not enough to save the battle for the Union. As so often in Civil War engagements, the victorious side failed to pursue panic-stricken and fleeing troops. This time, the Union troops were, with Rosecrans, heading straight back to Chattanooga. It being "after one o'clock" on a "hot and dry and dusty day," Longstreet later recalled, he decided to have his lunch instead.[7]

The outcome of the two-day Battle of Chickamauga, the largest engagement in the Western Theater and one of the bloodiest of the war, was a Confederate victory, but it was not the decisive one that the South needed, despite the presence of reinforcements from the Army of Northern Virginia. The fallout from Chickamauga was, perhaps inevitably, messy for both sides. In terms of casualties, it was a devastating battle to be fought for such an inconclusive victory. The Confederacy lost nearly 18,500 men. The Union had 16,000 troops that were killed, wounded, or missing. Many were taken prisoner. Foreign observers were appalled. One French newspaper reported that the "Americans are fighting on a military system inaugurated by the Kilkenny cats. The two armies meet and fight and slaughter each other with the utmost fury. Then they … reorganize for another general massacre. Positively, the war will end when the last man is killed." Some of the South's officers were equally appalled at the outcome. Bragg, according to Leonidas Polk, had "allowed the fruits of the great but sanguinary victory to pass from him by the most criminal incapacity … By that victory, and its heavy expenditure of the life-blood of the Confederacy," he fumed to Jefferson Davis, "we bought and paid for the whole State of Tennessee." In his memoirs, Longstreet, too, looked back on Chickamauga as a turning point. "In my judgment," he asserted, "our last opportunity was lost when we failed to follow the success at Chickamauga, and capture or disperse the Union army." At the time, Bragg was sufficiently unnerved by the criticism to call upon Jefferson Davis, who dutifully visited Bragg and his army in person. But, after hearing everyone's version of events (a process as lengthy as it must have been both embarrassing and tedious), Davis left matters as they were. Longstreet, one of Bragg's strongest critics, was sent to attack Knoxville, but Davis was unwilling to do what really needed to be done: replace Braxton Bragg. So, in mid-October 1863, Bragg was still in charge of the Army of Tennessee, the Union army was holed up in Chattanooga, and another painful waiting game began.[8]

Chickamauga did little for the reputations of either Bragg or Rosecrans. Although the spirits of Union troops remained high, the morale of Confederate troops suffered from the indecision of and infighting within, the high command. Many years later, Sam Watkins still remembered the horrors of that particular battle, made more poignant in his memory by the Confederacy's eventual defeat:

> All around us everywhere were the dead and wounded, lying scattered over the ground, and in many places piled in heaps. Many a heart-rending scene did I witness upon this battlefield of Chickamauga. Our men died the death of heroes. I sometimes think that surely our brave men have not died in vain. It is true, our cause is lost, but a people who loved those brave and noble heroes should ever cherish their memory as men who died for them. I shed a tear over their memory. They gave their all to their country.[9]

In the battle's immediate aftermath, both armies suffered. In the city itself, the Union troops endured a grueling few weeks of near-starvation while matters were not that much better, nor food any more plentiful, for the Confederates besieging them. Desertions increased as men, driven by frustration and hunger, gave up on the Confederate cause. "In all the history of the war," Sam Watkins recalled, "I cannot remember of more privations and hardships than we went through at Missionary Ridge." When Jefferson Davis came to hear the case against Bragg, Watkins remembered how the troops shouted at him: "Send us something to eat, Massa Jeff. Give us something to eat, Massa Jeff. I'm hungry. I'm hungry."[10]

If Jefferson Davis was content to leave leadership matters as they were at Chattanooga, Lincoln was not. It was clear to the Union that the Western Theater was the decisive one. "If we can hold Chattanooga and East Tennessee," Lincoln averred to Rosecrans, "I think the rebellion must dwindle and die." Reinforcements from the Army of the Potomac—some 20,000 troops—were removed from Virginia and sent to Tennessee by rail, under the command of Joe Hooker. From the West, William Sherman was heading toward Chattanooga with some 17,000 men. Placed in charge not only of both Hooker's and Sherman's groups, but in charge of the entire Division of the Mississippi (comprising the departments of the Ohio, the Cumberland, and the Tennessee—the Union in the West, in other words), was Ulysses S. Grant. When that happened, Rosecrans's fate was sealed. He had never enjoyed a good relationship with Grant, and Grant did not rate his abilities highly enough to retain him in command; he replaced Rosecrans with the "Rock of Chickamauga," and almost immediately issued Thomas his orders. "Hold Chattanooga at all hazards," he commanded, "I will be there as soon as possible." To which Thomas responded, grimly but decisively, "I will hold the town till we starve."[11]

Less than a week later, Grant arrived at Chattanooga, established a supply line for his troops, and began moving them into the city. Bragg was in a strong position on Missionary Ridge. Although his army was not as mentally strong (and certainly not as committed) as it appeared physically, it was arraigned in a solid, defensible line. Grant needed to wait for Sherman—to ensure numerical superiority—before he attempted a full-on engagement. By late November, Sherman had arrived, and the Union was as ready as it ever would be. Grant proposed to attack on both of Bragg's flanks—he certainly did not envisage a frontal assault on the Army of Tennessee—while Thomas distracted the center of the Confederate line. Hooker was dispatched to assault Lookout Mountain, which was the anchor-point for Bragg's left flank, and Sherman was detailed to aim for Tunnel Hill on the right. But the first day of the battle—November 24—did not go as planned. Hooker was successful at Lookout Mountain, but Sherman got bogged down in the ravines that separate Tunnel Hill from the rest of Missionary Ridge.

The first day of the battle ended with the Union in some disarray. The army's progress had been neither as fast nor as decisive as Grant wished. On the second day, therefore, he implemented his plan for Thomas to attack the Confederate center, but with a view to doing no more than distract the enemy and relieve Sherman. It did not work out quite as Grant planned. As Thomas moved on the Confederate line, the battle escalated—literally. Gaining the first line of trenches, Thomas's troops sustained heavy fire from the Confederates atop Missionary Ridge but, rather than retreat, they rushed the line. All previous evidence, from Malvern Hill, from Fredericksburg, from Gettysburg, suggested this was a bad move. But this time it worked. It worked for two main reasons. Firstly, Missionary Ridge is an actual ridge: 800 feet (250 meters) in height, it hampered the Confederates from firing accurately at the Union troops because they had to fire downhill, and was too short of space at the top for them to maneuver into a formation to mount an adequate defense. Secondly, the placement of Confederate troops at the base of the ridge meant that those at the top could not fire without endangering their comrades, who had been deployed there to delay the Union advance and then pull back, but, incomprehensibly, they stayed in position. Above all, the gradient was the decisive factor. Fredericksburg had seen Union troops mown down by Confederates entrenched behind a stone wall; Pickett had charged up a fairly gentle slope at Gettysburg; but the topography of the West, with its more extreme elevation changes, was an entirely different matter. Sam Watkins, on picket duty that day, recalled the confusion of the final hour-long assault. "The Yankees were swarming everywhere," he remembered, and "I was trying to stand aside and get out of their way, but the more I tried to get out of their way, the more in their way I got." Before long, he observed, the "whole army was routed." He was right. The Confederates retreated in the face of the Union army swarming up the hill toward them, and it did not stop retreating until they reached Dalton, Georgia.[12]

After the Union assault on Missionary Ridge, it was all over. Again, the losses were sobering, but they were not on the scale of previous engagements: 5,800 Union troops and 6,600 Confederates were killed, wounded, missing, or taken prisoner. Yet Chattanooga proved to be one of the most decisive battles of the war. Reputations were made—and lost—by it. On the Union side, Grant had been impressed by the tenacity of one of his division commanders, Phil Sheridan, who had charged after the retreating enemy at Missionary Ridge. Greater things lay ahead for both men. For Braxton Bragg, however, it was the end, and he was finally (and not a moment too soon in the opinion of many) replaced by Joe Johnston.

Chattanooga represented both an end and a beginning for the Union war effort. By the end of 1863, the Union had been victorious at three significant engagements: Gettysburg, Vicksburg and, now, Chattanooga. It was also the conclusion of over two years of fruitless searching for the general who might give the Union the overall victory it now so desperately needed. 1864 was an election year. Without victories, Lincoln's position was weak, and without Lincoln, the Union's position was precarious, at best. All the Confederacy really had left at the end of 1863 was the hope that the attrition of war would persuade the Northern populace to elect a peace candidate in 1864. William Sherman's brother John certainly saw the coming election as "a danger ... more ominous than any other," and wondered how, in the midst of war, it could be conducted at all. The Confederacy had merely to wait, he realized, and hold out until the North defeated itself politically, elected George McClellan, and offered a negotiated peace. With the victory at Chattanooga and the rise of Grant, however, that prospect seemed less likely than it had only a month before. By early December, George Templeton Strong reported an "almost universal feeling that rebellion has received its death blow and will not survive through the winter." This, he realized, was "premature, but being coupled with no suggestion that our efforts may safely be slackened, it will do no harm." When Lincoln gave his annual message to Congress he, too, evinced a more positive outlook at the end of a year of mixed fortunes for the Union. The Emancipation Proclamation had, he realized, given "to the future a new aspect, about which hope, and fear, and doubt contended in uncertain conflict." It seemed as if the Union might be through with its "dark and doubtful days," politically and militarily. At Chattanooga, the Union had identified Grant as the commander who offered it the best hope of success, and Lincoln knew that success in the field increased the likelihood of success in the polls.[13]

The Union had always had the superior resources, but until the end of 1863 had lacked the means to bring them to bear on the decisive point. It found those means in Grant, acting in concert with Sherman and Sheridan. As Bragg's star fell in the Confederacy, Grant's rose in the Union, and before many months had passed, he had become lieutenant general—the first since George Washington to hold that rank—and was facing Lee in the East. Grant's was a new and more aggressive style of warfare, and it operated within the context of a Union that was finally working decisively, and in concert, against the Confederacy. The battles to come would not much resemble the two- or three-day engagements that had been the norm in the war up to, and including, Chattanooga. In the following months, the Civil War became a very different, more intense war—a modern war—the kind of war that the twentieth century would experience. Grant was the new kind of commander required for this new kind of war, because he realized that organization combined with unrelenting pressure on the enemy was the road to victory. Unlike so many of the Union's generals, Grant was not prone to hesitation or prevarication. The endgame of the war would be a slugging match. Grant realized that, accepted it, and then got on with it. In the aftermath of Chattanooga, Confederate foot soldier Sam Watkins fully understood the stakes for which each side was now playing and the importance of leadership in the game. "More depends on a good general than the lives of many privates," he observed. "The private loses his life, the general his country."[14]

War Is Upon Us: the Move to Total War

The military situation at the start of 1864 was relatively quiet as both sides reconsidered their options. In the Virginia Theater, the Army of Northern Virginia took a long time to recover from the defeat at Gettysburg. Both Lee and his opponent, George Meade (still in command of the Army of the Potomac), were encamped in Virginia along the Rapidan River, and they would remain there for a while. The Confederacy's main force in the West, now under Johnston, remained in Georgia, at Dalton. This arrangement, given the Union's control of the Mississippi, bought the Union the time it needed to develop an overall plan of campaign aimed at hitting the Confederacy in both theaters simultaneously, for that was what Grant intended to do, come spring. Initially, Grant hoped to direct from the West, but on his arrival in Washington "it was plain that here was the point for the commanding general to be," as he later recalled. Having aligned himself with the Army of the Potomac—although Meade remained in overall command of that army—Grant personally oversaw the movement of the three main forces in the East in the spring. Throughout, Grant stayed in close contact with Meade and in almost constant contact with Lincoln, in person and via the telegraph network. In Washington he had the support of Halleck, who summarized for him the lengthy field reports coming in from all over the country, keeping him up to speed on the movements of the armies in the other theaters, on the supply lines, and on the extremely complex logistics system that the Union had in place by the final years of the war. This was no mean feat. Grant was in charge of a theater of war larger than any covered by Napoleon, with half a million troops spread over four main military divisions; it was the improved organization of the Union by 1864 that enabled Grant to control both numbers and distance, to attack all along the line, and to keep doing so until the Confederacy fell. His plan was designed to put pressure on Lee, now desperately trying to defend Richmond, from different directions. The Army of the James, under Ben Butler, was detailed to advance from Bermuda Hundred (the name of a fishing village at the point where the Appomattox and James rivers meet) to the south of Richmond and seize the city if it could, or, at the very least, to destroy the railroads at Petersburg. The Army of the Potomac under Meade was the major attack force; it would face Lee directly. Fritz Sigel was to occupy Confederate forces in the Shenandoah Valley (much as Jackson had done to the Union two years before) and block Confederate communications from the West. In the Western Theater, Sherman was to take on Johnston, in Georgia.[15]

The Union's spring 1864 offensive, when it got underway in May, relied not just on an improved level of organization within the Union command structure but also on the implementation of a 'hard war' policy that had been developing since mid-1862. In his 1846 study of the military arts, Henry Halleck had stressed that in "a country like ours, where large bodies of new and irregular forces are to be suddenly called into the field in case of war, it is important to establish very rigid rules in relation to forage and subsistence; otherwise the operations of such troops must be attended with great waste of public and private property, the want of means of subsistence, the consequent pillage of the inhabitants, and a general relaxation of discipline. Regular troops are far less liable to such excesses than inexperienced and undisciplined forces." He had not altered his opinion by 1863 as far as discipline went, but he had concluded that the "very rigid rules" that he had earlier advocated might not be appropriate to the war that the nation was now engaged in. Grant's decision to live off the land—

and by extrapolation, off the inhabitants of that land—in the aftermath of his supplies being destroyed at Holly Springs at the end of 1862, would not have met with censure from Halleck who, several months previously, had advised Grant that as "soon as the corn gets fit for forage get all the supplies you can from the rebels in Mississippi. It is time," Halleck averred, "that they should begin to feel the presence of war on our side." Grant did not advocate a policy of random pillaging, however. He took very seriously any reports of inappropriate conduct on the part of his troops, viewing such conduct as not only unacceptable but ineffectual. It "may serve to frighten women and children and helpless old men," he asserted, "but will never drive out an armed enemy." William Sherman, perhaps the most famous exemplar of hard war policy, also drew a clear distinction between random acts of violence and the need for a more aggressive policy toward Southern civilians. He pronounced himself ashamed of the "amount of burning, stealing, and plundering done by our army" (referring to the burning of a cotton gin in the summer of 1863), deeming them acts of vandalism that "in no way aided our military plans."[16]

By the final years of the war, however, it had become clear to the Union that attempting to tread a delicate line through Southern sensibilities and Southern property was not only unappreciated but also counterproductive. The hostility of the South's population hampered the Union's advance, leading to the realization that this population was not likely to be enticed back into the Union, but would have to be dragged back kicking and screaming. The amount of aid afforded the enemy by civilians also blurred the distinction between non-combatant and combatant, necessitating a new and more aggressive approach to the prosecution of the war. Early in 1863 Halleck argued that the "character of the war has very much changed within the last year. There is now no possible hope of reconciliation with the rebels ... There can be no peace but that which is forced by the sword. The North must conquer the rebels or be conquered by them." Sherman, who clearly had been giving the matter considerable thought, set out his understanding of the situation in the autumn of 1863 to the citizens of Warren County, Mississippi, who had complained that the Union was failing to support them. He reminded them that Union forces had been attacked by civilians, and that the government was therefore "justified in treating all the inhabitants as combatants" should it so wish. Aid, he stressed, was a reciprocal matter; if the citizens of Mississippi did not aid the government, the government was hardly likely to help them retain their goods. "You must first make a government," he told them, "before you can have property." To Halleck, Sherman was blunter:

War is upon us … none can deny it … In accepting war it should be pure and simple as applied to the belligerents. I would keep it so till all traces of the war are effaced; till those who appealed to it are sick and tired of it … I would not coax them or even meet them half way, but make them so sick of war that generations would pass before they would again appeal to it.[17]

Total war was what Sherman threatened and total war, in the South at least, was what he and the rest of the Union forces delivered, in a campaign of unrelenting pressure against the South's armies, its cities, and its people. This was no longer the same kind of conflict that had begun in 1861. Both commanders and troops were more experienced—although the armies of 1864 included many raw recruits—and the impact of the new weaponry and its possibilities had finally sunk in. The North's new kind of war was based on entrenchments and an overall campaign of attrition. Grant did not envisage achieving victory via any Napoleonic-style climactic battle, but by gradually—ideally, not too gradually—wearing down Confederate resistance. The Army of Northern Virginia, however, was Grant's immediate goal. As Grant advised Meade, "Lee's army will be your objective point. Wherever Lee goes, there you will go also." This was a method of warfare still susceptible to the sudden and daring maneuver, however—if any of the Confederate generals still had such a move within their grasp, or their imagination. It was clear that the Confederacy had some resources left. Nathan Bedford Forrest was continuing to disrupt the Union advance in Mississippi and Tennessee, eventually achieving—at horrific cost—the fall of Fort Pillow in April 1864. At the same time, Union general Nathaniel Prentiss Banks was floundering around in the misconceived Red River campaign, which was eventually abandoned in April. In the main theaters of the war, however, the Confederacy was weak numerically. Both Lee in the East and Johnston in the West had just over half the number of troops than the Union forces that opposed them, so any move on their part would have to be a smart one. In overall strategic terms, Lee's loyalty to his home state was, perhaps, beginning to be something of a liability by this stage of the conflict. In immediate, practical terms, fighting on home ground in May of 1864 was still an asset. A lack of familiarity with the terrain caused problems for the Union commanders, whereas their opponents, for the most part, knew where they were on the map.[18]

"Move at the time indicated in my instructions," Grant ordered Sherman at the start of May. "All will strike together"; and so the final push on the Confederacy began. When Grant crossed the Rapidan on May 5, he was anticipating a short campaign that would culminate in the seizure of Richmond by the end of the month. His intention to move around Lee's right, the better both to transport his own troops by water and to force Lee southward toward Butler and the Army of the James, meant that the Army of the Potomac would have to negotiate the fifteen square miles or so of dense forest lying between Orange Court House and Fredericksburg—the Wilderness—in which it would be hard to sustain any kind of coherent front. What numerical advantage Grant had would count for little in such an environment if he were forced to engage there, which he was.[19]

Lee did not oppose Grant's crossing of the Rapidan; his forces were scattered and he wanted Longstreet with him before taking on Meade and the Army of the Potomac again. By dawn on May 5, however, two corps of Lee's army, under Richard S. Ewell (2nd Corps) and A. P. Hill (3rd Corps), were approaching the Wilderness from the west via the Orange Turnpike and the Orange Plank Road. Meade's progress was slower than Grant would have wished; the Army of the Potomac had packed for rapid movement, but even so, its supply train stretched for 70 miles, so it could never travel especially fast. It was, perhaps, inevitable that the Union forces would be unable to get through the Wilderness before the Confederates blocked them, and so it turned out. By early morning on May 5, some of Ewell's troops encountered the Union army's 5th Corps and what began as a minor skirmish in Saunders Field soon escalated into a confusing set of engagements as more troops from both armies arrived and engaged in terrain sufficiently dense as to confuse attacker and defender alike. "It was next to impossible to move Artillery," Union soldier Elisha Hunt Rhodes recorded, "and the fighting was done by the Infantry ... The woods and brush were so thick and dark that the enemy could not be seen, but we knew they were there from the terrible fire we received ... The line surged backwards and forwards," he recalled, "now advancing and now retreating until darkness put an end to the carnage." After a fitful night during which the Confederates continued to snipe at the Union forces, Rhodes and his comrades endured a second day of fighting even worse—if that were possible—than the previous day's. Just when it looked as if Lee's right might be in trouble, Longstreet arrived and instigated a counterattack, but in the confusion history looked set to repeat itself when he was shot by his own forces, close to the very spot where, a year before at Chancellorsville, Stonewall Jackson had suffered exactly the same fate. Longstreet was luckier; although badly wounded—he had been shot through the throat—he survived to record his remarkably close call as one that "admonished me that my work for the day was done."[20]

The Battle of the Wilderness, as the series of engagements fought over May 5 and 6 were called, put paid to Grant's hopes for a quick conclusion to the Wilderness (Overland) campaign. In the end, the collapse of the Army of Northern Virginia "was not to be accomplished ... without as desperate fighting as the world has ever witnessed; not to be consummated in a day, a week, a month, or a single season ... The campaign now begun," Grant wrote years later, "was destined to result in heavier losses, to both armies, in a given time, than any previously suffered." The battle itself ended in stalemate. Union losses were close to 18,000; conservative estimates for Confederate losses suggested some 11,000. The dead and wounded lay scattered, and almost invisible to retrieval parties, amidst the trees and undergrowth that, again as at Chancellorsville, caught fire even as the battle was still underway, destroying those unfortunate enough to be in its path. Grant recalled the horror of the day in his memoirs:

> The woods were set on fire by the bursting shells, and the conflagration raged. The wounded who had not the strength to move themselves were either suffocated or burned to death. Finally the fire communicated with our breastworks, in places. Being constructed of wood, they burned with great fury. But the battle still raged, our men firing through the flames until it became too hot to remain longer.[21]

It was a grim finale to a terrible two-day ordeal for both armies, now equally exhausted. But Grant was not about to let the momentum ease. Unlike after Chancellorsville, the Army of the Potomac did not retreat back across the river, but kept going, southeast toward Spotsylvania, to try and get between Lee and Richmond. In terms of the morale of the army after such a devastating battle, it was the best move Grant could have made. "If we were under any other General except Grant I should expect a retreat," observed Elisha Hunt Rhodes, "but Grant is not that kind of a soldier, and we feel that we can trust him." The home front, too, was beginning to feel that it might put its faith in Grant. "Glorious News!," proclaimed the headlines in the *New York Times*, "Defeat and Retreat of Lee's Army." "Thank God," exclaimed George Templeton Strong, "Grant's victory seems established ... Lee is retreating and Grant is after him." Yet Strong also noted that Lee "shows no sign of demoralization." Lincoln, too, expressed himself "very glad at what happened," but reiterated his constant warning: "there is a great deal still to be done."[22]

Lee saw the danger from Grant, and moved fast to intercept it. Jeb Stuart's cavalry was instructed to hamper Meade's movements, and Meade had little to meet them with, having sent two divisions of his own cavalry to protect his supply trains. The Union's progress was again slower than it might have been. When the Union's advance troops finally arrived north of the Spotsylvania Court House on May 8, they found the way blocked by Confederate forces—some of Longstreet's corps now under Richard Anderson—who had themselves only just arrived after a grueling night march, and had quickly formed a line and begun firing at the approaching

Federals. Both sides soon entrenched, and settled in for what became an almost continuous encounter lasting two weeks—fought over ground familiar to many, but this time there was a level of violence and a death toll unimaginable in 1861 and 1862. Spotsylvania was not the Somme, but with its high casualty figures (for little gain), resulting from the Union's repeated attacks against the entrenched Confederate defenses, the Virginia landscape foreshadowed the battlefields of the twentieth century. As one soldier observed, neither army charged any more. "Instead we build fortifications and try to flank the enemy. The enemy does the same." Attempts at flanking the Confederates, however, failed, individual assaults against various apparently weak points on the Confederate salient failed—both at a greater cost in Union lives than in any previous battle. "Constant skirmishing going on in our front," Elisha Hunt Rhodes observed, "both Armies are evidently preparing for another death grapple. Shot and shell are constantly passing over us, and we are fast adding to the roll of dead and wounded." As he wrote, and the infantry struggled in front of Spotsylvania Court House, the Confederate cavalry—indeed the entire Confederacy—experienced a severe blow at Yellow Tavern near Richmond when Jeb Stuart fell in an engagement with the Union cavalry under Sheridan.[23]

Lee was greatly saddened by the loss of a man whom he described as "second to none in valor, in zeal, and in unfaltering devotion to his country." Combined with the wounding of Longstreet, the death of Stuart was too much for some Southerners. Soon, wrote Sallie Brock Putnam, in Richmond

the mournful strains of the Dead March, the solemn procession of military mourners, the funeral carriage, the coffin draped with the Confederate banner … told but too truly the story of the departure of another hero of the South. The laurel and the cypress strangely intertwined in the wreath of the South, and the mourning chaplet was growing almost too heavy to be borne on her brow.[24]

The Union's success in defeating Stuart, however, came at a price, and it was the troops at Spotsylvania who paid it. Without the cavalry—still harrassing Lee's rear and protecting the Union army's supply trains—Meade had no way of assessing his enemy's strength or position. This did not deter Grant. On May 11 he announced his "purpose to fight it out on this line if it takes all summer," and the next day he proved it when the Union attempted, again, to break through the center of the Confederate salient at what became known as the "Bloody Angle." The brutal hand-to-hand fighting lasted almost a full day, in conditions made worse by the weather. "The rain began to fall and soon we were deep in mud and water," Elisha Hunt Rhodes reported. "While we remained in the ditch we were sheltered from the enemy's fire, but if a head was shown above the works, bullets whistled immediately."[25]

The bad weather hampered operations, and Grant reported impassable roads that made even the transport of the wounded impossible. "You can assure the President and Secretary of War," he wrote to Halleck, "that the elements alone have suspended hostilities, and that it is in no manner due to weakness or exhaustion on our part." Elisha Hunt Rhodes was not concerned: "Grant is a fighter and is bound to win," he declared. As soon as the weather allowed, Grant was indeed back at Lee's throat. The Union's second major assault at the salient was on May 18, but Lee had reinforced the line, and the Federals were driven back—but not in retreat; they were still moving to try and get behind Lee. The following day it was the Confederates' turn to meet with a setback. Ewell's troops engaged with the Union at Harris Farm and encountered such heavy artillery fire that the dead fell in ranks, and lay on the field in almost perfect formation. The Union army still kept moving, probing for a way round, or through, the Army of Northern Virginia, trying to push toward Richmond or force Lee toward it. The confrontation shifted to the North Anna River, a strong defensive position for the Confederates, but it was just over twenty miles from the Confederate capital.[26]

All the time, Grant was striving to make the Army of the Potomac leaner, faster, and more efficient. He sent his excess artillery back to Washington before leaving Spotsylvania, and again before he reached the James. Yet although he may have had an excess of artillery, he did not have an unlimited supply of men. The casualties in the battles before Spotsylvania had taken their toll: some 18,000 Union dead, wounded, or missing. The Confederates, as usual, could afford their losses less, and estimates for their casualties range from less than half of those suffered by the Union to a figure closer to 11,000. In the race between Grant and Lee, the pressure remained on the South to defeat Grant before it ran out of men altogether.

The confrontation at the North Anna River took place toward the end of May—between the 23rd and 26th—as Grant sought a way through Lee's lines. It was a long shot at best. Despite the loss of Stuart and the temporary loss of Longstreet, Lee emerged from the battles around Spotsylvania in a solid position. For the Union, by contrast, the news from Sigel and Butler was not good; neither had achieved their objectives, and Butler was stuck on the James. While Lee could call on reinforcements, Grant had to forge ahead with only those reinforcements from Butler's army that could reach him, but they did not arrive in time for the battle at the North Anna. Again, Lee—despite being ill—had blocked the Union advance, and the Army of the Potomac failed to get through the Confederate lines. Grant's response was, as expected, to keep moving, again to the southeast, but again Lee anticipated the threat. At this point, Grant was confident, and advised Halleck that

> Lee's army is really whipped. The prisoners we take show it, and the action of his army shows it unmistakably ... Our men feel they have gained *morale* over the enemy, and attack him with confidence. I may be mistaken, but I feel that our success over Lee's army is already assured.[27]

Grant was mistaken. By the end of May, Lee had established a secure position along Totopotomoy Creek, which enabled him to make a stand against Grant. However, his position was dangerously close to Richmond. By the start of June, after several days of minor skirmishing between the armies, Sheridan and the Union cavalry managed to seize the crossroads at Cold Harbor, ten miles from the city. This was too close for comfort. Lee moved to deflect the threat, and did so successfully. Cold Harbor was a disaster for the Union. Despite the arrival of reinforcements from the Army of the James, an ill-planned frontal assault on June 3 resulted in the loss of some 7,000 troops in under an hour; Lee's casualties were less than 2,000. "I have always regretted that the last assault at Cold Harbor was ever made," Grant later wrote. "At Cold Harbor no advantage whatever was gained to compensate for the heavy loss we sustained." It was a terrible blow, made the more bitter by the fact that many of the troops in the Army of the Potomac had reached the end of their three-year enlistment. Cold Harbor was not the kind of engagement likely to persuade many to re-enlist, but amazingly, many did. Under Grant, the morale in the Army of the Potomac remained high and many soldiers, such as Elisha Hunt Rhodes, stayed not for the money, but for what he described as "higher and better motives for serving my country." Lee's troops, by contrast, had begun to refer to themselves as "Lee's Miserables," a pun on the popular novel *Les Miserables* by Victor Hugo. A cheap "Volunteers' Edition" was available in America, and was widely read by the troops on both sides. The pun was not wholly appropriate; Lee's forces (what was left of them) remained committed to their "country," too, especially because they were so close to Richmond. Nevertheless, the nickname carried a bitter truth about their condition and their cause, even if the irony of identifying themselves with a novel that was committed to the opposition of slavery—in all its forms—was lost in translation.[28]

After Cold Harbor, both armies remained in position, facing each other across their entrenchments, occasionally sniping at each other. The terrible Union defeat on June 3 marked, in many ways, a juncture in Grant's campaign, a campaign that had both shocked and enthused the Northern population as much as Lee's determined resistance had enthused and worried the South. The troops on both sides had sustained almost two months of unrelenting warfare, more brutal and more persistent (and so, more modern) than anything they had experienced before. In Grant, the Union may *not* have found the general that Lee did not understand; by the middle of June, Lee understood Grant very well. And what he understood worried him. As Longstreet had once advised him, Grant would never give up and never give in, not until his objective was achieved. In pursuit of that objective, Grant had one obvious move left in mid-June 1864: to attack the railway center at Petersburg. Confederate general D. H. Hill saw the danger in spreading the South's forces too thin by trying to cover Bermuda Hundred and Petersburg. Petersburg, he asserted, was the decisive point. "Its loss surely involves that of Richmond—perhaps of the Confederacy," he advised Beauregard, adding that in his view it was "arrant nonsense for Lee to say that Grant can't make a night march without his knowing it." Hill did not have second sight, but that was precisely what Grant was planning to do.[29]

Over the night of June 12–13, the Army of the Potomac began its retreat from Cold Harbor, moving south to the James River. As Hill had predicted, Lee was unaware of the movement. The crossing of the James via a pontoon bridge over 2,000 feet long was a remarkable feat of engineering and organization, but having gained the south bank of the river, the Union then stalled. The opportunity offered by Lee's brief ignorance of Grant's intentions was squandered by the Union commanders, who hesitated when they should have been decisive, and halted when they should have moved. When Grant crossed the river, Petersburg was vulnerable, and likely to remain so as long as Lee was unsure of Grant's position. On June 15, some 16,000 Union troops under W. F. "Baldy" Smith faced only 2,500 Confederates outside Petersburg, but Smith delayed. The arrival of Winfield Scott Hancock the next day doubled Union numbers, but Confederate general P. G. T. Beauregard was moving from Bermuda Hundred to counter the threat. This, in itself, was an opportunity for the Union because Beauregard had left barely 1,000 men to oppose Butler, but Butler did not seize the chance to break out and move on to Petersburg either. Beauregard, meanwhile, had arrived at Petersburg. His position was not yet secure and he struggled to hold off the Union assaults on Petersburg that finally came on June 16 and throughout the next day but when the Union failed to finish the job that evening, however, its chance to take Petersburg was gone, just at the point when Beauregard was advising Bragg—now Lee's military advisor—that without "immediate and strong re-enforcements results may be unfavorable." For the Union, it was not exactly a case of snatching defeat from the jaws of victory, because as soon as Lee was entrenched between Petersburg and Richmond the end was really inevitable. The failure to take Petersburg in the summer of 1864, however, delayed that end, allowing the Confederacy to hope that if Lee could hold the line, the line could hold the Confederacy.[30]

The Hard Hand of War

As the Army of the Potomac settled in for the long siege of Petersburg, the Army of the James was secure at Bermuda Hundred, and the war in the East became something of a stand-off for the next nine months, interspersed with the skirmishes and the type of brief, but brutal, engagements that characterized this early stage of trench warfare. The monotony was briefly broken by Grant's attempt to blow up Petersburg's defenses in the famous Battle of the Crater in mid-July. The creation of the crater in question went well enough. A complex series of tunnels was constructed under Petersburg's defenses and filled with gunpowder. The resultant explosion dispatched several Confederates and created the anticipated shock and confusion among the soldiers around Petersburg. Unfortunately, the Union was almost as surprised as the Confederacy, and hesitated to seize the opportunity that the explosion had afforded them, allowing the Confederates to rally and attack. The battle itself was also notable for the specialist unit of African-American troops that had been selected to lead the assault, but who were replaced at the last moment by untrained white troops, with tragic results. The Battle of the Crater witnesed the needless slaughter of much of the Union's IXth corps along with the hapless black troops sent in after them. As an attempt to pierce the Confederate defenses, the Battle of the Crater was, in all respects, as Grant later described it: "a stupendous failure."[31]

It would be a mistake, however, to envisage the siege of Petersburg as no more than a staring match between the Union and the Confederacy; it was, in fact, the ultimate static battlefield on which contact with the enemy was not merely prolonged, but continuous. African-American war correspondent Thomas Morris Chester's reports from the Virginia front in the last year of the war described an environment of "incessant fire," in which "bullets are incidentally flying through one's quarters, and flying about in a variety of directions." The tension prompted Chester to outbursts of levity, or possibly sarcasm, as when he announced "THE GRAND FIRE-WORKS" in August of 1864:

> The enterprising managers of the firm of Grant & Lee take pleasure in announcing to the public in and around Petersburg that they are now prepared, and will continue until further notice, to give every evening a grand exhibition of fireworks for the benefit of their respective employees. The past experience of the firm has enabled it

to acquire a success in this direction which it feels satisfied a liberal-minded public will concede.[32]

In the main, however, Chester's reports were serious, and frequently grim. His obvious interest in the welfare of the black regiments positioned along the Union line, and his focus on their fighting prowess, underscored for his readers not just the changed nature of the war in the aftermath of the Emancipation Proclamation, but the raised stakes—for black and white alike—in the aftermath of Fort Pillow. There was little room in the trenches of Petersburg for any racially exclusive camaraderie between Johnny Reb and Billy Yank, a camaraderie that had been in evidence in the war's earlier stages. The ideals for which the Union forces were fighting were, at that point, as evident as was their determination to win. In the end, the war had come to this: both sides were entrenched, literally and figuratively, in their respective positions and the struggle between them was to the death.

In the Shenandoah Valley and further west, however, both sides still had room to maneuver and the opportunity to turn the tide of the war. Following Fritz Sigel's failure to do the Confederacy any damage in the Shenandoah Valley in the spring of 1864, Grant had replaced him with David Hunter. Hunter, initially at least, had some success, defeating the Confederates at Piedmont in early June and getting as far as Lexington—where he burned down the Virginia Military Institute (VMI)—before heading toward Lynchburg. John C. Breckinridge, who had earlier repulsed Sigel with the aid of the cadets from the VMI, was dispatched to deal with this new threat, and Lee sent Jubal Early as support. Grant had also detailed Sheridan to meet up with Hunter at Charlottesville, but as Sheridan moved toward Hunter, he himself was being pursued by Confederate general Wade Hampton's cavalry, which was numerically almost as strong as Sheridan's force. However, when the two forces engaged in mid-June at Trevilian Station, it was to no obvious benefit for either side. With the Union advance in the Shenandoah running out of steam, Jubal Early had an almost clear road to Washington. He took it, reaching the city's outskirts in early July. It was unlikely that Early, with a force of only some 12,000, could ever have seized Washington itself, but he certainly gave it a fright, in the summer of 1864, before troops from the Army of the Potomac's 6th Corps reached the city. It was the last thing Lincoln needed in an election year, but the bigger problem that summer, both for Grant's strategic plan and for Lincoln's political future, lay further west—with Sherman, in Georgia.

Sherman's orders in the spring of 1864 were to attack Joe Johnston in Georgia and to damage, as much as possible, the Confederacy's war-making capacity and support network there. Given this remit, it was inevitable that the focus would be on Atlanta.

Like Grant, Sherman had three main armies, which were distributed across the Western Theater: the Army of the Cumberland, under George Thomas (Chattanooga); the Army of the Tennessee, now under James B. McPherson (Huntsville); and the Army of the Ohio (the 23rd Corps) under John Schofield (Knoxville). By early May, he had pulled most of these—some 100,000 men—together around Chattanooga. And also like Grant, Sherman believed that in a military campaign, less is more. Relying on the ability of the Union's chief quartermaster, Montgomery Meigs to ensure supplies en route, Sherman trimmed his armies' baggage to a minimum, the better to move fast and engage the enemy. "Soldiering as we have been doing for the past two years, with such trains and impediments, has been a farce," he exclaimed, "and nothing but absolute poverty will cure it." Sherman's opposite, Johnston, had also taken steps to improve the fighting ability of his 55,000 troops by drilling them over the winter months, ensuring that rifle practice was executed, and improving both food and clothing distribution. What he could not do, however, was prepare them for the fact that in the West, as in the East, contact with the enemy was likely to be fairly continuous from then on, and that much of it would be from an entrenched position. Although Union commanders in the West had constructed entrenchments at all three of the Western Theater's main engagements—Stones River, Chickamauga, and Chattanooga—Confederate commanders had been too focused on the offensive to attach much value to entrenchments. In the Atlanta Campaign, Sherman was the one more interested in the offensive, while Johnston's response was that Confederate ideal—offensive-defense. At first this took the form of fortifications just around Dalton but as his troops became as adept as their Union counterparts at quickly constructing fortifications, Johnston used them more frequently. As Sam Watkins of the Army of Tennessee recalled, the army "continued to change positions, and build new breast-works every night. One-third of the army had to keep awake in the trenches, while the other two-thirds slept." The western Confederate troops became as hardened as their eastern counterparts to almost continuous action; "it was battle, battle, battle, every day, for one hundred days," Watkins complained. "The boom of cannon, and the rattle of musketry was our reveille and retreat, and Sherman knew that it was no child's play."[33]

The summer of 1864 certainly saw battle after battle and no real gain for the Confederacy. Sherman and Johnston began a lengthy process of jockeying for position around each other, maneuvering, flanking, retreating—and all the time getting closer to Atlanta. The sole major engagement at Kennesaw Mountain, near Marietta, Georgia, at the end of June was

Sherman's Cold Harbor; it was another frontal assault that ended in defeat for the Union. Johnston's strategy was to wear the enemy down, but in Sherman he had picked the wrong enemy. Although defeated in that particular engagement, Sherman had not yet given up hope of winning the war. Like Grant, he simply picked himslf up and kept going.

For both the Union and the Confederacy that summer, the focus had narrowed to two strategic points: Richmond in the East; Atlanta in the West. By mid-June, Grant had Lee pinned down on the line between Petersburg and Richmond: Atlanta's fate, however, still hung in the balance. By mid-July, Jefferson Davis had grown tired of Johnston's apparently endless maneuvering and replaced him with John Bell Hood, an aggressive and opinionated fighter who was far from universally popular. When the army heard the news, it reacted with shock. According to Sam Watkins:

> It came like a flash of lightening, staggering and blinding every one. It was like applying a lighted match to an immense magazine. It was like the successful gambler, flushed with continual winnings, who staked his all and lost. It was like the end of the Southern Confederacy. Things that were, were not. It was the end.[34]

When Sherman heard the news—ironically, given his vitriol against newspaper correspondents, he read about it in a paper—he reacted with relative calm, but realized the game had just been raised a notch. The day of the Confederate retreat was over. Advising his corps commanders that the move on Atlanta would begin on July 20, he advised them to "accept battle on anything like fair terms," while to Halleck he announced, somewhat prematurely, that if "General Grant can keep Lee from re-enforcing this army for a week, I think I can dispose of it."[35]

His assault, when it came, was two-pronged: McPherson and Schofield would approach from the east, and Thomas from the north. Hood was ready, but his first attempt to block Thomas was repulsed. Undaunted, he swung round and went for McPherson, again to little effect—bar high Confederate casualties—although McPherson himself was a fatality of this engagement. At first, despite Hood's vigorous attacks, things looked promising for Sherman. But by the end of July, a breakthrough had still not been achieved. Union general Oliver Howard reported that his troops had been "invariably repulsed" at the end of July, in an assault that was "pertinaciously kept up for four hours with scarcely any intermission." For Sherman, it was important that he destroy the rail links south, especially the one to Savannah, but for much of August, Hood succeeded in holding Sherman back from that goal, and the Western, as the Eastern, battlefront became bogged down in siege warfare. The deadlock was broken at the end of August, when Sherman's forces succeeded in destroying the all-important rail links; by the start of September, Union forces occupied Atlanta. Major General Henry Slocum, whose 20th Corps entered the city first, reported its fall to Halleck, and the following day Sherman confirmed that "Atlanta is ours, and fairly taken." The taking of Atlanta was undoubtedly one of the great Union victories, but more because of its effect on the political battlefield in Washington than on the progress of the war in the West, or, indeed, overall. On hearing the news, George Templeton Strong observed that if "it be true, it is (coming at this political crisis) the greatest event of the war." In later years, Grant would describe Sherman's victory as

> the first great political campaign for the Republicans in their canvas of 1864. It was followed later by Sheridan's campaign in the Shenandoah Valley; and these two campaigns probably had more effect in settling the election of the following November than all the speeches, all the bonfires, and all the parading with banners and bands of music in the North.[36]

By September 1864, the Republicans, campaigning under the banner of the "National Union Party," had a wealth of support behind them, including that of the various Union and Loyal Leagues and Clubs across the North. As well, the Republicans had ensured that soldiers fighting in the field would, for the first time, be able to vote. When the issue really boiled down to whether to pursue the war and achieve peace through victory, or effectively give up and offer the South peace on its terms, it was almost a given on which side of the fence the soldier vote would fall. Peace without victory is not something many armies crave, and the Union Army in 1864 was no exception. For the Northern population as a whole, events on the battlefield also mattered, and the fall of Atlanta mattered more than most, but, as Grant wryly noted, the Union cavalry in the Shenandoah also played a part in forming public opinion. In the valley, Phil Sheridan very swiftly destroyed any hope on the part of the Confederacy that Jubal Early might hold the line there, via a series of engagements that began cautiously in September but soon evolved into a policy of hard war and destruction to match Sherman's. After the Battle of Cedar Creek in mid-October 1864, the Confederacy pulled back from the valley, drawing some its forces back to Virginia, to aid in what was building up to be the final showdown between Grant and Lee, the Union and the Confederacy.

Neither Sheridan's successes in the Shenandoah nor the fall of Atlanta presented a resolution to the problem the Union faced: how to terminate the war. The Confederacy was being neutralized in some areas, but Sherman never did dispose of Hood's army, and, having taken the city, Sherman's problem was how to hold it and how to protect his own long supply lines, which would enable him to keep possession of the city. Hood was down, but not necessarily out—and only some thirty miles away at Lovejoy's Station. Sherman had made it clear to Halleck that he did not intend to pursue Hood in September 1864, but would rest his army. After Atlanta, the pressing question for Sherman, and for the Union, was what to do next. Grant was not willing to lose any momentum, advising Sherman that as "soon as your men are sufficiently rested ... it is desirable that another campaign should be commenced. We want to keep the enemy constantly pressed to the end of the war," he stressed. "If we give him no peace ... the end cannot be distant." In the broader context of Grant's master strategy, Atlanta turned out to be only the midpoint of a larger maneuver that would eventually take Sherman all the way from the West to the Atlantic coast and then up through the Carolinas to meet up with the rest of the Union army, thereby tightening the noose on Lee in Virginia. Grant was initially uncertain, wanting Sherman to destroy Hood's army first, but Sherman averred that Hood's army was only part of the problem; the larger part was the continuing support that the Confederacy enjoyed across the South. The morale of the South, in effect, was what Sherman sought to attack. Having realized that the battle for hearts and minds had long since been lost, Sherman decided to take the war to the hearths and homes of the Confederacy instead. He proposed to Grant that his forces head out for Savannah. "Until we can repopulate Georgia, it is useless to occupy it," he argued, "but the utter destruction of its roads, houses, and people will cripple their military resources ... I can make the march," he assured Grant, "and make Georgia howl."[37]

In November 1864, Sherman saw the chance to implement the strategy he had long advocated; to make the South so sick of war that the war would cease. It was a chance he persuaded Grant to let him take. "We cannot remain now on the defensive," he insisted, "I would infinitely prefer to ... move through Georgia, smashing things to the sea." Grant concurred. Leaving the "Rock of Chickamauga" to hold the Union position in the West and deal with Hood, Sherman took four of his corps—some 60,000 men— and began his March to the Sea in mid-November 1864. By the time he reached Savannah in early December, he had cut a sixty-mile-wide swath through Georgia, covering about fifteen miles each day, destroying homes and railroads and seizing supplies wherever they were found; by the end, Sherman had ensured that the South was certainly sick of war, but in some respects, it was also more committed than ever to opposing the Union's will. Yet Sherman saw no other way to achieve the Union's ends. "We are not only fighting hostile armies, but a hostile people," he stressed, "and must make old and young, rich and poor, feel the hard hand of war." The bitterness induced by Sherman's march cut both ways, however. As Union troops came across evidence of cruelty to Union prisoners, the irreverent treatment of the dead, and casual cruelties enacted by a panicked population fleeing Sherman's advance, hostility to the South, and to the rebellion, increased. By the end of the year, Savannah was under Union control, and Sherman was making preparations for the return leg of his march through the Carolinas, fully aware that "the whole army is burning with an insatiable desire to wreak vengeance upon South Carolina. I almost tremble at her fate," he told Halleck, "but feel that she deserves all that seems to be in store for her."[38]

Endgame in the West: the Nashville Campaign

As Sherman marched through Georgia to engage in a more total form of warfare against hearts and minds as much as property and people, the men he left behind him had some of the traditional variety to contend with before Grant's goal of destroying the Army of Tennessee was met. With Atlanta having been partially destroyed, the next potential target was Nashville, Tennessee. Hoping to forestall this move on Thomas's part, Hood's plan was to attack Thomas before he could reach Nashville. The odds, this time, were not numerically in the Union's favor. The forces left by Sherman were scattered, and it took Thomas some time to pull them together. Hood also had the benefit of Nathan Bedford Forrest's cavalry, giving him a combined force of over 40,000 as against the 34,000 that his immediate opponent at Franklin, John Schofield, was fielding. By attacking the Union (hoping to prevent Schofield and Thomas from joining forces at Nashville), Hood anticipated the victory of the underdog against a more powerful force. This was not his fantasy alone; many in the Confederacy shared it. But the simple message conveyed by rifled weaponry—that the day of the frontal assault was probably over—was neither received nor understood by the Confederacy; although they were not completely alone in missing that message, some of the subtleties of the war eluded them. They never understood the effort it would take to transform its officer corps—no matter how much experience with slave patrols or slave ownership that the men might have had—into leaders capable of creating a functioning and effective army out of a disparate group of volunteer soldiers. When Hood sent his men against an entrenched Union position at Franklin, he was acting in the context of a Confederate military tradition that relied on outdated manuals, tactics, and strategy; the Confederacy failed to learn from their defeats. Union commanders proved more flexible. In the end, that was what Grant, Sherman, and Phil Sheridan brought to the art of war in the mid-nineteenth century; they dispensed with tradition and recognized that the face of battle in 1864 was no longer the visage of 1861—and certainly not that of 1776. The legacy of America's Revolution, so often invoked by Southerners as both justification for secession and anticipation of victory, in fact did the South few favors in the last year of the war.[39]

At the Battle of Franklin in 1864, Hood not only failed to destroy Thomas's forces, he destroyed his own instead. How or why he did so has traditionally been of less interest to historians than why Lee launched Longstreet at the Union line at Gettysburg, but Hood's ill-conceived assault on the Union in the West reflected like no other battle the desperation of the last days of the Confederacy—and the lingering (and perhaps bizarre) assumption that it could win despite the odds being against it. The disaster—for the Confederates—that the battles in Tennessee represented in the autumn of 1864 was not the fault of one man alone, not even a man as aggressive and possibly reckless as John Bell Hood. The South believed its own publicity; that was one of its strengths but, in the end, it was a fatal weakness. One Southerner could not whip ten, or even three Yankees, and the persistence of the belief in a martial South prevented a realistic assessment of the changing nature of the war and what it would take to win it. The last-ditch, suicidal frontal assault that Hood launched at Franklin at the end of November 1864, twenty miles south of Nashville, may have derived from different motives than Lee's similar move in Pennsylvania, but it was cut from the same cloth in terms of execution, and outcome.[40]

The battle that Sam Watkins described as "a grand holocaust of death," was, in his opinion, "the blackest page in the history of the war of the Lost Cause ... the finishing stroke to the independence of the Southern Confederacy." The slaughter was out of proportion to the battle, its goal, and its execution: Hood's casualties were over 6,000, more than twice as many as the Union sustained. Civil War battles had been bloodier, but it was the overwhelming nature of the defeat that shocked and numbed those involved. Among the dead was Theodrick (Tod) Carter, who had marched all over the battlefields of the West, only to die in his own backyard in Franklin in that futile and fatal assault against the Union in November 1864. His tragedy was the tragedy of the South. Although Hood did not accept it, Franklin was the end for the Army of Tennessee. He took what was left of his army on to Nashville, but to what ends he did so is anyone's guess. It was beyond Sam Watkins, who had lost all faith in Hood by that point (had he ever had any to start with). By December, the Union was in the city and behind entrenchments even less susceptible to an assault than those at Franklin had been. In the final battle, Thomas made short work of Hood and the Army of Tennessee. By the evening of December 16, it was all over. Sam Watkins recalled the terrible scenes of panic and confusion as the beaten and demoralized Confederates fled from Union pursuit, heading back across the Tennessee River toward Mississippi. There was a single Confederate truimph that day: Nathan Bedford Forrest staged a rearguard action against Thomas that prevented the total destruction of Hood's forces (which was not the least of the reasons for Forrest's enduring fame). Hood's forces were, in any case, already finished. In the retreat from Nashville, during one of the coldest winters of the war, the remnants of the "once proud Army of Tennessee had degenerated to a mob. We were pinched by hunger and cold," Watkins remembered. "The rains, and sleet, and snow never ceased falling from the winter sky, while the winds pierced the old, ragged, gray-back Rebel soldier to his very marrow."[41]

Endgame in the East: to Appomattox

By the opening months of 1865, the writing was on the wall for the Confederacy. Sheridan was in the process of finishing off the last remnants of the rebel threat in the Shenandoah. Fighting had pretty much ceased west of the Mississippi, and there was no major Confederate force left in the Western Theater. Sherman was on his way back through the Carolinas, to rendezvous with Schofield in North Carolina in early March, before moving on to join up with the Army of the Potomac on the James River. En route, Sherman's army seized Columbia, and prompted the panicked evacuation of Charleston. By the end of March, the confrontation between Lee and Grant in Virginia was almost all that remained of a war that had swept from the East through the South and West, across the Mississippi all the way to the Red River in Louisiana and even as far as Galveston, Texas; in the other direction Confederate forces had reached as far as the Ohio River and Gettysburg, Pennsylvania. It had been fought in environments as varied as the Wilderness of Virginia, the Shenandoah Valley, and the high seas. It had been fought between armies facing each other across a field, and between raiders swooping in on the enemy and civilians alike. It had been a war of many wars, encompassing the Napoleonic-style battle, the entrenched warfare that would become the norm in the future, and the guerilla campaign. The latter, waged predominantly in the border states, in Missouri and in Kansas, was a very different war from that fought in any of the recognized main theaters of the conflict; frequently more the result of personal vendettas than part of the war for each side, the guerilla war left its own legacy of bitterness for the populations of North and South alike.

The war to defend slavery—sometimes called a war to defend states' rights, but slavery's extension was the only right being contested—had resulted in the Emancipation Proclamation and, by the war's last months, even the Confederacy was contemplating arming the slaves (and one can only speculate on what the outcome of that would have been). As Sherman and Schofield finally reached each other, Lincoln delivered his Second Inaugural, in which he reminded his listeners of the origins of the war begun four years before, of slavery's role in the process, and of his own suspicion that "every drop of blood drawn with the lash, shall be paid by another drawn by the sword," before the "mighty scourge of war" finally passed away. Although the war continued in Virginia, Lincoln looked toward peace, a peace involving "malice toward none … charity for all." As Lincoln spoke, Grant was doing his utmost to achieve that peace, but whether it would be constructed in the spirit Lincoln had invoked remained to be seen.[42]

The winter weather that was causing Sam Watkins and the remains of the Army of Tennessee so much misery was having a similar effect on the forces gathered around Richmond in Virginia. Desertions from the beleaguered Confederate camps to the relative comfort of their Union opposites increased. "This kind of weather," observed Thomas Morris Chester, "has a very convicting effect upon the rebs toward stimulating them to a return to their allegiance, especially as their commissariat is well nigh exhausted." Lee knew the end was coming, and the Confederate government gave him, finally and far too late, overall control of the Confederate armies in February of 1865; by then, he really only had the Army of Northern Virginia left. As Sherman came on through Columbia, South Carolina and then Wilmington, North Carolina—the last port in Confederate hands—Lee sent Johnston to try to halt the advance, but by that stage such a plan was an impossibility. The Union forces were gathering and closing in on Richmond: Sherman from the Carolinas, Sheridan from the Shenandoah. By the end of March, Grant had nearly 125,000 troops west of the Confederate line, ready for his final assault on Lee's left. Lee had less than half that number, but he still fought. On his right flank, George Pickett briefly engaged Sheridan's cavalry at Dinwiddie Court House, only to get beaten back the next day and virtually wiped out at Five Forks on April 1. The following day, Grant renewed the assault on Lee's now seriously compromised right flank. By then, Petersburg and Richmond were no longer defensible; all Lee could do was hold Grant off long enough for the Confederate government to flee. After that, Lee himself abandoned the Petersburg-Richmond line, heading west, still hoping that he might be able to join forces with Johnston. Grant pursued, and for four days the Army of the Potomac and the remains of the Army of Northern Virginia fought a battle on the move, before Sheridan, having taken his cavalry to Appomattox Court House, blocked Lee's last line of retreat.[43]

On April 3, Lincoln arrived at Petersburg to congratulate Grant, and the next day he sailed up the James River to Richmond itself and walked up the main street to the Confederate Capitol before driving through the city with an escort of African-American cavalry. In New York on the same day, jubilation met the news, as it gradually filtered through and was confirmed, that Richmond had fallen. Standing in a newspaper office watching the vendor writing "Richmond is ... " on a notice, George Templeton Strong was beside himself. "What's that about Richmond?" he inquired. "He was too busy for speech," Strong noted, "but he went on with a capital C, and a capital A ... till I read the word CAPTURED!!!" After that, it was "like a Fourth of July night—such a fusillade and cannonade is going on," Strong recorded. "Broadway is a river of flags." In the South, Mary Chesnut was more behind the times. The telegraph line was down, and she did not learn of the fall of Richmond until several days later. In any case, she had "no heart to write about it. Grant broke through our lines, Sherman cut through them ... They are too many for us," she concluded in misery. Her misery turned to anger when Felix Gregory de Fontaine, one of the Confederacy's most prominent correspondents who wrote for the *Charleston Courier*, suggested that "Richmond is given up, because it was too heavy a load to carry, so we are stronger than ever." "Stronger than ever?" Chesnut railed. "Nine tenths of our army are under ground! Where is another to come from? Will they wait until we grow one?" It was over ten days before William Sherman heard the news, and he immediately telegraphed Grant: "I barely know how to express my feelings," he wrote, "but you can imagine them." Faced with the task of receiving Lee's surrender at Appomattox on April 9, Grant was in a more somber mood than most Northerners. "What General Lee's feelings were I do not know," he recalled, but he remembered that his own had been "sad and depressed. I felt like anything rather than rejoicing at the downfall of a foe who had fought so long and valiantly, and had suffered so much for a cause, though that cause was, I believe, one of the worst for which a people ever fought, and one for which there was the least excuse"[44]

Conclusion
Death of a President, Birth of a Nation

In this Confederate flag there is a meaning which cannot die—it marks the birthplace of a new nationality, and its place must know it forever. Even the flag of a rebellion leaves indelible colors in the political atmosphere. The hopes that sustained it may vanish in the gloom of night, but the national faith still believes that its sun will rise on some glorious morrow.

—William Howard Russell, *My Diary North and South,* **1861**[1]

Robert E. Lee's surrender to Ulysses S. Grant at Appomattox was by no means the final scene in the drama that had been the Civil War. For one thing, the war itself was not yet officially over: Johnston remained in North Carolina and Kirby Smith was still in the trans-Mississippi Theater. Yet in deciding to surrender at Appomattox, Lee had concluded that the Southern cause was irredeemably lost, and he was unwilling to prolong the conflict by shifting to a drawn-out and indecisive guerrilla campaign. Jefferson Davis, on the other hand, was among those who found defeat hard to accept, telling the few troops still around that "the cause is not yet dead." But John Breckinridge had a firmer grasp of the situation. He persuaded Davis that, "we can no longer contend with reasonable hope of success." More bluntly, Breckinridge urged: "This has been a magnificent epic, in God's name let it not terminate in farce." In fact, of course, it terminated in tragedy, with the assassination in mid-April of Abraham Lincoln. John Wilkes Booth's attack on Lincoln on Good Friday, 1865—Lincoln died the following day, April 15—came as a shock to North and South alike. When, two days later, Sherman met with Johnston to accept his surrender, he had just received the telegram bearing the grim news. Ensuring that no one said anything about its contents to Johnston, Sherman went into his meeting with his former adversary and only then showed Johnston the telegram. The Confederate general was shocked, as he realized the probable implications of Booth's actions and contemplated the retribution that might now be visited on the South. Rather than officially accept Johnston's surrender—as Grant had accepted Lee's at Appomattox—it was agreed that both sides would send their troops home, to try and reduce the possibility of retaliatory violence on either side.[2]

The possibility of uncontrolled violence breaking out was a real danger, and not just as a result of Lincoln's assassination. As Johnny Reb and Billy Yank came marching home, the enthusiasm that greeted their return was replaced by horror and anger when the released prisoners of war arrived. "The sight," according to Walt Whitman, "is worse than any sight of battle-fields, or any collection of wounded, even the bloodiest ... Can those be men," he asked, "those little livid brown, ash-streak'd, monkey-looking dwarfs?—are they really not mummied, dwindled corpses?" For Whitman, "no more appalling sight was ever seen on this earth." The Confederate prisoner of war camp at Andersonville, Georgia, was only the most notorious of a series of detention centers in both North and South; the conditions in none of them were acceptable or, in many cases, survivable. Some 22,600 Union soldiers and 26,500 Confederates died in the prison camps. The camps were part of a far from glorious and frequently hidden side of battle in the Civil War, but made suddenly visible to Americans, North and South, after April 1865, just at the point when thoughts on both sides needed to turn toward reconciliation.[3]

In the North, then, the ending of the war brought bitterness and frustration, both at the death of Lincoln and at the terrible human cost of the conflict, a cost that people now had time to dwell on in a way they could not while the war still continued. In the South, the humiliation of defeat was accompanied by more than a degree of fear, as white Southerners contemplated both a future without slavery and the possible reaction of black Southerners to the Confederacy's demise. African Americans themselves had been celebrating victory since Sherman had arrived in Georgia at the start of the year. Now, however, the problem of how to reconstruct their lives in the war's aftermath was pressing. The battle to win the war soon gave way to the even more bitter battle over the construction of the peace, and the reconstruction of a divided nation.

In the rebirth of one nation, however, another nation perished. Yet the Confederate nation, arguably, was never entirely laid to rest. When on May 26, Kirby Smith surrendered the trans-Mississippi forces, the Confederacy, as a military entity, ceased to exist. Death, however, was not entirely the end for the Confederacy; in many ways it was just the beginning. In defeat, some elements in the South found the fuel for a resurgent Confederate/Southern nationalism more persistent, more racially divisive, and ultimately stronger in form and expression than anything that emerged during the war itself. The open wound created by the Confederacy's defeat permitted a separatist, specifically Southern sentiment to enter the national body. The South became, in some respects, not only a putative nation that had challenged the American nation, but a nation within a nation, a stumbling block for years to come to the construction of any overarching American national identity and a challenge and a problem for those who, as Lincoln had said at Gettysburg, hoped that the nation might have "a new birth of freedom." For the North, the Civil War had undoubtedly reinforced, if not entirely constructed, a national sentiment that had been absent, or at least weaker, in the antebellum era. English journalist Edward Dicey had predicted as much at the war's outset, opining that "the effect of this civil war will be to consolidate the country. If it were not for the common interest in the war," he observed, "it would have been hard to realize that Boston formed part of the same country as Chicago, and St. Louis, and Nashville. There, as elsewhere, the war seemed to be the chief bond of union and identity between the different states of the North." How the South would factor into this new bond of identity when it was once again part of the nation was less obvious. Excluded from the new national cemeteries that soon began to define the physical and emotional landscape of the newly United States, white Southerners buried their own dead, and constructed around their sacrifice and loss a commemorative tradition that kept the memory—and, to a great extent, the bitterness—of the war alive. By the end of Reconstruction (1877), this tradition was fast becoming transformed into the core of a Confederate ideology that would come to revel in the title of the "Lost Cause," an overarching civil religion that for too long kept the white South as a land and a people apart.[4]

Nevertheless, the Civil War had settled, once and for all, the lingering questions over slavery and states' rights that had undermined the antebellum Union, and out of it emerged an integrated state with both territorial and political sovereignty. The validity of the American experiment in democratic government had been established. As Lincoln had hoped, the federal government had proved to the world "that those who can fairly carry an election, can also suppress a rebellion—that ballots are the rightful, and peaceful, successors of bullets; and that when ballots have fairly, and constitutionally, decided, there can be no successful appeal back to bullets." Yet the enmity between North and South, both a cause and a consequence of the Civil War, was not so easily dispelled. When reconciliation came, it came on the same ground that the war had been fought on. Both North and South used the war that had driven them apart as the means of bringing them back together again. For the troops who had fought, battlefield commemoration ceremonies provided the common ground—literally and figuratively—on which the opposing sides could meet. For Confederate veterans particularly, such ceremonies offered a way back into the American nation, but for some, participation in such ceremonies was also a way of reestablishing the conflict as a "white man's war." In an atmosphere of increasing racial exclusion and divisiveness— an atmosphere that would prevail during the period of Reconstruction and for many more years after that, reunification was achieved at the cost of the new birth of freedom that Lincoln had envisaged for his nation. During the war Lincoln had invoked—on countless occasions—the better angels of America's nature, instructing as much as reminding the people what was at stake in the cause the Union was fighting for. His own death, however, coupled with the coming betrayal of African-American hopes of equality, dashed the expectations of many Americans, North and South, that the Civil War might be productive of a new, inclusive American nationality that had no place for the racial divisions of the pre-war nation. As the hopes raised by emancipation gradually faded in the face of the rise of the Lost Cause and the reconceptualization of the war as a white man's conflict, the battle over the meaning of the war was perpetuated into the twentieth century. The legacy of the war was, for over a hundred years, one of bitterness and division, especially, but certainly not exclusively, in the South. This Lincoln never anticipated: "Our strife pertains to ourselves," he assured Americans in the second year of the war, "to the passing generations of men; and it can, without convulsion, be hushed forever with the passing of one generation."[5]

Endnotes

Introduction

1. Brian Holden Reid, *The Civil War and the Wars of the Nineteenth Century* (1999; paperback reprint, London: Cassell, 2002), 20.
2. Walt Whitman, *Specimen Days & Collect* (1883; reprint, New York: Dover Publications, 1995), 68.
3. Edward Dicey, *Spectator of America* (1863; reprint, Athens and London: University of Georgia Press, 1989), 139.

Chapter 1

1. "The Portent" was originally published in *Battle-Pieces and Aspects of the War* (1866; reprint, Amherst, NY: Prometheus Books, 2001), 50.
2. Philip L. Barbour (ed.), *The Complete Works of Captain John Smith, 1580–1631*, Vol. III (Chapel Hill: University of North Carolina Press, 1986), 274–75; Gouverneur Morris, speaking to the Federal Convention, July 5, 1787, in Max Farrand, *The Records of the Federal Convention of 1787*, Vol. I (New Haven: Yale University Press, 1911), 529–31. Three of Farrand's four volumes are available online at the Library of Congress website: http://memory.loc.gov/ammem/amlaw/lwfr.html (July 20, 2005); Washington's *Farewell Address* of 1796 can be accessed online at the Avalon Project at Yale Law School website: http://www.yale.edu/lawweb/avalon/washing.htm (July 21, 2005); Donald Ratcliffe, "The State of the Union, 1776–1860," in Susan-Mary Grant and Brian Holden Reid (eds.), *The American Civil War: Explorations and Reconsiderations* (Harlow, Essex: Longman, 2000), 3–38, quotation 5; Alexis de Tocqueville, *Democracy in America*, Henry Reeve (trans.), Phillips Bradley (ed.), Vol. I (1835, 1840; reprint, New York: Vintage Books, 1945), 401–2.
3. Linda Kerber, *Federalists in Dissent: Imagery and Ideology in Jeffersonian America* (1970; reprint, Ithaca, New York: Cornell University Press, 1993), 34; Ratcliffe, "The State of the Union," 5–6; David Waldstreicher, *In the Midst of Perpetual Fetes: The Making of American Nationalism, 1776–1820* (Chapel Hill: University of North Carolina Press, 1997), 112–13; John Murrin, "A Roof without Walls: The Dilemma of American National Identity," in Richard Beeman, Stephan Botein, and Edward C. Carter II (eds.), *Beyond Confederation: Origins of the Constitution and American National Identity* (Chapel Hill: University of

North Carolina Press, 1987), 333–48, quotation 344; Daniel J. Boorstin, *The Americans: The National Experience* (1965; reprint, New York: Cardinal, 1988), 401.

4. The five states were Louisiana (1812), Indiana (1816), Mississippi (1817), Illinois (1818), and Alabama (1819).

5. Duncan J. MacLeod, "Toward Caste," in Ira Berlin and Ronald Hoffman (eds.), *Slavery and Freedom in the Age of the American Revolution* (Charlottesville: University Press of Virginia, 1983), 229; Nell Irvin Painter, *Sojourner Truth: A Life, A Symbol* (1996; paperback reprint, New York: W. W. Norton, 1997), 9; James Madison, speaking to the Federal Convention, July 14, 1787, in Farrand, *Records of the Federal Convention*, Vol. II, 10. Accessed at http://memory.loc.gov/ammem/amlaw/lwfr.html (August 2, 2005).

6. Boorstin, *The National Experience*, 368; Reid Mitchell, *Civil War Soldiers: Their Expectations and their Experiences* (1988; reprint, New York, Simon & Schuster (Touchstone), 1989), 1–2; Susan-Mary Grant, "'The Charter of its Birthright': the Civil War and American Nationalism," *Nations and Nationalism*, 4, 2 (1998), 163–85.

7. Daniel Webster, Speech in the House of Representatives, January 14, 1814, in *The Debates and Proceedings in the Congress of the United States* (*Annals of Congress*), 13th Cong., 2nd sess., 940–51, quotations 945–46.

8. Albert Gallatin to Matthew Lyon, May 7, 1816, quoted in George Dangerfield, *The Awakening of American Nationalism, 1815–1828* (New York: Harper Torchbooks, 1965), 3–4.

9. The full text of the various amendments proposed by the Hartford Convention can be accessed online at the Avalon Project at Yale Law School website: http://www.yale.edu/lawweb/avalon/amerdoc/hartconv.htm (August 2, 2005); Maurice G. Baker, *One and Inseparable: Daniel Webster and the Union* (Cambridge, MA: Harvard University Press, 1984), 59, committee report quoted, 60.

10. Thomas Jefferson to John Holmes, April 22, 1820. This letter, and all of Jefferson's correspondence, can be accessed online at the University of Virginia's Jefferson Digital Archive website at: http://etext.virginia.edu/jefferson/texts/ (August 3, 2005).

11. John C. Calhoun, *Exposition and Protest*, in W. Edwin Hemphill, Robert L. Meriwether, and Clyde Wilson (eds.), *The Papers of John C. Calhoun*, Vol. 10 (Columbia: University of South Carolina Press, 1959–2001), 447.

12. Tocqueville, *Democracy in America*, Vol. I, 418, 420–21.

13. William R. Taylor, *Cavalier and Yankee: The Old South and American National Character* (1957; reprint, Cambridge, MA: Harvard University Press, 1979), 110: Daniel Webster, Speech in the Senate, January 26 and 27, 1830 in *Webster and Hayne's Speeches* (1850; reprint, New York: Books for Libraries Press, 1971), 50; Susan-Mary Grant, *North Over South: Northern Nationalism and American Identity in the Antebellum Era* (Lawrence: University Press of Kansas, 2000), 61–63.

14. McDuffie, quoted in Manisha Sinha, *The Counterrevolution of Slavery: Politics and Ideology in Antebellum South Carolina* (Chapel Hill: University of North Carolina Press, 2000), 36; Merrill D. Peterson, *The Great Triumvirate: Webster, Clay, and Calhoun* (New York: Oxford University Press, 1987), 183–233.

15. President Jackson's *Proclamation to the People of South Carolina* of December 10, 1832 can be accessed online at the Avalon Project at Yale Law School website: http://www.yale.edu/lawweb/avalon/presiden/proclamations/jack01.htm (August 4, 2005).

16. Edward Pessen, "How Different from Each Other Were the Antebellum North and South?" *The American Historical Review*, 85, 5 (December 1980), 1119–49, quotation, 1119.

17. Boorstin, *The National Experience*, 170; Grant, *North Over South*, 37–60.

18. David Walker, *Walker's Appeal, in Four Articles, together with a Preamble to the Colored Citizens of the World, but in Particular, and Very Expressly to Those of the United States of America* (1829) quoted in Charles S. Sydnor, *The Development of Southern Sectionalism, 1819–1848* (1948; reprint, Baton Rouge: Louisiana State University Press, 1968), 223; Thomas Wentworth Higginson, "Nat Turner's Insurrection," *The Atlantic Monthly*, 46, 8 (August 1861), 186–87, James McDowell quote, 186.

19. Susan-Mary Grant, "The Slavery Debate," in Richard Gray and Owen Robinson (eds.), *A Companion to the Literature and Culture of the American South* (Oxford: Blackwell, 2004), 76–92; William W. Freehling, *The Road to Disunion: Secessionists at Bay, 1776–1854* (New York: Oxford University Press, 1990), 190–91; Sydnor, *Development of Southern Sectionalism*, 226–30.

20. *Papers of John C. Calhoun*, Vol. XIII (1980), 394–95; Tocqueville, *Democracy in America*, Vol. I, 412, 420–22.
21. John O'Sullivan, "Annexation," *The United States Democratic Review*, 17 (July–August 1845), 5.
22. Ibid., 7.
23. Thomas Hart Benton, quoted in Peterson, *The Great Triumvirate*, 467.
24. David M. Potter, *The Impending Crisis, 1848–1861* (New York: Harper & Row, 1976), 145; *Papers of John C. Calhoun*, Vol. XIII, 394–95.
25. Lincoln, "Address at Sanitary Fair, Baltimore, Maryland," April 18, 1864, VII, 301–2; Leonard P. Richards, *The Slave Power: The Free North and Southern Domination, 1780–1860* (Baton Rouge: Louisiana State University Press, 2000), 58–59.
26. Stephen A Douglas, "Speech on the Kansas-Nebraska Bill," *Congressional Globe*, 33rd Cong., 1st sess., January 30, 1854, 275–80.
27. Grant, *North Over South*, 133–37, 141–45.
28. *Dred Scott v. Sandford* (60 U.S. 393 [1856]) can be accessed online at: http://supreme.lp.findlaw.com/supreme_court/landmark/dredscott.html (August 12, 2005).
29. Lincoln, "Speech at Springfield, Illinois," June 16, 1858 in Basler (ed.), *Collected Works of Abraham Lincoln*, II, 461; Victor Hugo, *Letters on American Slavery*, in Belle Becker Sideman and Lillian Friedman (eds.), *Europe Looks at the Civil War* (New York: Collier Books, 1962), 23.

Chapter 2

1. "Apathy and Enthusiasm" was originally published in *Battle-Pieces and Aspects of the War* (1866; reprint, Amherst, NY: Prometheus Books, 2001), 57–58.
2. Daniel Webster, "Speech at Marshfield, September 1, 1848," in Charles M. Wiltse (ed.), *The Papers of Daniel Webster: Speeches and Formal Writings, 1834–1852*, Vol. 2 (Hanover, NH: University Press of New England, 1988), 503.
3. The original broadside of the Republican Party Platform of 1860 can be accessed online via the Library of Congress website at: http://memory.loc.gov/cgi-bin/query/r?ammem/rbpe:@field(DOCID+@lit(rbpe0180010a (August 10, 2005).
4. James Henry Hammond, Speech in the Senate, March 4, 1858, *Congressional Globe*, 35th Cong., 1st sess., 961. Hammond's speech can be accessed online at: http://memory.loc.gov/cgi-bin/ampage (June 6, 2005); James R. Doolittle, Speech in the Senate, March 4, 1858, *Congressional Globe*, 35th Cong., 1st sess., 963–64; James A. Dorr, *Justice to the South!* (New York: 1856), 4. James A. Dorr papers, Congregational Library, Boston.
5. George Templeton Strong, diary entry, December 6, 1859, in Allan Nevins and Milton Halsey Thomas (eds.), *The Diary of George Templeton Strong: The Turbulent Fifties, 1850–1859*, Vol. II (New York: Macmillan, 1952), 475–76; Lydia Maria Child to Henry Wise, October 26, 1859; Henry Wise to Lydia Maria Child, October 29, 1859; Child to Wise [n.d.], 4. This correspondence was published under the title *Correspondence between Lydia Maria Child and Governor Wise and Mrs. Mason of Virginia* by the American Anti-Slavery Society in 1860 and also appeared in the *New York Tribune* in 1859. The full text can be accessed online via the Library of Congress website at: http://memory.loc.gov/ammem/ (June 2, 2005); Glenna Matthews, "'Little Women' Who Helped Make This Great War," in Gabor S. Boritt (ed.), *Why the Civil War Came* (New York: Oxford University Press, 1996), 33–49.
6. William H. Seward, Speech delivered at Rochester, New York, October 25, 1858. Seward's speech can be accessed online at: http://www.nyhistory.com/central/conflict.htm (May 2, 2005); Robert A. Toombs, Speech in the Senate, January 24, 1860, *Congressional Globe*, 36th Cong., 1st sess, appendix, 88.
7. C. Vann Woodward, "John Brown's Private War," in E. James Ferguson et al. (eds.), *The Random House Reader in American History: Essays on the National Past, 1607 to the Present* (New York: Random House, 1970), 327–44, quotation 339.
8. David M. Potter, *The Impending Crisis, 1848–1861* (New York: Harper & Row, 1976), 405–11; John McCardell, *The Idea of a Southern Nation: Southern Nationalists and Southern Nationalism, 1830–1860* (New York: W. W. Norton, 1979), 325–27; John S. Preston, quoted

in the *Charleston Daily Courier*, June 4, 1860, in Manisha Sinha, *The Counter-Revolution of Slavery: Politics and Ideology in Antebellum South Carolina* (Chapel Hill: University of South Carolina Press, 2000), 220.

9. Lincoln, "Address at Cooper Institute, New York City," February 27, 1860, in Roy F. Basler (ed.), *The Collected Works of Abraham Lincoln*, Vol. III (New Brunswick, NJ: Rutgers University Press, 1953), 522–50, quotations 543, 549–50.

10. Strong, diary entry for November 6, 1860, in Nevins and Thomas, *Diary: The Civil War, 1860–1865*, Vol. III, 58; for a detailed analysis of the election of 1860, the best source is Potter, *Impending Crisis*, 430–47, from which election figures are taken, 443; see also Brian Holden Reid, *The Origins of the American Civil War* (Harlow, Essex: Longman, 1996), 237–39.

11. Allan Nevins, *The Ordeal of the Union: The Emergence of Lincoln (Prologue to Civil War, 1859–1861)*, Vol. II (1950, 8 Vols.; reprint, New York: Macmillan, 1992), 4 Vols., 298; Douglas quotation, 295.

12. *Congressional Globe*, 36th Cong., 2nd sess., December 3, 1860, 1; Clingman and Crittenden comments, 3–5.

13. *Congressional Globe*, 36th Cong., 2nd sess., appendix, 1.

14. Strong, diary entries for November 7, 8, 10, and 15, in Nevins and Thomas, *Diary*, III, 60–63.

15. On the South and the territorial issue, see Michael A. Morrison, *Slavery and the American West: The Eclipse of Manifest Destiny and the Coming of the Civil War* (Chapel Hill: University of North Carolina Press, 1997), 276–77; Sinha, *Counter-Revolution of Slavery*, 243–54; An extract from South Carolina's Ordinance of Secession can be found in *The War of the Rebellion: A Compilation of the Official Records of the Union and Confederate Armies* (hereafter: ORA), Series IV (I) (Washington, D.C.: Government Printing Office, 1880–1900), 1. The full ordinance can be accessed online at: http://www.yale.edu/lawweb/avalon/csa/scarsec.htm (January 10, 2005).

16. Stephen F. Hale to Beriah Magoffin, December 27, 1860, in ORA, IV (I), 4–11, quotations 6, 9–10.

17. Georgia's Ordinance of Secession, ORA, IV (I), 81–85, quotation 85; Jeremiah Clemens to L. P. Walker, February 3, 1861, ORA, IV (I), 447; the Confederate Constitution can be accessed online at: http://www.yale.edu/lawweb/avalon/csa/csa.htm (January 10, 2005); Alexander H. Stephens, "Cornerstone Address, March 21, 1861," in Frank Moore (ed.), *The Rebellion Record: A Diary of American Events with Documents, Narratives, Illustrative Incidents, Poetry, etc.* Vol. I (New York: O. P. Putnam, 1862), 44–46; Stephens's address can be accessed online via Fordham University at: http://www.fordham.edu/halsall/mod/1861stephens.html (January 10, 2005); Potter, *Impending Crisis*, 473–74; Holden Reid, *Origins*, 297–98.

18. *New York Tribune*, January 16, 1861; *Springfield (Daily) Republican*, January 24, 1861; Jeremiah Clemens to L. P. Walker, February 3, 1861, ORA, IV (I), 447.

19. Lincoln, "Speech from the Balcony of the Bates House at Indianapolis, Indiana," February 11; "Speech at Steubenville, Ohio," February 14; "Speech at Cleveland, Ohio," February 15; "Address to the New Jersey General Assembly at Trenton," February 21, 1861 in *Collected Works*, IV, 195–96, 207, 215, 237; Potter, *Impending Crisis*, 557–62; Richard J. Carwardine, *Lincoln: Profiles in Power* (Harlow, Essex: Pearson/Longman, 2003), 144–48.

20. Lincoln, "First Inaugural Address," March 4, 1861, in Lincoln, *Collected Works*, 262–71; quotations 265, 268, 271; Holden Reid, *Origins*, 313.

21. Holden Reid, *Origins*, 312; from which statistics are taken, 341.

22. ORA, I (I), 5–7; 291; Lincoln, *Collected Works*, 323–24; F. W. Pickens to Jefferson Davis, April 9; to Hon. W. Walker (Secretary of War, CSA), April 9, 1861; Martin J. Crawford to Beauregard, April 9, 1861 in ORA, I (I), 292–93, 297; Gouverneur Morris speaking to the Federal Convention, July 5, 1787, in Max Farrand, *The Records of the Federal Convention of 1787*, Vol. I (New Haven: Yale University Press, 1911), 531.

23. Sarah Forbes Hughes (ed.), *Letters and Recollections of John Murray Forbes* (Boston and New York: Houghton Mifflin, 1899), 203; Major Robert Anderson to Col. L. Thomas, April 8, 1861, ORA, I (I), 294; Holden Reid, *Origins*, 358–59; *New York Tribune*, April 15, 1861; Strong, diary entry April 13, 1861, Nevins and Thomas, *Diary*, III, 119.

24. Emerson, quoted in James Elliot Cabot, *A Memoir of Ralph Waldo Emerson*, Vol. II (Boston, 1887), 600–601; William Howard Russell, *My Diary North and South* (Boston: T. O. H. P. Burnham, 1863), 105–6.
25. *Richmond Dispatch*, April 11, 1861.
26. Benjamin F. Butler to Winfield Scott, May 24 and 27, 1861; Simon Cameron to Butler, May 30, 1861, in ORA, II (I), 752, 754–55.

Chapter 3

1. Mary Boykin Chesnut, diary entry, April 15, 1861, in *A Diary from Dixie* (Boston: Houghton Mifflin, 1949), 38; *Louisville Courier*, quoted in Sarah Forbes Hughes (ed.), *Letters and Recollections of John Murray Forbes* (Boston: Houghton Mifflin, 1899), 202; Basil Liddell Hart, quoted in Charles Royster, "Fort Sumter: At Last the War," in Gabor S. Boritt (ed.), *Why the Civil War Came* (New York: Oxford University Press, 1996), 203; *New York Tribune*, April 3, 1861; *Springfield (Daily) Republican*, July 4, 1861; David Cannadine, "War and Death, Grief and Mourning in Modern Britain," in Joachim Whaley (ed.), *Mirrors of Mortality: Studies in the Social History of Death* (London: Europa Publications, 1981), 191–2; A. J. P. Taylor, *The First World War* (1966) and Mosley, quoted in Cannadine, 196; 2nd Michigan recruit, quoted in James M. McPherson, *For Cause and Comrades: Why Men Fought in the Civil War* (New York: Oxford University Press, 1997), 30.
2. Brian Holden Reid, "Command and Leadership in the Civil War, 1861–5," in Susan-Mary Grant and Brian Holden Reid (eds.), *The American Civil War: Explorations and Reconsiderations* (Harlow, Essex: Longman, 2000), 143; John Shy, *A People Numerous and Armed: Reflections on the Military Struggle for Independence* (Revised edition, Ann Arbor: University of Michigan Press, 1990), 260–62 and passim; Miller Wright to his brother, August 10, 1861, Augustus and Miller Wright Papers, Gilder Lehrman Collection (GLC 02691.11), Pierpont Morgan Library, New York.
3. William Howard Russell, *My Diary North and South* (Boston: T. O. H. P. Burnham, 1863), 96, 98.
4. Daniel Webster, House of Representatives, January 14, 1814, in *The Debates and Proceedings in the Congress of the United States* (*Annals of Congress*), 13th Cong., 2nd sess., 946; Brian Holden Reid, *The Civil War and the Wars of the Nineteenth Century* (1999; paperback reprint, London: Cassell, 2002), 73–76.
5. Russell, *My Diary North and South*, 132.
6. Russell, *My Diary North and South*, 118; Holden Reid, *Civil War*, 74–75; Jefferson Davis to William Howard Russell, May 9, 1861, in Russell, *My Diary North and South*, 173–74 (the diary date of May 9 is incorrect. Russell actually met Davis on May 7, 1861); see Martin Crawford (ed.), *William Howard Russell's Civil War: Private Diary and Letters, 1861–1862* (Athens and London: University of Georgia Press, 1992), 52; Mary Chesnut, diary entry, June 28, 1861, in Chesnut, *A Diary from Dixie*, 69.
7. *Detroit Free Press*, January 26, 1861; *Chicago Tribune*, April 15, 1861; *Boston Herald*, April 13, 1861; *Ottawa (IL) Free Trader*, April 27, 1861; John G. Nicolay, *The Outbreak of Rebellion* (1881; reprint, New York: Da Capo Press, 1995), 75; Russell, *My Diary North and South*, 369.
8. Samuel Wickliffe Melton to his wife, n.d., December 1860; March 23, April 24 and 25, 1861, in Samuel Wickliffe Melton Papers, USC South Caroliniana Library, South Carolina; Russell, *My Diary North and South*, 239; Jeremiah Tate to his sister Mary, May 12, 1861, Jeremiah Tate Papers, Gilder Lehrman Collection, Pierpont Morgan Library, New York; Russell, *My Diary North and South*, 311, 333.
9. Lincoln, "Proclamation Calling Militia and Convening Congress," April 15, 1861, in Roy F. Basler (ed.), *The Collected Works of Abraham Lincoln*, Vol. IV (New Brunswick, NJ: Rutgers University Press, 1953), 331–32.
10. James W. Geary, *We Need Men: The Union Draft in the Civil War* (Dekalb: Northern Illinois University Press, 1991), 6–7; Lincoln, "Proclamation Calling for 42,034 Volunteers," May 3, 1861, in Lincoln, *Collected Works*, IV, 353–54; Frederick Douglass, "'The Black Man's Future in the Southern States,' An Address Delivered in Boston, February 5, 1862," in Louis P. Masur, *The Real War Will Never Get in the Books: Selections from Writers during the Civil War* (New York: Oxford University Press, 1993), 110; Frederick Doug-

lass, quoted in Dudley Taylor Cornish, *The Sable Arm: Negro Troops in the Union Army, 1861–1865* (New York: Norton, 1956), 5–6.

11. Russell F. Weigley, *Quartermaster General of the Union Army: A Biography of M. C. Meigs* (New York: Columbia University Press, 1959), 203–4.

12. Gerald J. Prokopowicz, *All For the Regiment: The Army of the Ohio, 1861–1862* (Chapel Hill: University of North Carolina Press, 2001), 5; a detailed description of the size, organization, and command structures of the Civil War military units can be found in David J. Eicher, *The Longest Night: A Military History of the Civil War* (New York: Simon & Schuster, 2001; London: Pimlico, 2002), 58–70.

13. Edward K. Ward to his sister, June 18, 1861, June 14, 1862 in Edward K. Ward Papers, Gilder Lehrman Collection (GLC2232), Pierpont Morgan Library, New York.

14. Weigley, *Quartermaster General*, 204–5, 253–55.

15. William T. Sherman, Orders No. 19, April 4, 1861, *The War of the Rebellion: A Compilation of the Official Records of the Union and Confederate Armies* (hereafter: ORA), Series I, XII (I) (Washington, D.C.: Government Printing Office, 1880–1900), 92.

16. Edward Hagerman, *The American Civil War and the Origins of Modern Warfare: Idea, Organization, and Field Command* (1988; reprint, Bloomington: Indiana University Press, 1992), 16–17; *New York Times*, December 9, 1854.

17. Holden Reid, *Civil War*, 78–81; Eicher, *Longest Night*, 409–12; Laurens Wolcott to his brother, December 27, 1861 in Laurens W. Wolcott Papers, Gilder Lehrman Collection (GLC00653.11), Pierpont Morgan Library, New York.

18. Eicher, *Longest Night*, 413–16; Hagerman, *Origins of Modern Warfare*, 16; ORA, I, XXVII (I), 622–26; Joshua Lawrence Chamberlain, *Bayonet! Forward: My Civil War Reminiscences* (Gettysburg, Pennsylvania: Stan Clark Military Books, 1994), 32–33; Glenn LaFantasie, "Joshua Chamberlain and the American Dream," in Gabor S. Boritt (ed.), *The Gettysburg Nobody Knows* (New York: Oxford University Press, 1997), 31–55.

19. Montgomery C. Meigs to Simon Cameron, June 25, 1861, ORA, III, I, 295.

20. Holden Reid, *Civil War*, 80.

21. Russell, *Diary North and South*, 281; Holden Reid, "Command and Leadership," *Civil War*, 147; Lincoln to Edwin D. Morgan, May 20, 1861, in Lincoln, *Collected Works*, IV, 375.

22. Lincoln, quoted in James M. McPherson, *Battle Cry of Freedom: The Civil War Era* (New York: Oxford University Press, 1988), 336.

23. Eicher, *Longest Night*, 87–91; James B. Fry, "The South Triumphant, the North Disappointed: McDowell's Advance to Bull Run," in Ned Bradford (ed.), *Battles and Leaders of the Civil War* (New York: Appleton Century, 1956), 25–40; P. G. T. Beauregard, "Look at Jackson's Brigade! It Stands There like a Stone Wall!: The First Battle of Bull Run," in *Battles and Leaders*, 41–60; Irvin McDowell to E. D. Townsend, July 20, 1861, ORA, I (II), 308.

24. Eicher, *Longest Night*, 92–100; Bee, quoted in *Battles and Leaders*, 52; Nicolay, *Outbreak of Rebellion*, 198.

25. Irvin McDowell to E. D. Townsend, dispatches of July 21, ORA, I, II, 316; Russell, *Diary North and South*, 467–68, 470.

26. Russell, *My Diary North and South*, 467; Johnston, quoted in Nicolay, *Outbreak of Rebellion*, 211; *Springfield (Daily) Republican*, July, 24, 1861.

Chapter 4

1. Charles B. Haydon, diary entry for July 24, 1861 in Stephen W. Sears (ed.), *For Country, Cause and Leader: The Civil War Journal of Charles B. Haydon* (New York: Ticknor and Fields, 1993), 60; L. Thomas to McClellan, July 22, 1861, *The War of the Rebellion: A Compilation of the Official Records of the Union and Confederate Armies* (hereafter: ORA), Series I, II (Washington, D.C.: Government Printing Office, 1880–1900), 753; *New York Herald* and *New York Times*, both quoted in Stephen W. Sears, *George B. McClellan: The Young Napoleon* (New York: Ticknor and Fields, 1988), 93; McClellan to his wife Ellen, quoted in David E. Eicher, *The Longest Night: A Military History of the Civil War* (London: Pimlico, 2002), 101.

2. Ethel Lynn Beers, "The Picket Guard," *Harper's Weekly*, November 30, 1861; Sears, *George B. McClellan*, 93; William Howard Russell, *My Diary North and South* (Boston: T. O. H. P. Burnham, 1863), 473, 555.

3. Charles Colcock Jones, Jr. to his father, Rev. Charles Colcock Jones, July 24, 1861, in Robert Manson Myers, *The Children of Pride: A True Story of Georgia and the Civil War* (Abridged edition, New Haven: Yale University Press, 1984), 98; Henry Wager Halleck, *Elements of Military Art and Science Or, Course of Instruction in Strategy, Fortification, Tactics of Battles, &C.; Embracing the Duties of Staff, Infantry, Cavalry, Artillery, and Engineers; Adapted to the Use of Volunteers and Militia; Third Edition; with Critical Notes on the Mexican And Crimean Wars* (1846; reprint, New York and London, D. Appleton & Company, 1862), 16; William J. Cooper, Jr., *Jefferson Davis, American* (2000; paperback reprint, New York: Random House, 2001), 375–76.

4. Russell F. Weigley, *The American Way of War: A History of United States Military Strategy and Policy* (Bloomington: Indiana University Press, 1973), 96–97; Halleck, *Elements of Military Art and Science*, 17.

5. Weigley, *American Way of War*, 95; Edward Hagerman, *The American Civil War and the Origins of Modern Warfare: Ideas, Organization, and Field Command* (1988; reprint, Bloomington: Indiana University Press, 1992), 3–27; Lincoln to Don Carlos Buell and copy to Henry W. Halleck, January 13, 1862, in Roy F. Basler (ed.), *The Collected Works of Abraham Lincoln*, Vol. V (New Brunswick, NJ: Rutgers University Press, 1953), 98–99; Stonewall Jackson, quoted in John D. Imboden, "Jackson's Foot Cavalry: Stonewall Jackson in the Shenandoah," *Battles and Leaders*, Vol. II, 297.

6. *Official Records of the Union and Confederate Navies in the War of the Rebellion* (hereafter: ORN), Series I (VI) (Washington, D.C.: Government Printing Office, 1897), 120; William M. Fowler, Jr., *Under Two Flags: The American Navy in the Civil War* (New York: W. W. Norton, 1990), 62–64; ORN, I (VI), 121–22.

7. Russell, *My Diary North and South*, 513; *London Morning Chronicle*, November 28, 1861; Gustavus Fox to Stringham, September 14, 1861; F. H. Morse to William H. Seward, August 24, 1861; Stringham to Fox, September 16, 1861, ORN, I (VI), 210–11, 213–14; 216; Fowler, *Under Two Flags*, 68.

8. Report of du Pont to Gideon Welles, November 8 and 9, 1861, ORN, I (XII), 261–65; Weigley, *American Way of War*, 100; Fowler, *Under Two Flags*, 65, 71–78.

9. *New York Times*, March 10, 1861; Herman Melville, "The Temeraire," in *Battle-Pieces and Aspects of the War: Civil War Poems* (New York: Prometheus Books, 2001), 87–88; Fowler, *Under Two Flags*, 84–91; Michael J. Bennett, *Union Jacks: Yankee Sailors in the Civil War* (Chapel Hill: University of North Carolina Press, 2004), 78–79. The *Temeraire* went to the aid of Nelson's flagship, HMS *Victory*, at Trafalgar.

10. U. S. Grant to S. B. Buckner; Buckner to Grant, both February 16, 1862, ORA, I, VII, 160–61; Eicher, *Longest Night*, 219.

11. Ulysses S. Grant, *Personal Memoirs* (1885/6; London: Penguin, 1999), 195.

12. U. S. Grant to William T. Sherman, April 4, 1861; Sherman to Grant; Grant to Henry Halleck, both April 5; A. S. Johnston to the Army of the Mississippi, April 3; Grant to Commanding Officer, Advance Forces (Buell's Army); Wm. S. Hillyer (on behalf of Grant) to T. J. Wood, Clark Lagow (on behalf of Grant) to Gen. Nelson, all April 6, ORA, I, X (II), 91, 93–94, 389, 95–96; Eicher, *Longest Night*, 222–29; James M. McPherson (ed.), *The Atlas of the Civil War* (New York: Macmillan, 1994), 50–51.

13. Grant, *Memoirs*, 184, 192.

14. Braxton Bragg to Beauregard, April 8, 1862, ORA, I, XII (II), 398; Figures are extracted from Frederick H. Dyer, *A Compendium of the War of the Rebellion*, Vol. II (New York: Thomas Yoseloff, 1959).

15. Augustus R. Wright to his son Miller Wright, August 3, 1861, Augustus and Miller Wright Papers, Gilder Lehrman Collection (GLC 02691.11), Pierpont Morgan Library, New York; Henrietta Stratton Jaquette (ed.), *Letters of a Confederate Nurse: Cornelia Hancock, 1863–1865* (Lincoln: University of Nebraska Press, 1998), 5; Lieutenant Tuttle (3rd Kentucky), quoted in Gerald J. Prokopowicz, *All For the Regiment: The Army of the Ohio, 1861–1862* (Chapel Hill: University of North Carolina Press, 2001), 111; Grant, *Memoirs*, 188, 198; Torah Sampson, quoted in Prokopowicz, *All For the Regiment*, 110; Melville, "Shiloh: A Requiem," in *Battle-Pieces*, 63.

16. D. G. Farragut to Gideon Welles, April 29 and May 6, 1862; T. Bailey to Welles, May 8, 1862, all in ORN, I (XVIII), 158–59; 149–50; Fowler, *Under Two Flags*, 114–24; Mary Boykin Chesnut, diary entry April 27, 1862, in *A Diary from Dixie* (Boston: Houghton Mifflin, 1949), 215; Eicher, *Longest Night*, 237–41.

17. Rowena Reed, *Combined Operations in the Civil War* (1978; reprint, Lincoln: University of Nebraska Press, 1993), 190–223.

18. McClellan, quoted in Sears, "Lincoln and McClellan," 19; Reed, *Combined Operations*, 36–40; Sears, *George B. McClellan*, 95–114; Sears, *To The Gates of Richmond: The Peninsula Campaign* (New York: Ticknor and Fields, 1992), 3–9.

19. Sears, "Lincoln and McClellan," 28–29; *To the Gates of Richmond*, 9, 29–30.

20. Sears, *To the Gates of Richmond*, 23; Elisha Hunt Rhodes, diary entry March 27, 1862, Robert Hunt Rhodes (ed.), *All For the Union: The Civil War Diary and Letters of Elisha Hunt Rhodes* (1985; reprint, New York: Random House, 1992), 53; Russell, *My Diary North and South*, 546.

21. Lincoln to McClellan, April 9, 1862, in Lincoln, *Collected Works*, V, 184–85; D. H. Hill to George W. Randolph (CSA Secretary of War), April 21 and 24, 1862; J. E. Johnston to Robert E. Lee, April 22, 1862, ORA, I, XI (III), 454–56.

22. Sears, *For Country, Cause and Leader*, 216; George Templeton Strong, diary entry, April 12, 1862 in Allan Nevins and Milton Halsey Thomas (eds.), *The Diary of George Templeton Strong: The Turbulent Fifties, 1850–1859*, Vol. II (New York: Macmillan, 1952), 216.

23. D. H. Hill to George W. Randolph, April 24, 1862; J. E. Johnston to Robert E. Lee, April 30, 1862, ORA, I, XI (III), 461, 477.

24. J. E. Johnston to Robert E. Lee, April 30, May 10, 1862, ORA, I, XI (III), 477, 506;

25. Lincoln to McClellan, May 24, 25, and June 1, 1862, in *Lincoln Collected Works*, V, 232, 235–36, 237, 255; Sears, *George B. McClellan*, 192.

26. G. B. McClellan to the Army of the Potomac, June 2, 1862, ORA, I, XI (III), 210; Mary Chesnut, diary entry, June 16, 1862 in Chesnut, *A Diary from Dixie*, 252.

27. McClellan, quoted in Sears, *To the Gates of Richmond*, 162.

28. Lincoln to McClellan, June 18, 1862, in *Lincoln Collected Works*, V, 276; McClellan to Lincoln, June 18, 1862; James Longstreet's address to his troops, June 17, 1862, both ORA, I, XI (III), 233, 606; Sears, *To the Gates of Richmond*, 154–58; Emory M. Thomas, *Bold Dragoon: The Life of J. E. B. Stuart* (1986; reprint, Norman: University of Oklahoma Press, 1999), 113–25.

29. Robert E. Lee to Thomas J. Jackson, June 16, 1862, ORA I, XI (III), 602; McClellan to Stanton, June 26, 1862, ORA I, XI (III), 260.

30. McClellan to Stanton, June 25, 1862, ORA, I, XI (I), 51.

31. Sears, *To the Gates of Richmond*, 208–9; quotation in Sears, *George B. McClellan*, 211; McClellan to Stanton; and to Flag Officer Louis M. Goldsborough, June 27, 1862, ORA I, XI (III), 266–67.

32. McClellan to Stanton, June 28, 1862, ORA, I, XI (I), 61.

33. Elisha Hunt Rhodes, diary entry June 29, 1862, in Rhodes, *All For the Union*, 64; McClellan to Stanton, June 30; Stanton to McClellan, July 1, 1862, ORA, I, XI (III), 280–81.

34. Elisha Hunt Rhodes, diary entry, July 1, 1862, in Rhodes, *All For the Union*, 65.

35. McClellan to Lorenzo Thomas, July 5, 1862, ORA, I, XI (III), 299; Lincoln, quoted in Stephen W. Sears, "Lincoln and McClellan," in Gabor S. Boritt (ed.), *Lincoln's Generals* (New York: Oxford University Press, 1994), 3–50, 22; Elisha Hunt Rhodes, diary entry, July 4, 1862, in Rhodes, *All For the Union*, 66.

Chapter 5

1. Sallie Brock Putnam, *Richmond during the War: Four Years of Personal Observation* (1867; reprint, Lincoln: University of Nebraska Press, 1996), 149, 151.

2. George Templeton Strong, diary entry, August 19, 1862, in Allan Nevins and Milton Halsey Thomas (eds.), *The Diary of George Templeton Strong: The Civil War*, Vol. III (New York: Macmillan, 1952), 247; Edward Dicey, *Spectator of America* (1863; reprint, Athens: University of Georgia Press, 1989), 276.

3. Lincoln, "First Inaugural Address," March 4, 1861, and "Message to Congress," March 6, 1862, in Roy F. Basler (ed.), *The Collected Works of Abraham Lincoln*, Vol. IV (New Brunswick, NJ: Rutgers University Press, 1953), 282–83; Vol. V, 44–46; *National Intelligencer*, October 8, 1861; Dicey, *Spectator of America*, 277–79.

4. George W. Tillotson to his wife Libby, May 30, 1862, in George W. Tillotson Papers, Gilder Lehrman Collection (GLC04588), Pierpont Morgan Library, New York; Phillip Shaw Paludan, *A People's Contest: The Union and Civil War, 1861–1865*, 2nd ed. (Lawrence: University Press of Kansas, 1996), 65; George Julian, quoted in Bruce Tap, *Over Lincoln's Shoulder: The Committee on the Conduct of the War* (Lawrence: University Press of Kansas, 1998), 118.

5. Henrietta Stratton Jaquette (ed.), *Letters of a Confederate Nurse: Cornelia Hancock, 1863–1865* (Lincoln: University of Nebraska Press, 1998), 31.

6. Jacqueline Jones, *Labor of Love, Labor of Sorrow: Black Women, Work, and the Family from Slavery to the Present* (New York: Basic Books, 1985), 48–49; Leon F. Liwack, *Been in the Storm So Long: The Aftermath of Slavery* (1979; reprint, New York: Vintage Books, 1980), 129–31; on contraband women see also Thavolia Glymph, "'This Species of Property': Female Slave Contrabands in the Civil War," in Edward D. C. Campbell, Jr. and Kym S. Rice (eds.), *A Woman's War: Southern Women, Civil War, and the Confederate Legacy* (Richmond, The Museum of the Confederacy and Charlottesville: University Press of Virginia, 1996), 55–71; Wilma King, "'Suffer With Them Till Death': Slave Women and Their Children in Nineteenth-Century America," in David Barry Gaspar and Darlene Clark Hine (eds.), *More Than Chattel: Black Women and Slavery in the Americas* (Bloomington: Indiana University Press, 1996), 147–68.

7. Hancock, *Letters of a Civil War Nurse*, 43.

8. Thomas Wentworth Higginson, *Army Life in a Black Regiment* (1869; reprint, Boston: Beacon Press, 1962), 15.

9. Steven J. Ramold, *Slaves, Sailors, Citizens: African Americans in the Union Navy* (DeKalb: Northern Illinois University Press, 2002), 37–39; General Orders No. 27, Department of the South, August 17, 1862, *The War of the Rebellion: A Compilation of the Official Records of the Union and Confederate Armies* (hereafter: ORA), Series I, XIV (Washington, D.C.: Government Printing Office, 1880–1900), 376; Edwin M. Stanton to Rufus Saxton, August 25, 1862, ORA, I, XIV, 377.

10. Rufus Saxton to Edwin M. Stanton, August 16, 1862, ORA, I, XIV, 374–76.

11. William E. Gladstone, Speech at Newcastle, October 7, 1862, and Lord Russell's response, both in Belle Becker Sideman and Lillian Friedman (eds.), *Europe Looks at the Civil War* (New York: Collier Books, 1962), 157.

12. Lincoln, "Appeal to Border State Representatives to Favor Compensated Emancipation," July 12, 1862, in Lincoln, *Collected Works*, V, 317–18.

13. Lincoln to Horace Greeley, August 22, 1862, in Lincoln, *Collected Works*, V, 388–89.

14. Lincoln, "Reply to Emancipation Memorial Presented by Chicago Christians of All Denominations," September 13, 1862, in Lincoln, *Collected Works*, V, 419–25, quotations 420, 423.

15. George B. McClellan to Lincoln, July 7, 1862, McClellan's letter can be accessed online at: http://www.law.ou.edu/hist/mcclel.html (October 25, 2005).

16. E. D. Keyes to Lincoln, July 10, 1862, ORA, I, XI (III), 313–14; Allen C. Guelzo, *Abraham Lincoln: Redeemer President* (Cambridge, England: William B. Eerdmans Publishing, 1999), 305–6.

17. Robert E. Lee, quoted in Russell F. Weigley, *The American Way of War: A History of United States Military Strategy and Policy* (1973; paperback reprint, Bloomington: Indiana University Press, 1977), 108; R. E. Clary to General Meigs, August 26; H. Haupt to Jacob D. Cox, August 26; McClellan to Halleck, and Halleck to McClellan, August 27, all 1862, ORA, I, XII (III), 677–91.

18. Strong, diary entries for August 29 and September 4, 1862, in Nevins and Thomas, *Diary*, III, 249, 252; Elisha Hunt Rhodes, September 3, 1862, in Robert Hunt Rhodes (ed.), *All For the Union: The Civil War Diary and Letters of Elisha Hunt Rhodes* (1985; reprint, New York: Random House, 1992) 71; John Pope to Halleck, September 2, 1862, ORA, I, XII (III), 797.

19. Lincoln to McClellan, August 29, 1862, and McClellan's reply, in Lincoln, *Collected Works*, V, 399; Weigley, *American Way of War*, 109; Strong, diary entry, September 4, 1862, in Nevins and Thomas, *Diary*, III, 252.
20. Helmuth von Moltke, quoted in Jones, *Civil War Command and Strategy*, 74; and in Jay Luvaas, "The Influence of the German Wars of Unification on the United States," in Stig Förster and Jörg Nagler (eds.), *On the Road to Total War: The American Civil War and the German Wars of Unification, 1861–1871* (Washington, D.C. and Cambridge, England: German Historical Institute and Cambridge University Press, 1997), 597–619, quotation 605; Robert E. Lee to Jefferson Davis, September 3, 1862, ORA, I, XIX (II), 590–91.
21. Weigley, *American Way of War*, 109.
22. Robert E. Lee to Jefferson Davis, September 7, 1862, ORA, I, XIX (II), 596–97.
23. Private from 5th Wisconsin, quoted in James M. McPherson, *Crossroads of Freedom: Antietam: The Battle that Changed the Course of the American Civil War* (2002; reprint, London: Penguin Books, 2003), 104; McClellan to Lincoln, September 13, 1862, ORA, I, XIX (II), 281.
24. McClellan to Halleck, September 15, 1862, ORA, I, XIX (II), 294; Lincoln to Jesse K. Dubois; and to McClellan, September 15, 1862, both in Lincoln, *Collected Works*, V, 425–26; Gideon Welles, quoted in Stephen Sears, *Landscape Turned Red: The Battle of Antietam* (1983; paperback reprint, New York: Warner Books, 1985), 175; Dispatch sent by Lee to McLaws and R. H. Chilton, September 14, 1862, ORA, I, LI (II), 618–19.
25. Andrew G. Curtin to McClellan, September 15, 1862, ORA, I, XIX (II), 306; Herman Melville, "The Victor of Antietam (1862)," in *Battle-Pieces and Aspects of the War: Civil War Poems* (1866; reprint, New York: Prometheus Books, 2001), 95.
26. Report of Joseph Hooker; McClellan to Hooker, September 20, 1862, both in ORA I, XIX (I), 618–19; McClellan to Halleck, September 17, 1:20 PM, ORA, I, XIX (II), 312.
27. *New York Times*, October 20, 1862; Samuel Fiske (14th Connecticut); Diarist from 9th Pennsylvania, both quoted in Sears, *Landscape Turned Red*, 347; McClellan to Halleck, September 18 and 22, 1862, ORA, I, XIX (II), 330, 342.
28. Lincoln, "Preliminary Emancipation Proclamation," September 22, 1862, in Lincoln, *Collected Works*, V, 433–36, quotations 433–34.
29. Ira Berlin et al., *Slaves No More: Three Essays on Emancipation and the Civil War* (Cambridge: Cambridge University Press, 1992), 3; Frederick Douglass, "'The Day of Jubilee Comes,' An Address Delivered in Rochester, New York, December 28, 1862," in Masur, *The Real War Will Never Get in the Books*, 113–14.
30. George O. Bartlett to Ira Andrews, January 7, 1863, Bartlett Papers; George Tillotson to his wife, September 24, 1862, in Tillotson Papers, both in Gilder Lehrman Collection, Pierpont Morgan Library, New York; A New Yorker, quoted in James M. McPherson, *Marching Toward Freedom: The Negro in the Civil War, 1861–1865* (New York: Alfred A. Knopf, 1967), 10.
31. Mary Chesnut, diary entries June 9, 1862, March 4, 1861, in *A Diary from Dixie* (Boston: Houghton Mifflin , 1949), 242, 11; Chesnut, diary entry, October 19, 1861 in C. Vann Woodward and Elisabeth Muhlenfeld (eds.), *The Private Mary Chesnut: The Unpublished Civil War Diaries* (New York: Oxford University Press, 1984), 181.
32. Mary Chesnut, diary entry, May 4, 1865 in *A Diary from Dixie*, 527; Mary Jones; Eva B. Jones to Mary Jones, July 14, 1865, in Robert Manson Myers, *The Children of Pride: A True Story of Georgia and the Civil War* (Abridged edition, New Haven: Yale University Press, 1984), 523, 554.
33. Frederick Douglass, "'Fighting the Rebels With One Hand': An Address Delivered in Philadelphia, Pennsylvania, January 14, 1862," in Masur, *The Real War Will Never Get in the Books*, 108.
34. Lincoln, "Emancipation Proclamation," January 1, 1863, in Lincoln, *Collected Works*, VI, 28–31, quotation 30.
35. War Department instructions to Robert Dale Owen et al., ORA, III, III, 73.
36. "American Freedmen's Inquiry Commission Report," June 30, 1863, ORA, III (III), 430–54, quotation 438; Frederick Douglass quoted in McPherson, *Marching Toward Freedom*, 68.
37. AFIC Report, June 30, 1863, ORA, III, III, 440.

38. Johns, quoted in Leon F. Litwack, *Been in the Storm So Long: The Aftermath of Slavery* (1979; paperback reprint; New York: Vintage Books, 1980), 70; Lieutenant in 3rd Louisiana Native Guards, *New York Times*, June 11, 1863, quoted in Joseph T. Glatthaar, *Forged in Battle: The Civil War Alliance of Black Soldiers and White Officers* (New York: Meridian, 1991), 129–30.

39. Charles A. Dana; *Chicago Tribune*, November 10, 1862, both quoted in Glatthaar, *Forged in Battle*, 135, 122.

40. Northern soldier, quoted in Edward A. Miller, Jr., *The Black Civil War Soldiers of Illinois: The Story of the Twenty-Ninth U.S. Colored Infantry* (Columbia: South Carolina University Press, 1998), 5; Halpine, quoted in Ervin L. Jordan, Jr., *Black Confederates and Afro-Yankees in Civil War Virginia* (Charlottesville: Virginia University Press, 1995), 266.

41. Lincoln, "Annual Message to Congress," December 1, 1862, in Lincoln, *Collected Works*, V, 518–37, quotations 530, 536, 537.

42. Lincoln to James C. Conkling, August 26, 1863, in Lincoln, *Collected Works*, VI, 409–10.

43. Henry S. Harmon, Corporal, Co. B, 3rd USCI, Morris Island, South Carolina, to the *Christian Recorder*, October 23, 1863. The letter appeared in the paper on November 7, 1863. Edwin S. Redkey, (ed), *A Grand Army of Black Men: Letters from African-American Soldiers in the Union Army, 1861–1865* (New York: Cambridge University Press, 1992), 36.

44. Joint Committee on the Conduct of the War, *Report on the Fort Pillow Massacre* (Washington, D.C.: Government Printing Office, 1864), 2, 4. The full text can be accessed online at: http://www.hti.umich.edu/cgi/t/text/text-idx?c=moa;idno=AAW7861 (June 25, 2005).

Chapter 6

1. Marching song of the 1st Arkansas Colored Regiment, quoted in Robert F. Mullen, *Blacks in America's Wars* (New York: Monad Press, 1974), 23–24.

2. McClellan to William H. Aspinwall, September 26, 1862; Lincoln to Ozias M. Hatch, October 2, 1862, both quoted in Stephen Sears, *George B. McClellan: The Young Napoleon* (New York: Ticknor and Fields, 1988), 324, 331.

3. Lincoln to McClellan, October 13, October 24 [25], 1862, in Roy F. Basler (ed.), *The Collected Works of Abraham Lincoln*, Vol. V (New Brunswick, NJ: Rutgers University Press, 1953), 460–61, 474; Halleck to Governor Gamble (of Missouri), October 30, 1862, *The War of the Rebellion: A Compilation of the Official Records of the Union and Confederate Armies* (hereafter: ORA), Series II (II) (Washington, D.C.: Government Printing Office, 1880–1900), 703–4; Lincoln to Halleck, November 5, 1862, in Lincoln, *Collected Works*, V, 485; McClellan to the Army of the Potomac, November 7, 1862, ORA, I, XIX (II), 551; Elisha Hunt Rhodes, diary entry November 10, 1862, in Robert Hunt Rhodes (ed.), *All For the Union: The Civil War Diary and Letters of Elisha Hunt Rhodes* (1985; reprint, New York: Random House, 1992), 80.

4. Thomas Lawrence Connelly, *Army of the Heartland: The Army of Tennessee, 1861–1862* (1967; reprint, Baton Rouge: Louisiana State University Press, 1978), 3–7; Connelly, *Autumn of Glory: The Army of Tennessee, 1862–1865* (1971; reprint, Baton Rouge: Louisiana State University Press, 1974), 6.

5. Halleck to Buell, June 1, 1862; Halleck to Stanton, June 12, 1862, both ORA, I, XVI (II), 9, 10; Lincoln to Halleck, July 13, 1862, in Lincoln, *Collected Works*, V, 322; Archer Jones, *Civil War Command and Strategy: The Process of Victory and Defeat* (New York: Free Press, 1992), 84–86; Gerald Prokopowicz, *All For the Regiment: The Army of the Ohio, 1861–1862* (Chapel Hill: University of North Carolina Press, 2001), 129–30.

6. Braxton Bragg to S. Cooper, August 1, 1862, ORA, I, XVI (II), 741; Brigade commander's description of Bragg, quoted in Jones, *Civil War Command and Strategy*, 92.

7. Sam Jones, "Proclamation to the People of East Tennessee," September 30, 1862, ORA, I, XVI (II), 895; Bragg, quoted in David Urquhart, "Bragg's Advance and Retreat," *Battles and Leaders*, III, 601.

8. Prokopowicz, *All For the Regiment*, 158, 178.

9. Ambrose Burnside, General Orders No. 1, November 9, 1862; Burnside to General G. W. Cullen, November 7 (sent on November 9), 1862, ORA, I, XIX (II), 552–54; George

Templeton Strong, diary entry, November 13, 1862, in Allan Nevins and Milton Halsey Thomas (eds.), *The Diary of George Templeton Strong: The Civil War*, Vol. III (New York: Macmillan, 1952), 274–75; Joseph Jones, quoted in Erskine Clarke, *Dwelling Place: A Plantation Epic* (New Haven: Yale University Press, 2005), 424.

10. Mattie J. Jackson, *The Story of Mattie Jackson* (Lawrence, KS: Sentinel Office, 1866); cited in Emmy E. Werner, *Reluctant Witnesses: Children's Voices from the Civil War* (New York: Westview Press/Harper Collins, 1998), 44–46.

11. Céline's story is given in, and quotation taken from Werner, *Reluctant Witnesses*, 26–29.

12. Charles Haydon, diary entries, December 11 and 12, 1862 in Stephen W. Sears (ed.), *For Country, Cause and Leader: The Civil War Journal of Charles B. Haydon* (New York: Ticknor and Fields, 1993), 296–97; Lee to S. Cooper, December 11, 1862, ORA, I (XXI), 545.

13. David J. Eicher, *The Longest Night: A Military History of the Civil War* (2001; reprint, London: Pimlico, 2002), 401; George C. Rable, *Fredericksburg, Fredericksburg!* (Chapel Hill: University of North Carolina Press, 2002), 235; Craig A. Warren, "'Oh, God, What a Pity!': The Irish Brigade at Fredericksburg and the Creation of Myth," *Civil War History* 47, 3 (2001), 193–221; Lee quoted in Eicher, *Longest Night*, 403.

14. Charles Gordon Hutton to Burnside; William B. Franklin to Burnside; Darius N. Couch to Burnside, December 13, 1862, ORA, I (XXI), 112, 117–120; Haydon, December 13, 1862, in Sears, *For Country, Cause and Leader*, 298.

15. Report of Col. Rush C. Hawkins, 9th New York Infantry, December 19, 1862; Lee to James A. Seddon, December 16, 1862, both in ORA, I (XXI), 340, 549; Russell F. Weigley, *The American Way of War: A History of United States Military Strategy and Policy* (Bloomington: Indiana University Press, 1978), 113; Elisha Hunt Rhodes, diary entries, December 16 and 31, in Rhodes, *All For the Union*, 83–85.

16. John J. Hennessy, "'We Shall Make Richmond Howl': The Army of the Potomac on the Eve of Chancellorsville," in Gary Gallagher (ed.), *Chancellorsville: The Battle and its Aftermath* (Chapel Hill: University of North Carolina Press, 1996), 1–35, quotation 1; Lincoln to Hooker, January 26, 1863, in Lincoln, *Collected Works*, VI, 78–79.

17. General Orders No. 48, April 30, 1863; Stanton to Hooker, May 2, 1863, ORA, I, XXV (II), 316.

18. Lee to Jackson, May 3, 1863; Davis to Lee, May 11, 1863, ORA, I, XXV (II), 769, 791.

19. Rufus Ingalls to Dan Butterfield, May 3, 1863 (8:45 am, 12:45 pm); Hooker to Lincoln, May 3, 1863, ORA, I, XXV (II), 377, 379; Leonidas Torrence (23rd North Carolina), quoted in Stephen Sears, *Chancellorsville* (Boston: Houghton Mifflin, 1996), 365.

20. Robert E. Lee to Jefferson Davis, June 10, 1863, in Clifford Dowdey and Louis H. Manarin (eds.), *The Wartime Papers of R. E. Lee* (New York: Bramhall House, 1961), 508.

21. Gallagher, *Chancellorsville*, ix.

22. Sallie Brock Putnam, *Richmond During the War: Four Years of Personal Observation* (1867; reprint, Lincoln: University of Nebraska Press, 1996), 208–9.

23. Lincoln to Hooker May 14, June 10, and 16, 1863, in Lincoln, *Collected Works*, VI, 217, 257, 282; Hooker to Halleck, June 24, 27, 1863, ORA, I, XXVII (I), 56, 60; John F. Marszalek, *Commander of All Lincoln's Armies: A Life of General Henry W. Halleck* (Cambridge, MA: Harvard University Press, 2004), 172–75.

24. Lee to Samuel Cooper, January 20, 1864, in Dowdey and Manarin (eds.), *Wartime Papers of R. E. Lee*, 576; E. P. Alexander, quoted in Eicher, *Longest Night*, 546.

25. Rhodes, diary entries July 3, 4, and 9, in Rhodes, *All for the Union*, 108–9.

26. Lee to Samuel Cooper, January 20, 1864, in Dowdey and Manarin (eds.), *Wartime Papers of R. E. Lee*, 578; Pickett, quoted in Carol Reardon, "'I Think the Union Army Had Something to Do with It': The Pickett's Charge Nobody Knows," in Gabor S. Boritt (ed.), *The Gettysburg Nobody Knows* (New York: Oxford University Press, 1997), 122–143, quotation 122.

27. T. L. Crittenden to Col. Garesché, December 29, 1862, ORA, I, XX (II), 263.

28. Rosecrans, General Orders, December 31, 1862, ORA, I, XX (I), 183.

29. Eicher, *Longest Night*, 420–28; Peter Cozzens, *No Better Place to Die: The Battle of Stones River* (Urbana: University of Illinois Press, 1991), 177–98; Connelly, *Autumn of Glory*, 44–65; Lincoln to Rosecrans, January 5, August 31, 1863, in Lincoln, *Collected Works*, VI, 39, 424–25.

30. Ulysses S. Grant, *Personal Memoirs* (1885/86; reprint, London: Penguin Books, 1999), 239.
31. Grant, *Memoirs*, 262.
32. Grant, *Memoirs*, 236; Lincoln to Isaac Arnold, May 26, 1863, in Lincoln, *Collected Works*, VI, 230.
33. Grant, *Memoirs*, 291, 313; Pemberton, quoted on 311.

Chapter 7

1. Daniel Webster, House of Representatives, January 14, 1814, in *The Debates and Proceedings in the Congress of the United States (Annals of Congress)*, 13th Congress, 2nd sess., 945–6.
2. Lincoln, "Message to Congress in Special Session," July 4th, 1861, in Roy F. Basler (ed.), *The Collected Works of Abraham Lincoln*, Vol. IV (New Brunswick, NJ: Rutgers University Press, 1953), 438.
3. Edward Dicey, *Spectator of America* (1863; reprint, Athens: University of Georgia Press, 1989), 295.
4. George Templeton Strong, diary entries, November 4 and 5, 1862, in Allan Nevins and Milton Halsey Thomas (eds.), *The Diary of George Templeton Strong: The Civil War*, Vol. III (New York: Macmillan, 1952), 270–72.
5. *Chicago Tribune*, August 25, 1862; Edward Ingersoll, "Personal Liberty and Martial Law: A Review of Some Pamphlets of the Day (Philadelphia 1862)," in Frank Freidel (ed.), *Union Pamphlets of the Civil War* (Cambridge, MA.: Harvard University Press, 1967), 256.
6. *Congressional Globe*, 37th Cong., 2nd sess., appendix, 52–60.
7. Extract from Burnside's General Orders No. 38, quoted in Frank L. Klement, *The Copperheads in the Middle West* (Chicago: University of Chicago Press, 1960), 89–90; *Chicago Times*, January 3, 1863.
8. Melinda Lawson, *Patriot Fires: Forging a New American Nationalism in the Civil War North* (Lawrence: University Press of Kansas, 2002), 98–99; Strong, diary entries, March 20 and May 12, 1863, in Nevins and Thomas, *Diary*, III, 307, 321.
9. Jean H. Baker, *The Politics of Continuity: Maryland Political Parties From 1858 to 1870* (Baltimore: Johns Hopkins University Press, 1973), 129; Lincoln to Erastus Corning and others, [June 12] 1863, in Lincoln, *Collected Works*, VI, 264, 266–67.
10. Sam Watkins, *Co. Aytch: A Confederate Memoir of the Civil War* (New York: Simon & Schuster, 1992), 244.
11. "A Proclamation By The Governor of Virginia," August 30, 1862, *The War of the Rebellion: A Compilation of the Official Records of the Union and Confederate Armies* (hereafter: ORA), Series I, XI (III) (Washington, D.C.: Government Printing Office, 1880–1900), 947.
12. D. H. Hill to George Randolph, May 10; Joe Johnston to Lee, May 9, 1862, ORA, I, XI (III), 502–3, 506–7.
13. Watkins, *Co. Aytch*, 46–47.
14. William T. Sherman to John Sherman, March 14, 1863, in "Letters of Two Brothers: Passages from the Correspondence of General and Senator Sherman," *Century Magazine*, XLV (November 1892–April 1893), 436.
15. Michael Thomas Smith, "'The Most Desperate Scoundrels Unhung: Bounty Jumpers and Recruitment Fraud in the Civil War North," *American Nineteenth Century History*, 6.2 (June 2005), 149–72.
16. Strong, diary entry, July 13, 1863, in Nevins and Thomas, *Diary*, III, 335; Iver Bernstein, *The New York City Draft Riots: Their Significance for American Society and Politics in the Age of the Civil War* (New York: Oxford University Press, 1990), 18–29; Leslie M. Harris, *In the Shadow of Slavery: African Americans in New York City, 1626–1863* (Chicago: University of Chicago Press, 2003), 280–82; Strong, diary entry, July 19, in Nevins and Thomas, *Diary*, III, 342.
17. Lincoln to Charles D. Drake and others, October 5, 1863, in Lincoln, *Collected Works*, VI, 500.

18. Ibid.
19. Robert Gould Shaw to his parents, April 23, 1861, in Russell Duncan (ed.), *Blue-Eyed Child of Fortune: The Civil War Letters of Robert Gould Shaw* (Athens: University of Georgia Press, 1992), 77; William Haines Lytle in Ruth C. Carter (ed.), *For Honor, Glory and Union: the Mexican and Civil War Letters of Brig. Gen. William Haines Lytle* (Lexington: University Press of Kentucky, 1999), 219; James W. Geary, *We Need Men: The Union Draft in the Civil War* (Dekalb: Northern Illinois University Press, 1991), 6–7; James M. Maitland to his son, August 31, 1862, in Maitland Papers, Gilder Lehrman Collection, Pierpont Morgan Library, New York.
20. George Tillotson to his wife, October 24, 1862, in Tillotson Papers, Gilder Lehrman Collection, Pierpont Morgan Library, New York.
21. George Tillotson to his wife, January 1, 1863, in Tillotson Papers, Gilder Lehrman Collection, Pierpont Morgan Library, New York.
22. J. T. Boyle to J. B. Fry, June 25, Ambrose Burnside to Lincoln, June 26, David Tod to Stanton, June 26, 1863, ORA, III (III), 416, 418–19; Corporal James Henry Gooding to The *New Bedford Mercury*, March 21, 1863, in James Henry Gooding, *On the Altar of Freedom: A Black Soldier's Civil War Letters from the Front* (Amherst: University of Massachusetts Press, 1991), 7; Unnamed private to the *Christian Recorder*, March 1864 in Edwin S. Redkey (ed.), *A Grand Army of Black Men: Letters from African-American Soldiers in the Union Army, 1861-1865* (New York and Cambridge: Cambridge University Press, 1992), 48.
23. T. D. Freeman to William, March 26, 1864, in Nina Silber and Mary Beth Sievens (eds.), *Yankee Correspondence: Civil War Letters between New England Soldiers and the Home Front* (Charlottesville: University of Virginia Press, 1996), 47–48.
24. George E. Stephens, in Donald Yacovone (ed.), *A Voice of Thunder: The Civil War Letters of George E. Stephens* (Urbana: University of Illinois Press, 1997), 281.
25. George E. Stephens, in Yacovone, *A Voice of Thunder*, 288; Frederick Douglass, "'The Black Man's Future in the Southern States,' An Address Delivered in Boston, Massachusetts, February 5, 1862," in Masur (ed.), *The Real War Will Never Get in the Books*, 111; Gooding, May 11, 1863, *On the Altar of Freedom*, 19; George E. Stephens to the *Weekly Anglo-African*, August 7, 1863, Yacovone, *A Voice of Thunder*, 250–51, 254.
26. Henry Ward Beecher, quoted in Elizabeth Young, *Disarming the Nation: Women's Writing and the American Civil War* (Chicago: University of Chicago Press, 1999), 1; Linda K. Kerber, *Women of the Republic: Intellect and Ideology in Revolutionary America* (Chapel Hill: University of North Carolina Press, 1980), xi–xii.
27. Mattie Blanchard to Caleb Blanchard, March 26, 1863, in Nina Silber and Mary Beth Sievens (eds.), *Yankee Correspondence*, 115; Louisa McCord to Hiram Powers, December 24, 1860, in Richard C. Lounsbury (ed.), *Louisa S. McCord: Poems, Drama, Biography, Letters* (Charlottesville: University Press of Virginia, 1996), 364; Jane Stewart Woolsey and Louisa May Alcott, both quoted in Jeanie Attie, "Warwork and the Crisis of Domesticity in the North," in Catherine Clinton and Nina Silber (eds.), *Divided Houses: Gender and the Civil War* (New York: Oxford University Press, 1992), 253.
28. Mary A. Livermore, *My Story of the War* (Hartford, CT: A. D. Washington, 1889), 120; Statistics on nurses from Elizabeth Leonard, *Yankee Women: Gender Battles in the Civil War* (1994; paperback reprint, New York: W. W. Norton, 1995), 7–8; see also Elizabeth Leonard, *All the Daring of the Soldier: Women of the Civil War Armies* (New York: W. W. Norton, 1999; paperback reprint, London: Penguin Books, 2001), 165–68 (for estimated figures, see notes on 310–11).
29. LeeAnn Whites, *The Civil War as a Crisis in Gender: Augusta, Georgia 1860-1890* (Athens: University of Georgia Press, 1995), 39–40; DeAnne Blanton and Lauren M. Cook, *They Fought Like Demons: Women Soldiers of the American Civil War* (Baton Rouge: Louisiana State University Press, 2002), 201–2; ORA, I, XVII (I), 378; Elijah Cavins (107th Pennsylvania Regiment) quoted in Stephen W. Sears, *Chancellorsville* (Boston: Houghton Mifflin, 1996), 79; Rosecrans, quoted in Mary Elizabeth Massey, *Women in the Civil War* (Originally published as *Bonnet Brigades*, New York: Alfred A. Knopf, 1966; reprint, Lincoln: University of Nebraska Press, 1994), 84.
30. George Tillotson to his wife, May 15, 1862, in Tillotson Papers, Gilder Lehrman Collection, Pierpont Morgan Library, New York.

31. Loreta Velazquez's autobiography *The Woman in Battle* (1876) is available through the University of North Carolina's Documenting the American South website at: http://doc-south.unc.edu/velazquez/menu.html (May 3, 2005). It has also been republished with an introduction by Jesse Alemán, *The Woman in Battle: The Civil War Narrative of Loreta Velazquez, A Cuban Woman and Confederate Soldier* (Madison: University of Wisconsin Press, 2003); Clayton, quoted in Young, *Disarming the Nation*, 149. The work quoted is Ellen C. Clayton, *Female Warriors: Memorials of Female Valour and Heroism, from the Mythological Ages to the Present Era* (London, 1879); Livermore, *My Story of the War*, 112; Leonard, *All the Daring of the Soldier*, 106–9, 113.

32. Turchin quoted in Leonard, *All the Daring of the Soldier*, 140; see also 135–36; ORA, I, X (II), 212–23, 124–26.

33. Belle Z. Spencer, "From a Soldier's Wife," *Harper's New Monthly Magazine*, 26, 173 (October 1864), 622–29, quotation 622.

34. Spencer, "From a Soldier's Wife," 622, 629.

35. Leonard, *Yankee Women*, 13; Johnstone, quoted in George C. Rable, *Civil Wars: Women and the Crisis of Southern Nationalism* (Urbana: University of Illinois Press, 1989), 124, 127; Frederick Law Olmsted to Henry Whitney Bellows, September [25] 26, 1861, in Jane Turner Censer (ed.), *The Papers of Frederick Law Olmsted*, Vol. IV, *Defending the Union: The Civil War and the U.S. Sanitary Commission, 1861–1863* (Baltimore: Johns Hopkins University Press, 1986), 203.

36. Olmsted to Bellows, August 16, 1861; to John Foster Jenkins, May 20, 1862; to Henry Whitney Bellows, June 3, 1862, in *Papers of Frederick Law Olmsted*, Vol. IV, *Defending the Union*, 148, 340, 363–64.

37. Jeanie Attie, *Patriotic Toil: Northern Women and the American Civil War* (Ithaca: Cornell University Press, 1998), 5, 53.

38. Rable, *Civil Wars*, 236; Drew Gilpin Faust, "Altars of Sacrifice: Confederate Women and Narratives of War," in Clinton and Silber, *Divided Houses*, 171–199; Jacqueline Glass Campbell, *When Sherman Marched North from the Sea: Resistance on the Confederate Home Front* (Chapel Hill: University of North Carolina Press, 2003), passim. Earlier studies that stress the strengthening of women's resolve in the face of the enemy include Stephen V. Ash, *When the Yankees Came: Conflict and Chaos in the Occupied South 1861–1865* (1995; reprint, Chapel Hill: University of North Carolina Press, 2002), esp. 38ff; and Gary Gallagher, *The Confederate War* (Cambridge, MA: Harvard University Press, 1999).

39. Donald Ratcliffe, "The State of the Union, 1776–1860," in Susan-Mary Grant and Brian Holden Reid (eds.), *The American Civil War: Explorations and Reconsiderations* (Harlow, Essex: Longman, 2000), 30; Russell F. Weigley, *The American Way of War: A History of United States Military Strategy and Policy* (1973; paperback reprint, Bloomington: Indiana University Press, 1977), 78.

Chapter 8

1. William T. Sherman to Henry Halleck, September 17, 1863, September 17, 1863, *The War of the Rebellion: A Compilation of the Official Records of the Union and Confederate Armies* (hereafter: ORA), Series I, XXX (III) (Washington, D.C.: Government Printing Office, 1880–1900), 698.

2. William T. Sherman to John Sherman, July 19, 1863 in "Letters of Two Brothers: Passages from the Correspondence of General and Senator Sherman," *Century Magazine*, XLV (November 1892–April 1893), 439; Lincoln to James C. Conkling, August 26, 1863, in Roy F. Basler (ed.), *The Collected Works of Abraham Lincoln*, Vol. VI (New Brunswick, NJ: Rutgers University Press, 1953), 409–10.

3. Daniel H. Hill, "Chickamauga: The Great Battle of the West," in *Battles and Leaders of the Civil War*, III, 638–62, quotation 639, accessed online at the University of Ohio website: http://ehistory.osu.edu/uscw/library/books/battles/index.cfm (September 10, 2005).

4. General Orders No. 10, Ambrose Burnside, Army of the Ohio, September 15, 1863, ORA, I, XXX (III), 660.

5. Hill, "Chickamauga," 640–43.

6. Ibid., 644.

7. General James Longstreet, CSA, *From Manassas to Appomattox: Memoirs of the Civil War in America* (1893; reprint, New Jersey: Blue and Gray Press, 1984), 450. There are several versions of Longstreet's memoirs available—especially his response to the criticisms made of his Civil War career by, among others, Jubal Early. At least one version is available online at: http://www.wtj.com/archives/longstreet/ (June 3, 2005).

8. *Le Figaro* and Leonidas Polk, both quoted in Peter Cozzens, *This Terrible Sound: The Battle of Chickamauga* (1992; reprint, Urbana: University of Illinois Press, 1996), 534–35; Longstreet, *From Manassas to Appomattox*, 466.

9. Sam Watkins, *Co. Aytch: A Confederate Memoir of the Civil War* (New York: Simon & Schuster, 1997), 110.

10. Ibid., 113.

11. Lincoln to Rosecrans, October 4, 1863, in Lincoln, *Collected Works*, VI, 498; General Orders No. 1, October 18, 1863, ORA, I, XXX (IV), 450–51; U. S. Grant to G. H. Thomas and Thomas to Grant, October 19, 1863, ORA, I, XXX (IV), 479.

12. Sam Watkins, *Co. Aytch*, 117.

13. John Sherman to William T. Sherman, July 18, 1863, in "Letters of Two Brothers," 439; George Templeton Strong, diary entry, December 11, 1863, in Allan Nevins and Milton Halsey Thomas (eds.), *The Diary of George Templeton Strong: The Civil War*, Vol. III (New York: Macmillan, 1952), 379; Lincoln, "Annual Message to Congress," December 8, 1863, in Lincoln, *Collected Works*, VII, 49.

14. Peter Cozzens, *The Shipwreck of Their Hopes: The Battles for Chattanooga* (1994; reprint, Urbana: University of Illinois Press, 1996), 391–92; Sam Watkins, *Co. Aytch*, 118.

15. Ulysses S. Grant, *Personal Memoirs* (1885/6; reprint, London: Penguin Books, 1999), 377.

16. Henry Wager Halleck, *Elements of Military Art and Science Or, Course Of Instruction In Strategy, Fortification, Tactics Of Battles, &C.; Embracing The Duties Of Staff, Infantry, Cavalry, Artillery, And Engineers; Adapted To The Use Of Volunteers And Militia; Third Edition; With Critical Notes On The Mexican And Crimean Wars* (1846; reprint, New York and London, D. Appleton & Company, 1862), 42; Halleck to Grant, August 2, 1862, ORA, I, XVII (II), 150; Grant to C. S. Hamilton, January 20, 1863, ORA, I, XVII (II), 575; Sherman to John A. Rawlins, August 4, 1863, ORA, I, XXIV (III), 574–75.

17. Stephen V. Ash, *When the Yankees Came: Conflict and Chaos in the Occupied South, 1861–1865* (1995; reprint, Chapel Hill: University of North Carolina Press, 2002), 50–55; Halleck to Grant, March 31, 1863, ORA, I, XXIV (III), 156–57; Sherman to H. W. Hill, September 7, to Halleck, September 17, 1863, ORA, I, XXX (III), 401–4, 698.

18. Russell F. Weigley, *The American Way of War: A History of United States Military Strategy and Policy* (Bloomington: Indiana University Press, 1973), 141–42; Grant to Meade, April 9, 1864, in Grant, *Memoirs*, 389; David J. Eicher, *The Longest Night: A Military History of the Civil War* (2001; reprint, London: Pimlico, 2002), 666.

19. Grant to Sherman, May 2, 1864, ORA, I, XXXVIII (IV), 11.

20. Eicher, *Longest Night*, 665; Elisha Hunt Rhodes, diary entry, May 5, 1864, in Robert Hunt Rhodes (ed.), *All For the Union: The Civil War Diary and Letters of Elisha Hunt Rhodes* (1985; reprint, New York: Random House, 1992), 136; Longstreet, *From Manassas to Appomattox*, 564.

21. Grant, *Memoirs*, 413, 430.

22. Eicher, *Longest Night*, 671; Rhodes, diary entry, May 7, 1864, in Rhodes, *All for the Union*, 138; The *New York Times*, May 9, 1864; Strong, diary entry, May 9, 1864, in Nevins and Thomas, *Diary*, III, 442; Lincoln, "Response to Serenade," May 9, 1864, in Lincoln, *Collected Works*, VII, 334.

23. Mississippi soldier, quoted in Eicher, *Longest Night*, 680; Rhodes, diary entry, May 11, 1864, in Rhodes, *All For the Union*, 142.

24. Lee, General Orders No. 44, May 20, 1864, ORA, I, XXXVI (III), 800; Sallie Brock Putnam, *Richmond during the War: Four Years of Personal Observation* (1867; reprint, Lincoln: University of Nebraska Press, 1996), 292.

25. Grant to Halleck, May 11, 1864, in Grant, *Memoirs*, 445; Rhodes, diary entry, May 11, 1864, in Rhodes, *All for the Union*, 143.

26. Grant to Halleck, May 16, 1864 in Grant, *Memoirs*, 452; Rhodes, diary entry, May 16, 1864, in Rhodes, *All for the Union*, 145; Eicher, *Longest Night*, 679.

27. Grant to Halleck, May 26, 1864, in Grant, *Memoirs*, 461.
28. Grant, *Memoirs*, 477; Rhodes, diary entry, June 5, 1864, in Rhodes, *All for the Union*, 150.
29. D. H. Hill to Beauregard, June 11, 1864, ORA, I, XXXVI (III), 896.
30. Beauregard to Bragg, June 17 [18], 1864, ORA, I, XL (I), 666.
31. Grant, *Memoirs*, 500.
32. Thomas Morris Chester, August 14, 1864, in R. J. M. Blackett (ed.), *Thomas Morris Chester, Black Civil War Correspondent: His Dispatches from the Virginia Front* (Baton Rouge: Louisiana State University Press, 1989), 96, 98.
33. Sherman to Meigs, May 3, 1864, ORA I, XXXVIII (IV), 20; Andrew Haughton, *Training Tactics and Leadership in the Confederate Army of Tennessee* (London: Frank Cass, 2000), 150–54; Watkins, *Co. Aytch*, 153, 149.
34. Watkins, *Co. Aytch*, 172.
35. Special Field Orders No. 39, July 19, 1864; Sherman to Halleck, July 20, 1864, ORA, I, XXXVIII (V), 193, 195.
36. O. O. Howard to Sherman, July 28; Slocum to Halleck, September 2; Sherman to Halleck, September 3, 1864, ORA, I, XXXVIII (V), 282, 763, 777; Strong, diary entry, September 3, 1864, in Nevins and Thomas, *Diary*, III, 480–81; Grant, *Memoirs*, 413.
37. Grant to Sherman, September 10, 1864, in Grant, *Memoirs*, 519; Sherman to Grant, October 9, 1864, ORA, I, XXXIX (III), 162.
38. Sherman to Grant, October 11, 1864, ORA, I, XXXIX (III), 202; John E. Marszalek, *Sherman: A Soldier's Passion for Order* (1993; reprint, New York: Random House, 1994), 305–9; Sherman to Halleck, December 24, 1864, ORA, I, XLIV, 799.
39. Andrew Haughton, *Training, Tactics and Leadership in the Confederate Army of Tennessee* (London: Frank Cass, 2000), 25, 116, 119–20, 181.
40. Thomas L. Connelly, *Autumn of Glory: The Army of Tennessee, 1862–1865* (1971; reprint, Baton Rouge: Louisiana State University Press, 1974), 503–6; on Hood and the "frustration-aggression hypothesis," see Robert Pois and Philip Langer, *Command Failure in War: Psychology and Leadership* (Bloomington: Indiana University Press, 2004), 106–8.
41. Watkins, *Co. Aytch*, 234–35, 242.
42. Lincoln, "Second Inaugural Address," March 4, 1865, in Lincoln, *Collected Works*, VIII, 333.
43. Chester, January 22, 1865, in *Dispatches from the Virginia Front*, 230.
44. Strong, diary entries, April 3 and 4, 1865, in Nevins and Thomas, *Diary*, III, 574, 576; Mary Chesnut, diary entry, April 7, 1865 in *A Diary from Dixie* (Boston: Houghton Mifflin, 1949), 518–19; Sherman to Grant, April 12, 1865, ORA, I, XLVII (III), 177; Grant, *Memoirs*, 601–2.

Chapter 9

1. William Howard Russell, *My Diary North and South* (Boston: T. O. H. P. Burnham, 1863).
2. Davis and Breckinridge, quoted in William J. Cooper, Jr., *Jefferson Davis: American* (2000; reprint, New York: Random House, 2001) 568; Breckinridge, quoted in Mark O. Hatfield, Senate Historical Office, *Vice Presidents of the United States, 1789–1993* (Washington, D.C.: U.S. Government Printing Office, 1997), 193–99, quotation 198; John E. Marszalek, *Sherman: A Soldier's Passion for Order* (1993; reprint, New York: Random House, 1994), 342.
3. Walt Whitman, *Specimen Days & Collect* (1883; reprint, New York: Dover Publications, 1995), 70; POW death estimates from David J. Eicher, *The Longest Night: A Military History of the Civil War* (2001; reprint, London: Pimlico, 2002), 628.
4. Edward Dicey, *Spectator of America* (1863; reprint, Athens: University of Georgia Press, 1989) 274.
5. Lincoln, "Message to Congress in Special Session," July, 4 1861; "Annual Message to Congress," December 1, 1862, in Roy F. Basler (ed.), *The Collected Works of Abraham Lincoln*, Vols. IV, V (New Brunswick, NJ: Rutgers University Press, 1953), 439, 529.

Short Guide to Secondary Reading

The literature on the Civil War is voluminous—entire studies are devoted to the historiography alone, never mind the war itself—so the following offers merely some suggestions for further reading. On the origins of the war, a good starting point is Brian Holden Reid, *The Origins of the American Civil War* (Harlow, Essex: Longman, 1996), although David M. Potter, *The Impending Crisis, 1848–1861* (New York: Harper & Row, 1976) remains extremely valuable for the political context and the intricacies of the infighting of the 1850s. A more recent and extremely sophisticated treatment of the growth of sectional thinking can be found in Michael A. Morrison, *Slavery and the American West: The Eclipse of Manifest Destiny and the Coming of the Civil War* (Chapel Hill: University of North Carolina Press, 1997) and, for sectional sentiment in South Carolina, Manisha Sinha, *The Counterrevolution of Slavery: Politics and Ideology in Antebellum South Carolina* (Chapel Hill: University of North Carolina Press, 2000). On the growth of a specifically Northern sectional/national sentiment at odds with the whole idea of the South, see Susan-Mary Grant, *North Over South: Northern Nationalism and American Identity in the Antebellum Era* (Lawrence: University Press of Kansas, 2000).

On the war itself there are a number of longer comprehensive treatments. The best known of these remains James M. McPherson, *Battle Cry of Freedom: The Civil War Era* (New York: Oxford University Press, 1988), although for anyone wholly unfamiliar with the topic the clear organization and overarching sweep of Peter J. Parish's, *The American Civil War* (New York: Holmes and Meier, 1975) remains a valuable introduction to the war in all its complexities. On the military history of the war, David J. Eicher's *The Longest Night: A Military History of the Civil War* (New York: Simon & Schuster 2001; London: Pimlico, 2002) is lively and detailed, and packed with information on battles and weaponry as well as the individuals involved. A shorter but more focused study of the war that might be of more use to anyone new to the topic is Charles Royster's, *The Destructive War: William Tecumseh Sherman, Stonewall Jackson, and the Americans* (1991; reprint, New York: Random House, 1993).

On the various campaigns and individual battles, the choice is virtually endless. The work of Stephen Sears on McClellan and the Peninsula Campaign, *To The Gates of Richmond: The Peninsula Campaign* (New York: Ticknor and Fields, 1992) offers an excellent starting point for an understanding of the Union war effort in the opening years of the conflict, and his studies of the war's bloodiest day, *Landscape Turned Red: The Battle of Antietam* (1983; paperback reprint, New York: Warner Books, 1985) and the Confederacy's finest hour in the East, *Chancellorsville* (Boston: Houghton Mifflin, 1996) are detailed and packed with information without ever becoming turgid. George C. Rable's *Fredericksburg, Fredericksburg!* (Chapel Hill: University of North Carolina Press, 2002) may look daunting at over six hundred pages, but it is an approachable study that places the battle in the broader context of its impact on those who fought it and on the civilian population. It is an excellent introduction to two armies and two societies at war.

The Battle of Gettysburg falls into a category of its own by dint of the sheer amount published on it. Here, the best place to start is with a relatively short book, Kent Gramm's *Gettysburg: A Meditation on War and Values* (Bloomington: Indiana University Press, 1994), before launching into detailed studies of the first, second, and third days of that battle, studies that of necessity assume a working knowledge of the battle's aims, objectives, and highlights. Having read that, Gabor S. Boritt, ed., *The Gettysburg Nobody Knows* (New York: Oxford University Press, 1997) is the next accessible stage in understanding that battle. For anyone wishing to explore Gettysburg's centrality to the Civil War as battle and national shrine, the two best studies are: Garry Wills, *Lincoln at Gettysburg: The Words that Remade America* (New York: Simon & Schuster, 1992), and Jim Weeks, *Gettysburg: Memory, Market, and an American Shrine* (Princeton and Oxford: Princeton University Press, 2003).

On the Western Theater, the two-volume study of the Army of Tennessee by Thomas Lawrence Connelly remains the best place to begin: *Army of the Heartland: The Army of Tennessee, 1861–1862* (1967; reprint, Baton Rouge: Louisiana State University Press, 1978); and *Autumn of Glory: The Army of Tennessee, 1862–1865* (1971; reprint, Baton Rouge: Louisiana State University Press, 1974). Peter Cozzens's trilogy on that army's three most famous engagements—*No Better Place to Die: The Battle of Stones River* (Urbana: University of Illinois Press, 1991); *This Terrible Sound: The Battle of Chickamauga* (1992; reprint, Urbana: University of Illinois Press, 1996); and *The Shipwreck of Their Hopes: The Battles for Chattanooga* (1994; reprint, Urbana: University of Illinois Press, 1996)—is detailed, accessible, and sweeping in its coverage. The best single-volume study of the Union's Army of the Tennessee is Steven Woodworth, *Nothing But Victory: The Army of the Tennessee, 1861–1865* (New York: Alfred A. Knopf, 2005).

If those works published on the Civil War generally would fill an Olympic-size swimming pool, those on women in the war might just about fill a sink, but good places to start are Elizabeth Leonard's works, *Yankee Women: Gender Battles in the Civil War* (1994; paperback reprint, New York: W. W. Norton, 1995) and *All the Daring of the Soldier: Women of the Civil War Armies* (New York: W. W. Norton, 1999; paperback reprint, London: Penguin Books, 2001); Drew Gilpin Faust, *Mothers of Invention: Women of the Slaveholding South in the American Civil War* (Chapel Hill: University of North Carolina Press, 1996); Noralee Frankel, *Freedom's Women: Black Women and Families in Civil War Era Mississippi* (Bloomington: Indiana University Press, 1999); and Edward D. C. Campbell, Jr., and Kym S. Rice (eds.), *A Woman's War: Southern Women, Civil War, and the Confederate Legacy* (Richmond, The Museum of the Confederacy and Charlottesville: University Press of Virginia, 1996). On African-American troops the choices are between detailed studies of individual regiments, very good collections of primary material, and rather gung-ho sweeping treatments that sometimes fail to convey the complexities of the black Civil War. Start with Joseph T. Glatthaar, *Forged in Battle: The Civil War Alliance of Black Soldiers and White Officers* (New York: Meridian, 1991).

On the Civil War's leaders, the choice is, again, daunting. Before launching into the detailed historiographical debates over Lincoln, Davis, or Lee, look at: Richard J. Carwardine, *Lincoln: Profiles in Power* (Harlow, Essex: Pearson/Longman, 2003), now republished in a revised edition as *Lincoln: A Life of Purpose and Power* (New York: Alfred A. Knopf, 2006); William J. Cooper, Jr., *Jefferson Davis: American* (2000; reprint, New York: Random House, 2001); and Brian Holden Reid, *Robert E. Lee: Icon for a Nation* (London: Weidenfeld & Nicolson, 2005). For Ulysses S. Grant, the best place to start is his own *Personal Memoirs* (1885–6; London: Penguin Edition, 1999).

Finally, the web offers a valuable—if sometimes erratic and biased (as if books are not) resource. Anyone seeking to understand a particular battle should begin with the excellent National Parks Service websites that are available for most of the major battles; many of these provide an overview of the engagement concerned and, crucially, color maps. William G. Thomas and Alice E. Carter, *The Civil War on the Web: A Guide to the Very Best Sites* (Wilmington, DE: Scholarly Resources, 2001) remains valuable, as many of the sites that are of interest to the serious scholar and general reader are stable—the Library of Congress, for example, or the Making of America (MOA)—and updated regularly.

Index

A

abolitionism 16, 17, 18, 22, 24, 26–7, 30
African-Americans
  post-war 226
  racist attacks against 135–6, 177–8
  in Union army 62, 109-14, 128, 129-
    37, 177, 180–2, 193, 211, 212
  women 111, 183
agriculture 15
Alabama 4, 5, 10, 36, 42, 87, 186, 196
Alabama Platform 34, 36
Albermale Sound 81
Alcott, Louisa May 183
Alexander, E. P. 150, 159
Alexandria 119
American nationalism 2–3, 7, 8
American System 9-10
Anderson, Richard 206
Anderson, Robert 39, 44, 48–9
Andersonville, Georgia 224
Antietam 123–6
Appomattox 220–1, 223
Aquia Creek 71, 119
Arkansas 36, 43, 50
armies 47, 60
  medical care 90–1, 135, 187, 188–9
  naming of 63
  support services 64–5
  uniforms 65–6
  weaponry 66–9
  women as soldiers 183–4, 185, 186

  see also Confederate armies;
    Union armies; and names of
    individual armies
Army of the Cumberland 63, 141, 146,
  156, 161, 195, 196–7, 213
Army of the James 63, 202, 205, 209, 211
Army of Kentucky 141, 145
Army of the Mississippi (Confederate)
  63, 88, 93
Army of the Mississippi (Union) 63, 93,
  163
Army of Northeastern Virginia,
  see Army of the Potomac
Army of Northern Virginia 63, 118, 121,
  122, 154–5, 164, 194, 204, 220
  and Battle of the Wilderness 205–6
  and Gettysburg 156, 157, 158–60, 201
  and Seven Days Battles 101, 104, 107
  at Chickamauga 195, 197
Army of the Ohio 63, 87, 88, 89, 93, 141,
  143, 145, 146, 213
Army of Pensacola 87
Army of the Potomac 65, 78, 101, 117–18,
  120, 121, 131, 146–7, 164, 198,
  201, 202, 208, 219, 220
  and Battle of the Wilderness 205–6
  and Chancellorsville 152, 153, 154
  and Cold Harbor 209, 210
  creation of 63
  and Fredericksburg 148, 149–50
  and Gettysburg 157–8, 159, 160–1
  Lincoln visits 117, 140

morale of 122, 151, 209
'Mud March' 151
and Peninsula Campaign 94–5, 96,
97
and Seven
Days Battles 102, 103, 104, 105
and Spotsylvania 206–7
Army of the Shenandoah 73
Army of Tennessee (Confederate) 63,
141–2, 145, 161, 163, 195, 198,
218, 219
Army of the Tennessee (Union) 87, 88,
89, 93, 161, 213
Army of the Trans-Mississippi 163
Army of Virginia 118, 120
Army of the West 93
Athens, Alabama 186, 196
Atlanta, Georgia 80, 213–15
Atlantic Blockading Squadron 81, 84, 87

B

Bailey, Theodorus 92
Baker, Maurice 9
Baltimore 15
Bank of the United States 8
Banks, Nathaniel P. 94, 135, 165, 204
Baton Rouge 93, 165
Bay Point Island 84
Bay State 4
Beauregard, P. G. T. 45, 63, 71, 72–3, 74,
87–8, 89–90, 93, 210
Beaver Dam Creek 102
Bee, Barnard E. 73
Beecher, Henry Ward 182
Beers, Ethel Lynn 77
Bell, John 35, 36
Belmont, Battle of 87
Benton, Thomas Hart 21
Berlin, Ira 127
Bermuda, British steamer 82
Bermuda Hundred 202, 210, 211
Big Bethel, Virginia 72
Blackburn's Ford 73
Blair, Montgomery 95
Blanchard, Mattie 182–3
'Bloody Angle' 207–8

Boorstin, Daniel 3, 16
Booth, John Wilkes 223
Border States 50, 56, 70, 114, 115–16,
168
see also Delaware
Kentucky
Maryland
Missouri
Boston, Massachusetts 108
Boyd, Belle 185
Bradley, Amy Morris 189
Brady, Matthew 126, 147
Bragg, Braxton 87, 88, 89, 90, 118, 156,
163, 164, 194, 200
at Chickamauga 195–6, 197, 198
at Stones River 161, 162
Kentucky campaign 143–6
bread riots 156
Breckinridge, John C. 36, 37, 51, 174,
212, 223
Britain 7, 8, 17, 18, 19, 82, 83, 114–15
Brooks, Preston 25, 29
Brown, John 25, 26–7, 29, 32
Brown, Joseph E. 174
Bruinsburg 164–5
Buchanan, James 25–6, 38–9
Buckner, Simon Bolivar 87
Buell, Don Carlos 80, 86, 87, 89, 93, 143,
144–6, 146
Buford, Harry T. 185
Buford, John 158
Bull Run/Manassas
First Battle of 63, 72–5, 77, 78, 81
Second Battle of 119-20, 121
Bureau of Colored Troops 132–3
Burnside, Ambrose E. 73, 87, 131, 171,
180, 195
and Antietam 125, 126
and Battle of Fredericksburg 148, 149
as commander of Army of the
Potomac 141, 146–7
'Mud March' 151
resignation from Army of the
Potomac 151
Burnside's (Rohrbach) Bridge 125, 126
Butler, Andrew P. 25
Butler, Benjamin 51, 62, 71, 72, 81, 92,
110, 132, 135, 202, 208

C

Calhoun, John C. 10, 13, 14, 15, 16, 17,
    20, 21, 22
  defense of slavery 18–19
  Exposition and Protest 11, 13
California 19, 20, 21
Cameron, Simon 51, 62
Canada 7
Cannadine, David 54
Carter, Theodrick (Tod) 218
Cass, Lewis P. 20–1
Castle Pinckney 46
casualties 90, 103, 104, 105, 121, 124,
    125, 150, 154, 160, 163, 197,
    200, 206, 207, 208, 209
Cayuga, Union gunboat 92
Cedar Creek, Battle of 215
Cemetery Hill 158, 160
Cemetery Ridge 159
Chamberlain, Joshua Lawrence 68, 159
Chancellorsville 151–5, 190
Chaplin Hills 145
Charles City Crossroads 104
Charleston 38–9, 44–5
  evacuation of 219
  federal arsenal at 44, 48
Charlottesville 212
Chase, Salmon P. 35, 95, 169
Chattanooga 80, 143, 145, 161, 194–5,
    198–201, 213
Chesnut, Mary Boykin 53, 58, 92–3, 100,
    221
Chester, Thomas Morris 211–12, 220
Chew, Robert S. 48
Chicago Times 171
Chicago Tribune 58, 170
Chickahominy River 99
Chickamauga 195–8, 213
Chickasaw Bluffs 161, 169
Child, Lydia Maria 32–3
Cincinnati 3
Clay, Henry 10, 15, 21, 24
Clayton, Ellen 185
Clemens, Jeremiah 42
Clingman, Thomas 38
Cobb, Howell 39
Cobb, Thomas 150
Cold Harbor 209, 210

First (Gaines Mill) 102–3
Colt rifles 68
Columbia, South Carolina 219, 220
Columbus, Kentucky 86, 87
Compromise of 1850 21, 23
Confederacy 47, 190–1, 224–5
  capital at Richmond, Virginia 50, 51
  Constitution 42–3
  formation of 42–3
  government and political
    environment 173–5
  motivations for fighting 59-60
  recognition as
objective of 57, 114, 118, 191
Confederate armies 55, 57, 61, 97–8
  casualties 90, 103, 104, 105, 121, 125,
    150, 154, 160, 163, 197, 200,
    206, 208, 209
  commanders/command structure 64,
    71–2
  conscription 175–6
  names 63
  slaves as resource for 57
  strategy 78–9, 80–1, 100
  support services 64–5
  treatment of black Union troops
    135–6
  uniform 65
  volunteers 64
  weaponry 67, 68
  see also under names of individual
    armies
Confederate navy 55, 84, 85
Confederation, Articles of 3
Confiscation Acts 112, 113, 130
Congress, USS 85
Conkling, James 134
Connecticut 133
Connelly, Thomas 141–2
conscription 98, 173, 175–7, 193
Constitution 3, 5, 6
  Confederate 42–3
Constitutional Union Party 35
Copperheads 170–1
Corinth, Mississippi 68, 87, 93, 146
cotton 4, 5, 12, 13, 31–2, 55
Couch, Darius 150
Crater, Battle of the 211
Crawford, Martin J. 48

Crittenden, John J. 38
Cross Keys 94
Crump's Landing 88
Culp's Hill 158
Cumberland Gap 86
Cumberland River 80, 87, 161
Cumberland, USS 85
Cumming, Kate 189-90
Curtis, Samuel R. 91

D

Dalton, Georgia 201
Dana, Charles A. 132
Davis, Jefferson xi-xii, 43, 58, 72, 74, 78,
    84, 97, 121, 197, 214, 223
  and Confederate strategy 79, 100
  on death of Stonewall Jackson 153-4
  election as president of Confederacy
    42
  and one-party
politics 173
Declaration of Independence 6, 33, 107
Delaware 44, 50
Democratic Convention (1860) 34-5
Democratic Review 19, 20
Democrats 16, 24, 34-5, 36, 168, 170-1,
    172
Denmark Vesey conspiracy 15
desertion 122, 175
Devil's Den 158
Dew, Roderick 18
Dicey, Edward xiii, 107, 108, 115, 168-9,
    225
Dinwiddie Court House 220
Dix, Dorothea 'Dragon' 188
doctors, female 188
Doolittle, James R. 32
Dorr, James A. 32
Douglas, Stephen A. 21, 24, 26, 36, 37
Douglass, Frederick 62, 110, 127, 129,
    130, 131, 181
draft, *see* conscription
Draft Riots (July 1863) 177-8
Dred Scott v. Sandford 26, 30
du Pont, Samuel Francis 84

E

Early, Jubal 73, 212, 215
Eastern theater 71, 81-2, 84, 85-6,
    93-105, 146-51, 205-12
  see also Antietam
  Appomattox
  Bull Run/Manassas
economic nationalism 9-10
Edmonds, Sarah Emma 184
Eicher, David 149
elections
  1844 20
  1848 21
  1856 25
  1860 34-7
  mid-term 1862 169
  1864 170, 172
Elkhorn Tavern 91
Emancipation Proclamation 117, 124,
    126-8, 129, 130, 140, 151, 168,
    170, 177, 200, 219
emancipation of slaves 126-31, 133-4,
    136-7, 168, 169, 170, 171, 178
Emerson, Ralph Waldo 49
Enfield rifle 68
Erie Canal 12
Etheridge, Annie 185-6
Ewell, Richard S. 73, 157, 158, 159, 160,
    205, 208

F

Fair Oaks 99-100
Farragut, David Glasgow 91, 92, 93
Federal Convention (1787) 2, 5
Federalists 7
5th Colored Heavy Artillery 132
54th Massachusetts 163
1st Arkansas Infantry 139-40
1st Kansas Colored Volunteers 112, 130
1st Minnesota Volunteers 179
1st South Carolina Volunteers 112, 130,
    132
Five Forks 220
Florida 7, 36, 42
Fontaine, Felix Gregory de 221
food shortages 155-6
Foote, Andrew 87

foraging 165, 202–3
Forbes, John Murray 48
Forrest, Nathan Bedford 136, 143, 161, 196, 204, 217, 218–19
Fort Beauregard 84
Fort Clark 81
Fort Donelson 87
Fort Hatteras, *see* Hatteras Inlet
Fort Henry 87
Fort Jackson 92
Fort Johnson 46
Fort Monroe 51, 71
Fort Moultrie 38–9, 44, 46, 48
Fort Pickens 46, 48
Fort Pillow 136–7, 204, 212
Fort St. Philip 92
Fort Sumter 38–9, 44, 46–7, 48–9, 53
Fort Wagner 163
Fort Walker 84
Foster, C. W. 132
Founding Fathers 33
Fowler, William 84
Fox, Gustavus V. 81, 92
France 7
Franklin, Battle of 217–18
Franklin, William B. 95, 149–50
Frederick, Maryland 121
Fredericksburg 146–51, 169, 190, 199
Free-Soil Party 16, 21, 30
Freedmen's Inquiry Commission 130–1
Freeman, Thomas 180–1
Frémaux, C,line 148
Frémont, John C. 25, 94, 112
Fugitive Slave Act 23, 51, 113

G

Gag Rule (the 21st Rule) (1836) 18
Gaines Mill 102–3
Gallagher, Gary 155
Gallatin, Albert 8
Gardner, Alexander 126
Garibaldi Guard 61
Garrison, William Lloyd 17
Georgia 4, 36, 42, 141, 201, 202, 212–17
Gettysburg 68, 155–61, 190, 194, 200, 201
Ghent, Treaty of (1814) 7

Gladstone, W. E. 115
Goldsborough, Louis M. 87
Gooding, James Henry 180, 181
Grand Gulf 164
Grant, Ulysses S. 54, 63, 93, 141, 201–10, 211, 215, 217, 221
    and Battle of Belmont 87
    and Chattanooga 198–9, 200, 201
    and North Anna River 208
    and Battle of Shiloh 88, 89, 90, 91
    and Spotsylvania 206–7
    and Vicksburg 146, 156, 161, 163, 164–6
    and Battle of the Wilderness 204–6
Great Seal 6
Greeley, Horace 25
Greenbow, Rose 185
Gregg, Maxcy 150
Grierson, Benjamin 165
growth, *see* population growth
    territorial expansion
    urban growth
guerrilla war 219

H

habeas corpus, suspension of 140, 170, 173
Hagerstown 122, 123
Hale, Stephen F. 41–2
Halleck, Henry W. 86, 87, 120, 142–3, 151
    as general in chief of Union armies 93, 118
    on military affairs in the East 140–1
    relations with Hooker 157
    on rules relating to forage and subsistence 202, 203
    on strategy 78–9
Halpine, Charles 133
Hamlin, Hannibal 36
Hammond, James Henry 55
    'Mudsill Speech' 31–2
Hampton Roads, Virginia 84, 85–6
Hampton, Wade 212
Hancock, Cornelia 90–1, 110–11
Hancock, Winfield Scott 210

Hardee, William J. 89, 162
Harmon, Henry S. 134
Harpers Ferry 122–3
    John Brown's attack on 26, 27, 29
Harriet Lane steamer 81
Harris Farm 208
Harrison's Landing 105, 119
Hartford Convention (1814) 8–9, 30
Hatteras Inlet 81–2, 83, 84
Haupt, Herman 119
Haydon, Charles 77, 149, 150
Hayne, Robert Y. 13, 16, 30
Hazen, William B. 162
'Hells' Half Acre' 162
Hennessy, John 151
Henry House Hill 73
Herbert, Philemon T. 25
Heth, Harry 158
Higginson, Thomas Wentworth 17, 112, 132
Hill, A. P. 102, 125, 157, 159
Hill, Benjamin 174, 205
Hill, Daniel H. 97–8, 175, 194, 195, 196, 210
Hilton Head 84
Hodgers, Jennie 184
Holly Springs, Mississippi 165, 203
Holmes, John 11
Holmes, Oliver Wendell Jr. 126
Holmes, Theophilus H. 71, 163
Hood, John Bell 149, 214, 215, 216, 217, 218, 219
Hooker, Joseph 'Fighting Joe' 124–5, 149, 151–3, 157, 164, 198, 199
'Hornet's Nest' 89
Horseshoe Ridge 197
Hospital Bill (1862) 189
Howard, Oliver 158, 214
Howland, Eliza Newton Woolsey 189
Hudson River 12
Huger, Benjamin 71
Hugo, Victor 27
Hunter, David 112, 212
Huntsville 213

I

Illinois 4, 10, 36

immigration 12, 16, 24
Indiana 4, 10, 36
industry 9-10, 55–6
intelligence 153
Irish Brigade 149
ironclads 84–6
Island Mound, Missouri 130
Iuka 146

J

Jackson, Andrew 7, 8, 13, 14, 15
Jackson, Mattie 147–8
Jackson, Thomas J. 'Stonewall' 54, 73, 93–4, 100, 124, 125, 142, 149
    at Harper's Ferry 122–3
    death at Chancellorsville 153–4
    and Seven Days Battles 102, 103
    Shenandoah Valley Campaign 93, 118, 143
    on tactics 80–1
James Peninsula 93, 96
James River 103, 104, 105, 119, 210, 219
Jefferson, Thomas 6–7, 10, 11
Johns, Henry T. 132
Johnston, Albert Sidney 86, 87–9
Johnston, Joseph E. 43, 74–5, 86, 95, 97, 98, 155, 175, 212, 220, 223–4
    and battle of Fair Oaks 99, 100
    in Shenandoah Valley 71, 72, 73
    on the Western Front 163–4, 165, 174, 200, 201, 202, 204, 212, 213–14, 220
Johnstone, Mary 188
Joint Committee on the Conduct of the War 110, 136
Jomini, Antoine Henri 79
Jones, Archer 143
Jones, Charles Colcock 78, 129
Jones, Joseph 147
Jones, Sam 144

K

Kansas 3, 25, 29, 219
Kansas-Nebraska Act (1854) 24–5
Kennesaw Mountain 213–14

Kentucky 4, 5, 44, 50, 70, 143–5, 146, 156, 161, 180
Kerber, Linda 2, 182
Key, Francis Scott 8
Keyes, Erasmus 117–18
Know-Nothing Party 24
Knoxville 213

L

Lane, Jim 112, 130, 132, 135
Latané, William 101–2
Lawson, Melinda 172
Lee, Robert E. xii, 35, 43, 54, 63, 84, 94, 97, 100–2, 118–19, 120, 142, 164, 194, 201, 204–5, 206, 208, 209, 220
   and Antietam 123–6
   and Chancellorsville 153–5
   and Fredericksburg 147, 148, 150
   and Gettysburg 156, 157–8, 159, 160, 161
   in Maryland 121–2, 123
   and Second Battle of Bull Run 120
   and Seven Days Battles 103, 104–5
   and Shenandoah Valley Campaign 93
   surrender at Appomattox 220, 221, 223
'Lee's Miserables' 209
Leonard, Elizabeth 183, 186
The Liberator 17
liberty 22–3
Liberty Party 16, 20
Liddell Hart, Basil 53
Lincoln, Abraham xi, xii, 49, 71, 72, 80, 120, 193, 206, 225, 226
   Annual Message to Congress (1862) 133–4
   Annual Message to Congress (1863) 200–1
   visits Army of the Potomac 117, 140
   assassination of 223–4
   Cooper Union address 35–6
   election of 36–7
   Emancipation Proclamation 117, 124, 126–8, 129, 130, 140, 151, 168, 200
   inaugural address 46, 109

inauguration 45–6
   letter to
Hooker 151–2
   assumption of war powers 170
   letter to James Conkling 134
   on liberty 22–3
   and McClellan 95, 96–7, 101, 105, 123, 140
   on Northern war aims 178
   reaction to secession 45, 46
   on Rosecrans victory at Stones River 163
   Second Inaugural (1865) 219-20
   and slavery issue 26, 31, 35, 38, 109, 112, 114, 115–17, 126–8, 129, 130, 133–4, 136, 178
   and state militias 60–1
   suspension of habeas corpus 140, 170, 173
   on the Union 46
Little Round Top 68, 158, 159
Livermore, Mary Ashton 183, 185
Longstreet, James 73, 101, 118, 123, 142, 148
   and battle of Fair Oaks 99
   and Battle of the Wilderness 205
   and Chickamauga 197–8
   and Fredericksburg 149
   and Gettysburg 157, 159
   and Second Battle of Bull Run 120
Lookout Mountain 195, 199
Loudon Heights 123
Louisiana 4, 10, 36, 42
Louisiana Native Guards 130, 132
Louisiana Purchase 7
Louisville Courier 53
Louisville, Kentucky 86
Lovejoy's Station 216
Loyal Leagues 171–2, 215
Loyal Publication Society, Philadelphia 171
loyalty to the Union 171–3
Lynchburg 212
Lytle, William Haines 179

M

McClellan, George B. 54, 78, 93, 100–1, 117, 121, 122, 123, 140, 144
  and Battle of Antietam 123–6
  hostility to emancipation 168
  Peninsula Campaign 94–100, 105
  as presidential candidate 170
  relieved of command of Army of the Potomac 141
  Savage Station dispatch 103–4
  and Second Manassas 120
  and Seven Days Battles 102, 103, 104
McClernand, John 164
McCook, Alexander 162
McCord, Louisa 183
McDowell, Irvin 71, 72, 73, 78, 94, 95, 96, 118
McDowell, James 17
McDuffie, George 14
McFadden's Ford 162
McLaws, Lafayette 123
MacLeod, Duncan 5
McPherson, James B. 213, 214
McPherson, James M. 124
Madison, James 6
Magoffin, Beriah 41
Magruder, John B. 71, 96, 97, 103, 105
Maine 10
Mallory, Stephen R. 84, 85
Malvern Hill 104–5, 107
Manassas 71, 95
  First and Second battles of, see Bull Run/Manassas
Manassas, Confederate ironclad 92
'Manifest Destiny' 19
'March to the Sea' 65, 216
maritime law 82–3
Marye's Heights 148, 149
Maryland 44, 50, 121–6
Mason, James 83
Massachusetts 4, 10, 36, 56, 133
Meade, George C. 157, 158, 201, 202, 205, 206, 207
Mechanicsville 102
medical care 90–1, 135, 187, 188–9
Meigs, Montgomery 65, 69, 95, 213
Melton, Samuel Wickliffe 53, 59
Melville, Herman 1, 29, 86, 91, 124

Memphis and Charleston Railroad 87, 93, 142–3
Merrimack, USS, see Virginia
Mexican War (1846–8) 20
Mexico 19
Militia Act (1862) 130, 135
Miller Cornfield 124–5, 126
Milliken's Bend 164
  Battle of 132, 134
Mini, ball 66, 68
Minnesota, USS 81, 85
Missionary Ridge 195, 199, 200
Mississippi 5, 10, 21, 36, 42, 141, 146, 163–6, 204
Mississippi River 80, 86, 87, 92, 93, 161
Mississippi River Expedition 86
Missouri 10, 43, 50, 219
Missouri Compromise (1820) 10, 24, 26, 38
Mobile, Alabama 87
Mobile and Ohio Railroad 86, 93
Moltke, Helmuth von 121
Monitor, USS 85, 86
Monticello steamer 81
Moore, Andrew B. 41
Morgan, John Hunt 143, 194
Morris, Gouverneur 2, 48
Morris Island 48
Mosley, Sir Edward 54
'Mud March' 151
Mudsill Speech 31–2
Murfreesboro, Tennessee 87, 143, 161, 162
Murrin, John 3
mythology, national 6

N

Nashville 80, 87, 144, 161, 217–19
Natchez 93
national anthem 8
National Intelligencer 109
national symbols 6
'National Union Party' 215
nationalism 13, 15
  American 2–3, 7, 8
  economic 9-10
  Southern 190–1, 225

naval operations 81–6, 92–3
navy
  Confederate 55, 84, 85
  pre-war 84–5
  Union 55, 81–2, 83, 84, 85, 112–13
Nevada 3
Nevins, Allan 37
New England 4, 7
  and sectional division 8–9, 13
New England Loyal Publication Society
    171
New Jersey 4, 7, 36
New Mexico 20, 21
New Orleans 15, 80, 91–3
New Orleans, battle of (1815) 7
New York city, Draft Riots (1863) 177
New York state 4, 7, 20, 56
New York Times 66, 85, 126, 132, 206
New York Tribune 44, 49, 53, 70, 116
Nicolay, John G. 59, 73, 75
9th Louisiana Infantry 132
Norfolk, Virginia 98
North Anna River 208–9
North Atlantic Blockading Squadron 87
North Carolina 36, 44, 50, 219, 220, 223
North, the
  and controversy over emancipation
      168, 169, 170, 171
  as free society 5–6
  and growth and development 12–13,
      22
  immigration 12
  increasing hostility to the South
      108–9
  industrial capacity 55–6
  motivations for fighting 58–9, 178–82
  population 22, 56
  reaction to secession 43–4
  sectional thinking in 30
  slavery in 4, 5
  see also Union
  Union armies
  Union navy
Northwest Ordinance 5, 10
Nullification Crisis 12, 13, 14–15, 40
nurses 183, 184, 187, 188–9

O

Oak Grove 102, 105
Ohio 4, 10
Olmsted, Frederick Law 188, 189
Orange and Alexandria railroad 72
Orange Plank Road 205
Orange Turnpike 205
Oregon 19, 20
'O'Reilly, Miles' 133
O'Sullivan, John 19, 20

P

Painter, Nell 5
Pakenham, Sir Edward 7
Palfrey, John Gorham 23
Pamlico Sound 81
Paris, Declaration of (1856) 82–3
patriotism 2, 13
Patterson, Robert 71, 72–3
Pawnee steamer 81
payment of troops 135, 180–1
Pea Ridge 91
Peace Democrats 170–1
Peach Orchard 158, 159
Pemberton, John C. 163, 164, 165, 166
Peninsula Campaign 84, 85–6, 94–100,
    105, 118
Pennsylvania 4, 36, 56, 157
Perryville 145
Pessen, Edward 15
Petersburg 202, 210–12, 214
Philippi 70
Pickens, Francis W. 48
Pickett, George 158, 161, 199–200, 220
Piedmont 212
Pilgrim Fathers 6
Pittsburg Landing, *see* Shiloh, Battle of
Polk, James K. 20
Polk, Leonidas S. 87, 88, 162, 195, 197
Pope, John 93, 118, 119-20
popular sovereignty, doctrine of 21, 24
population
    Northern 22, 56
    Southern 22, 56, 57
population growth 3–4, 12, 22
Port Hudson, Louisiana 132, 193
Port Republic 94

Port Royal Sound 84
Porter, David Dixon 92, 164
Porter, Fitz John 102, 120, 125
Pottawatomie Creek 25
Potter, David 22, 36
Preston, John S. 35
prisoners of war 224
Puritans 6
Putnam, Sallie Brock 107–8, 156, 207

R

Rable, George 190
race relations 177–8
racial discrimination 135, 180–1
radical politics 16
raiding, as offensive strategy 143
railroads 12, 56, 72, 81, 86, 87, 93, 141, 142
Randolph, George 97, 175
Rapidan River 201, 204
Rappahannock River 146, 157
Ratcliffe, Donald 2
Reardon, Carol 160–1
Reconstruction 225, 226
Red River campaign 204
Republicans 7, 24, 25, 30–1, 33, 35–7, 168, 169, 170, 172, 215
    antislavery stance 30–1
    election victory (1860) 36–7
    support for the union 30–1
Revolutionary War 54–5, 217–18
Reynolds, John F. 158, 195
Rhett, Robert Barnwell 40
Rhode Island 133
Rhodes, Elisha Hunt 96, 104, 105, 120, 141, 151, 160, 205, 206, 207–8, 209
Rich Mountain, West Virginia 78
Richmond Dispatch 50
Richmond, Virginia 80, 95, 96, 105, 107–8, 146, 155–6, 204, 214
    fall of 220–1
Roanoke Island 87
Rohrbach (Burnside's) Bridge 125
Rosecrans, William S. 146, 161–3, 168, 184, 194, 195, 198–9
Round Forest 162

Round Top 158
Ruffin, Edmund 40
Ruggles, Daniel 88
Russell, Lord John (Earl) 115
Russell, William Howard 49-50, 55, 57, 58, 59, 60, 70, 74, 78, 82, 96, 223
Rust, Albert 25

S

San Jancinto ship 83
Sanford, Edward 104
Sanitary Commission 147, 188, 189
Sanitary Fairs 189
Saunders Field 205
Savage Station 104
Savannah 65, 216–17
Saxton, Rufus 113–14, 130
Schofield, John 213, 214, 219
Scott, Thomas A. 95
Scott, Winfield 47, 51, 70–1, 78, 100
Sea Islands 113, 114
Sears, Stephen 102
secession 2, 3, 14, 15, 29, 34, 37, 40–2, 43–4, 50
    Northern reaction to 43–4
Second Party System 21, 24
sectionalism 1–3, 8–11, 12–21, 33–4, 38
    Northern 30
    slavery and 5–6, 10–11, 16–19, 20–7
    and tariff debates 9-10, 11, 13, 14–15
    and voting in 1860 election 36
Seddon, James 151
Seminary Ridge 158
Seven Days Battles 100–5, 107
Seven Pines (Fair Oaks) 99-100
74th U.S. Colored Infantry 132
79th U.S. Colored Infantry 130
Seward, William H. 33, 35, 82, 95, 169
Sharpsburg, see Antietam
Shaw, Robert Gould 179
Shenandoah Valley 71, 72, 93–4, 118, 143, 202, 212, 215, 219
Sheridan, Philip H. 200, 201, 207, 209, 212, 215, 217, 219, 220
Sherman, John 200

Sherman, William T. 65–6, 73, 88, 91, 121, 165, 193, 201, 202, 203, 212–16, 217, 220, 221, 223–4
   Atlanta Campaign 213–15
   and Chattanooga 198, 199
   defeat at Chickasaw Bluffs 161
   and hard war policy 203–4
   'March to the Sea' 65, 216
   on Union draft 176
Shiloh, Battle of (1862) 88–90, 91
Sickles, Dan 159
Sigel, Fritz 202, 208, 212
Slave Power 20, 23, 24, 31
slavery 4–6, 10–11, 15, 16–19, 20–7, 109-17, 219-20, 225
   abolition of 4, 17–18, 21, 109, *see also* slaves, emancipation of
   antislavery/abolitionist thinking 10, 16, 17, 18, 21, 22, 24, 26–7, 30–1, 32–3, 35
   and Confederate Constitution 42–3
   defense of 18–19, 31–2, 34, 35, 41, 170
   and doctrine of popular sovereignty 21, 24
   in the North 4, 5
   and sectional division 5–6, 10–11, 16–19, 20–7
   in the territories 20–1, 22, 24–5, 30, 31, 34, 38, 40
slaves 147–8
   as Confederate resource 57
   emancipation of 126–31, 133–4, 136–7, 168, 169, 170, 171, 178
   fear of possible uprising of 39, 40
   fugitive, within Union lines (contrabands) 51, 109-14, 128–9
   as threat to Confederate war effort 57
Slidell, John 83
Slocum, Henry 215
Smith, John 1–2
Smith, Kirby 118, 144, 145, 163, 223, 224
Smith, W. F. 'Baldy' 210
Smith, William 25
South Atlantic Blockading Squadron 84
South Carolina 4, 11, 12, 13–15, 21, 34, 36, 217, 219, 220
   secession of 41
South Mountain 123

South, the
   economic value of 16, 31–2
   and growth and development 12–13, 15, 22
   idea of 16
   industrial capacity 55–6
   military tradition 57–8
   population 22, 56, 57
   positive versus negative images 16
   as slave society 5, 6, 15, 16
   as source of national leaders 58
   see also Confederacy Confederate armies Confederate navy
Southern nationalism 190–1, 225
Spain 7
Spencer, Belle 186–7, 188
spies, female 185
Spotsylvania 206–7
Springfield Republican 44, 53–4, 75
Springfield rifle 66, 67, 68
Stanton, Edwin M. 62, 102, 130, 143, 153
Star of the West steamer 44–5, 46
state militias 55, 60–1
states
   admission to the Union 3, 10, 19, 20, 21
   loyalty to 2–3
states' rights 13, 40, 43, 45, 173, 174–5, 225
Stephens, Alexander H. 43, 188
Stephens, George 181, 182
Stones River 161–3, 168, 213
Stowe, Harriet Beecher 23
strategy 79-80
   Confederate 78–9, 80–1, 100
   Union 70–1, 79–80, 86, 94–5
St. Louis, Missouri 86
Stringham, Silas H. 81, 82, 83
Strong, George Templeton 32, 37, 40, 49, 97, 108, 147, 200, 206
   on Draft Riots (July 1863) 177, 178
   on fall of Richmond 221
   on mid-term elections (1862) 169
   on Union defeat at Second Bull Run 119, 120
   on Union occupation of Atlanta 215

Stuart, J. E. B. (Jeb) 73, 101, 123, 142, 157–8, 206, 207
Sumner, Charles 25, 29
Sumner, Edwin V. 149
Sunken Road 125, 126
Susquehanna 81

T

Tallmadge, James 10
Taney, Roger B. 26, 30
Tariff of Abominations 11, 12
tariffs 9-10, 11, 12, 13, 14–15
Taylor, A. J. P. 54
Tennessee 5, 36, 44, 50, 141–2, 144, 156, 161, 194, 204, 217–19
    East 194–5
Tennessee River 80, 87
territorial expansion 6–7, 12, 19-20, 22
Texas 19-20, 36
textile industry 4
    see also cotton
33rd U.S. Colored Infantry 112, 135
Thomas, George H. 93, 195, 196, 197, 199, 213, 217, 219
Thoroughfare Gap 119, 120
three-fifths clause 5, 23
Tillotson, George 110, 128, 179-80, 184–5
Tocqueville, Alexis de 2, 12, 19
Tod, David 180
Toombs, Robert 34
topography, as barrier to Union invasion of the South 56–7
total war 204
Totopotomoy Creek 209
trade embargo, British 8
training, Union armies 66, 134–5
trans-Mississippi Theater 71, 223, 224
transport 12, 56, 119
    see also railroads
trench warfare 204, 207, 209, 211, 213, 219
Trent, British mail packet 83
Trevilian Station 212
Tubman, Harriet 185
Tunnel Hill 199
Turchin, John Basil 186, 196

Turchin, Nadine 185, 186
Turner, Nat 17, 26

U

Uncle Tom's Cabin 23
uniforms 65–6
Union
    admission of states to 3, 10, 19, 20, 21
    and controversy over emancipation 168, 169, 170, 171
    loyalty to 171–3
Union armies 55, 60–3
    African-Americans in 62, 109-14, 128, 129-37, 177, 180–2, 193, 211, 212
    casualties 90, 103, 104, 105, 121, 125, 150, 154, 160, 163, 197, 200, 206, 208, 209
    commanders/command structure 62, 63, 71, 72, 77–8
    conscription 176–7, 193
    views on emancipation of slaves 128
    hard war policy 202–3
    medical care 90–1, 135, 187, 188–9
    names 63
    organizational
structure 63
    payment of troops 135, 180–1
    soldiers' motivations for fighting 178–82
    strategy 70–1, 79-80, 86, 94–5
    support services 64–5, 119
    training 66, 134–5
    uniform 65–6
    volunteer regiments 61–3
    weaponry 67, 68
    see also under names of individual armies
Union Army of West Tennessee 87
    see also Army of the Tennessee
Union Club of Boston 171
Union Leagues 171–2, 215
Union Mills Ford 72
Union navy 55, 81–2, 83, 84, 85, 112–13
United States v. Colonel Gorman 179
urban growth 15

Urbanna 95
Utah 21

V

Vallandigham, Clement Laird 170–1
Van Dorn, Earl 91, 93, 161, 165
Vance, Zebulon B. 174–5
Velazquez, Loreta 185
Vicksburg 93, 146, 156, 160, 161, 163–6
    siege of 166, 193
Vienna, Congress of (1815) 18
Virginia 4, 5, 18, 29, 43, 50, 51, 70, 71,
    201, 216
    see also West Virginia
Virginia ironclad vessel 85–6, 96, 98
Virginia Military Institute 212

W

Wabash steamer 81, 84
Wakeman, Sarah Rosetta 184
Waldstreicher, David 3
Walker, David 17
Walker, John G. 123
Walker, Mary Edwards 188
Wallace, Lewis 88, 89
War of 1812 7–8
Warrenton Turnpike 72
Washington 29, 50, 212
Washington, George 2, 6
Watkins, Sam 139, 175, 176, 198, 200,
    201, 213, 214, 218, 219
wealth 15–16
weaponry 66–9
Webster, Daniel 7, 13, 16, 24, 30, 56, 167,
    181
Weigley, Russell 190
Welles, Gideon B. 81, 84, 112–13,
    123
West Virginia 3, 50, 118
West Wood 125

West/westward expansion 4, 19
Western Theater 71, 86–93, 141–6, 156,
    161–6, 194–201, 202, 204,
    212–19
Wheat Field 158
Wheeler, Joseph 143
Whigs 16, 23–4
White Oak Swamp 104
Whites, LeeAnn 183
Whitman, Walt xii, 224
Whitney, Eli 4
Wigfall, Louis T. 40
Wilderness, Battle of the 205–6
Wilkes, Charles 83
Wilmington, North Carolina 220
Wilmot, David 20
Wilmot Proviso 20, 34
Wise, Henry 32
Wolcott, Laurens 67
women 182–90
    black 111, 183
    Confederate 155–6, 183, 185, 189-90
    doctors 188
    nurses 183, 184, 187, 188–9
    soldiers 183–4, 185, 186
    spies 185
    Union 182–3, 184, 185–7, 188–9
Women's Central Association of Relief
    for the Sick and Wounded of
    the Army 189
Wood, T. J. 89
Woodward, C. Vann 34
Woolsey, Georgeanna Muir 189
Woolsey, Jane Stewart 183
Wright, Augustus 90
Wright, Miller 55

Y

Yancey, William Lowndes 34, 36, 40, 174
Yellow Tavern 207
Yorktown 97, 98